MEMORY AND LEGACY

THE SHOAH NARRATIVE OF THE ILLINOIS HOLOCAUST MUSEUM

Michael Berenbaum

Yitzchak Mais

ILLINOIS
Holocaust
Museum & Education
Center

Michael Berenbaum is a writer, lecturer, and teacher who consults in the conceptual development of museums and the development of historical films. He is director of the Sigi Ziering Institute: Exploring the Ethical and Religious Implications of the Holocaust at the American Jewish University (formerly the University of Judaism), where he is also a professor of Jewish studies. He was the executive editor of the *Encyclopaedia Judaica (Second Edition),* which reworked, transformed, improved, broadened, and deepened the now classic 1972 work. In the past, he was president and chief executive officer of the Survivors of the Shoah Visual History Foundation, and project director overseeing the creation of the United States Holocaust Memorial Museum. The author and editor of 18 books, he also has won an Emmy Award for his work in film. He was the senior consultant and conceptual developer, along with Yitzchak Mais, of the Illinois Holocaust Museum and Education Center.

Yitzchak Mais was director of the Yad Vashem Historical Museum in Jerusalem and founding chief curator of the Museum of Jewish Heritage—A Living Memorial to the Holocaust (MJH) in New York. A distinguished public historian who has contributed to numerous scholarly and educational publications, he has consulted and developed museum projects on the Holocaust and Jewish history worldwide, including those in Jerusalem, Kiev, Montreal, Moscow, and New York. Some of his other projects include the Basketball Hall of Fame Museum in Springfield, Massachusetts, and educational and historical consultant for *Voices of the Holocaust: Children Speak,* an interactive educational CD produced by Steven Spielberg's Survivors of the Shoah Visual History Foundation. His recent publication, *Daring to Resist—Jewish Defiance in the Holocaust,* which he edited and contributed to, was the companion volume to the exhibit of the same name. The exhibition opened at MJH in 2007. It was one of four exhibitions honored in the Excellence in Exhibition Competition, awarded by the American Association of Museums (AAM) in 2008.

"About the Building" essay © Stanley Tigerman, 2008.

Factual verification: Chris Smith and Marci McGrath.

Photograph on cover: Hungarian Jews arriving at Auschwitz-Birkenau in 1944.

Artifacts on cover: Jewish Star, with the word *Jew* in German; Scroll of Esther, burned during *Kristallnacht;* German rail car, built in 1913 and refurbished in 1943, of the type used by the Nazis to transport Jews to the death camps. Each of these artifacts is part of the Museum's collection.

Illinois Holocaust Museum and Education Center
9603 Woods Drive
Skokie, IL 60077

Published by:
Louis Weber, CEO
Publications International, Ltd.
7373 North Cicero Ave.
Lincolnwood, IL 60712

ISBN: 0-9816334-0-4
ISBN13: 978-0-9816334-0-4

Manufactured in China.

8 7 6 5 4 3 2 1

Library of Congress Control Number: 2008941963

Printed with the kind assistance of:

LEO PAPER GROUP

Authors' Acknowledgments

Words of gratitude are in order. The content of this work is solely the responsibility of its authors, and yet it could not have been accomplished without the assistance of others.

We have been privileged to work on the development of the Illinois Holocaust Museum and Education Center. Having worked on projects throughout the world, we frequently marvel at how wonderful its leadership has been; their requests are straightforward, their demands for excellence genuine. We have worked together in true harmony, united by a cause that each of us knows is far greater than ourselves. Working together, we have achieved much; the whole is far greater than the sum of its parts.

We would like to express our gratitude for the survivors who trusted us to tell their stories. There are 18 portraits of survivors in *Memory and Legacy.* Each story was captured from the testimony that the survivors gave for posterity. We trust that we have been equal to their trust in us.

We are grateful to those who contributed to this book with descriptions of their individual projects. Clifford Chanin contributed an insightful essay about his groundbreaking exhibition, *The Legacy of Absence.* Noreen Brand, Esther Netter, and Vince Beggs added a succinct description of the Museum's Youth Exhibition. We are also grateful to our colleagues at Northern Light Productions—Ken Winukur, Benjamin Avishai, Beth Sternheimer, and Bestor Cram—who shaped the Museum's films and crystallized massive amounts of survivor testimonies into usable themes. They were assisted by the indispensable research of Ita Gordon. Thanks also to David Layman and his team for the exhibition's skillful and moving design.

We are grateful to:

• Stanley Tigerman, project architect, for his brilliant and powerful design of the Museum as both a monument and memorial. Readers will deepen their appreciation of his concept by reading his essay.

• Sam Harris, president of the Museum, whose spirited leadership has galvanized the survivor generation to carry forward the lessons of the Holocaust to a new generation. His voice is often heard in the Museum and in the pages of this book.

• J. B. Pritzker, Capital Campaign chair, for his steadfast commitment and vision of the new Museum as an international human rights center that will apply the universal lessons of the Holocaust to our world today.

• Our colleague and friend, Rick Hirschhaut, project and executive director, whose visionary leadership, organizational acumen, and unwavering dedication have established the Museum as a major institution. He has demonstrated again and again that former Cubs manager Leo Durocher was wrong when he said: "Nice guys finish last." Rick is a nice guy who has finished on time and within budget. He has been an excellent boss and a real mensch.

Nearly five years ago, Rick took a detour from the security of a 21-year career with the Anti-Defamation League to help realize the dream of the Illinois Holocaust Museum and Education Center. He began this remarkable journey with the love and support of his family, whose patience and understanding have never wavered. To his dear wife, Susan, and his precious children, Rachel and Ben, we are forever grateful. We are also grateful to Violet Satmary, z"l, Susan's mother and beloved grandmother Ibi, a Holocaust survivor and a true woman of valor, whose unending love inspired Rick and the entire Hirschhaut family. Her beautiful spirit was essential to the accomplishment of this important task.

• The dedicated staff of the IHMEC, who contributed in many and different ways to creating the Museum. We ask their forgiveness, as we can single out only a few: Director of Operations Evette Simon and Assistant Director of Operations Julie Avchen, as well as Kelley Szany, Lillian Polus Gerstner, and the dedicated staff and docents of the Education Department.

• Bethany Fleming, director of Collections and Exhibitions and a full partner in this endeavor. Her depth of knowledge of the Museum's collections and overall management of the production schedule assured this book's successful completion.

• Susan Lerner, registrar, whose photo research and acquisition were instrumental to this book's visual appeal.

• Renny Bergeron, collections manager, who assisted in artifact photography and coordination as well as photo coordination.

• Tobias Etzel and Bettina Augue, Action Reconciliation Service for Peace (ARSP) volunteers, for their translation work and outreach to German archives.

• Tom Fields-Meyer for cutting and cutting and cutting the manuscript and thus improving it substantively.

• Louis Weber, CEO of Publications International, Ltd., who graciously donated money and resources to publish and print this special book. We want to thank the PIL staff members who worked on the project, particularly David Hogan, Doug Brooks, Marissa Conner, David Aretha, Pat Murray, Valerie Iglar-Mobley, and Joanna Liff. They brought the book in on time and with a visual quality appropriate to the Museum.

Finally, permit us a personal word. We are grateful to Richard Salomon, who recruited us for this project and who had the foresight to engage both of us knowing that two is better than one. And our thanks to Howard Swibel, whose counsel has been wise, effective, efficient, and gracious.

We are always grateful to our families: The Berenbaums—Melissa, Joshua, Mira, Llana and her family as well as Lev—for their forbearance and inspiration, as well as Vicky Mais, who is often left in Jerusalem without her husband, but who well understands why.

Michael Berenbaum and Yitzchak Mais

CONTENTS

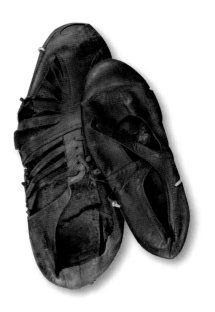

FOREWORD

The pages of this book illuminate a journey into the spirit and soul of the Illinois Holocaust Museum and Education Center. For this institution not only honors the memory of the millions who were murdered during the Holocaust, it salutes the courage and resilience of the survivors, who rebuilt their lives and awoke the conscience of humanity to never forget. Their collective exhortation of "Never Again," to any people at any time, is the guiding principle underlying the Museum's educational mission.

The fascinating architectural features of the Museum affirm its place as both monument and memorial. Yet it is within the walls of this structure that its enormous capacity to change lives is fully revealed. In these spaces, individual stories are told: personal encounters with unimaginable evil as well as precious moments of human kindness—testimonies that make it possible for us to better understand an otherwise incomprehensible atrocity.

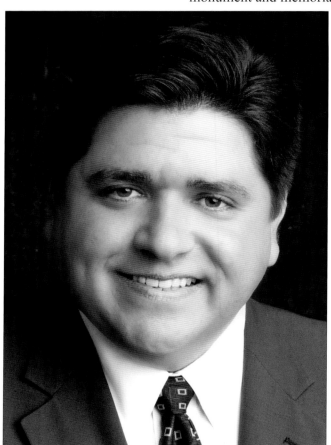

J. B. Pritzker

In the Museum's Core Exhibition, featured throughout this book, we present many of the literally thousands of precious artifacts entrusted to the institution. The voices of our region's survivors are expressed throughout the exhibition, via film, audio, and the written word. Many of the films are a montage of actual survivor testimony, so it becomes possible to literally "follow" the survivors through this history.

In our Youth Exhibition, younger visitors have the opportunity to explore issues of character and individual identity, to better understand how the choices we make affect those around us. Building awareness of the responsibility we all share toward our fellow human beings can encourage their taking a stand when witnessing bullying or bigotry among their peers. This experience will lay the groundwork for an even more powerful encounter when they eventually visit the Core Exhibition.

The Midwest Collection of survivor testimonies, created by the USC Shoah Visual History Institute and located in the Museum's Brill Family Resource Center, contains the testimonies of nearly 2,100 Holocaust survivors from across the Midwest—neighbors, friends, survivors, liberators, and rescuers. This fully digitized and indexed database offers an invaluable archive of eyewitness accounts of Holocaust experiences, presented in a most personal and compelling way.

The Legacy of Absence Gallery on the second floor explores how Holocaust memory is made tangible in contemporary art. It explores how the Holocaust has touched the lives and work of artists from every continent. Shaped by so many diverse experiences, these artists struggled to give expression to absence where presence had been. In attempting to deal with their losses and their history, they forged a common vocabulary of protest, of outrage, of loss. This international collection examines how a new visual vocabulary was required to commemorate both the Holocaust and other episodes of genocide or mass violence—in Armenia, Cambodia, Rwanda, and elsewhere. These artistic works, so very particular to their creators and their historical experience, manifest a universal language of creativity.

The Museum's Temporary Exhibitions Gallery and Goodman Auditorium offer myriad opportunities for special exhibitions, lectures, music, film, and drama, further illuminating the personal dimensions of the Holocaust.

From our Education Center emanates many outreach programs, including our traveling education trunks. These educational materials assist teachers in classrooms and our speakers bureau, which brings survivors and educators to local communities to teach the universal lessons of the Holocaust.

Richard S. Hirschhaut

When the creators of the Museum approached this awesome task, they were committed not only to remembering the past but to establishing a center for learning, where young people in particular are taught to make good, ethical choices, to stand up for fairness, to raise their voices against hatred and injustice. We seek to present the Holocaust narrative in ways that enable visitors to relate this experience to their own lives—values they hold dear, moral choices they face. It is our hope that they will recognize that the power to stand up to bigotry and hate resides within us all.

The origins of this Museum are modest. Survivors came together in the aftermath of the proposed neo-Nazi march on Skokie realizing that the succeeding generations' memory of the Holocaust was fading. They were determined to ensure that the legacy of their experience was carried forward. At the time, they did not aim to have an international impact; they simply wanted to make an impact in their communities. They began with a small storefront and made it available to the public, especially to schoolchildren. In the center of that building stood the Book of Remembrance. Created to honor the dead, it contains the names of those who were murdered and whose ashes were sent into the sky. We have brought that book of names with us to its new visionary shrine. We are still committed to remembering the names of the lost and giving them a hallowed place from which they can be remembered.

As we honor the survivor generation, we who were fortunate enough to be born in a later time and another place accept the responsibility to protect, cherish, and transmit their precious legacy. For they have given us a tremendous gift, a genuine sense of hope and optimism for the future. Their lesson, their inspiration to generations to come, is the affirmation of life itself. May we honor their legacy and their vision of a better tomorrow through our own vigilance and activism today.

J. B. Pritzker
Chairman, Board of Trustees
Museum Campaign Chairman

Richard S. Hirschhaut
Museum Director
Project and Executive Director

It is within the walls of this structure that individual stories are told: personal encounters with unimaginable evil as well as precious moments of human kindness.

INTRODUCTION

Names are chosen deliberately and, if chosen wisely, stand for something significant.

The founders of the Illinois Holocaust Museum and Education Center chose its name deliberately and wisely. It is a museum, but much more than a museum. It is an education center, but not just an education center.

Once a museum, any museum, opens its doors, it offers itself as a place to visit. The Illinois Holocaust Museum and Education Center is no exception. We invite you to visit the Museum. And yet, there are now other ways to visit the

A boy rests his head on a soup pail in a doorway in the Lodz ghetto; German-occupied Poland, c. 1941

Museum without entering the building. The website, www.ilholocaustmuseum. org, is one such avenue, and this book, *Memory and Legacy: The Shoah Narrative of the Illinois Holocaust Museum,* is another.

This book is intended for three audiences. One audience includes those who have visited the Museum and want to take something home that they can read and view at their convenience. The book will underscore and reinforce what they have seen in the Museum. To those who have not yet visited the Museum, *Memory and Legacy* serves as an invitation, a way of exploring its many offerings, a means of preparation for a more informed and engrossing experience. This book also offers a general introduction to the Holocaust, a history that is rooted in scholarship but, like the Museum, is intended for a general audience beginning with older middle school students.

A word about the Museum and therefore also about *Memory and Legacy:*

Unlike most artifact-centered historical museums, which tell the stories of the artifacts they possess, the Illinois Holocaust Museum is a storytelling museum, driven by the history of the Holocaust. It is on the basis of this story that artifacts have been collected and exhibited, photographs gathered and presented, and media—film, video, narrative tale, text, design, and atmosphere—chosen.

The Museum must address its visitors and must be responsive to its community. We have kept this in mind when shaping the Museum and this book, both of which include personal histories and memories about survivors who made Chicagoland and the Midwest their home. A determined effort was made to gather and present the precious few enduring photographs, artifacts,

A charcoal drawing by "feb,"
Ferdinand Bloch, created in
Theresienstadt; c. 1943.

and testimonies of local survivors. It is their legacy that we seek to convey in our depiction of the events now universally known as the Holocaust—an event so singular in its ramifications to our understanding of the world we live in that Holocaust memorials and museums have been established worldwide as well as in numerous cities throughout the United States. Moreover, the history of the Holocaust has become an integral part of numerous educational curricula taught in schools, public and private, Jewish and Christian, which underscores and highlights the universal relevance of the *Shoah*.

Perhaps because the survivors have been neighbors, friends, and teachers, they can best transport us back more than 70 years in time, moving us a continent away. They take us with them into Jewish life before the war and then into the unforeseen shock of a world of anguish and suffering, but also one of endurance and resilience. Future generations who have not lived in the presence of survivors will now realize that they have walked our streets, lived in our neighborhoods, and rebuilt their lives within our communities.

Museums that are located on historical sites must reflect the significance of those sites. Thus, for example, the museum at Auschwitz tells the story of Auschwitz, not the entire story of the Holocaust and the emergence of the Final Solution. Among our younger visitors and readers, Skokie is merely a pleasant suburb of Chicago, a village—a quaint term that implies friendship, neighbors, and community. And yet to an older generation, Skokie is a symbol, a place deliberately chosen by American neo-Nazis in the late 1970s who planned to march on its quiet streets because it was then the home of some 7,000 survivors of the Holocaust.

The neo-Nazis chose Skokie to amplify their message by provoking anguish among those who had seen real Nazis march. Their intention to march caused a communal uproar that made Skokie a national symbol. The legal case reached the Supreme Court and gained international notoriety. It pitted the principles of free speech and freedom of assembly against those whose tranquility and sense of security were threatened by such hate speech. It also roused the survivors into action—to speak for

We have tried to create a sense of identification and empathy with the victims of the Holocaust.

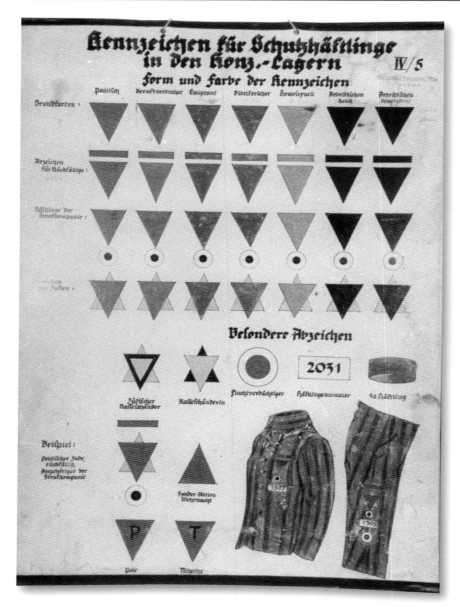

A chart of prisoner markings used in German concentration camps; c. 1940.

tims—appearing as emaciated skeletons by the end of their ordeal—they were people. Thus, we begin with the world of the Jews before the Holocaust when they lived in their homes, worked in their communities, lived out their values, and coped with their circumstances. Only from that point can we begin our journey into the darkness.

Many Holocaust museums and historians do not take into account how the Jews lived under oppression. It is sufficient for them to describe the unprecedented circumstances created by Nazi policies and practice. Too often the ghettos and the death camps are viewed from without, and we neglect to examine the Jewish world that was shaped under domination by Nazi Germany as the Jewish community struggled to cope with their deteriorating situation. The timetable most often considered is solely a Nazi timetable. The various survivor stories integrated in our Museum's exhibits and this book, as well as the chronology that appears at the end of this volume, employ an unusual and innovative approach. By highlighting the manifold and diverse actions undertaken by Jews to cope with, defy, and resist Nazi policies, the victims and survivors are not depicted—as in many Holocaust narratives—as passive objects, but as historical actors who responded with a surprisingly wide range of resourceful and often dangerous initiatives.

In the Museum and within *Memory and Legacy,* we enter the ghettos and see life within; we enter the camps and let those who were there tell us what it was like to live in the shadow of mass murder, death, and dehumanization. We view the event that we call the Holocaust from the perspective of both the perpetrators and the victims, and also from the vantage point of the rescuers, the collaborators, and the bystanders so that a more complete understanding is possible. We do not end in May 1945 with the conclusion of World War II in Europe and the liberation of the

themselves and to transmit their stories. The original storefront Illinois Holocaust Museum in Skokie may be the most profound result of that attempted march. Survivors and their supporters responded to hatred by building community, by creating an educational center that espoused respect for human dignity and diversity.

The new Museum and this book reflect several commitments that are the guiding principles of our entire project. We seek to rectify a historical wrong. The Nazis dehumanized their victims before they killed them. We seek to tell a human story. Before they were vic-

camps. Instead, we take you through the efforts of survivors to rebuild their lives, to move to new countries, and adapt to new lands. We also discuss the efforts of the world to come to terms with the Holocaust. We explore the legacy of the Holocaust to the present day in this new century, as we are the last to live in the presence of those who were there.

The Museum focuses on Jews, for they were the central focus of Nazi ideology; the central focus but not the sole focus. In order to understand the singularity of the Jewish experience, we portray all the victims of Nazism, from political dissidents to Jehovah's Witnesses, homosexuals, the handicapped, non-Jewish Poles, and Gypsies. We are deeply concerned about portraying the particularity of the Jewish experience, yet we must portray the Jewish story as a human story, reflecting traits and emotions—hope, fear, desire, courage, adaptability, survival, and triumph—that are common to all people. Hence, the more universal a story is in its appeal, the more it can successfully bridge cultural differences.

We have tried to create a sense of identification and empathy with the victims of the Holocaust. We also aim to create an understanding of, and ultimately rejection of, its perpetrators and collaborators, as well as insight into the pressures that led bystanders to be bystanders.

We have also endeavored to show you other aspects of the Museum, including the *Legacy of Absence Gallery,* which considers how people who have lived through and in the shadow of mass murder and destruction respond to it artistically and creatively. It brings us forward from the Holocaust to other genocides that have occurred since, and to the efforts of recent generations to deal with the presence of absence and the absence of presence. We explore the Youth Exhibition, a unique area designed for younger visitors who are offered an entrance point into this historical narrative in an age-appropri-

ate manner and also to the issues raised by the Holocaust. We offer a depiction of the unique building that houses this museum, the work of a master architect who wanted to respond to the event and to the survivors in a space that gives dimension and voice to the experience. And we tell of the origins of the Museum—the origins and the significant aspirations of its creators.

Despite the fact that the Holocaust was a horrific event, the Museum is not a chamber of horrors. Horror will be used as a vehicle to encounter the truth of the Holocaust, but never for its own sake. Shock is an element of discovery, never an end in itself. So when we use harsh language or difficult imagery, it is to convey the reality of what happened—nothing less and nothing more.

Our aim is to present this history as a catalyst to moral engagement rather than as a cathartic experience with an easy resolution. We will not make a cliché out of an event of such magnitude.

Memory and Legacy and the Museum are shaped by two commitments to memory: The Holocaust must be remembered, and memory of the Holocaust must be in service of conscience—individual and communal, political and national, religious and secular.

Michael Berenbaum
Los Angeles, California
September 29, 2008

Yitzchak Mais
Jerusalem, Israel
Erev Rosh Hashanah 5769

A dress worn by Judith Kolb when she was a child living in Shanghai, China, after her family found refuge there; 1941.

WHO ARE THE JEWS?

Edward Lust in his bar mitzvah suit and tallit; Belgium, 1935.

The Jewish People are direct descendents of the ancient Israelites (Hebrews), the children of Abraham, Isaac, and Jacob and their wives—Sarah, Rebecca, Leah, and Rachel. God called Abraham to leave the place of his birth and journey to a land that would be given to him and his descendants. In the biblical account, the Lord renamed the patriarch Jacob "Israel" after wrestling with him through the night. Later, Jacob and his family of 70 left Canaan because of a famine and dwelt in Egypt, where the Egyptians eventually enslaved future Hebrew generations.

In slavery, the Israelites became a people, and the Exodus from Egypt under the leadership of Moses became a formative event of the Jewish story—and a widely shared narrative of oppressed people across diverse cultures. The famous spiritual sung by African American slaves was only one of many songs, stories, and poems that were used by people in anguish to dream

of their liberation and to empower themselves to achieve it.

> *When Israel was in Egypt's land,*
> *let my people go;*
> *oppressed so hard they could not*
> *stand,*
> *let my people go.*
>
> Refrain:
> *Go down, Moses,*
> *way down in Egypt's land;*
> *tell old Pharaoh*
> *to let my people go.*

The Exodus story—the tale of enslavement, liberation, and the journey through the desert to the Promised Land—was one of two formative experiences of the ancient Israelites.

The other was Sinai. Moses in the Biblical narrative ascended the mountain and heard the word of the Lord, who spoke to the people, instructing them with Ten Commandments, four that embody their relationship to God

Jewish Population of European Countries, c. 1933–39:
Many Jews at the time also lived in North Africa, including 210,000 in Morocco, 120,000 in Algeria, 85,000 in Tunisia, and 30,000 in Libya.

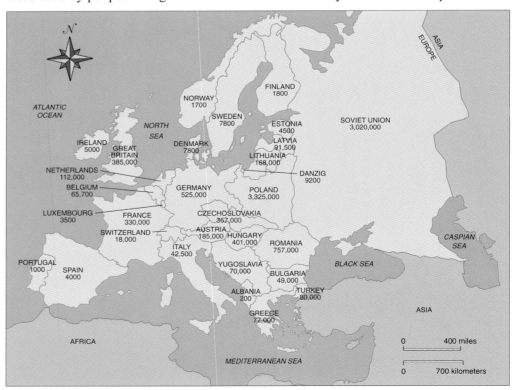

and six that form the ethical code for all civilizations: prohibiting murder, adultery, stealing, and bearing false witness; and honoring one's father and mother. The Ten Commandments became the foundation of Jewish faith, the genesis of ethical monotheism.

From the desert the Israelites entered the Promised Land, where they lived as a nation of tribes with charismatic leaders; only later was a monarchy established. Eventually King David moved the capital to Jerusalem, where his son Solomon erected the Holy Temple.

For the Jews, sacred scripture is called the *Tanach,* composed of the Torah (called also the Five Books of Moses—Genesis, Exodus, Leviticus, Numbers, and Deuteronomy), the Prophets, and the Writings. (Called by Christians the Old Testament, for Jews it is the sole Testament.) The prophets of ancient Israel were men—and on occasion women—who provided spiritual leadership, advising and rebuking kings, princes, and priests in the name of justice and mercy, and for the sake of God.

Biblical Israelites experienced attacks and occasionally defeats. Living at a crossroads amid major powers— Egypt, Assyria, and Babylonia—they could sustain independence only if there was a balance that checked the undisputed might of one of those powers.

Under aggressive kings or in a period of weakness, the Israelites would face attack. When the power they faced was overwhelming, they were defeated. Such was the case in 586 BCE (Before the Common Era), when the Babylonians under King Nebuchadnezzar captured Jerusalem and destroyed the Temple, sending the Israelites into exile. Decades later, Persia's King Cyrus permitted the return to Jerusalem that was followed by the rebuilding of the Second Temple.

For five centuries, the Israelites navigated the dangerous terrain on which they lived, finding a niche among the major powers. In a world dominated by Greek civilization and later

the Roman Empire, they practiced their faith, absorbing the surrounding culture, yet resisting what conflicted with their own religion. During this time, the third segment of the Hebrew Bible, the Writings, took form: books as diverse as Psalms and Proverbs, the Scroll of Esther and Lamentation, Job, and Ecclesiastes. Hellenism (the principles and ideals associated with classical Greek civilization) had a tremendous impact on Jewish life. Some Jews were attracted to Hellenic thought to the point of thorough assimilation; others incorporated it into their own tradition.

By the 1st century, Jews were living under Roman domination, with three competing religious perspectives: The Sadducees sought accommodation with Rome, the Pharisees sought spiritual independence, and the Zealots pursued political independence. It was into this world that Jesus of Nazareth was born, lived, and taught.

Jesus of Nazareth lived as a Jew, died as a Jew, and was crucified by Rome. The Jews of his time lacked the power to inflict capital punishment; crucifixion was a common form of Roman death, alien to Jewish practice.

In the year 67 C.E. (Common Era), a war broke out between the Jews and Rome, which conquered Jerusalem and destroyed the Temple in 70 C.E. The Jews were a defeated people who would live without political independence under Roman domination.

Challenged to survive without a homeland or Temple, the Jewish leader Rabbi Yochanan ben Zakkai made the

For five centuries, the Israelites navigated the dangerous terrain on which they lived, finding a niche among the major powers. In a world dominated by Greek civilization and later the Roman Empire, they practiced their faith, absorbing the surrounding culture, yet resisting what conflicted with their own religion.

These shofars (ram's horns), blown on Rosh Hashanah, were brought to the Chicago area from Germany by founding members of the congregation Ezra Habonim, now part of Ner Tamid Ezra Habonim.

center of Jewish life the synagogue, which could move from place to place. All that was required for worship was a quorum of at least 10 Jews and a Torah scroll. Religious worship and study of sacred texts would replace Temple worship, and sacred time would substitute for the sacred land. In this context, the Jewish people endured exile, with synagogue and Torah study the centerpieces of Jewish life.

To Christians, the Temple's destruction symbolized God's abandonment of the Jewish people, who had refused to accept the teaching of Jesus. Sometime later, the Jews stood accused of crucifying Jesus.

Originally a form of Judaism, Christianity became its rival, making different claims about faith and God. Later, with Christianity's transformation into Rome's official state religion, persecution and discrimination followed.

Three issues became central to the divisions between the two religions:

- For Christians, Jesus is the Messiah. Jews believed the Messiah was yet to come.
- Some Christians believed the New Testament superseded the Old Testament. For Jews the Hebrew Bible remains God's sacred word, which all of Judaism seeks to apply to human life.
  - For Christians, Jesus is a divine figure, God incarnate. For Jews, Jesus is a human figure whose

teaching has strong roots in Scripture and in Judaism, and finds echoes in the Rabbinic tradition developed in his time.

Unique in the Jewish-Christian confrontation was the charge that Jews had killed the Christian God. The Gospel of Matthew, written after Jesus lived and after the destruction of the Temple, alleges that Jews accepted that responsibility on themselves and on their children. (The Second Vatican Council of 1962–65 absolved the Jews of blame for the crucifixion and rejected the centuries-old, slanderous "Teaching of Contempt.")

In the 4th century, Christianity became the Roman Empire's official religion and Jews lived as a despised minority, facing religious antagonism and the social and economic discrimination that resulted. Internally, Judaism flourished. Jews compiled sacred literature, such as the Babylonian Talmud (composed between the 2nd and 6th centuries), and developed codes of law, philosophy and liturgy, religious practices, and tradition.

Holidays set the rhythm of the Jewish community. Annual festivals and weekly Sabbath observances lent structure and stability from year to year, generation to generation. They worshiped in synagogues, with the Torah as the central symbol, placed in an ark facing Jerusalem. One portion was read each Sabbath

Below: *Moishe Rental, chief cantor of Radom, Poland; 1938. He was the last cantor of Radom before the destruction of the community.* Below, right: *A ritual Torah binder (wimple) made from the swaddling cloth of a baby boy. It is hand-painted with the boy's name, his birth date, and the traditional blessing: that he grow to a life filled with Torah (religious learning), marriage, and good deeds.*

to the congregation from a handwritten parchment scroll. Jews continued to observe the seventh day, Saturday, as their Sabbath, refraining from all labors. On the Sabbath, religious Jews did not travel, light fires, or do physical labor. This is still true today.

The most sacred days on the Jewish calendar are the High Holidays: Rosh Hashanah (the Jewish New Year) and Yom Kippur (the Day of Atonement), whose themes are sin and repentance. Tradition teaches that on Rosh Hashanah, God sits in judgment; on Yom Kippur, the observant fast and pray as an act of atonement, in hopes of forgiveness and reconciliation. Unlike the frivolity that marks the secular New Year, this time is sacred and somber, a time when many Jews flock to the synagogue.

Many holidays are both seasonal and historical, reflecting roots in the land of Israel, with its annual agricultural cycle and holiday pilgrimages to Jerusalem. Passover, the spring festival, commemorates the Exodus from Egypt. Families eat matzah (unleavened bread), gather for the Seder, and retell the liberation story. The final words of the Seder elaborate on the dream of freedom, "Next Year in Jerusalem," which for centuries was recited in the depth of exile and even in death camps. Shavuot (Pentecost) in early summer commemorates the giving of the Torah at Sinai. During Succot (Tabernacles), the joyous fall harvest festival, Jews build temporary booths to commemorate the sojourn in the desert.

Other holidays derive from Jewish history. The most widely known (though not the most religiously significant) is Hanukah, when candles are lit to recall the successful Maccabean revolt against the ancient Greeks in 165 BCE and the rededication of the Temple in Jerusalem. Purim, in late winter or early spring, retells the story of Esther, the Jewish

Queen of Persia, saving her people from destruction by Haman. Elaborate costumes are worn as the Scroll of Esther is read. Days of fasting mark Jewish tragedies or defeats in centuries of history.

Traditionally, the Jewish home was kosher: Two sets of dishes were required, milk and meat were not eaten together, and only certain meats were allowed. Pork and shellfish were prohibited. Animals had to be slaughtered according to a prescribed ritual, an act performed by a well-trained *shochet* (ritual slaughter).

Jews mark the major milestones of life with a rich tapestry of traditions and rituals, varying with geography. Jewish boys are circumcised on the eighth day of life—as was Isaac, their biblical ancestor—entering into the covenant of Israel with an indelible sign of the covenant on their flesh as they are given their name. (Jewish girls traditionally are named in synagogue.)

At age 13, a Jewish boy comes of age, becoming *bar mitzvah*—literally, one obligated to observe the commandments. Since 1922 in the United States, in liberal traditions, Jewish girls have observed bat mitzvah ceremonies.

Above: *The Baum Family; Gissen, Germany, November 1930.* Below: *A samovar, for boiling water, and Shabbat candlesticks, kindled on Friday evening and holiday eve. These items were brought to the United States from Russia early in the 20th century.*

Top: *A ketubah (marriage contract) for Adolph Brandis and Ruth Rosenbaum, who were married on May 28, 1929, in Germany. The signed text is in Hebrew and German.* Bottom: *Wedding portrait of Adam and Pela Starkopf; Warsaw, 1936.*

Jews embrace their religious traditions in diverse ways, from ardent traditionalists to Liberal, paying heed to both tradition and modernity.

During weddings—held under a *chuppah,* a canopy symbolizing the home—a glass is broken; for even at the height of joy, Jews remember the destruction of Jerusalem. Blessings are recited, and a *ketubah,* a marriage contract, is read.

A Jewish funeral is simple, usually within a day or sometimes two after death, with burial traditionally in a plain pine box. Mourners sit *shiva* (meaning sitting for seven days), receiving guests who bring comfort. The mourner recites the *Kaddish* at prayer services for 11 months following the death of a parent.

Jews embrace their religious traditions in diverse ways, from ardent traditionalists (known now as Orthodox) to Liberal, paying heed to both tradition and modernity. Some are distant from tradition, either estranged or uninformed, but still acknowledge—or even embrace—their identity as Jews. Some choose to observe some teachings and disregard others but proudly continue their tradition.

Through the centuries, Jews remained self-reliant, preserving a strong identity as a distinct people. Generally excluded from the society around them, they established their own schools, hospitals, charities, and clubs. Even as Jews increasingly participated in the surrounding culture, Jewish organizations endured, often serving the general community as well.

At the heart of each community is a rabbi and synagogue. And observant Jews, no matter where they live, need a *shohet* (who properly prepares the animal for the kosher butcher), *mohel* (circumciser), and *mikveh* (ritual bath).

Before the French Revolution in 1789, European Jews were denied equality and had limited social contact with the surrounding society. Hence, they generally lived as a community apart from the state, separate from society.

The French Revolution began a century-long process of emancipation throughout Western Europe. Jews gained rights of citizenship and participation in the countries in which they lived. When emancipation worked well, Jews became part of the countries in which they dwelled. Social and political integration did not necessarily keep pace with legal equality. Emancipation was actively opposed by segments of each society. And emancipation posed a challenge for Jewish continuity: No longer set apart by law, Jews had to navigate the challenges of communal survival along with the opportunities of assimilation and participation.

The process of emancipation proceeded at different paces in different countries and had different levels of support from the general public. The United States, which was established 13 years before the French Revolution, is the first post-emancipation country, the first in which Jews were citizens from the nation's inception.

Left: *Jews at an outdoor cafe; Vienna, 1938.*

schools taught Yiddish. In the Sephardic community, the *Alliance Israelite Universelle* sponsored schools throughout North Africa and the Middle East that emphasized French language and culture.

Rabbi Azriel Hildesheimer founded a Berlin rabbinic seminary in 1873, combining Orthodoxy with *wissenschaft,* the scientific study of Judaism. It was the first of many schools to offer a broader historical approach to Jewish studies rather than a purely traditional religious education.

Nonreligious institutions for Jewish scholarship also thrived, included YIVO (Yiddish Scientific Institute), founded in Vilna in 1925, and Warsaw's Institute of Jewish Studies. The Hebrew University of Jerusalem was established in 1925. Jews also founded modern rabbinical seminaries in Berlin and across Europe.

In the United States, this dynamic has continued with the establishment of numerous Jewish institutions of higher learning. These include: Cincinnati's Hebrew Union College (Reform); New York's Jewish Theological Seminary (Conservative) and Yeshiva University (Orthodox); and the Reconstructionist Rabbinical College in suburban Philadelphia. In the Chicago area, the Spertus Institute of Jewish Studies and the Hebrew Theological College in Skokie have continued this tradition.

Jewish communities throughout the world were known for a wide variety of charitable agencies as well as self-help and self-governing organizations. Jews submitted their monetary disputes to rabbinical courts, and kosher slaughtering was administered by the *kehilla* (community). Most large communities boasted an array of charities that served impoverished Jews, including free-loan societies, orphanages, old-age homes, and soup kitchens.

Education has always played a central role in the Jewish community. Before the modern era, private schools for boys (*heders,* or *meldar* among Sephardic Jews) helped establish universal male Jewish literacy. (Until the 20th century, most girls in Eastern Europe did not study formally; many learned to recite the prayers and read Yiddish translations of the Bible.)

Promising students or those from wealthier homes continued their religious studies with an advanced teacher (*melamed*), or in the local synagogue's study hall (*beit midrash*). The most capable studied at the famous Talmudic academies (*yeshivot*) throughout Europe; the most renowned of these were in Poland and Lithuania.

With the mid-19th century came new types of secular Jewish schools. Various Jewish political movements formed schools that helped boys and girls preserve their Jewish identity while gaining a broad education. Zionist schools taught Hebrew as a modern language; socialist

Above: *A Jewish woman reads a book under a hanging portrait of Theodor Herzl, journalist, statesman, and founder of political Zionism; Danzig, Germany/Gdansk, Poland, c. 1925.* Left: *A Sabbath oil lamp used by the Baum family in Germany in the early 1900s and brought to the United States in 1933.*

RISE OF NAZISM

Top: The Mystery of Jewish Success, *authored by German antisemite Theodor Fritsch.* Bottom: *A 1935 German propaganda poster advertising a special issue of the Nazi weekly newspaper* Der Sturmer. *"Rassenschande" (race pollution) supposedly explains and justifies the Nuremberg race laws.*

From 1914 to 1918, World War I engulfed Europe with massive loss of life and unprecedented horror. On average, more than 5,000 people were killed every day for more than 1,500 days—8.5 million dead. At the Battle of Verdun (February to July 1916), there were one million casualties; 500,000 men on each side. Yet neither France nor Germany gained significant territory. The battle lines in France remained basically the same.

Germany was unprepared for losing the war, especially as there were no enemy troops on German soil. The population had been told of heroic victories and not of the anguish of the war or of setbacks on the battlefront. There was a major gap between the soldiers who had fought in the trenches and those back at home who spoke of the war and its glory. Germany was exhausted, without gas for its trucks or rubber for its tires.

For many Germans, the shock of losing the war was compounded by the terms of the peace treaty, signed in Versailles in 1919.

The late-entering Americans fought largely for idealistic reasons. President Woodrow Wilson called World War I "The War to End All Wars." In the aftermath, the Allies were determined that Germany could never again rise to instigate another world war. Germany was forced to reduce the size of its army, cede territory, and pay stiff wartime reparations. Germany's monarchy, the second Reich, was abolished, and in its place the Allies supported an experiment in democracy, the Weimar Republic, in a country that had no deep democratic tradition.

The Allies envisioned the Weimar Republic as a robust liberal democracy in the heart of Europe. But in practice, it was a weak and unstable government. Conceived in defeat, it lacked legitimacy for many of its citizens. Ultimately, the Weimar Republic's lackluster performance did not gain the assent of the governed.

By 1923 rampant inflation made Germany's currency worthless. Citizens pushed wheelbarrows full of *Deutsche Marks* to the store for bread. Economic failures led to massive unemployment and food shortages. The savings of the middle class became worthless, and the people lost hope for the future.

The political center was weakened and German politics became polarized. Communism on the left and National Socialism on the extreme right became most vocal.

Into this combustible mix stepped Adolf Hitler, who manipulated Germans' fear and frustration into a vision of national rebirth through a racial ideology and the utter elimination of their enemies. The real enemies were still in their midst, Hitler said—Communists, liberals, and, above all, Jews.

The 1929 worldwide depression fueled Hitler's appeal. Unemployment in Germany increased fivefold, and exports fell by more than half. In the December 1924 elections, the Nazis won only 14 seats in the *Reichstag* (parliament). By 1930 support for the Nazi party increased to 6.3 million votes and 107 seats in the *Reichstag.*

In 1932 Hitler ran for president, but he lost in a runoff election to World War I hero Paul von Hindenburg. In the July parliamentary election, the Nazis drew 37.3 percent of the vote, gained 230 seats, and became the largest of

Into this combustible mix stepped Adolf Hitler, who manipulated Germans' fear and frustration into a vision of national rebirth through a racial ideology and the utter elimination of their enemies.

Germany's numerous political parties. Master Nazi propagandist Joseph Goebbels had predicted: "We come like wolves descending upon a herd of sheep.... We will become members of the *Reichstag* in order to disable the Weimar order with its own acquiescence." In the November elections, called because the divisions were so deep that a stable government could not be formed, support for the Nazis decreased by two million votes, down to 33.1 percent of the electorate.

A series of brief-lived governments of ineffective leaders brought a reluctant and disdainful President Hindenburg to name Hitler chancellor (prime minister),

as head of a coalition government with only three Nazi cabinet seats. Hindenburg and his advisers presumed that once in power Hitler would be moderated by the other eight cabinet members, all more experienced politically and seemingly more sophisticated.

Hitler came to power legally on January 30, 1933, as the head of a coalition government. Aging President Hindenburg appointed him knowing that Hitler and the Nazi Party were a major source of German political instability, terror, and violence. Hindenburg figured that being chancellor as a minority leader in a coalition government would force Hitler to the center. Political lead-

A Nazi mass rally in the Berlin Sportspalast in 1935. The banners bear antisemitic slogans, including, "The Jews are our misfortune."

> **The books were tossed into bonfires in an effort to purify German culture from "un-Germanic" writings. Some were by Jewish authors, others by the likes of Jack London, Ernest Hemingway, and Helen Keller. Works that were politically offensive to Nazism were destroyed.**

ers assumed that he could be controlled. They overestimated their own resources and underestimated Hitler.

Once in office, Hitler's first objective was to consolidate power and to eliminate political opposition. The burning of the *Reichstag* on February 27, 1933, which the Nazis claimed was ostensibly set by a Communist, provided a pretext for the strengthening of Hitler's position. The next day, he received emergency powers from President Hindenburg, and immediately 100 Communists were arrested. In a March election, the Nazi Party received 288 seats in the *Reichstag*—44 percent of the vote but still short of a majority. That same month, special Nazi courts were established to deal with dissidents, and the first concentration camp, Dachau, was established outside of Munich to house the newly arrested.

A provision of the Weimar Constitution was employed to dismantle constitutional protections and to give Hitler dictatorial powers. Two emergency provisions of the Constitution allowed the president to usurp the powers of state governments and suspend constitutional guarantees of civil liberties. With a two-thirds majority of those *present and voting,* the chancellor could be granted temporary legislative powers.

Hitler could not ordinarily command a two-thirds majority, but the *Reichstag* burning provided just such an opportunity. One hundred and seven legislators—Communists and some Social Democrats—were prevented from attending the *Reichstag* session; therefore, they could not be present and were prevented from voting. On March 23, 1933, the Enabling Act was passed, which gave Hitler just such legislative powers. In the first 60 days, there were random attacks against the Jews, but the major focus was on the political opposition.

The Assault Against the Jews

The assault against the Jews began with the April 1, 1933, boycott of Jewish businesses, which lasted just one day.

Some non-Jewish Germans supported the boycott; others made it a point of honor to call on Jewish friends and patronize Jewish shops. Signs declaring the boycott were printed in English as well as German. They were intended as a warning to the Jews of America that any strong response to the Nazis' rise to power, such as the proposed boycott of German products and a repeat of the mass rally sponsored by the American Jewish Congress in Madison Square Garden on March 27, would endanger German Jews. German Jews urged caution to American coreligionists, lest they make worse an already difficult situation. The question of how publicly Jews in the free world could oppose the persecution of Jews in other countries without endangering their situation was not new to Jewish history. It remained a problem throughout the Nazi years.

On April 7, the Law for the Restoration of the Professional Civil Service was promulgated. Jews were dismissed from the civil service. These included lawyers working for the state, physicians employed by state-run health plans and hospitals, and even university professors employed by the state universities. By the end of the month, Jewish participation in German schools was restricted by a quota.

On May 10, Hitler's 100th day in office, thousands of Nazi students along with many professors stormed university libraries and bookstores in 30 cities throughout Germany to remove tens of thousands of books written by non-"Aryans" and those opposed to Nazi ideology. The books were tossed into bonfires in an effort to purify German culture from "un-Germanic" writings. Some were by Jewish authors, others by the likes of Jack London, Ernest Hemingway, and Helen Keller.

Works that were politically offensive to Nazism were destroyed alongside the works of Karl Marx, Sigmund Freud, Albert Einstein, and other Jewish writers. Joseph Goebbels proclaimed at the book burning that was staged near the Berlin Opera House, "the age of Jewish intellectual domination has ended."

After a period of intensity came a certain settling in and a further consolidation of Nazi power. By July 14, the Nazi Party was the only legal political party. Unopposed in the next election, it received 92 percent of the vote. A law regarding the Revocation of Naturalization and the Annulment of German Citizenship stripped citizenship from Eastern European Jews who had immigrated to Germany. A law for the Prevention of Offspring with Hereditary Diseases provided for the sterilization of "unfit" parents or potential parents, and the euthanasia of defective offspring. "Useless eaters," they were termed. Jews felt their condition was precarious, but so did others who had politically or racially run afoul of Nazi domination.

On July 20, 1933, the Vatican signed a concordat with Germany. Pope Pius XI believed that he had protected Catholic rights in Germany.

In August 1934, President Hindenburg died of old age and Hitler consolidated his powers. Henceforth, he was the unchallenged and unchecked *Fuhrer* of Germany, the one supreme leader.

Right: *A Nazi anti-Jewish propaganda poster entitled "Das Judische Komplott" ("The Jewish Conspiracy"); Germany, 1941.* Below: *Spectators salute passing formations during a Nazi Labor Corps parade.*

ADOLF HITLER

Hitler emerged from World War I bitter and disillusioned. Germany, he felt, had not been defeated on battlefields but betrayed— "stabbed in the back," he falsely claimed—by socialists, liberals, and Jews.

Adolf Hitler was born in Braunau, Austria, on April 20, 1889, the son of Alois Hitler and Alois's third wife, Klara. His father worked hard to achieve his position as a comfortable Austrian customs official, and he expected his son to do the same. There were tensions between father and son, especially about young Hitler's poor schoolwork. The family moved to Linz, where Hitler attended a Roman Catholic school. His mother died from cancer in 1907. Some historians have attributed his hatred of Jews to the treatment his mother received from her Jewish physician. In fact, Hitler praised the doctor and later personally allowed him to emigrate from Germany in 1940. For years, rumors circulated that Hitler was of Jewish origin, but the story has no factual basis.

To pursue his interests in painting and architecture, Hitler moved to Vienna in 1908, but he failed the entrance exam to the Academy of Fine Arts. Living on his now-deceased father's pension and inadequate family support, he sustained himself meagerly, painting postcards and sketching for tourists.

Hitler's sojourn in Vienna shaped his worldview. In that large Austrian city, Jews were culturally active and prominent but anti-Jewish attitudes were rampant. "This was the time of greatest spiritual upheaval I have ever had to go through," Hitler wrote. "I had ceased to be a weak-kneed cosmopolitan and became an antisemite."

In May 1913, Hitler left Vienna for Munich, where he tried unsuccessfully to escape the Austrian draft. He was forced to return and flunked his physical. He volunteered for the German Army in World War I, serving on the Western Front. Decorated for bravery, he achieved only the rank of lance corporal. Suffering from temporary blindness and hallucinations after a British gas attack, he was still in the hospital when Germany surrendered in November 1918. The subsequent Weimar Republic was formed out of the rubble of both the Second Reich and the failed, Munich-based Soviet Republic led by Jewish peace activist Kurt Eisner.

Hitler emerged from the war bitter and disillusioned. Germany, he felt, had not been defeated on battlefields but betrayed—"stabbed in the back," he falsely claimed—by socialists, liberals, and Jews. Hitler and his cohorts considered the Allied terms at the Versailles Peace Conference—requiring reparations and limiting the German military—as a national humiliation and the Weimar Republic leaders who signed the Peace Treaty to be traitors.

Just after the war, Hitler came into contact with a small party that he would dominate: the German Workers' Party. Its name soon became the National Socialist German Workers Party (Nazis).

Hitler's obsession with racial purity was no secret. He clearly stated this belief in speeches. As early as 1919 he wrote: "Rational antisemitism must lead to systematic legal opposition. Its final objective must be the removal of the Jews altogether." (He was then speaking in societal and territorial terms, not in terms of total annihilation.)

By 1923 he and his party staged a military coup in Munich, the "Beer Hall Putsch," which was quickly crushed. Hitler was arrested for treason. He used his subsequent trial as a soapbox and soon became a household name. Sentenced to just five years in Landsberg Prison, he served but less than nine months and used his time to articulate his political views, writing an autobiography, *Mein Kampf* (*My Struggle*), published in 1925.

In the book, Hitler wrote that it was the "sacred mission of the German people . . . to assemble and preserve the most valuable racial elements . . . and raise them to a dominant position."

"All who are not of a good race are chaff," Hitler wrote. The Aryan race was destined to be superior; therefore the German people "are the highest species of humanity on earth." In the racial struggle of history, the "master race" would dominate if it preserved its purity. Otherwise, it would be polluted, corrupted, and destroyed by inferior races.

Hitler's worldview revolved around two concepts: nationalism (including greater "living space" for the German people) and racial supremacy. He considered Jews to be the most inferior and singularly dangerous group of people because of, he insisted, their inclination to infiltrate other races and societies and to dominate them. They were therefore, in Hitler's opinion, the greatest threat to Germany's ability to reach its destiny. Hitler defined the Jews racially, based on blood—not religiously, as a matter of faith and tradition.

After the failed coup, the Nazi Party entered electoral politics, using the tools of democracy to undermine it. Hitler allied the Nazi Party with those parties that opposed the Weimar Republic and the Communists. He attained an increasingly wide audience, especially among the lower middle class. He used the violence of his paramilitary organization, the SA, to promote the Party's agenda.

Short and dark, Hitler could nevertheless extol the image of a tall, blond "Aryan" and instill the German people with national pride and a sense of purpose. A spellbinding orator, he held great appeal for German youth, including university students, and for the frightened middle class, offering them links to their celebrated past and instilling in them a vision for a glorious German future.

Antisemitism alone did not draw German voters to the Nazi Party, though it attracted some. It did not disqualify Hitler in the eyes of most of his supporters. They were far more interested in ending chaos and violence; they were disillusioned by the Weimar government and welcomed an alternative, nationalist vision. Once Hitler was in power in 1933, his hatred of the Jews and his zest for German territorial expansion— *Lebensraum* (living space), as he called it—shaped his policies.

Racism was the dominant theme in Nazi ideology. It directed German social policy throughout the Nazi regime. It was a major factor in the conduct of World War II, and it found expression in German policy in the occupied territories. Though none could imagine it at the time, it gave rise to the Holocaust.

Standing above Heinrich Himmler (head of the SS), Adolf Hitler reviews SS troops during a Reich Party Day mass parade in Nuremberg, Germany, in 1938.

THE NAZIS IN POWER

Laws in increasing severity, scope, and detail were promulgated against the Jews, and eventually other groups were targeted for discrimination and persecution.

Discrimination began in 1933: Germany's Jews were banned from journalism and music, broadcasting and theater—even farming. April 1 brought a boycott of Jewish businesses, and the April 7 Law for the Restoration of the Professional Civil Service barred Jews from the civil service.

Laws in increasing severity, scope, and detail were promulgated against the Jews, and eventually other groups were targeted for discrimination and persecution. The Jewish situation appeared insecure, but the scope of what would happen was ill defined.

German strategy was aimed at making it difficult for Jews to remain in Germany and forcing their "voluntary" emigration. The Nazis were sensitive to public opinion. They did not want to push too far, too fast, or be perceived as lawless. Often after a flurry of activity, conditions stabilized briefly, giving hope that the worst had passed.

Seeking greater legitimacy for his regime, Hitler was pleased with 1933's concordat, the agreement negotiated with the Vatican that sealed his relationship with the Roman Catholic Church and gave him much needed international support.

In 1934 Hitler and the Nazis consolidated power and eliminated their enemies within the German body politic and their rivals within the party. In July, they purged the SA (Storm Troopers) and murdered its leader, Ernst Rohm. They got rid of Gregor Strasser—the second-ranking Nazi Party leader—and in August, with the death of President Hindenburg, Hitler became Germany's sole ruler. Even the army swore allegiance directly to the man—not to the Constitution and not to the country. The judiciary soon followed suit. The *Fuhrer Princip* took effect—Hitler's decrees had the effect of law.

The Nuremberg Laws

In the following years, Germany severely restricted Jewish public activities and participation in professions.

As discrimination against Jews increased, German law required a legal definition of who was a Jew. The "Nuremberg Laws" were promulgated at the annual Nazi Party rally in Nuremberg on September 15, 1935. The Law for the Protection of German Blood and the Reich Citizenship Law became the centerpieces of anti-Jewish legislation. Marriage—and sexual relations—between Jews and citizens of "German or kindred

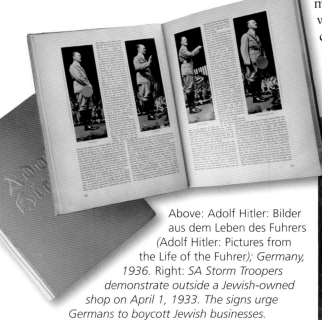

Above: Adolf Hitler: Bilder aus dem Leben des Fuhrers (Adolf Hitler: Pictures from the Life of the Fuhrer); Germany, 1936. Right: SA Storm Troopers demonstrate outside a Jewish-owned shop on April 1, 1933. The signs urge Germans to boycott Jewish businesses.

blood" was prohibited. Women under 45 could not work in Jewish homes. Only racial Germans were entitled to civil and political rights. Jews were reduced to subjects of the state. They could not even fly the flags of the Reich.

The Nuremberg Laws formally divided Germans and Jews, yet neither the word "German" nor "Jew" was defined. That task was left to the bureaucracy, which filled in the gap by November. Two basic categories were established:

- A Jew: anyone with three Jewish grandparents
- A *mischlinge* (mixed blood)

Thus, the definition of Jews was based not upon the identity they affirmed or the religion they practiced, but by blood. Holocaust historian Raul Hilberg argued that categorization had consequences. It was the first stage towards removal from German society and ultimately genocide, though that could not be foreseen at the time. In 1936 an opportunity presented itself.

The 1936 Berlin Olympics

Long before the Nazis rose to power, Berlin had been scheduled to host the 1936 Olympic Games. Two unsettled questions arose: Would Hitler allow the games to take place? And who would come?

Hitler originally saw the Olympics as an "infamous festival organized by Jews," but he soon became convinced by Propaganda Minister Joseph Goebbels that it was an opportunity to feature the "New Germany."

First, German sports associations banned Jews. German Olympic officials with Jewish ties lost their positions. The exclusion created a stir in the International Olympic Committee, which forbade restricting participation based on "class, color, or creed." After a carefully controlled trip to Germany, the American Olympic Committee—led by Avery Brundage—accepted the German invitation.

The American Athletic Association demurred. Its president, Jeremiah Mahoney, organized a Committee on Fair Play in Sports, which quickly gained the support of university presidents and former Olympic medalists, politicians, and clergy. Brundage countered that U.S. athletes should stay clear of the "Jew-Nazi" fight. Brundage ultimately prevailed, and the U.S. Olympic team went, though several Jewish athletes refused to participate. Germany was forced to permit a few—but by no means all—Jewish athletes to participate on German teams.

The issue became more acute when—one month after the Winter Olympics, which Germany also hosted—the German army marched into

Top: *Students carry Nazi flags and march around a bonfire of "un-German" books on the Opera Square in Berlin, on May 10, 1933.* Above: *German passports stamped with a red "J," inserted at the request of the neutral Swiss government in 1938. Also included are the middle names "Israel" and "Sara," a legal requirement for all Jewish documents after 1938.* Bottom: *An instructional chart used by the Nazis to distinguish "Aryans" from Jews and* mischlinge.

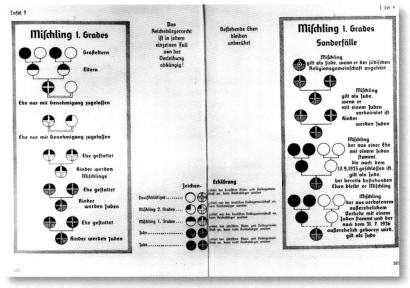

THE NUREMBERG LAWS

Reich Citizenship Law
September 15, 1935

The *Reichstag* unanimously enacts the following law, which is promulgated herewith:

1

1) A subject of the State is a person who enjoys the protection of the German Reich and who in consequence has specific obligations toward it.
2) The status of a subject of the State is acquired in accordance with the provisions of the Reich and State Citizenship Law.

2

1) A Reich citizen is a subject of the State who is of German and related blood, who proves by his conduct that he is willing and fit faithfully to serve the German people and the Reich.
2) Reich citizenship is acquired through the granting of a Reich Citizenship Certificate.
3) The Reich citizen is the sole bearer of full political rights in accordance with the Law.

3

The Reich Minister of the Interior, in coordination with the Deputy of the *Fuhrer*, will issue the Legal and Administrative orders required to implement and complete this Law.

Nuremberg, September 15, 1935, at the Reich Party
    Congress of Freedom
The *Fuhrer* and Reich Chancellor Adolf Hitler
The Reich Minister of the Interior Frick

Law for the Protection of German Blood and German Honor
September 15, 1935

Imbued with the insight that the purity of German blood is prerequisite for the continued existence of the German people and inspired by the inflexible will to ensure the existence of the German nation for all times, the *Reichstag* has unanimously adopted the following law, which is hereby promulgated:

1

(1) Marriages between Jews and subjects of German or kindred blood are forbidden. Marriages neverthe-less concluded are invalid, even if concluded abroad to circumvent this law.
(2) Only the State Attorney may initiate the annulment suit.

2

Extramarital intercourse between Jews and subjects of German or kindred blood is forbidden.

3

Jews must not employ in their households female subjects of German or kindred blood who are under 45 years old.

4

(1) Jews are forbidden to fly the Reich and national flag and to display the Reich colors.
(2) They are, on the other hand, allowed to display the Jewish colors. The exercise of this right enjoys the protection of the state.

5

(1) Whoever violates the prohibition in paragraph 1 will be punished by penal servitude.
(2) A male who violates the prohibition in paragraph 2 will be punished either by imprisonment or penal servitude.
(3) Whoever violates the provisions of paragraphs 3 or 4 will be punished by imprisonment up to one year and by a fine, or by either of these penalties.

6

The Reich Minister of the Interior, in agreement with the Deputy of the *Fuhrer* and the Reich Minister of Justice, will issue the legal and administrative orders required to implement and supplement this law.

7

The law takes effect on the day following promulgation, except for 3, which goes into force January 1, 1936.

Nuremberg, September 15 1935, at the Reich Party
Congress of Freedom
The *Fuhrer* and Reich Chancellor
The Reich Minister of the Interior
The Reich Minister of Justice
The Deputy of the *Fuhrer*

the Rhineland, in direct violation of the Versailles agreement.

In anticipation of the Summer Games, Berlin was scrubbed clean and antisemitic signs were taken down. Graffiti was painted over. Gypsies were spirited out of the city. Optimists felt that perhaps the worst had passed.

The 1936 Olympics are remembered for pageantry and precision, with grand parades and a smiling Hitler receiving flowers from a young German girl. It was also a moment of triumph for racial equality, as Jesse Owens—an African American sprinter—won four gold medals, then an Olympic record. Little attention was paid to the exclusion of Jewish athletes. Marty Glickman and Sam Stoller, two American Jewish athletes, had qualified to run the final lap of the 400-meter relay. They were replaced by Frank Metcalfe and Owens, who had already won three gold medals. Stoller called it the most "humiliating moment of my life."

The façade of normalcy worked well. President Franklin D. Roosevelt told Rabbi Stephen Wise, head of the World Jewish Congress, that "the [German] synagogues are full and apparently there is nothing wrong."

By late 1937 the process of "Aryanization," in which Jewish businesses were transferred to non-Jewish "Aryan" ownership, was intensified. Jews were forbidden from remaining corporate officers or stockholders. Their property was purchased at well below its value. When business owners held out for more favorable conditions, they often found themselves in more vulnerable positions, which in turn diminished the value of their assets. In time, the formerly well-established German Jewish community became impoverished.

In 1938 conditions again deteriorated for Jews. In March, Germany invaded Austria and incorporated that country into the Reich. Discriminatory measures were imposed overnight on Austria's nearly 200,000 Jews. Violence against Jews intensified, as Austrian Nazis were unleashed to commit violence. Hitler triumphantly rode into Vienna, and the Jews of Vienna saw their future turn bleak.

In September at the Munich talks, Britain and France agreed to let Hitler take control of parts of Czechoslovakia, further signaling Allied weakness and the desire to avoid war at all costs.

In October, the neutral Swiss government requested that the Germans stamp all Jewish passports. Afraid of being overrun by Austrian Jews seeking refuge in their country but willing to receive other Germans as visitors, vacationers, and businessmen, they insisted—and Germany willingly complied—on the distinction between "Aryan" and Jew.

Also in October, Germany expelled tens of thousands of Polish Jews living in Germany without German citizenship. Sent to the Polish border at Zbaszyn and other sites, these Jews were caught in no-man's land. They were not permitted to return to Poland, nor could they live in Germany. Instead, they dwelled in temporary huts along the Polish-German border as winter set in.

By the end of the year, male Jews had to add the name "Israel" to their identification cards; females had to add "Sara." Jews were marked.

Top left: *Anti-Jewish poster that reads "German patriots, do not buy from these Jews"; Germany, 1933.* Top right: *An anti-Jewish propaganda leaflet; Germany, c. 1939.* Bottom: *Page from the antisemitic German children's book* Der Giftpilz (The Poisonous Mushroom)*; Germany, 1938. The text reads: "Money is the god of the Jews. He commits the greatest crimes to earn money. He won't rest until he can sit on a great sack of money, until he has become king of money."*

JOHN FINK
1920–2000

Hans Finke (later known as John Fink) was born in Berlin. His mother died when he was a toddler, while his father, Julius, had been awarded the Iron Cross for heroism during World War I. Almost one in six German Jews served in that war, and many earned honors for bravery.

Julius operated a dry goods store, which he lost during the massive inflation of 1923, when a wheelbarrow of German currency was needed to buy bread. Later, Julius worked in a large Berlin department store, but he lost that job during the Depression and was out of work for many years. He became a peddler, going from door to door. At night, he addressed envelopes for a mail order house. Hans's childhood was poor. "We never had bananas," Hans said. His father remarried. Ella Finke became his stepmother, and Ursula was his new stepsister. "She was the good one, and I was the troublemaker," he recalled.

The family lived in impoverished circumstances, and Hans was one of just two Jews in his elementary school class. He received religious instruction weekly, and had his bar mitzvah during the year that Adolf Hitler came to power.

"We played soccer, cops and robbers, never had a big problem," Hans remembered. That ended when the Nazis came to power. Since the tavern below their apartment was an SA hangout, the Finke family moved yet again. When school became uncomfortable for Hans because he was Jewish, he was sent to a Jewish middle school near the synagogue and an old age home. He had wonderful teachers, most of whom had been dismissed from prestigious jobs. The young were being trained not for careers in Germany but for emigration. Some were

anxious to go to Palestine. Hans became an apprentice electrician working for a Jew. That man taught him what he needed to know but did not pay him a salary.

The Nuremberg Laws, which defined Jews on the basis of their grandparents, were promulgated in 1935. Hans's employer understood that both he and his son would be classified as Jews, despite the fact that his wife was a non-Jew. Shortly thereafter, the employer immigrated to South Africa, leaving Hans without a job and without a mentor.

Hans took the test as a journeyman worker, but Jews were not allowed to see the results. He did find work for a time with a contractor who could still employ Jews. "We remodeled newly confiscated Jewish homes," Hans recalled.

When World War II began, a series of laws further restricted the movement of Jews in Berlin, and Hans got a job with the Siemens Company doing electrical installations. "Every week people disappeared from our group," he said. They either were victims of deportation or they went underground.

In 1941 Hans was forced to wear the Jewish star. Sometime later, bicycles were confiscated from Jews. His parents were deported in February 1943, and their apartment was sealed. Hans later assumed that they were murdered in Auschwitz upon arrival.

One month later, on March 12, 1943, Hans himself was sent to Auschwitz. Upon arrival, two SS officers made *Selektionen* (selections). "Everything went fast," he remembered. "Women and children disappeared." Hans was one of 964 Jews taken on one of the last transports from Berlin. He was sent to Auschwitz III, the slave labor camp known as Buna-Monowitz. His hair was cut, his body doused in kerosene to kill lice. The number 107821 was tattooed on his left arm, and he was sent to the showers—real showers, not gas chambers.

One day, the Germans announced that "people with a trade should report." Hans reported as an electrician.

He was assigned to Block 11, housed with musicians from a band, who—in one of the maudlin aspects of life in the camps—played music as workers left for work and returned from the slave labor. For Hans, it was better than carrying cement bags back and forth each day.

As to what was happening in Birkenau, the death camp at Auschwitz, Hans said: "We could see the sky red with the flames. And smell the flesh burning."

After a few months, he became an old-timer. He was made foreman of a small commando, and he could sit on a bench when he came after work—great luxuries in the world of Auschwitz III. He made a heating plate for a *Kapo* (prisoner who worked as a guard), and was given a tin with marmalade in return.

Hans witnessed many new arrivals: Warsaw Jews after the April 1943 Ghetto Uprising; Hungarian Jews after the German invasion in 1944; Jews from Holland and Norway; Ukrainian civil laborers; even German and French women. Hans used a non-Jewish prisoner to smuggle a letter to his sister, Ursula, informing her he was alive.

After the bombing of Buna-Monowitz in the summer of 1944 (the nearby gas cham-

"We played soccer, cops and robbers, never had a big problem until the Nazis came to power."

bers were not bombed), the power station was blown up. There was no heating, no hot water.

When asked what was the worst aspect of Auschwitz, Hans replied: "nature: The cold of winter, the heat of summer, snow and rain." He thought again: "The treatment, the *Selektionen.*"

Hans left Auschwitz on January 17, 1945, in the forced evacuations that became known as death marches. The SS marched with warm clothing. Many prisoners were barefoot and in rags. Prisoners who collapsed or fell behind were killed. Hans was walked to Gleiwitz and then boarded an open coal car in Poland's cold January. When the prisoners traveled through Czechoslovakia, the Czechs threw food into the wagons from the bridges. The SS shot people in front of the villagers.

The captives arrived in Mauthausen and were turned away because the camp was too crowded. They arrived in Sachsenhausen and, after a brief stay, were again sent away. They arrived next in Flossenberg, where they were sent to work in the quarries, and then were sent to Bergen-Belsen. There, the camp system had completely broken down under

John and Alice's marriage, performed in the Bergen-Belsen DP camp; 1948.

Alice and John in 1948.

John has four children, a son and three daughters. Two daughters teach the deaf, inspired by their deaf sister. One child was president of the Children of Holocaust Survivors in Chicago. And John worked as an electrician for many years. He joined an electrical workers union, where he experienced ethnic diversity not as a license for murder and persecution, but for cooperation and celebration.

When asked why he survived, his response was simple: "Pure luck." Yet he spoke with confidence: "If I could make it through Auschwitz, if I can make it in Auschwitz, I can make it anywhere."

After retirement, John began to think about the Holocaust and its impact on his life and the youth he lost. "I don't know how to dance," he said. "I don't know the smell of a bar. I don't know how to play cards. When my grandson wants to play chess, I don't know how to play that game either.

"I lived 4,454 days under Nazism, and I was in a concentration camp for 764 days."

the pressure of new arrivals, and a typhus epidemic was rampant.

On April 15, 1945, Hans was liberated by the British, who then employed him to restore electricity and water while they coped with a medical epidemic that caused 13,000 people to die after liberation. Hans stayed there until October and witnessed the transformation of the Bergen-Belsen concentration camp into a thriving displaced-persons camp, complete with its own schools and Yiddish theater, its own leadership and the glimmer of hope.

On the eve of his first Rosh Hashanah in freedom, Hans met his future wife, Alice, who was working as a nurse in Bergen-Belsen with a Jewish relief organization. In October 1945, he was strong enough to go back to Berlin, where he learned that his sister was alive, and then worked at a children's home for the American Jewish Joint Distribution Committee, known as the Joint.

Hans returned to Bergen-Belsen in 1945 and lived in the hospital. He married in 1948. The couple applied to leave, and his wife's cousin supplied an affidavit that brought the Finke family to Chicago. No longer Hans Finke, he became John Fink. In 1948 they traveled to the United States on a DC–6 military transport aircraft. John and Alice traveled with 100 pregnant women who could not endure the rough seas. John and his wife settled in Chicago.

John and Alice during their 50th year of marriage.

JEWISH LIFE UNDER THE SWASTIKA

Well integrated into society and comfortably assimilated, Germany's Jews were shocked by the Nazis' rise to power. As a rule, the more acculturated the Jews—the more they thought of themselves as Germans—the greater the shock.

German Jews had been granted civic equality—citizenship and the right to vote—in 1871 after Otto von Bismarck united Germany into one nation. Despite legal emancipation, Jews were often still restricted socially and barred from senior government and academic positions.

One hundred thousand Jews, almost 20 percent of Germany's approximately 530,000 Jews, had fought for Germany during World War I; 12,000 died in battle. Full legal emancipation came after the war, during the progressive Weimar Republic. Under Weimar, Jews served as judges in court and full professors in the leading German universities. They played major roles in all aspects of Germany's flourishing and avant-garde cultural life and arts, as well as in journalism and politics. From 1901 to 1933, ten German Jews were among the more than 30 Germans who had won Nobel Prizes. They felt at home in German society and even spoke of the unique German-Jewish symbiosis.

Years later Gershom Scholem, the great scholar of Jewish mysticism and Zionist dissenter from German Jewish culture, described the "symbiosis" as a German-Jewish monologue: Jews, he said, were telling themselves how deeply German they were.

Religiously and culturally, the community had also been flourishing during Weimar times as some young Jews were rediscovering their roots.

A small Zionist movement had emerged. Theological seminaries—liberal and Orthodox—and great German universities were attracting not only German Jews but Eastern European men and women who wanted to share the best of Western culture and integrate it into their Jewish learning and living. Among them: Shmuel Yosef Agnon, Zalman Rubashov (Shazar), Joseph Dov Baer Soloveitchik, Abraham Joshua Heschel, and Menachem Mendel Schneerson. Safety, freedom, and opportunity were to be found by moving westward toward Germany. The remnant that survived would come to prominence on three continents in the next generation.

With the rise of Hitler, few perceived the full extent of what was to follow, but how could they? A small minority—mostly political leaders targeted by the Nazis, cultural figures banned from their fields, and young people—prepared to leave. The majority regarded Nazism as an aberration, as antithetical to German values and German tradition, abhorrent to the neighbors and colleagues they knew so well.

In response to the April 1, 1933, boycott, Robert Weltsch, editor of the Zionist weekly *Juedische Rundschau,* metaphorically proclaimed: "Wear it with pride, the Yellow badge." Deprived of their confidence as Germans, some Jews turned inward and embraced their Jewishness. Others despaired; a few committed suicide. Still others decided to wait out the crisis, presuming that the

A Hanukah menorah is proudly placed in a window across from the town hall and a Nazi banner in Kiel, Germany; 1932.

Deprived of their confidence as Germans, some Jews turned inward and embraced their Jewishness. Others despaired; a few committed suicide.

Germans would wake up and the nightmare would end.

The initial Jewish reaction to Nazi anti-Jewish measures, on both the individual and communal level, was an attempt to continue to lead normal lives. This striving for normalcy was evident in numerous initiatives undertaken by leaders of the Jewish community, by Jewish organizations, and by individual Jews, all of whom responded to what they believed was a brutal—but temporary—situation.

One response to Germany's increasingly hostile environment was the creation of alternative activities and organizations for Jews, to replace those from which they were excluded. A major achievement was uniting the often-conflicting ideological groups under a single umbrella organization, *Reichsvertretung der deutschen Juden* (Reich Representation of German Jews). Led by Rabbi Leo Baeck, this official representative body was founded on September 17, 1933. It served two roles: as both a much-needed liaison with the hostile Nazi government and as a source of material aid, education, and emigration assistance for its Jewish constituents.

That same year also witnessed the creation of the *Kulturbund* (Cultural Union of German Jews), which allowed Jewish artists and audiences, who were excluded from public cultural life, to engage in and to enjoy cultural activities in newly organized theaters and orchestras throughout the country.

In the field of social welfare, Jews were excluded from 1935's general Winter Relief programs. In response, Jews established their own *Winterhilfe,* which aided and supported many impoverished Jews who, for the first time, needed assistance.

Finally, throughout this period, the Jewish community initiated practical alternatives for banned Jews in a variety of disciplines—medicine, law, education, sports—allowing them, at least for a time, to pursue their interests and professions after being "legally" excluded by the regime.

For Jewish children, the first blow of persecution often came in school, where

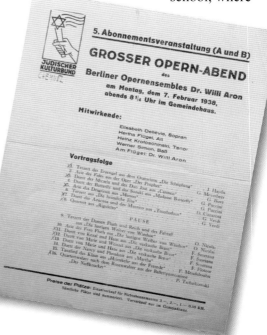

Above left: *Students from the Youth Aliyah School pose with teacher Jizchak Schwersenz; Berlin, 1940. The partial Hebrew caption above reads: "The People Israel Lives."* Above right: *A program for a concert put on by the Cultural Union of German Jews; Berlin, February 1938.*

they met with hostility from their classmates and teachers, and where appeals to school administrators were often met with silence—if not with sympathy for the harassers. The Jewish community enlarged its schools and established new ones, where Jewish children could feel safe even if they met with dangers en route to and from school.

Synagogues became the center of Jewish life, havens from the hostile outside world, comparable to the schools that protected the children. In addition to serving its religious function, a temple might be used as a lecture hall, theater, concert hall, or training center.

Until he left for Palestine in 1938, Jewish philosopher Martin Buber led an effort to educate Jewish adults, preparing the Jewish community for the long ordeal ahead.

Emigration came in waves, with sudden upsurges after the rise of Hitler, after 1937's economic confiscation of businesses, and especially after the November 1938 pogroms. During periods of quiet, Jews adjusted to their new circumstances, feeling that the situation had stabilized and could not worsen. They certainly did not perceive how precarious their situation was—or how much worse it would soon become.

Young people were trained for portable professions. For those hoping to go to Palestine, agricultural training was preferable—although unfamiliar to Germany's urban Jews. Architects, doctors, filmmakers, and musicians had an easier time contemplating emigration since they could practice their livelihoods elsewhere. Lawyers, though, had been trained in German laws, and writers needed the German language. By the outbreak of World War II in September 1939, more than half of German Jews had left Germany, despite worldwide restrictions on Jewish emigrants.

In August 1933, the *Haavara* (Transfer) Agreement was signed between the German Ministry of the Economy and the Jewish Agency for Palestine. It permitted German Jews to

THE KINDERTRANSPORT

After the November pogroms known as *Kristallnacht,* Jews recognized that the situation would not get better. One opportunity for escape developed when British Jews advanced the idea that some 10,000 children would be admitted to safety in Britain. The Cabinet approved and a rescue was organized.

In a mission called the *Kindertransport,* the German Jewish community organized the exodus of 8,000 Jewish children under age 18 to Great Britain. The British were willing to receive these children precisely because they would not work and take away British jobs. Parents were faced with an impossible dilemma: To protect their children, they had to let them go, perhaps never to see them again.

In Germany, a network of organizers was established. These volunteers worked around the clock to make priority lists of those most endangered, including orphans and those whose parents were in concentration camps or too poor to sustain them.

How did parents and children react to their separation? Eva Heyman recalled:

We had about two weeks before we left and into that fortnight, both mother and father were trying to give instructions, the guidance that they hoped to have their whole life to give.

What did they take with them? Lorry Cahn remembered:

I think I took my teddy bear. And my mother always slept on a little pillow on top of her big pillow. And I asked her whether I could take that with me. So she said: "Sure."

The first *Kindertransport* left Berlin on December 1, 1938. In March 1939, after the German entry into Czechoslovakia, transports were sent from Prague. The last transport of children left Germany on September 1, 1939, the day World War II began. Its adult leader, Norbert Wollheim, either had to escort the children to England or stay to be with his wife and his son. He remained in Berlin and survived. His wife and his son did not.

A similar effort by Senator Robert Wagner (D-NY) and Representative Edith Rogers (R-MA) to save 20,000 German Jewish children by bringing them to the United States, outside the allotted quotas, was tied up in committee and never reached the floor. So, no such effort was undertaken by the United States.

From 1933 to the outbreak of World War II in 1939, more than 5,000 children arrived without their parents in Palestine, through *Youth Aliya* (Youth Immigration). The effort was run by Recha Freier, the wife of a Berlin rabbi, in an attempt to rescue endangered Jewish youth in Germany. Housed in *kibbutzim* and youth villages in Palestine, many of these young Jews never saw their families again.

bypass British restrictions and migrate to Palestine. As with all Jewish negotiations with the Nazis during this era, and especially during World War II, it was a meeting of unequals. The imbalance of power was only to deepen. Under the provisions of the agreement, the assets of Jews leaving for Palestine were placed in special accounts; portions of these accounts could be drawn upon in Palestine in the form of German goods. The arrangement enabled more than 50,000 Jews to leave Germany for Palestine and arrive there with at least some resources to begin their new lives. The German language could be heard in the streets of Haifa, in the cafes of Tel Aviv, and in the neighborhoods of Jerusalem.

This agreement was consistent with the view that the goal of German policy during the prewar period was the "voluntary" emigration of Jews, to make Germany *Judenrein,* free of Jews, not by murder but by making it unbearable for Jews to continue to live in Germany.

The name and the functions of the Jewish community changed over time in response to its deteriorating condition:

1933: Reich Representation of German Jews

1935: Reich Representation of Jews in Germany

1938: Reich Federation of Jews in Germany

1939: Reich Association of Jews in Germany

Beginning as representative of Jewish communities, the formal body of Jews gradually was forced to adapt its constituents' new situation not as German Jews but as Jews in Germany. Not entitled to representation, the most they could assume was an association.

Below: *Young Michael Strauss sails with a family friend aboard a ship to Beirut. The Strauss family made its way to Palestine from Germany in 1933.* Bottom: *A Jewish men's field hockey team; Berlin, 1930s.*

WALTER REED
1924–

Werner Moritz Rindsberg (Walter Reed) was born in the southern German city of Wuerzburg, but he lived in a small nearby village called Mainstockheim. Werner was the oldest of three brothers. In the basement of the family home and in leased facilities, his father, Siegfried, operated a winery, which his own father had founded in 1898. "In our town, Jews were either cattle dealers or winemakers," Walter recalled.

The Jewish community was small but dedicated: All were Orthodox. His family observed the Sabbath scrupulously. Werner would neither ride in a car nor on a bicycle on the Sabbath.

Werner excelled at Mainstockheim's strict Jewish elementary school, whose teacher and Jewish community cantor was the uncle of Henry Kissinger (who attended a junior high school in a town two miles away). There, Werner was sometimes taunted for being Jewish. Some teachers made it clear that they were Nazis; a few made it a point of honor to show their solidarity with Jewish students. However, Werner was respected on the soccer field, where his skills as a defenseman served him well.

Since Siegfried's business was dependent on his contacts with non-Jews, the family's circumstances grew more precarious year by year. Customers were concerned about buying from a Jew. His main worker and his freight hauler kept working for Siegfried, even though they were castigated for doing so.

Werner's family started looking for opportunities to flee Germany. His mother's six siblings had emigrated from the country by the mid-1930s. Siegfried was torn between staying to care for his elderly mother and res-

cuing himself and his family. He hesitated and did not begin looking for an exit until 1939.

Walter's memory of the November pogroms, known as *Kristallnacht,* begins with loud knocks at the door. He and his father, along with a few dozen other Jewish men, were arrested and hauled away to the county jail.

Werner, age 14, was released, but his father was sent to Dachau, which in March 1933 had become the first of the Nazi concentration camps. After five or six weeks at the notorious camp, Siegfried was released. To Werner, his father seemed broken, haggard, and much older than he had been just weeks earlier.

Now there was no question whether or not to leave Germany. The only questions were *how* to leave and *where* would a Jew be accepted?

Werner was the first to leave. His parents heard of a Belgian rescue program and sent him there in June 1939. Meanwhile his parents and brothers were working to get visas to America. Werner journeyed to Cologne and then to Brussels, where, thanks to the rescue efforts of the Belgian *Comite d'Assistance aux Enfants Refugies Juif* (CAEJR)—which saved nearly 1,000 Jewish children from Germany and Austria—he was taken to a children's home in Brussels with some 40 other refugee boys.

The summer of 1939 was wonderful for Werner. The world looked safe. He was no longer persecuted.

Werner (first row, far right) during Purim; c. 1930.

He had time to explore museums and go on outings with the other children. Away from the small town where everyone knew his family, Werner enjoyed the freedom and anonymity of a large city.

He also started to reexamine his own religious faith, the path of his parents and their forebears. "Jews set themselves apart," he thought. "We chose to be different."

On May 10, 1940, the Germans invaded Belgium and Werner's days of freedom ended. He was on the run again, leaving Belgium on a refugee freight train for northern France with 92 other children under the committee's care. He later moved south to a village near Toulouse.

"In our town, Jews were either cattle dealers or winemakers."

Werner (center) with brothers Kurt (left) and Herbert; 1942.

After he lived more than a year in Vichy France (which collaborated with Germany) under very harsh conditions, his aunt Sarah secured immigration papers for him. She was assisted by a Belgian committee woman, who worked from the Hebrew Immigrant Aid Society office in New York. Werner traveled to neutral Portugal, where he boarded a boat in 1941 for a dangerous Atlantic crossing.

Greeted by his mother's siblings in New York, Werner went to work immediately as a tool and die maker's apprentice, attending high school at night. Werner's last communication with his parents was in mid-June 1941.

In 1943 Werner was drafted into the U.S. Army, where he worked as a machinist and joined a replacement battalion for the invasion of Normandy. Because of his military service, he became a U.S. citizen in 1943 without the mandatory five-year wait. After choosing a new name, Walter Reed, he returned to Europe in March 1944—three years after he had left—and landed in Normandy as a combat engineer just after the June 6

invasion. He was trained to lay pontoon bridges to assist advancing infantry forces.

Skilled in German and French and fluent in English, Walter was transferred to military intelligence in France, where he interrogated German prisoners and civilians at the front. During the Battle of the Bulge at the end of 1944, he returned to Belgium not as a refugee but as a liberating soldier. He later returned to Germany as part of the victorious U.S. Army. His task: help occupation forces rid Germany of its Nazi leadership. Once ejected from his German junior high school for being Jewish, he was now deciding the fate of professors at the University of Marburg.

When he returned to Mainstockheim in 1945 as an American soldier, he learned that his parents and brothers had been deported to Izbica, Poland. Later he found out that they had been among the early mass-murder victims of Germany. Walter returned to his native village, now in a position to reclaim his family's property. But with his parents and brothers dead, the property seemed insignificant.

After his discharge in 1946, Walter studied journalism at the University of Missouri, where he hid his religion and his past, and explained that he was from Brooklyn. Walter Reed was fully American. More than 20 years later, before he proposed to his wife, he felt compelled to reveal to her the truth of his background.

Walter pursued a career in public relations and worked for more than three decades for the National Automatic Merchandising Association. He remained in contact with his relatives even as he married and raised three sons of his own. Only in the 1990s did Walter begin to talk publicly of his background.

NOVEMBER POGROMS–KRISTALLNACHT

On the evening of November 9, 1938, the 15th anniversary of the failed Nazi *Putsch* in Munich, anti-Jewish violence erupted throughout the Reich, which now included Austria. The outburst was staged to *appear* as the spontaneous eruption of national anger at a young Jewish youth's assassination of a minor German Embassy official in Paris. In fact, the violence was choreographed in detail.

Two events earlier in 1938 foreshadowed things to come for German Jews:

- The Evian Conference in July 1938—in which delegates of 32 nations met to discuss the absorption of Jews seeking to flee Nazi Germany—had yielded no realistic new havens and convinced Germany that no one wanted to take its Jews.
- The Munich Conference, hastily convened in September to deal with Hitler's demands to annex the Sudetenland area of Czechoslovakia, had resulted in appeasement, which indicated to Germany that the West would not oppose its expansionist goals.

On the night of October 28, some 17,000 Polish Jews living in Germany were rounded up and expelled. Many had lived comfortably in Germany for years but had never acquired German citizenship. Poland would not readmit them, and they lived in desperate conditions in no-man's land, most in the border town of Zbaszyn.

On November 3, 17-year-old Herschel Grynszpan received a postcard in Paris from his sister that described the family's desperate plight. Pushed over the edge, he avenged the persecution by shooting a German official in Paris. His revenge replicated the 1936 assassination in Davos, Switzerland, of Wilhelm Gustloff, head of the Swiss Nazi Party, by a young Yugoslavian Jew, David Frankfurter, which did not result in any "spontaneous" eruption of anti-Jewish violence.

Left: *Interior of the architecturally impressive* Fasanenstrasse Synagogue; Berlin, c. 1912. Below: *The* Fasanenstrasse Synagogue after being destroyed during Kristallnacht *in November 1938.*

Within 48 hours, some 1,400 synagogues were attacked and many burned, along with their Torah scrolls, Bibles, and prayer books. Some 30,000 Jewish men aged 16 to 60 were arrested and sent to newly expanded concentration camps within Germany.

The assassination in Paris was the pretext for what was to follow.

Around midnight on the evening of November 9, a senior Gestapo officer, Heinrich Mueller, sent a telegram to all police units: "In shortest order, actions against Jews and especially their synagogues will take place in all Germany. These are not to be interfered with...." Bystanders to the violence, the police were to arrest its *victims*. Fire companies were instructed to stand by—not to protect the synagogues, but to ensure that the flames did not spread to adjacent "Aryan" property.

Within 48 hours, some 1,400 synagogues were attacked and many burned, along with their Torah scrolls, Bibles, and prayer books. Some 30,000 Jewish men aged 16 to 60 were arrested and sent to newly expanded concentration camps within Germany—foremost among them Buchenwald, Dachau, and Sachsenhausen—which were overflowing with newly arrested Jewish inmates and where up to 1,000 died. Some 7,500 businesses were smashed and looted, and more

The Scroll of Esther, saved from the fires of a burning synagogue on Kristallnacht; Germany, *November 9–10, 1938.*

than 100 Jews were killed. Jewish cemeteries, hospitals, schools, and homes were ransacked, and many were destroyed.

Hour after hour, the pogrom's pace intensified and the toll increased. No Jewish institution, business, or home was safe. The terror directed at the Jews was often not the action of strangers but neighbors.

In the aftermath of these pogroms, the Jews in Germany were left without their synagogues. Many Jews had lost their businesses, their homes, and, above all, any hope that their situation could be managed if only they held on. *All* Jews were now convinced: Jewish life in the German Reich was no longer possible.

As the fury subsided, the pogrom was given a name: *Kristallnacht* (Crystal Night; Night of Broken Glass).

Germans also had learned important lessons. Because of their bourgeois sensibilities, many were uncomfortable with *Kristallnacht.* The sloppiness of the November pogroms and the explosive violence of the SA Storm Troopers would soon be replaced by the cold, calculated violence of the SS, Hitler's elite troops. They would dispose of the Jews out of the view of most Germans.

On November 12, 1938, Hermann Goring convened Nazi officials to deal with the problems that had resulted from *Kristallnacht.* One industry had much at stake: the insurance industry, which stood to lose huge sums paying claims from those whose property had been destroyed.

Goring was clearly disturbed by the two-day rampage's damage—to the German economy. "It's insane to burn a Jewish warehouse and then have a

German insurance company pay for the loss," he said. "We suffer, not the Jews."

The discussion centered on how to solve the "Jewish problem" once and for all, but in 1938 its meaning was in economic terms and in implementation of "voluntary" emigration. Only later, by 1941, would the language turn genocidal. In 1938 there remained a concern for legality, for maintaining economic stability. Thus, while the economic elimination of the Jews transpired over time, the direction was clear: Jews were to disappear from German life.

Several concrete results were achieved—all economically lethal to Jewish life. By a series of policy decisions, the Nazis transformed *Kristallnacht* into the ultimate platform to eliminate Jews from German life:

- Jewish compensation claims were confiscated and insurance companies instructed to forward the compensation funds to the Reich.
- Jewish property owners were forced to repair their property.
- The rubble of ruined synagogues had to be cleared by the community.
- A collective fine of one billion Reichsmarks ($400 million) was imposed on the Jewish community.

- The "Aryanization" process of seizing Jewish businesses was finalized.
- Jewish organizations were dissolved and their newspapers banned.
- The Central Office for Jewish Emigration was created to "encourage" Jews to leave Germany.

In the end, Goring expressed regrets over the whole event. "I wish you had killed 200 Jews and not destroyed such value," he concluded with irony. "I would not like to be a Jew in Germany!"

The November pogroms were the last occasion for street violence against Jews in Germany proper. In 1939 additional restrictions banned Jews from residing and working with Germans. Moreover, a curfew was imposed that banned Jews from streets after 8 P.M. While Jews were no longer subject to mass organized attacks, a lethal process of destruction that was more effective and more virulent was set in place.

Above: *The schedule of a tax assessment levied on Walter Hesse by the Nazi Party. Jews had to pay for damages incurred during* Kristallnacht. Left: *Two men walk past the shattered display window of a Jewish-owned cafe that was vandalized during* Kristallnacht; *Berlin, November 11, 1938.* Below: *The release document for Max Gottschalk from Buchenwald, dated November 14, 1938. Along with 30,000 Jewish men, he had been taken into custody immediately after* Kristallnacht.

RALPH REHBOCK

1934–

Ralph Rehbock was born in 1934 in Gotha, Germany, a midsized town in the center of the country. His mother, Ruth, was a dental hygienist, and his father, Hans, was a businessman working in metal fabrication for a company run by Ralph's grandfather. They exported products throughout Europe and the United States. Among their customers was Marshall Field's, the famed Chicago department store. Because they were exporters, Hans was able to keep his passport and driver's license well into the Nazi period.

Ralph enjoyed a wonderful family life, living in an apartment building that housed his grandmother and her mother as well. His middle-class home was an integral part of the small community of some 350 Jews in Gotha. His parents were keenly aware of their Jewishness. Although they were not devoutly religious, they celebrated major holidays. Their home was graced with Jewish ceremonial objects, including a family prayer book that had been passed down for five generations.

Among Ralph's fondest memories were his trips to Ohrdruf, where his maternal grandparents—who lived on a farm—were the town's only Jews, as Ralph remembered it. The farm was the gathering place of their extended family. (Ohrdruf would later become the site of a concentration camp.)

Ralph was young during the rise of Nazism, too young to remember firsthand but not too young to have impressions deepened by family lore. The neighbors were friendly before Hitler's rise to power in 1933. Afterward, he recalled, "some stopped talking to our family. People shied away from us, but I was very well taken care of." Ralph's mother was dismissed from her job, although his father was allowed to continue to work in his business as it produced much-needed foreign currency for the German economy. For a time, his parents made no plans to leave Germany, where they were rooted and prosperous. One uncle was a decorated, disabled German World War I veteran.

In 1938 Ralph's family decided to leave Germany. They sought a visitor's visa to the United States, but the German official would not let the entire family leave. Only one could go; the official worried that otherwise they would not return. Ralph's father insisted that Ralph's mother go. She went to Chicago, where she met with family members who had previously settled in the city. On her first Passover in Chicago, she drew down the blinds to celebrate the holiday. She had forgotten that in a free, tolerant country, one could celebrate religious festivals openly. She returned to Germany with the appropriate papers needed for immigration.

Ralph's most vivid recollection is of the November 1938 pogrom, known as *Kristallnacht.* His parents had received word from the American Embassy to come and pick up their valuable immigration certificate. The date was set for November 10, 1938. By custom, the Rehbocks were never on time; they always arrived early. So they went to Berlin on November 8, and they were in their hotel when the adjacent synagogue was set on fire on the 9th. His father received an urgent telephone call from Ralph's teenaged Jewish nanny: "The English lesson is canceled," she told Hans.

Hans understood immediately. The Nazis were looking for him that night. For on *Kristallnacht,* synagogues throughout Germany and Austria were set on fire, businesses were looted and destroyed, and

30,000 Jewish men aged 16 to 60 were arrested and sent to newly expanded concentration camps. Hans had been on a list. Fortuitously, he had been out of town. He never returned to Gotha and spent the next weeks hiding from the Nazis. Ralph was sent back home, where he was cared for by a Jewish nanny. (Since the 1935 Nuremberg Laws, non-Jewish women younger than 45 were not permitted to work in Jewish homes.) Before departing their Berlin hotel, they noticed a newly displayed sign: "No Jews allowed!"

Ralph recalled that he—and, he presumed, his parents—had no knowledge of what would happen later, so the experience of leaving Germany was filled with fear and trepidation. He traveled with his mother to the German-Holland border, where all Jews were forced off the train and his mother strip-searched. For reasons still unknown, a Dutchman, a stranger, at the border quietly separated his mother and Ralph from the other Jews and signaled to them to take a local train on a different track to Holland. They had to jump the track, but they arrived safely.

Ralph's grandparents were left behind. They were not concerned about their well-being. After all, what would the Nazis do to old people?

From Holland, Ralph and his mother went to England, where they met his father, who had fled Germany by stowing away on an airplane bound for London.

Before departing their Berlin hotel, they noticed a newly displayed sign: "No Jews allowed!"

From there they journeyed to the United States, arriving in December 1938 and settling in Chicago's Hyde Park/Kenwood area. Hans was fortunate: He began to work the day after he arrived, and Ralph, now five, began school.

As to the family left behind, his mother was one of six children—three girls and three boys. One of her brothers committed suicide. The two remaining brothers went to South Africa in 1936, and one sister, with her husband, escaped to the Soviet Union and then to Shanghai, China.

An uncle was killed when the Nazis came to deport him. Ralph's aunt (one of his mother's sisters) and his 10-year-old cousin were murdered in Auschwitz. His maternal grandparents were on a ship that was not admitted to South Africa and had to return them to Germany. They were then allowed to join the family in the United States. His other grandmother spent the war years safely in England before joining her family in Chicago.

In contrast to many other German Jews, they were fortunate. They had resources and, similar to the nearly 60 percent of German Jews who escaped, had initiative. They despaired of their life in Germany just in time to get out, and their contacts in the United States proved invaluable. But how, specifically, did Hans Rehbock survive?

Most of all, because he was not home, but in Berlin, when the Nazis came to arrest his father. Luck had smiled upon him.

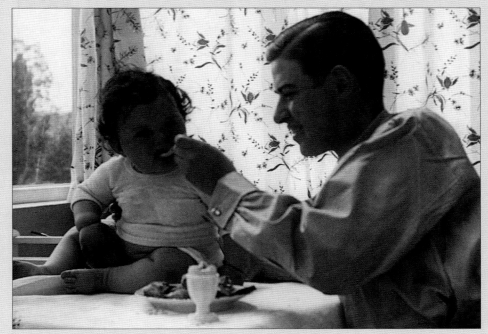

Ralph with his father, Hans Rehbock; Gotha, Germany, 1935.

WORLD RESPONSE: 1933–39

In the 1930s, Germany's actions against the Jews took place in full view of the Western world, which looked on apprehensively at the rise of Hitler and the remilitarization of the German army. Western leaders, however, considered the "Jewish question" as but one of the many issues it had with Hitler's Germany.

Even significant opposition did not translate into policies that aided the Jews. The plight of the Jews was viewed as an internal German issue. The more abstract issue of human rights was not yet a central concern in foreign policy. In a segregated United States—where in many places blacks could not use the same restrooms as whites—a great deal of discrimination was overlooked.

America and Isolationism

The 1924 immigration laws had restricted entry to the United States on a quota system enacted to preserve the United States along the "racial stock" of of its founders. Government officials had erected what one historian has called "paper walls": Would-be immigrants needed certification that they would not become public charges, and they needed certificates of good conduct from their local police. Judgments about who was eligible for immigration were left to individual American diplomats, most of whom viewed immigrants as a drain on an economy already weakened by the Great Depression.

American law at the time did not include provisions for admitting refugees fleeing persecution. Indeed, after the outbreak of war in Europe in 1939, the U.S. excluded Jews as potential spies.

After World War I, United States foreign policy was driven by isolationism. Americans felt safe, and they opposed foreign entanglements. If Germany oppressed its minorities, that was a German problem. If a rearmed Germany threatened its neighbors, that was a European problem.

Antisemitism was more prevalent in the United States during the interwar years than ever before, or since. Henry Ford, the famed auto magnate, published anti-Jewish editorials in his newspaper, *The Dearborn Independent,* and financed the American publication of a fabricated antisemitic book, *The Protocols of the Elders of Zion.* Father Charles Coughlin, a Detroit priest and radio broadcaster, led antisemitic diatribes. Quotas limited Jewish admission to colleges, the presence of Jews on faculties, and Jewish participation in banking and industry. Jews were restricted in where they could live and where they could stay on vacation; "No Jews or Dogs Allowed" was not an unfamiliar sign. They also were restricted in the workplace; "Gentile Only" was often part of want ads. "American First" advocates, supported by famed aviator Charles Lindbergh and others, favored isolation and opposed America entering another war.

American Jews—many of them immigrants, or just making their way into the middle class—could not comfortably leverage power. Some feared

A pedestrian in New York City reads a notice that announces an upcoming public meeting at the Mecca Temple. The purpose was to urge Americans to boycott the 1936 Berlin Olympics.

they might provoke anti-semitism by advocating too forcefully. Jews feared that they would be accused of dual loyalty if they pushed policy changes that would aid Jews in danger at the expense of American self-interest.

When the Nazis organized 1933's boycott of Jewish businesses, American Jewish leaders hesitated to take bold action for fear of endangering German Jews. Letters and telegrams from German Jewish leaders—possibly coerced—urged restraint.

In 1935–36, the U.S. debate over Nazism centered on the 1936 Olympics. Advocates of boycotting stressed that U.S. participation would condone Hitler's policies. Opponents said that politics had no place at athletic events and, furthermore, that participation would provide leverage with which to combat these policies.

In 1938 President Franklin Roosevelt called for a conference in Evian, France, to consider the refugee problem. Attended by 32 western nations that July, it did not yield effective action.

After the November pogroms known as *Kristallnacht*, American response was intense. The president issued a blistering statement condemning such action. Roosevelt said: "I could scarcely believe that such things could occur in a 20th century civilization." The U.S. ambassador was called home. Politicians and religious leaders loudly attacked the violence in Germany, but such condemnation—though genuine—did not result in a change in immigration policy. According to Roper polls, 95 percent of Americans disapproved of the German regime, but fewer than 9 percent supported changing the system to allow more refugees into the country.

Realizing the country's isolationist mood, President Roosevelt would not risk losing congressional support. It was critical for his legislative agenda

to allocate significant funds for militarily preparing America for war. Any proposed change to immigration policy would be torpedoed by Congress and endanger rearmament. The issue of Jewish refugees from Germany was a lower priority.

Even so, after *Kristallnacht,* Roosevelt ordered that 15,000 Germans, mostly Jews, in the U.S. on visitor visas were to have their visas extended without a time limit. He was widely condemned, thus constraining his room for further action.

Two other events were to illustrate the limits of American goodwill. The Wagner-Rogers bill, which called for the acceptance of 20,000 children from Germany and Austria—above the existing quotas—failed to emerge from committee.

Voyage of the Damned

On May 13, 1939, the SS *St. Louis,* a German luxury liner, left Germany for Cuba carrying 936 passengers—all but six of them Jews. Each one had a visa to Cuba. They were fortunate, or so it seemed. When the *St. Louis* reached Havana's port on May 27, the Cuban

Top: *Special U.S. presidential envoy Myron Taylor addresses the International Conference on Refugees at Evian-les-Bains, France, in July 1938.* Above: *Renate and Innes Spanier, twin girls on board the ill-fated refugee ship* St. Louis, *look from a porthole while waiting to set sail for Cuba. The* St. Louis *was denied entrance to both Cuba and the United States and forced to return to Europe.*

Ninety-five percent of Americans disapproved of the German regime, but fewer than 9 percent supported changing the system to allow more refugees into the country.

government refused to honor the passengers' visas and asked for $1 million in bribe money.

The American Joint Distribution Committee, the Jewish organization responsible for relief and rehabilitation work overseas, was faced with a difficult choice: To pay a ransom would invite other regimes to hold Jewish immigrants captive; not to pay was to condemn these refugees to be forcibly returned to Europe.

Press attention was riveted on these unfortunate passengers. Newsreels covered the story in movie theaters, and newspapers followed the story carefully. A *New York Times* editorial stated:

We can only hope that some hearts will soften and some refuge will be found. The cruise of the St. Louis *cries to high heaven of man's inhumanity to man.*

Appeals were made to the State Department and to other governments, but to no avail. The sympathetic German captain, Gustav Schroeder, sailed the *St. Louis* to waters off Florida to call attention to his passengers' plight. In the end, the ship returned to Europe, where England, France, Belgium, and the Netherlands agreed to receive these refugees.

Appeasement

If the United States was committed to isolationism, Europe manifested a desire for appeasement. If Hitler's demands could be met, war could be avoided. European powers did not respond to Germany's army expansion and the remilitarization of the Rhine valley. They also did not respond to German annexation of Austria—all in direct violation of the Treaty of Versailles.

In 1938 Hitler threatened war unless he received the Sudetenland, a Czechoslovakian territory that bordered Germany and contained many ethnic Germans. On September 29–30, 1938, a conference was called in Munich with the leaders of Germany, Italy, Great Britain, and France. Britain and France accepted Hitler's promise that this was his last territorial demand and acceded, granting him the Sudetenland and thus dooming the Czech democracy.

In London, British prime minister Neville Chamberlain was greeted enthusiastically. He spoke triumphantly.

We regard the agreement signed last night ... as symbolic of the desire of our two people to never war with one another again.

But by March 15, 1939, Hitler had occupied all of Czechoslovakia. The peace of Munich was short-lived. In less than a year, Poland was conquered—and hopes for peace disappeared.

Of less importance to world history but of direct importance to the fate of the Jews was a White Paper, issued by Britain in 1939, which restricted Jewish immigration to Palestine to 15,000 a year for the next five years. Thus, on the eve of the war, the one territory willing to receive Jews was closed to significant immigration.

Adolf Hitler greets Neville Chamberlain upon the British prime minister's arrival in Munich on September 29, 1938, the day before the signing of the Munich Agreement.

WORLD AT WAR

If British prime minister Neville Chamberlain thought that he had brought "peace in our time" back to his nation, Hitler learned a rather different lesson from the Munich Conference. The West was weak, Hitler believed, and unwilling to take on Germany. His proof: the policy of "appeasement" at Munich, in which Britain and France agreed to Germany's demands regarding annexation of the Czech Sudetenland, increased Hitler's appetite for domination. Ultimately, Czechoslovakia disappeared from the map, as Germany took over Bohemia and Moravia and established a puppet government in Slovakia in March 1939.

In an address to the German *Reichstag* on January 30, 1939, the sixth anniversary of his rise to power, Hitler linked the threat of a possible world war with the fate of the Jews. He proclaimed:

*If international-finance Jewry [Hitler's term for the supposed con-*spiracy of Jewish bankers] inside and outside of Europe should succeed once more in plunging nations into another world war, the consequence will not be the Bolshevization of the Earth and thereby the victory of Jewry, but the destruction of the Jewish race in Europe.*

According to Propaganda Minister Joseph Goebbels, war made possible "the solution of a whole series of problems that could never have been solved in peacetime."

On September 1, 1939, Germany invaded Poland. Two days later, France and Great Britain declared war on Germany. World War II had begun. The United States remained officially neutral for more than two years; only the December 7, 1941, attack by Japan on Pearl Harbor impelled America to enter the war.

On August 22, 1939, speaking to German army generals, Hitler defined a

German panzer tanks advance during the invasion of Poland in 1939.

new type of war. "Our war aim does not consist in reaching certain lines, but in the physical destruction of the enemy," he declared. "Accordingly, I have placed my death head formations in readiness— for present only in the East—with orders to send to death mercilessly and without compassion, men, women, and children of Polish derivation and language. Only thus shall we gain the living space [*Lebensraum*] which we need." War was initiated in part to achieve one of the Nazis' most enduring goals, territorial expansion to the East.

In a surprise move, especially considering Hitler's oft-stated hostility to communism, the Ribbentrop-Molotov Pact was signed by Germany and the Soviet Union on August 23, 1939, with the two sides pledging nonaggression. A secret protocol called for the division of Poland. German troops would enter from the west and Soviet troops from the east. German progress was swift. Within six days,

Krakow was conquered. Within eight days, Lodz, Radom, and Tarnow—and within four weeks, Warsaw—fell to the Germans. Polish Jews quickly felt the ramifications of the Nazis' racial ideology, as they were immediately singled out for brutal persecution.

The Germans also targeted non-Jewish Poles. Polish priests and politicians were murdered, Polish leadership was decimated, and, over time, the children of the Polish elite were kidnapped and raised as "Aryans" by new German "parents." A common enemy (the occupying *Wehrmacht*) and even the fury that the Nazis unleashed against Polish culture and Polish nationalism did not lead to solidarity between Poland's Catholics (the dominant population) and Jews. Instead, the German invasion only heightened tensions that were already high between the two communities.

Jews living in border areas between German and Soviet zones of occupa-

French refugees flee the German advance; France, June 10, 1940.

tion had to decide in which direction to move. In World War I, the Germans had been a far more benign occupying power than the Russians, and for more than a century freedom and opportunity had been found in migration from Russia toward the West. So experience had taught the lesson that a Jew would be best off under German, not Soviet, domination. Yet, some 300,000 Jews escaped to Soviet-occupied Polish territories. Many escapees who fled German-occupied areas seemed to have operated counter-intuitively, against the grain of history, against the hard-won insights of experience.

But Germany was anything but a safe haven. In an order given in mid-October but backdated to September 1, 1939 (to give it the appearance of a wartime measure), Hitler instructed his personal physician and the chief of the Chancellery to put to death those Germans who were considered "life unworthy of living." His signed order read:

> *Reich leader Philip Bouhler and Dr. Brandt are charged with the responsibility for expanding the authority of physicians, to be designated by name, to the end that patients considered incurable according to the best available human judgment of their state of health, can be granted a mercy killing.*

War would provide not only *Lebensraum,* but the option to impose euthanasia.

Having conquered Poland with ease, Germany waited until the following year to widen its military expansion. On April 9, 1940, Germany invaded Denmark and Norway. On May 10, German troops stormed into Holland, Belgium, France, and Luxembourg. German victories were swift. The attacks, like the earlier Polish campaign, utilized unprecedented massive use of mechanized warfare techniques that were called a *Blitzkreig,* a lightning war. By June, an armistice had been signed with France. Part of France was now under German occupation, while another part was ruled by Italy in the southwest. The remainder was under the control of a collaborationist French government based in Vichy.

The nature of German occupation differed by country, but as a rule the Germans treated Western countries more respectfully than they did the populations in the East, who were considered racially inferior by Nazi ideology. In Denmark, the civil service remained in place and German occupation was restrained.

On April 6, 1941, German troops invaded Greece and Yugoslavia, setting off a war in the Balkans. German progress was slower than expected, which proved to be an omen of things to come. When German troops invaded the Soviet Union in the summer of 1941, they made significant—but less significant than expected—advances before the onset of the cold Russian winter. While Europe and much of North Africa were gradually subjugated to German domination, only Britain stood as the sole defender of Western democracy opposing the Nazi forces and their Fascist allies.

German soldiers fire a field howitzer during the attack on the Polish capital of Warsaw in September 1939. Warsaw fell on September 27.

A MOSAIC OF VICTIMS

By September 1939, a state-sponsored murder program was in place. Historian Henry Friedlander has argued that the roots of genocide must be seen in this so-called "euthanasia" program.

Throughout Hitler's reign, Jews were the major Nazi target—but they were not the only one. The Nazis targeted a mosaic of victims. Diverse groups of people were persecuted for different purposes and according to varied policies.

- **Political dissidents**—Communists, socialists, and liberals alike—and trade unionists were persecuted and often imprisoned in concentration camps because of their politics. Jews among these groups were subject to especially brutal treatment.
- **Dissenting clergy** were arrested when they spoke out against the regime.
- **Roma and Sinti** (pejoratively called Gypsies), traditional outsiders, were distrusted and despised. Regarded as a menace, they were deported and incarcerated. Still later, many were killed.
- **Jehovah's Witnesses,** who would not swear allegiance to the state or serve in the army of the Third Reich, were targeted, as were pacifists.
- **Homosexuals in Germany** were arrested and incarcerated in concentration camps, and they found their institutions destroyed because of their sexual practices. Lesbians were not specifically targeted, nor were homosexuals in non-Germanic lands.
- **Mentally retarded, physically handicapped, congenitally ill, and emotionally disturbed Germans** were not considered suitable raw material for breeding the "master race." They too suffered at the hands of the Nazis. They were defined as "useless eaters," "life unworthy of living," a drain on the resources of the state. By October 1939, a state-sponsored murder program was in place. Historian Henry Friedlander has argued that the roots of genocide must be seen in this so-called "euthanasia" program.
- **Poles:** With the onset of war, the Germans decimated Polish political, religious, and intellectual leadership. They murdered priests and kidnapped "German-looking" Polish children for resettlement with German families. The Nazi goal was to make the Poles a subservient people.
- **Soviet prisoners of war:** More than 3.3 million Soviet POWs died after capture. Due to starvation rations and lack of shelter, they died at a rate in excess of 50 percent—compared to 3.6 percent of Anglo-American POWs in German incarceration.

Thus, some groups were victimized for what they did; others for what they refused to do; still others, simply for what they were.

According to the Nazis' race ideology, the world included a "superior" race (their own) and "inferior" races, as determined by skin color, ethnicity, and/or geography. Blacks and Slavs were special targets of Nazi animosity. Thus, the "Rhineland bastards"—the children of French North African occupiers of World War I and German women—were also targeted.

Roma and Sinti

Unlike the Jews, who were accorded full civil and legal rights in the Weimar Republic, Roma and Sinti were subjected to official discrimination long before 1933, yet no comprehensive Roma and Sinti law was ever promulgated.

The Nazi treatment of Roma and Sinti was primarily determined by whether specific Roma and Sinti were "pure" or of mixed blood, and whether they lived a traditional nomadic Roma and Sinti life. Often, Nazi policy was inconsistent: Some Roma and Sinti were

Gypsies deported to Poland; c. 1940.

deported, others were sterilized; some were murdered, and others were basically left alone.

Until 1942 pure Roma and Sinti were not targeted. Only those who intermarried with Germans were considered a threat to the "purity of the race." Local initiatives against Roma and Sinti preceded policy decisions from Berlin. For example, in 1935 the city of Frankfurt established a fenced and guarded Roma and Sinti camp.

In 1937 concentration camp imprisonment was authorized for Roma and Sinti. In 1938 SS Chief Heinrich Himmler issued guidelines for "Combating the Gypsy Plague," which required the photographing and fingerprinting of Roma and Sinti. This information proved lethal when persecution and incarceration later gave way to murder.

During World War II, a "Gypsy camp" was established at Auschwitz-Birkenau. By the end of 1943, some 18,500 Roma and Sinti (two-thirds from Germany) were registered at the main camp. They were tattooed with the letter Z. However, Roma and Sinti were allowed to live as families—an exceptional situation in the death camp of Birkenau. Many brought along musical instruments and were allowed to form small bands.

Roma and Sinti were the victims of medical experiments. Children at Auschwitz were a peculiar fascination of Dr. Josef Mengele. He thought nothing of giving them candy before he experimented upon them. During the height of the murder of Hungarian Jews in May 1944, the Nazis "liquidated" the Roma and Sinti camp, killing the men, women, and children.

Euthanasia of the Handicapped

Mass murder of the handicapped began slowly. At first, authorization was informal and secret. Narrow in scope, it was limited only to the most serious cases. From the Berlin Chancellery *Tiergarten 4* (hence the code name T-4), officials ordered a statistical survey of all psychiatric institutions, hospitals, and homes for chronic patients. Within months the T-4 program involved virtually the entire German psychiatric community.

Three medical experts reviewed forms submitted during the survey, often without examining individual patients or reading detailed records. Theirs was the power to decide life or death. Patients ordered killed were transported to six killing centers: Hartheim, Sonnenstein, Grafeneck, Bernburg, Hadamar, and Brandenburg. The SS donned white coats for the transports to impersonate medical personnel.

The first killings were by starvation. Then injections were used. Children were simply put to sleep, never again to awake. Sedatives became overdoses. Gassing soon became the preferred method of killing. False showers were constructed, and Ph.D. chemists were employed. The process was administered by doctors, and many people were killed at a time. Afterward, black smoke billowed

Smoke rises from a chimney at the Hadamar, Germany, euthanasia center in 1941. The smoke is black not from the burning of wood or coal but of human flesh.

from the chimneys as the bodies were burned.

A few doctors protested. Carl Bonhoeffer, a leading psychiatrist, helped his son Dietrich contact church groups urging them not to turn patients over to the SS. A few physicians refused to fill out the forms.

Growing public pressure, including a sermon on August 3, 1941, by Bishop Clemens August von Galen of Muenster, openly challenged the euthanasia program. "We must oppose the taking of innocent human life even if it were to cost us our lives," he argued.

On August 24, 1941, almost two years after it began, the operation was seemingly discontinued. However, it was merely driven underground. "Mercy killings" secretly continued until the end of the war. Some 200,000 Germans were victims of this program.

While T-4 continued in secret, mass murder was just beginning. Physicians trained in the medical killing centers graduated to bigger tasks. Irmfried Eberl, M.D., who began his career in the T-4 program, became the commandant of Treblinka. His colleagues went on to Belzec, Sobibor, Treblinka, and Auschwitz, where killing took on massive dimensions.

The murder of the handicapped demonstrates that even the Nazis were not immune to public pressure: Religious leaders protested the murder of the handicapped, and the killing was driven underground. When Jews were killed, however, the Church did not protest.

Poles

In the aftermath of the German invasion of Poland, Poles—who in Nazi racial ideology were considered "inferior" Slavs—were targeted for persecution and ultimate enslavement. Hitler called the war against Poland a new type of war.

Terror intensified after Poland's surrender. Killing was a tool of dominance, not merely an instrument of war. The first group to be targeted for systematic murder was the Polish leadership class. In a terror operation code-named "Tannenberg," some 60,000 Poles whose names had been compiled before the invasion were to be eliminated. Hitler, while touring the Polish battlefields, declared to his commanders on September 12, 1939, the need for "political housecleaning." Hitler said that it was "imperative to break all elements of the Polish will to resist. It is especially necessary to eliminate the clergy, the aristocracy, the intelligentsia, and the Jews."

In areas adjacent to Germany, Poles were expelled and more than 200,000 ethnic Germans were moved into these areas. Thousands of teachers, priests, and other intellectuals were murdered in mass killings in and around Warsaw, especially in the city's Pawiak prison. The rest of the Polish population was to be trained to be subservient to the Germans. Heinrich Himmler said about young children: "They should learn to count to 500. I don't believe that reading and writing are necessary."

Thousands of other Poles were sent to concentration camps in Germany and to the newly built Auschwitz concentration camp in Poland, where non-Jewish Poles constituted the majority of inmates until Jews began to arrive in early 1942. In November 1942, the Germans expelled more than 100,000 people from the Zamosc region; many were deported to the Auschwitz and Majdanek camps. Approximately 50,000 Polish children were taken from their families, transferred to the Reich, and subjected to a program of "Aryanization": adopted by German families, raised as Germans, and denied all knowledge of their past.

Physicians trained in the medical killing centers graduated to bigger tasks.

Piotr Sosnowski, a Polish priest, is executed in Poland's Tuchola Forest on October 27, 1939.

NAZI RACISM SPREADS

From 1939 to 1941, the German Reich expanded dramatically by conquest and by alliance. Within the countries that they occupied, the Germans set different policies. As noted, policy was driven by two commitments: *Lebensraum* (living space) and racial domination.

In general, those countries west and north of Germany were accorded greater respect; those to the East, most especially the Slavic countries, were regarded as inferior. German policy was also determined by the nature of German occupation, the number of troops available, and its reliance on assistance from the local population and their government for the implementation of their anti-Jewish measures.

As a general rule, once the Final Solution became the policy of the Reich, transit camps were employed near major Jewish population centers. Jews were first deported to these internment camps; from there, they were deported to death camps in the East.

From the moment that Germany invaded a country, discrimination and persecution began. The implementation of the Final Solution would follow later. The Final Solution would only be hindered by a willingness of native people to resist German occupation and to assist the Jews (though resistance and assistance did not necessarily go hand-in-hand).

Belgium

When the Germans invaded Belgium in May 1940, the government fled; a government-in-exile was established in Great Britain. King Leopold II remained with his people and was placed under house arrest. The Belgium Civil Service, which remained in place, worked with the German military occupation.

Anti-Jewish laws were introduced shortly after occupation. Jewish property was confiscated, and Jews were barred from professions. Belgium's Jews, some

Above: *Yellow Stars with the word* Jew *in German (*Jude*), French (*Juif*), and Dutch (*Jood*).* Left: *German troops advance through a burning village near Brest-Litovsk, Belorussia, during the opening days of Operation Barbarossa in the summer of 1941.*

Belgian firefighters converse outside a synagogue in Antwerp after its destruction by Belgian antisemites in April 1941.

66,000, resided mostly in Brussels, the capital, and in Antwerp. Most were foreign-born, many stateless—immigrants from World War I. By 1942 they were forced to wear a Jewish Star.

Belgian civil administration refused to cooperate in the deportation of Jews, so the German military police had to do it themselves. Jews were sent to the transit camps Breendonk and Mechelen, and from there to death camps. More than 25,000 Jews were hidden by Belgians in a well-organized clandestine operation that depended upon the good will of the native population. Belgian Jews were active initiators and participants in these attempts to hide. Roman Catholic institutions, most especially convents, were instrumental in saving Jewish children. Of the 25,000 Jews deported from Belgium, fewer than 2,000 survived.

The Netherlands

When the Germans conquered Holland in 1940, a civil administration was installed under SS auspices and Arthur Seyss-Inquart was appointed Reich commissar. Anti-Jewish decrees were issued in 1940. Jews were barred from civil service. All Jewish-owned business assets had to be registered, and in 1941 all Jews had to be registered. There were 159,806 Jews in the Netherlands, including 19,561 of mixed marriages. Almost one in six were Jews from Germany who had fled to safety in Holland in the prewar years, including Otto Frank and his family.

The arrest and deportation of several hundred Jewish youngsters led to a general strike by Dutch workers and to the enduring reputation of Dutch support for their Jewish neighbors. It also led to a crackdown.

Dutch Jews were concentrated in Amsterdam, the Dutch capital. Foreign and stateless Jews were sent to Westerbork, a transit camp, and later to Vught. On April 29, 1942, Jews were forced to wear the Yellow Star of David with *Jood* (Jew) emblazoned in the center of the star.

Deportations began in the summer of 1942 and continued until September 3, 1944. Most Jews were sent to Auschwitz, where there was a slim chance for survival, and Sobibor, where less than a handful of Dutch Jews survived. Some 25,000 to 30,000 were able to hide in Holland; two-thirds of that group survived.

For many years, little was said about the cooperation of the Dutch police in the deportation of Dutch Jews. Such cooperation is now understood to have been virtually universal.

Anne Frank

Anne Frank was one of more than one million children under the age of 18 who were murdered by the Nazis. Her diary, found by her father after the war, remains one of the most widely translated and read books in the world. Published in more than 100 editions, it has sold more than 20 million copies. The play that was based on the diary is performed in high schools throughout the world. Two major films, made more than four decades apart, focus on Anne's life.

Anne Frank was born in Germany on June 12, 1929. Her parents had the foresight to flee to Amsterdam soon after

Hitler came to power. The Germans invaded when Anne was a month shy of 11. She was given her diary at the age of 13, just before the family went into hiding.

On July 5, 1942, Anne's older sister, Margot, received a summons to report for forced labor. The Frank family immediately went into hiding at a vacant annex of Otto Frank's office. They remained there for almost two years because of the help of Miep Gies, one of the women who worked in Otto's office, and her comrades in the Dutch underground.

Anne understood what would happen if the attic were discovered. On October 9, 1943, she wrote:

Our many Jewish friends are being taken away by the dozen. These people are treated by the Gestapo without a shred of decency,

Below: *Anne Frank, whose insightful and poignant diary has enlightened millions about the Holocaust.* Bottom: *Samuel Schryver poses beneath a sign that indicates the entrance to the "restricted" Jewish quarter of Amsterdam; German-occupied Netherlands, 1942.*

> *being loaded into cattle trucks and sent to Westerbork. . . . It is impossible to escape; most of the people in the camp are branded as inmates by their shaven heads. If it is as bad as this in Holland, whatever will it be like in the distant and barbarous regions they are sent to. We must assume that most of them are murdered. The British radio speaks of their being gassed.*

On August 4, 1944, the Security Service received an anonymous call informing them of the hiding place. Anne and her family followed the path of many Dutch Jews. They were taken to the Westerbork transport camp. From there they were sent to Auschwitz on September 3, on the last transport to leave the camp.

Anne, Margot, and their mother, Edith, were sent to the women's camp as workers. Edith died at Auschwitz early in January 1945, days before Anne and Margot were forcibly evacuated and sent on death marches to Bergen-Belsen. Both girls died of the typhus epidemic that broke out in the camp in March 1945, just weeks before liberation.

Of the eight who lived in the attic, only Otto Frank survived.

A poet once said that the birth of a child is the genesis of infinite possibility. What then of a child's loss, a child's murder? Anne Frank was just one of a million Jewish children who were murdered solely because their grandparents were Jews. She is the emblem of lost possibility.

Denmark

See "Denmark" in the section on "Rescue," p. 148.

Luxembourg

When the Germans invaded Luxembourg, the grand duchess fled to Great Britain along with her government. So Luxembourg was under a military administration only, and later under German civil administration, until it was formally annexed in August 1942.

The Jewish population of Luxembourg was some 3,600, the vast majority of whom fled to France before Germany outlawed emigration. The Nuremberg Laws, defining the Jew, were introduced in September 1940. Discriminatory policies against Jews, their businesses, and holdings followed.

From October 1941 to April 1943, 674 Jews were deported from the transit camp in Funfbrunnen to the Lodz ghetto, Auschwitz, and Theresienstadt. Only 36 Jews are known to have survived the death camps.

France

When France was conquered by Germany in June 1940, it was divided primarily between German occupation in the north and a quasi-independent collaborationist government headed by Marshal Henri Philippe Petain in Vichy France, which governed the south. The only exception was a small area of the southeast occupied by Italy. Alsace and Lorraine were annexed to Germany itself.

Jews were safest in the Italian-occupied zone; Fascist Italy had little interest in the Final Solution. The rulers of Vichy France, in contrast, instituted their own antisemitic laws. They identified the Jews, registered them and their property, expelled them from the professions, and restricted their movements. Jews were sent to internment camps in Gurs in the south of France. Foreign Jews were sent to internment camps in Les Mills, Rivesaltes, Saint Cyprien, and le Vernet.

In the summer of 1942, 13,000 Jews in Paris were arrested by French police, and many were interned in the *Velodrome d'Hiver* sports arena in Paris. From there they were taken to Drancy, a transit camp near Paris, and then deported to Auschwitz, where they were murdered upon arrival.

The last deportation from France to Auschwitz took place in August 1944, shortly before the liberation of France by Allied armies. More than

---

Jews were safest in the Italian occupied zone; Fascist Italy had little interest in the "Final Solution." The rulers of Vichy France, in contrast, instituted their own antisemitic laws.

A Jewish woman in Paris who was required to wear a Yellow Star; German-occupied France, c. 1942.

77,000 Jews were deported from France and murdered in Nazi camps. Eight thousand of them were children, and one-third of the 77,000 were French—not foreign citizens

For several reasons, three out of four Jews in France were able to survive the war. Unlike in other countries, German occupation of France was light; they did not have many troops to spare. Another reason that Jews survived was that they lived in many different places in France, not in one or two major cities. Also, many had lived in France for generations and could pass as non-Jewish French.

For a long time, some could escape to the Italian occupied zone, and the French Resistance cooperated in the rescue of Jews. It was not their top priority, but they were not particularly antisemitic compared to citizens of other countries.

Norway

The Germans invaded Norway in April 1940. They hoped to use Norway, which was across the North Sea from Great Britain, in the battle against England. Norway surrendered on June 10, but King Haakon VII and his government escaped to London. Vidkun Quisling, a pro-Nazi Fascist who had modeled his own political party after the Nazis, established himself as prime minister. So willing an accomplice of Hitler was the Norwegian leader that today the word *quisling* is a synonym for unprincipled collaboration.

Norway, home to 1,700 Jews, did not have a tradition of antisemitism. At first, the Germans and Quisling proceeded slowly, but with the Final Solution fully operative in the fall of 1942, Germany, with the assistance of the Norwegian police, moved against Norway's Jews. In early October, Jewish men in Trondheim were arrested.

On October 26 and 27, Jewish men, women, and children were arrested in Oslo, Norway's capital city. Instead of a transit camp, they were placed on a ship, the *Donau,* bound for Germany and from there to Auschwitz. Warned by the Norwegian underground and helpful citizens, more than half of Norway's Jews escaped to neutral Sweden. In the end, 760 Jews were deported and only 25 returned.

HELGA LESSER FRANKS

1926–

Helga Lesser was born in Berlin. Her father, Leo, was a manufacturer of women's clothing, and her mother, Meta, worked with designers, bringing the latest Paris fashions to Berlin. Helga grew up surrounded by a large family—many aunts, uncles, and cousins.

From an early age, Helga was taught to be proud of being Jewish, despite the oppressive climate of her youth. In her earlier years, she recalled, antisemitism was less rampant in Berlin, with its large Jewish population, than elsewhere in Germany. Nevertheless, she can remember her mother tensing as the brown-shirted SA (Storm Troopers) passed by. In the beginning, Helga had several non-Jewish friends, but after 1935 or 1936, those friends were not as available for play.

Leo and Meta tried to leave Germany. On a vacation in Sweden, they looked into relocating their businesses to Malmo, but the Swedish government refused their request to stay. Deep in his heart, Helga recalled, her father did not believe that Hitler would last. Still, as the Lessers searched for a place that would accept them, they found it almost impossible.

Helga remembered that when she was 10, "We led a normal life, not knowing how abnormal it was." The Lesser family's comfortable Berlin apartment was next to a gorgeous synagogue. Helga went to a Jewish school; public schools were no longer safe for Jewish children in the mid-1930s. The curriculum was rigorous. Jewish students in Germany studied English in anticipation of life in the United States or England.

Helga's recollection of the November 1938 pogroms known as *Kristallnacht* is clear. When she left for school, she smelled something burning. She noticed the synagogue on fire and firefighters standing by—not to extinguish the flames, but to make sure that adjacent buildings did not catch fire. Not understanding what was happening, she went to school as usual by tram, noticing stores with their windows shattered. En route to school, she met her teacher, who told her to go home. Her school, situated in a Berlin synagogue, was on fire.

When she returned home, her mother took the family to the apartment of Helga's widowed grandmother. The police were arresting Jewish men, and with no man in the apartment, it seemed safe. "We spent five or six days there," Helga recalled.

Helga's family was able to secure French visas through relatives in France and escaped by train. Her family was able to smuggle enough money out of Germany to obtain visas for the large family to flee. Helga's father was successful in getting visas to Bolivia. When the war started on September 1, 1939, the Lesser family members were categorized as enemy aliens because they were Germans. France had declared war on Germany, and the French made no distinction between Jewish refugees fleeing Nazism and Germans loyal to the Nazi regime.

Sent to an internment camp, Helga's father tried to join the Foreign Legion, but he was rejected because of a heart condition. Helga's mother had a nervous breakdown. Ironically, Germany's 1940 invasion of France led to her father's release from the internment camp. He was told to leave before the Germans conquered the region, and so he went home.

Helga went to schools in France, where she was subject to ridicule because she was German. Her classmates, like the French government, did not distinguish between Germans and German-Jewish refugees.

Helga's father died in January 1942, and in Helga's words, "things became tougher and tougher." She tried to carry on her father's business, and enjoyed considerable short-term success. The money she earned would prove to be a lifesaver in the years to come.

On July 16, 1942, the French police came to arrest Helga. She and her mother were among 13,000 Jews rounded up in Paris (by now in the occupied zone of France). They were taken to the *Velodrome d'Hiver* sports arena along with some 7,000 other Jews, and held without food or water. Because of strange circumstances and connections, they were eventually released and not deported. Most of those who were arrested were eventually deported to Auschwitz and killed.

It was time to go into hiding. The Lesser family lived on the outskirts of Paris with a woman—perhaps a Jewish woman—who rented them a room and asked no questions.

"She wanted to help, and it brought her some money," said Helga. "Without money, nobody would have taken us."

Joining the underground, Helga acted as a kind of social worker, bringing comfort and support to some of the many Jewish children hiding in the Paris suburbs. Helga had heard of death camps, gas chambers, and gassing from a BBC broadcast by Thomas Mann in 1943.

Some suspected that Helga was American or English. When liberation came in August 1944, she was told "your compatriots arrived." Because of her fluency in English, she was hired by a Jewish organization to work with the refugees.

Soon thereafter, Helga met an American soldier, Gerald Franks, himself a Jewish refugee from Berlin who had lived in her old neighborhood and whose sister had gone to school with Helga. Gerald had fled to the United States before returning to fight as an American to free Germany from Nazism. Gerald and Helga married, and she immigrated to the United States.

Unlike many survivors, Helga spoke English when she arrived and was prepared to tell her story. However, she soon found that people could not grasp what she was saying. Even relatives felt uncomfortable and pulled away. She understood. "Even in France, it was difficult to believe what went on in Auschwitz," she said.

With the Illinois Holocaust Museum and Education Center, Helga found an outlet to share her story. She is an active member of the Speaker's Bureau, and addresses hundreds of students every year.

She can remember her mother tensing as the brown-shirted SA (Storm Troopers) passed by.

Helga with her family; France, c. 1942.

THE GHETTOS

After Germany invaded Poland, it imposed a process of ghettoization on the Jewish population. "Jewish residential quarters"—the sanitized German name for ghettos—were established in each major Polish city, and Jews were forcibly resettled from smaller villages. Warsaw contained the largest of Poland's approximately 400 ghettos. Lodz, the Polish industrial city, held some 164,000 Jews.

When Warsaw was sealed in the fall of 1940, some 400,000 Jews—30 percent of Warsaw's population as well as refugees from other cities—were forced into an area covering just 2.4 percent of the city, with a population density of more than 200,000 per square mile and approximately 9.2 people per room. The population, peaking at 445,000 in March 1941, faced hunger, then famine, and soon diseases that developed into epidemics.

In 1941 Warsaw's death rate was one in ten, with 43,239 deaths, before the deportations and planned systematic killing.

To the German occupiers, the ghetto was a temporary measure, a holding pen to contain the Jews until it was determined what to do with them.

To the Jews, the ghetto was where they would be forced to live until the end of the war, until the Germans came to their senses, until...they knew not what.

Mordecai Chaim Rumkowski, chairman of the Lodz ghetto Judenrat, *speaks with Hans Biebow, head of the German ghetto administration, in 1941.*

In the directive establishing German policy toward Jews in the occupied territories of Poland, dated September 21, 1939, Reinhard Heydrich, head of the Reich Security Services, listed the intermediate—but not final—goals. He wrote of the *Endzeil,* the final goal (which must be distinguished from the *Endloesung,* "Final Solution," the later German euphemism for the murder of the Jews). The final goal is unarticulated in Heydrich's memo. The first intermediate goals, though, are clearly stated:

- Jews are to be moved from the countryside to the larger cities.
- Certain areas are to be *Judenrein,* free of Jews.
- Local authorities are to establish a council of Jewish elders, specifically 24 Jewish men to be appointed from established Jewish leaders and rabbis and "made fully responsible in the literal sense of the word" to implement future decrees.
- A census must be taken.
- Care must be exercised to minimize the economic consequences.
- An inventory must be taken of resources, industries, and personnel.

The Jewish Perspective

Jews believed this was how they would be forced to live until the end of the war.

Like non-Jews in occupied Europe, Jews overwhelmingly believed that the forces of good would eventually triumph over evil and that Germany would ultimately lose the war. Moreover, Jewish history demonstrated that Jews had repeatedly survived the enemies who sought to destroy them.

Jews were biding their time. They used the term *iberleben:* to survive and outlast. Meanwhile, Jewish leaders were placed in an impossible situation. Their authority was given by their German masters, and their resources were ever more limited. To the Jews, the Jewish Councils (*Judenraete*) represented German orders and were responsible for their implementation. To the Germans, the Councils represented Jewish needs, to which the Germans were to become ever more unresponsive.

Jewish Councils had all the responsibilities of local mayors: providing food and water, education and sanitation, health services and police protection, and overseeing taxation and labor. The forces around them were at best unresponsive and routinely hostile. Men of varying skills and integrity, they were to be sorely tested as they faced ever more dire circumstances. Often, members of the Jewish Councils were killed for not fulfilling German orders—then replaced by less experienced and less morally responsible leaders.

Four Phases

Ghetto life can be divided into four stages: moving in and initial adjustments, mainly in 1940; sealing of the ghetto, severely limiting contact with the outside world; enduring life in the ghetto with ever diminishing resources, 1941 and early 1942; and finally, the deportations.

In Poland, ghettoization occurred before the systematic killing of Jews had begun. In the eastern areas—those first occupied by the Soviet Union and then by Germany—ghettos came after the *Einsatzgruppen* killings. A small minority of political activists began to suspect a possible shift of anti-Jewish policies: Were mass shootings the omens of an unprecedented reality—even if they could not grasp its dimensions?

In Hungary, ghettoization was only a matter of months (in 1944). In Poland, ghettoization lasted approximately two to three years—and in Lodz almost four.

Moving In

The Germans usually set up the ghetto in an impoverished, run-down part of a city. If a family was relatively fortunate, the boundaries of the ghetto included

The Jewish Council tried to educate the young and provide for the orphans, but their resources were extremely limited.

their home. If not, they had to find a place to live.

Liza Silbert recalled being evicted from her home in Vilna and forced into the ghetto:

> We didn't know what was going on. My mother said, "What did I do? What kind of crime?" They yelled at her and they said, "No questions asked! You're a Jew. You have to go from your house."

Robert Emery described moving into the ghetto:

> I am down, helping my mother and sisters and family in a very sad procession . . . a pillow, a bed sheet and some photographs of the family. Just what you could put in a bundle.

Peter Hersch remembered his move as a young boy:

> . . . my mother dressed me. I don't know how many shirts I had on. And jackets and sweaters. I was looking like a barrel. I could hardly walk, but she said: "You will need it, because it will be cold."

Ghettos had different modes of organization. In Warsaw, Jewish Coun-

Top: *Children study in a clandestine school held in a stable in the Kovno ghetto; c. 1941. Above: A Lodz ghetto work permit issued to Margola Checinska; July 2, 1943.*

Above: *Food is smuggled into the Warsaw ghetto. This photo is from the* Oyneg Shabbes *underground archive.* Right: *Residents of the Lodz ghetto wait outside public soup kitchen #452 in 1941 to receive food rations distributed by the Jewish Council.*

cil chairman Adam Czerniakow permitted laissez faire capitalism, turning a blind eye to those who smuggled in food by piercing the walls or traveling through the sewer system. The Jewish Council tried to educate the young and provide for the orphans, but their resources were extremely limited. Czerniakow's diary reflects his daily struggle to be responsive to the needs of the ghetto residents despite having few resources at his disposal.

His counterpart in Lodz, Mordecai Chaim Rumkowski, centralized power. He controlled food distribution and health services and transformed his ghetto into a labor camp, believing that the Germans would not destroy a vital industrial center that produced required goods for the war effort.

Meeting Hate with Humanity

In ghettos, the scent of death was all around. Winters were more difficult than summers.

Max Epstein remembered the very cold winter of 1941 in Lodz:

That was one of the worst winters . . . wood disappeared. Everything, all the fences, everything was taken. Trees were cut. Everybody was stealing wood to burn.

Renny Kurschenbaum described her experience early in the Warsaw ghetto:

People would take out all their best belongings, and put them on little tables and hope somebody would buy them from them. Anything, for a few potatoes, for a little bread, for a bag of flour.

Later, when there were no longer any possessions to sell, she recalled:

You would line up in lines—big lines and a little bit of water, soup, and a piece of bread. That was in the beginning. After that, they took

even this away. That's when people started to lay in the street, hungry, swollen from hunger.

Until December 7, 1941, when the United States cut off diplomatic relations with Nazi Germany, the American Jewish Joint Distribution Committee operated in the ghettos, providing funds for soup kitchens and food. Afterward, the institutions that had previously functioned broke down under the strain.

Felicia Brenner, a resident of the Lodz ghetto, reflected:

I would see eight-year-olds, 10-year-olds. And they became like the head of the family after the father was taken away. The mother would hold discussions with the 10-year-old.

Inhabitants, Felicia reflected, faced impossible choices:

If you drank the water, you got typhus. I was sick. I had typhus also. Sanitation was terrible.

Sylvia Fishman described the Warsaw ghetto:

You had people lying on the sidewalks covered with paper. They couldn't bury them.

Wood became so expensive and scarce in Warsaw that the burial society buried the dead covered only by a sheet. Later they used mass graves, with bodies covered in paper or nothing at all.

Still, Herculean efforts were made to preserve some semblance of humanity, the scaffolding of a culture under attack.

Resistance

Before even considering armed resistance, Jews practiced three other types of resistance:

- Symbolic and personal resistance: maintaining dignity, identity, and continuity
- Polemical resistance: gathering and disseminating information regarding the German crimes
- Defensive resistance: individual and organized attempts to aid, protect, and rescue

Affirming hope: Henryk Ross and Stefania Schoenberg stand beneath a chuppah *during their wedding in the Lodz ghetto in 1941.*

Lisa Derman described her education in Slonim:

We met with a teacher in a dark basement. Six girls.... You would go out and you would hear the shooting in the street. But it [the classes] took away from the moroseness. It made you feel that you are human.

Warsaw had a Jewish theater. Even in smaller cities, such as Kovno and Lodz, theater groups performed, music was played, lectures were held, and synagogue services were conducted clandestinely. Underground Jewish newspapers warned of the true nature of German policies. Jewish youth organizations met: Zionists sang songs of the *halutzim* (pioneers), and Bundists continued to imagine autonomous Jewish existence in a world filled with social justice.

The various prewar political parties, such as the Bund and Zionist movements, initiated social and cultural activities. The diverse Zionist youth movements helped sustain and nurture ghetto youth, both physically (through their soup kitchens) and spiritually (through their educational and social initiatives).

Lodz had its Chronicles, a daily recording of events that systematically documented the history of the ghetto. In

Wood became so expensive and scarce in Warsaw that the burial society buried the dead covered only by a sheet. Later they used mass graves, with bodies covered in paper or nothing at all.

EMANUEL RINGELBLUM

Born in eastern Galicia, Emanuel Ringelblum earned a Ph.D. in history from Warsaw University. With universities closed to all but the most fortunate Jews, Ringelblum taught high school. He was a member of YIVO (Jewish Scientific Institute) and in 1923 became a founder of the Circle of Young Historians in Warsaw. He was also a political activist and a left-wing Zionist. In 1938 he was dispatched to Zbaszyn to direct the relief work for Jews stranded in no-man's land between Germany and Poland.

From the moment of the German invasion, Ringelblum helped run a Jewish aid association, which later evolved into ZETOS (Jewish Society for Social Help). The group organized soup kitchens, health clinics, and numerous house committees that supported families living in shared courtyards.

His involvement made Ringelblum highly informed about the fate of Warsaw's Jews and their changing conditions. It was this gathering and preserving of information that formed the essence of his clandestine works within the ghetto. Ringelblum understood that the situation in Poland was unprecedented, and he used his formidable talents—both academic and organizational—to document the situation in the Warsaw ghetto and in all of Poland.

His *Oyneg Shabbes*—Yiddish for "Joy of Sabbath" and the code name for his underground archives—was a sterling example of spiritual defiance. Ringelblum believed that the Germans could not be allowed to write the history of the ghettos; it was the responsibility of its inhabitants to leave a lasting record from which this history could be told from the perspective of the victims, not their tormentors.

Guided by a love of his people and a fascination with the raw material of historical writing, Ringelblum led a diverse and large team effort at documentation. He reviewed every item in the archive, maintaining balance among all segments of the population. Scientific work was included, alongside literary works. Most noteworthy is the collection of clandestine Jewish underground newspapers in various languages.

Ringelblum worked to have this information transmitted to London, and on to the U.S. His efforts led to the first reports of the mass killings at the Chelmno and Treblinka death camps and the deportations of Warsaw Jewry. He was critical of *Judenrat* chairman Adam Czerniakow's decision to commit suicide rather than preside over the deportation, writing: "a weak man, he should have called for resistance." After the massive deportation during the summer of 1942, Ringelblum became a firm believer in armed resistance.

The great deportation changed his perspective. Afterward, he no longer dealt with small details but with the larger picture of the situation. He created biographical notes on some of the great figures in the ghetto. Before the ghetto was destroyed, collections of material were put in containers (including the one pictured) and buried in three—or perhaps more—caches. (Two were discovered after the war.)

Together with his wife and young son, Ringelblum left the ghetto and was hidden. He returned to the ghetto during the uprising, alone. He was taken to Trawniki's prison and, with the help of others, managed to escape. Once again, he was hidden on the "Aryan" side. He worked to the end, writing a portrait of Polish-Jewish relations during the occupation. When the Gestapo discovered his hiding place on March 7, 1944, he and his family were arrested and murdered.

The Ringelblum Archives is housed in the Jewish Historical Institute in Warsaw. Copies are available at Yad Vashem and the U.S. Holocaust Memorial Museum. Extensive efforts were made to preserve this material, which is now available in Hebrew and English translations. It is an indispensable source for the study of Polish Jews under occupation.

Ringelblum's legacy is secure: No one can write this history without considering the work that he and his colleagues undertook during the height of their oppression, under penalty of death.

Warsaw, Emanuel Ringelblum organized a clandestine effort at documentation, an underground archive that brought together a diverse spectrum of Jews to record life in the largest of Poland's ghettos and elsewhere. He was adamant that the history of the ghetto be written by the Jews, even children, in every zone of occupation.

Theresienstadt—the Nazis' so-called model ghetto and transit camp—became the destination and death place of many prominent Czech, Austrian, and German writers, scientists, jurists, diplomats, musicians, professors, and artists. The density of such talent and the severity of their situation gave rise to a rich cultural life in the shadow of death. Leo Baeck, Germany's best-known rabbi, offered courses in philosophy and theology. Though he had the opportunity to leave Germany, Baeck had opted to remain with his congregants.

In Theresienstadt, symphonic music was written and performed; there was even a children's opera, *Brundibar.* By day, artists in the workshops painted what was acceptable to their Nazi overseers. By night, they secretly painted a true picture of camp life. Also at Theresienstadt, Mina Pachter and a group of women compiled their favorite recipes in a cookbook, coping with hunger and starvation by connecting with the world they had left behind.

Rabbi Yitzhak Nissenbaum of Warsaw understood the magnitude of the situation. He gave voice to the uniqueness of the Jewish condition under Nazism, which was unprecedented in Jewish historical experience. Nissenbaum spoke of *Kiddush Hahayim* (the sanctification of life):

"In the past our enemies demanded our soul and the Jew sacrificed his body in sanctifying God's name (*Kiddush Hashem*)," Nissenbaum said. "Now the enemy demands the body of the Jew. That makes it imperative for the Jew to defend it and protect it."

Self-help was organized: house committees in Warsaw, soup kitchens in

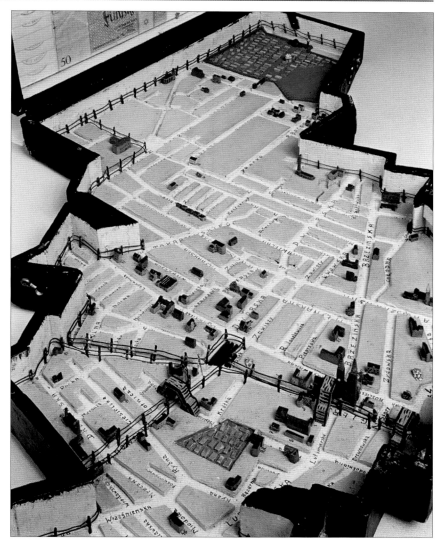

almost all of the ghettos, charity drives in Kovno.

When the mass deportations began in 1942–43, Jews were told that they were being "resettled in the East." Some also heard rumors of more dire conditions: death, murder, and gassing. But it was impossible for them to imagine the unimaginable.

Jewish Responses to Deportation

When the orders for resettlement were issued in the ghettos, Jews responded in a variety of ways.

Some hid—either by passing for non-Jews or hiding in secret. Posing as a non-Jew was dependent on obtaining forged identification documents—as well as how one looked and spoke, and

A model of the Lodz ghetto details the ghetto's administrative and cultural sites. Resident Leon Jacobson, a shoemaker, created the model in 1940.

Non-Jewish Poles could be killed for hiding a Jew. Some who offered to shelter Jews could not withstand the pressure, fearing their neighbors.

how disciplined one could be in concealing one's true identity.

Finding a place to hide depended on the goodwill of others. Non-Jewish Poles could be killed for hiding a Jew. Some who offered to shelter Jews could not withstand the pressure, fearing their neighbors.

Powerless as they were, Jews took all sorts of initiatives, some remarkably bold.

Following mass deportations from the Warsaw ghetto in July 1942, Adam Starkopf—the blond, blue-eyed father of a one-year-old blonde, blue-eyed daughter and married to a blonde, blue-eyed wife—obtained false papers for his family. He sedated his infant daughter and brought her to the Jewish cemetery as if for burial. From there, they fled to the adjoining Tartar cemetery and then into "Aryan" Warsaw. His Polish was flawless. His plan was as precise as it was desperate. Any glitch and all would be killed.

When the deportations from the Minsk ghetto began, Matus Stolov found shelter in the home of his non-Jewish aunt along with her Jewish husband, his half-Jewish cousin, and his mother. His aunt's underground connections brought them to the Russian partisans, who rejected the mother and child but allowed them to move eastward to Soviet-held territories, where they survived the war.

If ghettos were located near forests as in some sectors of Eastern Europe, Jews could take to the countryside and try to survive that way.

Lisa Nussbaum and Aron Dereczunski (Derman) walked from the Vilna ghetto for eight days to join the partisans in the woods. Lisa was startled to discover that Jews were living in freedom so close to Vilna.

Even going to the forest had its costs. Most Jews could not hide, and even many of those who could were betrayed by informers—or simply ran out of options. Miles Lerman said: "They would take me in the forest, I was young and able-bodied, but they would not accept my mother or my sister and her children."

In the end, the imbalance of forces between the powerful Germans and the isolated Jews was simply too much; ghettos were temporary and ultimately Jews were to be resettled. After years of enduring starvation and disease, they believed that they had experienced hell on earth and nothing could be worse. They could not imagine what lay ahead. Surely, they feared for their future, but they never imagined that the Germans had embarked on a new and totally unprecedented policy of killing all Jews.

Rampant starvation: A man lies dead in front of a shop in the Warsaw ghetto. Dead bodies were routinely found on the ghetto's streets.

ADAM, PELA & JASIA STARKOPF

1914–2005   1914–1999   1941–

When the Germans invaded Poland on September 1, 1939, blond and blue-eyed Adam Starkopf was 25 years old. He had been married for three years to Pela, who was also blond and blue-eyed. He was an office manager and chief accountant at a Warsaw leather-goods factory, living near his parents and in-laws.

The beginning of the war was a time of anxiety. Moods shifted with the news and, in the absence of news, with rumors. Adam heeded the patriotic call to all young men to head to Brzesc, where he assumed that he was to be inducted into the army. He set off to do his duty, but first he had to say goodbye to his wife, her parents, and his. He was never to see his mother again.

Traveling to Brzesc by wagon and later on foot, he soon understood that Poland had lost the war with Germany—that no army would be established, at least not in time to do combat. So he traveled to Kletzk, where he was surprised to encounter not Germans but Russians. At first, he assumed that the Soviet Union had come to Poland's defense. But he soon learned that Poland was to be divided. Germany would rule western Poland and the Soviet Union would control the eastern half.

Safely ensconced in Kletzk, Adam had escaped the Germans, but he had left his wife and their parents behind. Unable to accept the separation, he returned to Warsaw, first to rescue his wife and later to send for their parents.

Adam, Pela, and Jasia Starkopf at the Feldafing DP camp; Germany, 1946.

Fortune smiled, and both Pela and Adam were able to escape to Kletzk. But when Pela returned to Warsaw for her mother and father and for Adam's father, the older people refused to leave. A harrowing journey back reunited Pela and Adam, but they came to a decisive conclusion, appropriate for normal times but extremely difficult in the world that they were about to face. Pela said: "Whatever happens, the family cannot be separated."

Adam remembered: "I was unable to put up an effective argument. I knew she was right." So they returned to Warsaw, en route catching a train at Malkinia, which in 1942 was to become a transit point for Jews being shipped from Warsaw to the death camp of Treblinka.

What to do in the Warsaw ghetto?

Individual enterprise was still possible, so Adam started a toy store, which survived for a time until the Germans looted his stock. He gave one of his father's friends a significant quantity of ladies' stockings for storage on Warsaw's "Aryan" side, presuming that it would be his financial protection when needed.

In the spring of 1940, Pela became pregnant. They knew it was going to be extremely difficult bringing a Jewish child into the world of German occupation. By the summer of 1940, the city of Warsaw was separated into three sectors: German, Polish (non-Jewish), and Jewish. During the summer, the construction of the ghetto wall began.

Among the first to be deported were the prisoners, and Adam used the commotion of the truck boardings to escape. His one thought: *How can I give my family a chance for survival?*

Adam Starkopf;
c. 1940.

On October 16, 1940, the ghetto was established. Two hundred thousand Jews were forced to move in, and 80,000 Poles were expelled. On November 15, the ghetto was sealed, surrounded by miles of walls, absolutely separated from the Aryan sector. Adam and his family were relatively fortunate that their homes were in the Jewish sector. They were not deported from their homes—at least not yet. They had their possessions, which over time they would be forced to sell.

For the Jews, the ghetto was a way to live until . . . until what, they did not know. For the Germans, the ghetto was a holding pen to isolate and contain the Jews until a decision was made about their fate.

Adam went to his father's friend for stockings, only to be told that the stockings had been stolen. Adam was not convinced, but there was nothing he could do. On January 19, 1941 Pela gave birth to a daughter, Jasia, whom they named after her paternal great grandfather. The couple's struggle for survival would now include a vulnerable infant.

Food in the ghetto, Adam recalled, was sufficient to offer an opportunity for slow death by starvation. Indeed, one in 10 Jews in the Warsaw ghetto died in 1941 from starvation, malnutrition, disease, and/or despair. Pela organized tenants in their building to gather food and clothing for newly arrived Jews. Poor Jews gave to those who were even more impoverished. Available buildings were turned into shelters; people slept on the floor.

Smugglers were indispensable to the ghetto's survival. Some smugglers ran large enterprises. Others were just children who could swiftly move from one

sector to another so that they could provide for their parents.

Pela also worked imaginatively to save her family. When the Germans "organized a collection of Jewish furniture"—stealing whatever they could get their hands on—she posted a crude quarantine sign on the door for typhus. The Germans dared not enter.

Others could not quite hold up to the pressure, could not quite deal with starvation and humiliation. Adam's father attempted suicide before Jasia's first birthday. Pela's father, ordinarily proud, was depressed. When Adam was arrested and imprisoned, Pela bribed the appropriate official and got him released. He was arrested again in the spring, and that time no release could be arranged.

On July 22, the great *Aktion* began. Hundreds of thousands of Jews were deported from Warsaw to Treblinka, which they later learned was a death camp. Among the first to be deported were the prisoners, and Adam used the commotion of the truck boardings to escape. His one thought: *How can I give my family a chance for survival?*

His most important need was false papers that would show that he and Pela were non-Jews. Through contacts with family friends, he received crudely forged papers. He was now Adam Bludowski, and Adam would try to pass as a Pole. He would hide not in an attic or a basement but in the open by pretending to be what he was not.

But first he, Pela, and Jasia had to escape from the ghetto. How do you take an infant out of the ghetto when you never know when she could wake up, or cry, or laugh? Taking a bold initiative, they sedated Jasia, placed her in a coffin and then on a board that was covered with cloth, and went with her to the morgue. From there, they went into the Jewish cemetery and then to the adjoining Tartar cemetery on the Ayran side of Warsaw. Their plan was precisely executed on July 31, 1942.

They found temporary shelter in an underground "safe apartment," strategically located in the same building as the German railway administration. Adam, Pela, and Jasia traveled to Luchow and found a place to live in a village a short distance from the town. He returned to Warsaw for his parents and in-laws, but by then it was too late. They had been deported shortly before his return.

Adam obtained a *Kenkarte* and an *Arbeitskarte,* an identity card and work card, offering him some protection as an Aryan. He found work in a lumberyard, and he rented a room from an antisemitic Polish couple. They brought two more people to live with them: Christina, formerly a nanny to a Jewish family, and Marysia, a child whom Christina called her daughter—actually a Jewish child entrusted to her when her parents were deported. When the baby became ill, Christina took her to Warsaw, where the child died. Christina, an Aryan, no longer needed Adam and Pela.

Trying to pass as non-Jews, Adam and Pela could not show excessive interest in Jews or any such sympathy. From time to time, they risked their safety. For example, they gave food to desperate Jews who reached their door. However, they did not open their home to Jews whose train had been derailed en route to Treblinka. Protecting Jasia was paramount.

Adam and Pela were always in danger as Jews and were often in danger as Poles, especially when the Germans retaliated for the activities of the Polish Underground by randomly arresting and murdering Poles. In one such harrowing moment, when the Polish railway station became the scene of a roundup of Poles, a kind stranger bought Pela a train ticket and signaled to her when she could safely board a train.

For two years, Adam, Pela, and Jasia lived as Polish Christians. Sometimes they were suspected as Jews. On the rarest of occasions, they revealed their identity to those with whom they had become close, those they

Adam and Pela Starkcpf; Warsaw, 1937.

Johanna (Jasia) Starkopf Brainin with her father, Adam Starkopf; Skokie, Illinois, 2005.

After several days, Adam and Pela revealed their true identity and applied for admission to a shelter. Desperate to learn what had become of their parents, they met a survivor of Treblinka, one of a hundred or so people who had survived the death camps where more than 700,000 Jews had been murdered in 18 months. He knew Adam and Pela's parents and told them for certain what had happened to them: They had been gassed upon arrival.

In September 1945, Adam, Pela, and Jasia observed the High Holidays for the first time in three long years. They had looked forward to the opportunity to reaffirm their Judaism together with other Jews, to live openly as Jews. Until then, Jasia did not know that she was Jewish. Raised as a Polish Catholic, she did not want to be Jewish; only Christians could pray to Jesus Christ. Her return to the traditions of her ancestors took time and required much security and love.

As conditions deteriorated for Jews in Poland, Adam and Pela undertook another journey—across borders from Poland to Czechoslovakia to the American occupied zone of western Germany, where they stayed in the Feldafing displaced-persons camp.

They faced a decision about their future: Should they go to Palestine, where Adam could join his brother, or the United States? They were fearful of going to Palestine with their young child, and when an invitation presented itself to come to the United States, they took it and moved to Chicago.

After all, Adam commented, there is always time to die.

trusted with their lives. To their surprise, two such friends were fellow Jews, also living as Christian Poles.

When Jasia became ill, she was placed in a convent for safekeeping. When Pela got sick, she had to go to the hospital. She not only feared that she might die because of her illness, but she was anxious that in her fever and anguish she might use a Jewish word that would reveal her true identity and doom her chances for survival.

Adam remembered the day of his liberation:
Suddenly through the mist and smoke, human figures appeared: Russian soldiers, their faces and uniforms black with caked mud and dirt, many of them barefoot but they all carried weapons. Then came the German soldiers, looking as we had never seen them before: dazed with the shock of defeat. Pela and I looked at each other, still unable to grasp that we were free at last.
We were still alive together.
We were free but we were homeless.

In July 1944, Lublin was freed and Majdanek, the death camp in the valley just outside the city, was liberated.

BARBARA ZYSKIND STEINER

1925–

Basia [Barbara] Zyskind was born in Warsaw, Poland, a city of some 1.3 million—one-third of them Jews. Living amid a thriving Jewish community, Barbara's family was devoutly religious and wealthy. Her grandfather, who was in the scrap metal business and real estate, was one of the first Jews to build apartment houses in Warsaw. Her parents, Fraida Kuperman and Moshe Zyskind, lived in Moshe's father's home.

On September 1, 1939, when the Germans invaded Poland, Barbara's pampered childhood abruptly ended. In January 1940, two SS officers appropriated the family apartment, forcing the family to move into a much smaller place within what soon became the ghetto. Their new flat was crowded, and suddenly they had no income. The Zyskind family was forced to sell their possessions for bread.

With schools closed, Barbara earned money by tutoring younger children. Her father, once prominent and successful, could never ask for work, so Barbara solicited additional students for him to tutor. On Yom Kippur 5701 (1940), the day that the Nazis proclaimed that the Jews of Warsaw would be confined to a Jewish quarter—ghettoized—Barbara's father led clandestine, illegal services. Dressed in the traditional white *kittel* (shroud), he appealed for divine mercy.

More than 100,000 Jews died in the Warsaw ghetto of malnutrition, disease, and despair *before* the deportations of 1942. Among them were Barbara's father, mother, and brother. That left her to fend for herself. From July 22 to September 21, 1942, some 265,000 Jews were deported from Warsaw to Treblinka, where they were gassed upon arrival. Warsaw's Jews continued to be sent to the *Umshlagplatz,* the deportation point. Most were seemingly unaware of what was waiting for them at the other end of the line. Barbara recalled:

I remember one guy named Rubinstein; he escaped from Treblinka. He ran through the streets screaming, "They are gassing us! They are burning us!" In the beginning no one believed him.

Barbara lived with various acquaintances and scrounged for food and work, eventually landing a job in a German broom factory. It came with a room and work permit. With so many deported, the emptied ghetto suddenly had room.

On April 19, 1943, the night of the Passover seder, the Warsaw Ghetto Uprising began. Jews rose in armed rebellion, refusing at all costs to report for deportation. "We said no!" Barbara said. "Never again would we allow them to take us to kill. We would fight to the end.... The atmosphere in the bunker was tense. We each felt that we were in the last hours of our life." Trained in first aid, Barbara served as a medic, tending to the wounded.

On the first day, the Jews held off the German invaders, forcing them to retreat from the ghetto. German general Jurgen Stroop returned with his troops, who burned the ghetto, building by building, street by street. Barbara remembered that by the third week...

We knew that there was no place to hide, knew that we would have suffocated or burned alive had we stayed in the bunker, and knew that no one was listening to our cries, so we just held our cloths to our mouths, tried to hide as best we could, prayed and cried, prayed and cried.

On May 5, Barbara was captured and deported to Majdanek, a Nazi death camp outside Lublin. What did the local Polish population know of the fate of the Jews? Barbara did not answer that question abstractly. On the train, she recalled, people from the outside shouted:

"Throw us your diamonds and your gold. You are going to die anyway."

Arriving, she said, "we were given no underwear, but I was able to fashion a bra and a pair of underpants from parts of the shirt." Instinctively, she grasped that preserving her dignity was essential to any hope for survival:

It was impossible to survive by yourself, so we tended to find someone on whose shoulders we could cry. My friend was Paula. She was everything to me: friend, sister, mother, and angel.

While many prisoners tended to view the perpetrators as nameless and faceless oppressors, without any shred of compassion, Barbara experienced one guard, Mawa Parelca, or Little Pearl, who was "small and completely different than the rest. She would tell us to huddle together to keep warm and would place girls in four corners of the field to look out for other SS." Her compassion made seemingly endless work, work without purpose, almost bearable.

From Majdanek, Barbara was sent to Skarzysko Kamienna, a labor camp where she met three girls who became like sisters, and from there to a camp in Czestochowa, where another prisoner, Arnold Steiner, took an interest in her and protected her. It was from Czestochowa that she was liberated by the Russians.

I was just out of hell liberated on my own. But what did I feel? I knew that I loved being with Arnold. He was almost like a father figure to me. He took care of me. I didn't know my emotions at the time.

When Arnold proposed, Barbara said yes. With no rabbis available, they were married by a Jewish man

"I was a broken person, consumed with survivors' guilt, not wanting to live."

Barbara and Arnold Steiner; Czestochowa, Poland, 1948.

who remembered the prayers, the blessings of marriage. *We were man and wife. Instead of laughter, we hugged each other and cried for hours. That was our wedding day.*

Returning to Warsaw, she found no trace of her past. "I was a broken person," she said, "consumed with survivors' guilt, not wanting to live." Twice she tried to take her own life. Arnold rescued her each time. To overcome despair, she was told that she had to have a stake in the future: She was advised to get pregnant.

A son was born bearing the names of Barbara's and Arnold's fathers, Moshe Peretz (now Marvin Paul). The young couple and their son soon immigrated to newly independent Israel, where conditions were difficult—too difficult for survivors who had endured so much. So they moved in 1952 to Chicago, where Arnold worked for Hart Schaffner Marx, the clothing manufacturer, and Barbara became a bookkeeper for Sears. Barbara gave birth to a daughter, giving the Steiners two sources of joy and stakes in the future.

Barbara had the opportunity to confront one of her oppressors at the trial of Majdanek guards. Not until the late 1970s did she begin to speak of her experiences. Still later, she became deeply involved in the museum established by the survivors in Skokie. Her accomplishments have been significant, her aspirations profound yet simple.

I hope that my story will, in some way, help young people realize what prejudice, hatred, and inhumane behavior can do. I hope that this will inspire them to create a better world for themselves and for future generations to come.

MASS MURDER

Three thousand members of the *Einsatzgruppen,* special killing units, entered the Soviet Union in June 1941 on the heels of the invading German army. Their assignment: to round up Jews, Soviet commissars, and other opponents of the Reich—in cities and towns, villages and hamlets—confiscate their property, and then systematically kill them.

They could not operate alone; they did not operate alone. The *Wehrmacht* (German army) and other Axis armies, local gendarmeries, native antisemitic groups, and even ordinary citizens assisted them in their task.

They would enter a city, gather their intended victims (often by using deceptive promises of relocation), march them to the edge of dug-out pits, and execute them one by one, bullet by bullet.

Their victims were men, women, and children; entire families; whole communities; entire regions. Historians can plot their progress week by week. Reports were written to their superiors, and maps were drawn up signifying their accomplishments with symbolic coffins and numbers of Jews killed.

Sometimes, the mere presence of German troops in the vicinity was sufficient to spur a massacre. In July 1941, the Polish population of the village of Jedwabne slaughtered their 1,600 Jewish neighbors. Though the massacre was blamed on the Germans for years, the local population knew that it was they who had turned against their Jewish neighbors. Recent research in Ukraine, which involved interviews with the local population and archaeological digs of the killing fields, reveals who the killers were. Sometimes it was the *Wehrmacht;* sometimes Romanian troops accompanying the German army. Other villages were decimated by *Einsatzgruppen,* still others by the local police or armed locals. Romanian troops were so harsh in their treatment of Jews that they aroused the ire of even the Germans.

In some cases, the killing fields were adjacent to major cities. These are just some of the massacres:

- In Babi Yar, Kiev, now Ukraine, 33,771 Jews were murdered on September 28–29, 1941, during the week between Rosh Hashanah and Yom Kippur.
- In the Rumbula Forest outside the ghetto in Riga, Latvia, some 28,000 Jews were murdered from November 29 to December 9, 1941.
- In Ponar, the killing fields neighboring Vilna (Vilnius) in present-day Lithuania, more than 60,000 Jews were murdered beginning in the summer of 1941.
- At the Ninth Fort outside of Kovno (Kaunus), Lithuania, 9,000 Jews—more than half of them children—were killed on October 28, 1941, alone.

Mass shootings continued unabated, wave after wave. In the face of a Soviet counter-offensive in the fall of 1943, special units returned to dig up the dead and burn their bodies in an attempt to destroy the evidence of the crime. The operation, conducted by *Kommando 1005* under the command of Paul Blobel, was called "Operation Blot Out." Erasing the evidence would per-

A young mother with her two children sits among a large group of Jews from Lubny, Ukraine, who are assembled for mass execution by the Germans; October 1941.

mit the denial of the crime. It is conservatively estimated that these shootings killed approximately 1.25 million Jews and hundreds of thousands of Soviet citizens, including POWs.

The Killers

Who were these men? What were their motivations? After the war, many claimed that they were merely following orders. Raul Hilberg, the preeminent Holocaust historian, described them:

The great majority of the officers of the Einsatzgruppen *were professional men. They included a physician, a professional opera singer and a large number of lawyers. They were in no sense hoodlums, delinquents, common criminals or sex maniacs. Most were intellectuals. . . . There is no indication that any of them requested an assignment to a* Kommando *[Einsatzgruppen sub-units]. All we know is that they brought to their new task all the skills and training that they were capable of contributing. In short, they became efficient killers.*

In his book *Ordinary Men: Reserve Police Battalion 101 and the Final Solution in Poland,* Christopher Browning described the members of a German police reserve battalion unit that also participated in the killing as ordinary men placed in extraordinary circumstances. Conformity, peer pressure, careerism, obedience to orders, and group solidarity gradually overcame their moral

inhibitions. Daniel Jonah Goldhagen, whose book *Hitler's Willing Executioners* was an international bestseller, disputes Browning's account. He views them not as ordinary men but ordinary Germans who had accepted Hitler's vision of eliminationist antisemitism and were able to embrace its next phase, exterminationist antisemitism. The systematic murder, what the Germans called extermination—something done to rodents or insects, not people—was in their minds not a pleasant task but a necessary one.

Both Browning and Goldhagen concur that no *Einsatzgruppen* member faced punishment if he asked to be excused. Not participating in the killing may have slowed their career advancement—and they may have lost face and disappointed their comrades—but they had a choice whether to participate or not. Almost all chose to become killers.

The SS remained proud of its achievement. In a speech to SS major generals at Poznan on October 4, 1943, SS Commander Heinrich Himmler paused to speak openly and directly of the Jews: "The Jewish people are going to be annihilated."

He spoke with pride of his men's toughness and moral integrity: "Most

Above right: *German soldiers look on as a member of an* Einsatzgruppe *prepares to shoot a Ukrainian Jew; Vinnitsa, German-occupied Ukraine, c. 1941.* Below: *Members of a mobile killing unit shoot Jews in a field in Dubossary, Moldova, in German-occupied Soviet Union.*

ONE EVENT, THREE ACCOUNTS

Perpetrators

Operational Situation Report USSR No. 101
Einsatzgruppe C
Location: Kiev
Sonderkommando 4a in collaboration with *Einsatzgruppe* HQ and two *Kommandos* of police regiment South, executed 33,771 Jews in Kiev on September 29 and 30, 1941.

The Victims

From *The Black Book of Soviet Jewry*, edited by Ilya Ehrenburg and Vasily Grossman shortly after liberation (the book was banned by Soviet authorities):

They took our clothing, confiscating all our possessions, and led us about fifty yards away, where they took our documents, money, rings, and earrings. They wanted to remove the gold teeth of one old man and he tried to resist. Then one of the Germans grabbed him by the beard and threw him on the ground. There were tufts of beard in the German's hand, and the old man was covered in blood. When my child saw that, she started to cry.

Don't take me there, Mama. Look, they're killing the old man.

Don't shout, sweetie, because if you shout, we won't be able to run away, and the Germans will kill us.

She was a patient child, so she kept quiet, but she was shaking all over. She was four years old then. Everyone was stripped naked, but since I wore only underwear, I didn't have to take if off.

At about midnight the command was given in German for us to line up. I didn't wait for the next command, but threw my girl into the ditch and fell on top of her. A second later, bodies started falling on me. Then everything fell silent. There were more shots, and again bloody dying and dead people began falling into the pit.

I sensed that my daughter wasn't moving. I leaned up against her, covering her with my body. To keep her from suffocating, I made fists out of my hands and put them under her chin. She stirred. I tried to raise my body to keep from crushing her. The execution had been going on since 9:00 A.M. and there was blood all over the place. We were sandwiched between bodies.

I felt someone walk across the bodies and swear in German. A German soldier was checking with a bayonet to sure no one was still alive. By chance he was standing on me, so the bayonet blow passed me.

When he left, I raised my head. The Germans were quarrelling over the booty.

The Bystanders

Also from *The Black Book of Soviet Jewry:*

An entire office operation with desks had been set up in an open area. The crowd waiting at the barriers erected by the Germans at the end of the street could not see the desks.

Thirty to forty persons at a time were separated from the crowd and led under armed guard for "registration." Documents and valuables were taken away. The documents were immediately thrown to the ground and away. Witnesses testified that the square was covered with a thick layer of discarded papers, torn passports and union identification cards. Then the Germans forced everyone to strip naked, girls, women, children and old men. No exceptions were made. Their clothing was gathered up and carefully folded. Rings were ripped from the fingers of the naked men and women and these doomed people were forced to stand at the edge of a deep ravine where the executioners shot them at point-blank range. Their bodies fell over the cliff, and small children were thrown in alive. Many went insane when they reached the place of execution.

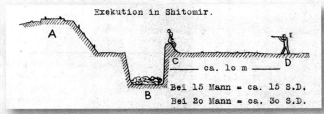

A diagram drawn by an unidentified German soldier describes details of an Aktion at Zhitomir in the Ukraine, during which about 500 Jews were shot.

Above: *A mass grave containing the bodies of 7,000 Jews; Proskurov, German-occupied Ukraine, September 1941.*
Below: *German police look through the clothing of people killed during a shooting action at Babi Yar, Kiev, in German-occupied Ukraine, 1941.*

of you know what it means to see a hundred corpses lie side by side, or five hundred, or a thousand. To have stuck this out and—excepting cases of human weakness—to have kept our integrity, that is what has made us hard."

He spoke the unspoken. He spoke but urged silence. "This is an unwritten and never-to-be-written page of glory in our history."

Himmler spoke of the Jews, but not only the Jews. Of the Soviet POWs who were killed or allowed to die by the millions, he spoke with regret in the most utilitarian of tones. He regretted the loss of their labor potential: "At that time we did not value this human mass the way we value it today as raw material, as labor." He expressed no such regret regarding the murder of Jews.

He spoke candidly: "What happens to others is a matter of total indifference." Germany was the center. Other nations concerned him only insofar as needed. "It is a crime against our own blood to worry about them."

This form of killing imposed a psychological burden on the killers. Alcohol was often needed after the killing—and sometimes before and during. Some broke under the strain. Many found their duty difficult. And the killing was public, which had significant consequences even for an acquiescent native population.

The experience of Jews in the Soviet territories, where the *Einsatzgruppen* killers engaged in mass shootings, differed from the Jews of Poland in two major respects: Ghettoization in Poland preceded the mass killing by some 18 months. Farther to the east, killing came first. The new ghettos created after June 1941 in Soviet territories were established in the wake of mass shootings. A few Jews, particularly members of the Bund and Zionist youth movements, began to perceive the possibility of a shift in anti-Jewish policies, the omens of an unimaginable and radical new reality of mass murder. Secondly, some ghettos were surrounded by large and very dense forests that could be used for hiding. The forests facilitated escape because there was somewhere to go. They served as a base for some partisan groups.

THE FINAL SOLUTION

On January 20, 1942, 15 men gathered at a magnificent lakeside villa in Berlin for a meeting that was critical to the fate of the Jews. As they gathered, more than 80 percent of those who were to die in the Holocaust were still alive; 18 months later, four of five would be dead.

The meeting had been scheduled for December 9, 1941, but the Japanese attack on Pearl Harbor and America's entry into the war had forced a postponement.

At the table were senior representatives of the German state ministries with responsibility for the "Jewish question." Wilhelm Stuckart, a veteran Nazi party member who had drafted the original Nuremberg Laws, represented the Interior Ministry. Roland Freisler represented the Justice Ministry—everything was to be done within the law. Eric Neuman, who directed the Four Year Plan—Germany's economic blueprint—was there because the decision on the Jews' fate would have significant impact

on the supply of skilled and unskilled labor. The Reich Chancellery, Hitler's own office, was represented by Freidrich Kritzinger. Martin Luther was there on behalf of the Foreign Ministry.

The SS was also at the table, with representatives of the Nazi Party Chancellery, the Race and Resettlement Office, and the Office of Reich Commissar for Strengthening of Germandom. Reinhard Heydrich, head of the Reich Security Services and deputy protector of Bohemia and Moravia, had his own staff present, including Gestapo Chief Heinrich Mueller and Adolf Eichmann, who would later play a key role in the administration of the deportation of Jews.

Representatives of the occupied territories were invited. An *Einsatzkommando* officer from Riga joined personnel from the General Government, the area in Poland with the largest concentration of Jews—all in ghettos. These men were added to the list of original invitees after they pressured higher authorities to do something about the

View of the Wannsee villa outside of Berlin, where the details of the Final Solution to the "Jewish problem" were discussed.

By then it was clear that all Jews were to be killed. The unresolved questions were *how* and by *whom.*

dire conditions in their territories and to solve jurisdictional disputes between the SS and the governor general of occupied Poland.

The 15 men—Germany's "best" and brightest—were not of one mind regarding the Jews. None supported the Jews, but there was competition between the Nazi Party and the governmental ministries. Racial purists in the party wanted to eliminate all Jewish blood, even among the *Mischlinge*—those of mixed ancestry. German ministries felt duty-bound to protect German blood. Stuckart was anxious to preserve his authority. Eliminating a labor force in the midst of war would have serious economic consequences. Those in Poland feared epidemics that would spread beyond the ghetto and threaten both the Polish population and the

Reinhard Heydrich, chief of the RSHA (Foreign Office), chaired the Wannsee Conference.

German military. Nazi official Josef Buehler pleaded for speed: "Jews should be removed... as fast as possible, because it is precisely here that the Jew constitutes a substantial danger as carrier of epidemics.... Moreover, the majority of the 2½ million Jews involved are not capable of work."

They were not there to make the decision to annihilate the Jews. That decision had been made earlier—and at a much higher

level of authority. They were not even there to arrange for the deportation of Jews; logistical arrangements were coordinated at a much lower level.

By then it was clear that all Jews were to be killed. The unresolved questions were *how* and *by whom.*

A variety of options had been tried, including shooting, starving, working them to death—and even gassing. The representatives also considered at length what to do about those of mixed lineage—sterilize or execute—and how to manage those on the home front who would be concerned about their relatives.

The meeting was convened by Reinhard Heydrich, then a 38-year-old rising star described as the "pacesetter" on the Jewish question. He had received instructions in July 1941 from Hermann Goring to make "all necessary preparation of the organizational, practical and financial measures for the execution of the intended Final Solution of the Jewish question." Recent discoveries in archives of the former Soviet Union indicate that Heydrich had indeed composed the instruction that Goring was to sign back in March. So indeed he may have been self chosen to accomplish a historic task. A man of foresight and meticulous planning, he was never unprepared for a meeting. Heydrich may have wanted to establish an independent, indispensable base of operations, since his superior, Heinrich Himmler, was only three years his senior.

The agenda was set forth by Heydrich:

Another possible solution of the [Jewish] problem has now taken the place of migration, i.e. evacuation of the Jews to the East.... Such activities are, however, to be considered as provisional actions, but practical experience is already being collected, which is of greatest importance in relation to the future Final Solution of the Jewish question.

The men at the table understood that "evacuation to the East" was a euphemism for concentration camps, and that the Final Solution meant systematic murder.

From 1933 onward, the German state's policy was to rid itself of Jews by forced migration—creating conditions that would make it difficult if not impossible for Jews to live in Germany. That policy failed because some Jews could not find anywhere to go and German military policy kept expanding the number of Jews under their control. The Final Solution would now be final: total annihilation.

The Nazis soon perfected gassing, with which they had already experimented. Mobile gas vans and later stationary gas facilities had been used in Hadamar and other "euthanasia centers." Seventy thousand Germans deemed incurable had been gassed in what the Germans had deemed a "medicalized operation." Their personnel soon played a key role in the Final Solution. Since December 1941, mobile gas vans had been used at Chelmno to murder Jews from surrounding communities. Experiments had been conducted in Poltava and Kharkov in the Soviet Union. After Wannsee, gassing became the preferred solution at the six killing centers created in German-occupied Poland.

What did Heydrich accomplish at the conference? Scholars suggests three concrete achievements:

- There was collective acknowledgement that the Final Solution, killing all Jews, was the policy of the German state. With this came a shared complicity.
- The participants' language was openly murderous, even as the secret protocols deliberately used euphemisms.
- Above all, control came into the hands of the SS. Civilian bureau-

The dining room where the Wannsee Conference was convened. Fifteen men, many with doctorates, discussed how to murder the remaining Jews of Europe.

crats dared not challenge their authority. Those responsible for the occupied territories, including the military, recognized SS primacy. The ingredients for centralization were set in place.

And they were swiftly implemented. That spring, the death camps were established. By midsummer the deportations of ghettoized Polish Jews were underway, and by mid-1943 Polish Jewry had been mostly annihilated.

Yet this meeting almost passed undetected. Thirty copies of the "Top Secret" protocol were prepared using language that would reveal the full scope of what was being done only to those in the know. A single copy—the one sent to Martin Luther in the Foreign Ministry—was found after the war. Several participants denied having seen the protocol—and for good reason; it would have revealed the scope of their participation. Adolf Eichmann was more candid: "At the end, Heydrich was smoking and drinking brandy in a corner near a stove. We all sat together like comrades . . . not to talk shop, but to rest after long hours of work."

DECEPTION

The Nazis were masters of deception. They created a rich language of doublespeak, saying one thing and meaning another. They succeeded in masking what they intended to do: lulling their victims into inactivity or paralysis, at least for a time.

But they also spoke of what they did and what they were doing, because they were proud of it. They regarded the murder of the Jews as a significant accomplishment, perhaps the proudest achievement of the Third Reich.

In 1939 Hitler spoke openly of his plans. In a speech to the *Reichstag* marking the sixth anniversary of his ascent to power, Hitler warned:

If international-finance Jewry [Hitler's term for the supposed con-spiracy of Jewish bankers] inside and outside of Europe should succeed once more in plunging nations into another world war, the consequence will not be the Bolshevization of the earth and thereby the victory of Jewry, but the destruction of the Jewish race in Europe.

But at that time, no one—at least no sane person—believed him.

Still, the danger to German Jewry was taken seriously. More than half of the Jews of Germany and Austria left in the years 1933–39. And undoubtedly more would have left had countries been willing to receive them. As former U.S. secretary of state Henry Kissinger said of his parents' escape from Germany:

Joseph Goebbels, Hitler's minister of propaganda. Goebbels once stated, "If you tell a lie big enough and keep repeating it, people will eventually come to believe it."

"When my parents left, it took no foresight, merely opportunity."

Hitler repeated his promise to annihilate the Jews in September 1942. At that time, he well knew that the death camps were in full operation and that more than 200,000 Jews were being killed each month.

Speaking to the *Reichstag,* he boasted:

> *Once the German Jews laughed at my prophecy [that a world war would lead to the destruction of Jewry]. I do not know whether they are still laughing, or whether they are laughing on the other side of their faces. I can simply repeat—they will stop laughing altogether, and I will fulfill my prophecy in this field, too.*

Reading these two speeches with the benefit of hindsight, it is clear that Hitler said what he was going to do and set out to do it. At the time, however, the crime was unprecedented: Who would believe that the nation of Goethe and Schiller, of Kant and Hegel could contemplate the murder of an entire people? One could imagine these as the deeds of barbarians, not a cultured people.

The Nazis practiced an elaborate language of deception with regard to the camps; they practiced what George Orwell referred to as doublespeak:

- *Mercy killings* was the term they used for the murder of the handicapped, the mentally ill.
- *Jewish residential district* was the term used for a ghetto.
- *Evacuation to the East* meant deportation to death camps.
- *Resettlement* also meant deportation to death camps.
- A *shipment* referred to Jews en route to death camps.
- *Special trains* signified transport to death camps.

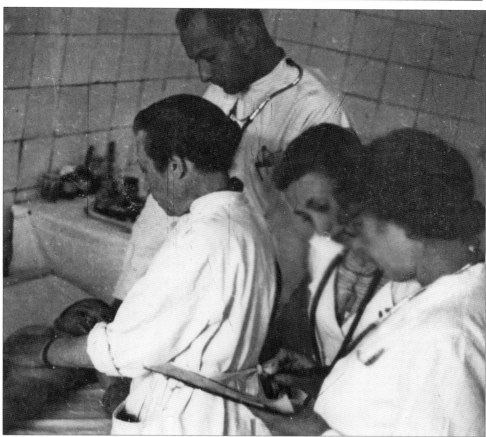

The Nazis used the term mercy killings to describe the murder of the handicapped and the mentally ill.

- *Special actions* was a euphemism for mass murder.
- *Special treatment* singled Jews out for immediate death upon arrival.
- Gas chambers were labeled as *showers.*
- Jews going to the gas chambers were told that they were to undergo *disinfection.*
- When a place was made *free of Jews,* it meant that all Jews in that area had been killed.

The entire effort was labeled the *Final Solution of the Jewish question.* In this the Nazis were quite truthful. Murder was the Final Solution. The murder of all Jews—adults and children, believers and nonbelievers, converts and those of partial Jewish ancestry— would resolve the presence of Jews forever.

Some people partially internalized what was happening, but they were few and far between. On January 1, 1942—three weeks before the Wannsee

When a place was made *free of Jews,* it meant that all Jews in that area had been killed.

Conference—Jewish poet Abba Kovner proclaimed in a manifesto: "Hitler wants to kill all the Jews, and the Jews of Lithuania are first in line." Years later, Kovner was asked: "How did you know?" He responded that it was a poet's intuition.

Most Jews could not imagine or comprehend that a plan was in place to kill all the Jews and that the infrastructure had been created for their destruction. The death camps were unprecedented—and unimaginable.

Humans are naturally inclined to ignore bad news. It is why a woman might avoid going to the doctor when she discovers a lump in her breast, or why intelligent people avoid the emergency room when they have pains in their arms or their chests. It also explains why in cases of infidelity, often the betrayed spouse is the last to know.

THE HOAX OF THERESIENSTADT

Alone among the many occupied countries of Europe, Denmark continued to concern itself with the fate of its citizens even after they were deported. While most Danish Jews were ferried to safety in Sweden in October 1943, 456 Danes were incarcerated in Theresienstadt, near Prague. Denmark formally inquired as to their fate and insisted on a Red Cross visit.

Under pressure, the Germans consented to the Red Cross inspection. In anticipation of the visit, the Germans thinned the ghetto population, deporting Jews to Auschwitz, where most were gassed upon arrival. They beautified the "model" ghetto, growing gardens, preparing a village green, opening a community center, and even establishing a concert hall and synagogue. A café was opened, and it was filled with customers; its menu was elaborate. An orchestra played music in the background. A soccer game was played and a goal was scored on cue. The head of the *Judenrat,* Paul Epstein, greeted the visiting dignitaries dressed in a black suit and a top hat. A children's opera, *Brundibar,* was performed for the visitors. The entire event was filmed and later used for a Nazi propaganda film.

When the visit was over, reality again set in, as most of the performers were shipped to Auschwitz.

A pencil drawing, signed by Georg Wolff, that depicts a building in Theresienstadt; c. 1943.

Some people are paralyzed by the bad information they hear. It robs them of hope; it leads to depression and lethargy. Others are empowered by bad news to take chances that they would never take if they were expected to live.

Jews were unprepared for the death camps. They had heard rumors about the camps, but these were just some of the many rumors that were disseminated, most of which turned out to be incorrect, incomplete, or unconvincing.

Arriving on railcars after days of travel—without water, without food, and without provisions for sanitation—they felt relieved when the doors to the cars were opened; they thought the worst had passed.

Neighboring Poles often seemingly understood what was about to happen to the Jews. Survivors report seeing Polish children gesture with a hand slicing across their necks: "Goodbye, Jews, you are doing to die." One survivor recalled that en route to the trains, the Poles said: "Throw out your money and your jewels. You won't need them where you are going."

In Elie Wiesel's depiction of his experience as a young boy, his teacher Moshe escaped from a scene of mass murder to warn the Jews of Sighet of what was about to happen. They took him for a madman. When the underground press published reports of the gassing, the stories were dismissed as exaggeration or uncorroborated rumors.

Yitzhak Zuckerman, a commander of the Warsaw Ghetto Uprising, wrote:

Warsaw did not believe. Simple common sense refused to accept the possibility of the mass destruction of tens and hundreds of thousand of Jews. The press was decried for panic mongering.

As for the Germans, top personnel were sworn to silence, but not all could keep what was happening to themselves. Husbands would unburden themselves

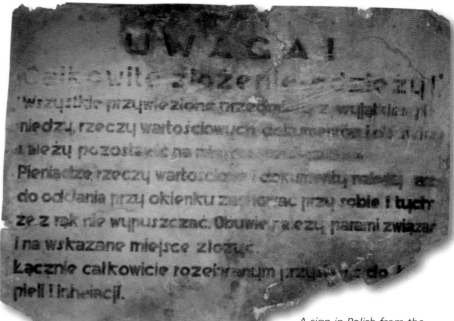

A sign in Polish from the Belzec death camp reads, "Attention! All belongings must be handed in at the counter except for money.... Afterward, one must go completely naked to the showers."

to their wives; young guards would try to impress their girlfriends.

One reason that the killing centers replaced the *Einsatzgruppen* as the means of murder was efficiency and the effective use of personnel. Another consideration was secrecy. The internal *Einsatzgruppen* reports are direct, explicit, and open with regard to the number of Jews killed and the nature of the actions. The camps were in restricted areas. Visitors were limited and the camps generally were off-limits to all but those deeply committed to the efforts. Still, everyone knew that the Jews were being deported; everyone knew that they were not going to return. If citizens did not connect the dots, it was largely because they did not want to connect the dots and learn the truth about what their government was doing.

Walter Laqueur, in his book *The Terrible Secret: Suppression of the Truth About Hitler's Final Solution,* concluded:

These defense mechanisms [against the news of the Final Solution] spring from deep and inherent qualities shared by all mankind—a love of life, a fear of death and an understandable inability to grasp the reality of the greatest crime in the history of humanity.

DEPORTATION

Trains were essential to the killing process. They made the victims mobile and enabled the creation of a new mode of industrialized killing: factories of death.

At first, the Nazis sent mobile killers to stationary victims. *Einsatzgruppen* (mobile killing units) were ordered to round up Jews, Soviet commissars, and Gypsies and kill them one by one—a process that was difficult for the killers and all too public for the local populations.

With the creation of death camps, the killing process was reversed. Instead of sending mobile killing units to stationary victims, the victims were made mobile and sent by train to stationary killing centers where the process was further depersonalized and the killing proceeded in an assembly-line fashion.

In the fall of 1941—months before the Wannsee Conference of January 1942—Odilo Globocnik was told to organize what became known as "*Aktion Reinhard*"—the annihilation of all Jews from German-occupied Poland. Globocnik built the death camps of Belzec, Sobibor, and Treblinka. He also supervised the construction of Majdanek. The infrastructure for industrialized killing was built, the death camps were opened, and the order was given. Shortly after the Wannsee Conference, the deportation of European Jews to death camps began.

The killing centers in German-occupied Poland generally employed stationary gas chambers and were situated along major railroad lines. Auschwitz had 44 parallel railroad tracks. (New York's Pennsylvania Station has but 21.) The existing infrastructure enabled Auschwitz to serve as a gathering point for the murder of the Jews of Europe.

Majdanek was in a valley just below the large city of Lublin. Belzec, where 500,000 Jews were killed in just 10 months, was on the rail connection between Lublin and Lvov (Lemberg). It was the murder site for the Jews of Galicia.

Some deportations were small, local: Belzec received several transports a day as town after town in Galicia was emptied. Jews were killed just miles from their homes. Other deportations were massive. More than 265,000 Jews were transported from the Warsaw ghetto to Treblinka (60 kilometers away) from July 22 to September 21, 1942.

In the largest single deportation of the war, more than 430,000 Hungarian Jews on 147 trains were transported primarily to Auschwitz from May 15 to July 8, 1944. One German document gives a precise count of 437,402 Jews.

How Did the Booking Work?

The SS employed travel agents, who billed for the passage of prisoners at four pfennig (a few cents) per kilometer. Children under four got free passage, and those aged four to 10 paid half fare. A group rate was used for deportations of 400 or more, so there was incentive for the SS to organize passage precisely.

In the West, ordinary passenger trains were often used. In the East, Jews routinely traveled to death camps in cattle cars—or even open cars. No

A column of Jews with their belongings in sacks awaits deportation, while German police officers supervise and keep guard; German-occupied Poland, c. 1943.

provision was made for food, and only buckets were provided for sanitation. If water was provided, it was only at infrequent stops.

The German *Reichsbahn,* the railway, was one of the largest organizations in the country, employing some 1.4 million people, of whom 500,000 were civil servants.

Trains were not easily available. Extensive coordination was needed to ensure the availability of cars, passengers, clear tracks, and funds. As the war progressed, the supply lines were extended well into the Soviet Union to the east and expanded north, south, and west. Other elements of the German state wanted the very same trains to move munitions, supplies, and German war casualties.

The civilian economy required trains to ship products and receive the raw materials required for manufacture. Adolf Eichmann, in charge of supplying the trains for the deportation of Jews, was a superb bureaucratic infighter who operated with the implied imprimatur of the *Fuhrer* and the authority of the much-feared Himmler. Eichmann got what he needed, when he needed it. Deportations were rarely delayed for lack of trains.

What Did the Railway Workers Know?

When the deportations from Warsaw began on July 22, 1942, the anti-Nazi underground was anxious—even desperate—to learn more about Treblinka, the destination point of the transports leaving the ghetto. Zygmunt Friedrich, a member of the Underground who had connections with railway men through the Bund (Jewish Workers Party), was able to follow the trail of deportees and head toward Treblinka, where he proceeded to speak with the local Poles. They told him that:

- Trains were arriving daily, sometimes twice a day.
- The trains were filled with Jews.
- The trains arrived in the station filled; they left empty.

- No food was brought into the camp.
- No wells were dug to provide water.
- No supplies were being delivered to the camp.
- The camp was virtually silent.

Friedrich had to connect the dots— something others had avoided, perhaps because they did not want to know. Wandering around Sokolow, Friedrich met an escapee, a friend from before the ghetto. The man, Wallach, described the gassing process.

"How can I be certain?" Friedrich asked.

"Take a deep breath," Wallach told him.

The smell of burning human flesh is unmistakable. The two men proceeded back to Warsaw together. They had news—real news.

Why Did Jews Board the Trains?

- They did not know what awaited them.
- They could not know what was to happen next.
- They had been resettled before and believed that they were being resettled again.

This German rail car is on permanent display at the Illinois Holocaust Museum. Built in 1913 and refurbished in 1943, it is of the type used by the Nazis to transport Jews to the death camps.

The victims were made mobile and sent by train to stationary killing centers, where the killing proceeded in an assembly-line fashion.

This class of Jewish girls was deported in June 1943 from Paris to the Drancy transit camp to Auschwitz, where they were killed.

- They were starving, dying. A journey elsewhere, anywhere—was sufficient to lure them.
- Some Jews knew what awaited them—and still boarded the trains.

Although *we now know* that German trains led to Auschwitz and other death camps, *Jews, at the time, did not.* Many Jews believed the Germans when they told them that they were going to be "resettled in the East."

Some had previously been resettled. From 1939 to 1941, Jews from small Polish towns were deported into larger ghettos, such as Lodz, Lublin, and Warsaw. In July 1940, 7,500 Jews from southern Germany were deported to transit camps in France. In November 1941, some 20,000 German and Austrian Jews were sent to the Lodz ghetto. In the West, Jews were sent from cities to transit camps such as Drancy in France, Westerbork in Holland, and Malines (Mechelen) in Belgium. In the German-annexed areas of Czechoslovakia in 1941, the Nazis established "the model Jewish ghetto" at Terezin (Theresienstadt) in November, to which almost all the Jews from annexed Czechoslovakia were forcibly relocated.

When Jews arrived in the ghettos and transit camps, they spoke of their resettlement. Based on experience, then, Jews could believe that resettlement in the East was just one more instance of forced relocation to places where conditions would be difficult, persecution intense, but where life would go on.

In Warsaw, some Jews were lured to the trains by the promise of food. Faigele Peitel, who worked on the "Aryan" side of Warsaw, reported:

My mother sent out a note that they were hungry and that they are going [to the trains]. At that time they were giving bread and marmalade for the people to make them believe that they were going to be resettled in other cities— when the truth was that they were being taken to Treblinka. So my mother went with my brother.

Polish contacts told Janusz Korczak (Henryk Goldszmit)—a famed educator, radio personality, author, and pediatrician—that he could leave the ghetto and would not be sent to Treblinka. But he was told that the children of his orphanage could not be saved. He went with them to Treblinka, knowing full well what awaited them.

For most Jews what was at the other end of the railroad was inconceivable. Not so for their killers.

On the Train

Author Primo Levi wrote:

We suffered from thirst and cold: at every stop we clamored for water; or even a handful of snow, but we were rarely heard; the soldiers drove off anybody who tried to reach the convoy. Two young mothers, nursing their children, groaned night and day, begging for water. Our state of nervous tension made the hunger and exhaustion and lack of sleep seem less of a torment. But the hours of darkness were nightmares without end.

Lilly Appelbaum remembered:

There was a small little window with barbed wire over it, and we had no air except what came from that little window.

Fritzie Weiss, then 16, recalled:

Jews did not know where they were going so they tried to ascertain it anyway they could.

They would lift a child up that could read. A man would lift the child up as the train would pass a station, so that the child could read what direction the train was going in, what stations we passed.

Food was scarce, conditions horrible. Sanitation was minimal. Helen Herskovic described the smell:

They had like a bucket in the corner where everybody went. The stench was horrible.

Stops provided an opportunity to cry for help, to barter for urgently needed food and to discard the dead.

Sandor Kirsche remembered the ordeal:

Every few hours, they stopped the train, and they were harassing us: "You got money?. . . You give us the gold. You give us the money."

Olga Astor Weiss recounted: "The dead were tossed out, and then we went back in and resumed the ride."

Still, Jews made efforts to raise each others' spirits. Norbert Wollheim remembered with astonishment one such morale booster:

It was Friday night and when it became dark, one of the ladies there, aware this was a Friday night, took out some candles she had prepared, was lighting the candles, was blessing the candles . . . to welcome the Sabbath. . . . In that wagon of a hundred people, most probably 90 percent of them did not live to see the next evening, but still riding in that car, they were blessing God and welcoming the Sabbath in that mobile prison going from Berlin to we still did not know where.

Israel Stark was transported to Auschwitz during the major deporta-tions of the spring of 1944. He remem-bered his arrival:

Finally, the train slowed down. . . . And finally, they lifted me up again and said, "What do you see?" And I says, "I see a gate.". . . . So, they said, "What else do you see?" And then as we came in further and further, I say, "Oh, there's a lot of suitcases and bundles and all sitting near the railroad. I wonder why?"

Elaine Mortkovic described her arrival at Auschwitz:

We heard the Germans, "Raus! Raus!" In German that meant we had to get off. They slide open the doors. We had to get off the train and we saw the sign at this last station: "Auschwitz. . . . "

Hannah Messinger, who had already been in Theresienstadt, the transit camp that was a model ghetto, recalled her arrival at Auschwitz:

Suddenly the train stopped and we heard screaming, and it was, "Raus! Raus!"—"Get out! Get out!" and some Jewish prisoners came and said, "You are in Aus-chwitz."

German police officers super-vise the boarding of Jews onto a train during a deportation action in the Lodz ghetto; German-occupied Poland, c. 1942.

DEATH CAMPS

During a conference in Lublin on October 17, 1941—three months before the Wannsee Conference—Heinrich Himmler designated *SS-Brigadefuhrer* (Brigadier General) Odilo Globocnik to build a new type of institution, the death camp. It was to be a factory of murder, where an assembly-line process would culminate in lethal gas chambers.

The Nazis built the death camps on two foundations they had developed earlier in their regime: concentration camps and gassing installations.

Concentration camps had first been used as an instrument of Nazi persecution within weeks of Hitler's rise to power. He became chancellor on January 30, 1933, and by March, Dachau was opened to house the regime's "enemies."

Later, the Germans established slave labor camps. They not only housed inmates but also utilized their labor for the war economy. Initially, industries were established near slave labor camps to employ prisoners for the SS's benefit. Later, the camps were built near German industries, which willingly used these workers in order to minimize labor costs.

The next step was to establish an efficient method of gassing. Mobile gas vans gave way to stationary gassing installations, including gas chambers complete with dissecting rooms and crematoria.

The death camp was a singular innovation in history.

For the Germans, the death camp was an efficient way of conducting industrialized murder, which was essential for the full implementation of the Final Solution. For the Jews, they were the places where they faced death, where they worked in the shadow of death, and where they sought out any way to avoid death.

For the Nazis, the death camps had one purpose: the planned execution of all Jews with maximum efficiency and minimum use of resources. They employed a depersonalized process that limited contact between the killers and their victims—one that could be operated in relative secrecy, leaving little trace of the crime and enabling the confiscation of remaining Jewish property and the disposition of bodies.

Six major death camps were established:
- Chelmno
- Belzec
- Sobibor
- Treblinka
- Auschwitz
- Majdanek

> **The death camps had one purpose: the planned execution of all Jews with maximum efficiency and minimum use of resources.**

Above right: *An inmate uniform jacket worn in one of the death camps.*

Murder at Chelmno

Chelmno—the Germans called it Kulmhof—was the first death camp. It was located west of Lodz in territory that Germany had annexed from Poland. The gassing of Jews began on December 8, 1941, the day after Japan's attack on Pearl Harbor, and continued through March 1943. The camp reopened in June and July 1944 to carry out the gassing of 7,000 Jews from Lodz; the ghetto's remaining Jews were sent to Auschwitz. In the autumn of 1944, special units under *Aktion* 1005 were sent to Chelmno to dig up the bodies and burn them, destroying evidence of the crime. The SS abandoned Chelmno on January 17, 1945, burning it and killing the remaining Jewish prisoners.

The dead at Chelmno numbered at least 160,000, including 60,000 Jews from Lodz, 11,000 Western European Jews who had been shipped to the Lodz ghetto, and 5,000 Gypsies who had been deported to Lodz. Also killed were an unknown number of Soviet prisoners of war and 88 children from the Czech village of Lidice. The camp personnel consisted of fewer than 20 SS men and about 120 German regular police for auxiliary functions.

How did the killing work?

Unlike the other death camps, which were on major railroad lines, Chelmno could not be reached directly by train. Jews were transported to the Kolo Station, transferred to a narrow-gauge track, which took them to Powiercie Station, and then transported by truck to the *Schloss,* a palace. Jews were concentrated there in groups of 50 and taken to the cellar, where their valuables were confiscated and they were told to undress. To deceive the victims, a sign read: "To the Washroom." They proceeded by ramp to gas vans— trucks disguised as delivery vans to deceive the local population.

Next, the rear doors were shut and a flexible hose was connected from the exhaust pipe directly to the rear compartment of the truck. Death by gassing took just a few minutes, as it was a short trip to Waldlager, the camp for cremation and burial some 2.5 miles away in the forest. The Germans constructed three crematoria after a typhoid epidemic in the district (caused by decaying corpses) in the summer of 1942. A few Jews were forced to strip the corpses of valuables, burn the corpses, and bury the remains.

A few Jews survived the camp. Jacob Grojanowski escaped on January 19, 1942, fleeing to Warsaw. His account of the camp's activities was received there, just as the gassing began, by Ringelblum's *Oyneg Shabbes* archives. Ringelblum transmitted it, via the underground, to the Polish government-in-exile in London in June 1942. The American Jewish publication *The Jewish Frontier* ran a detailed article on Chelmno in November 1942.

Aktion Reinhard

Aktion Reinhard was the German code name for the elimination of the Jews in the General Government, the German-occupied areas of Poland.

For this purpose, three death camps were constructed: Treblinka, Sobibor, and Belzec. Each was located far from major population centers, yet next to railway lines so that the killing

Jewish belongings at a synagogue in Kolo, German-occupied Poland. After shedding these personal items, the Jews were sent to the death camp at Chelmno.

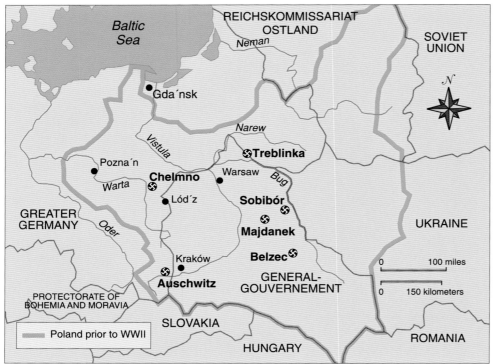

Nazi Death Camps: *All six of the death camps were located in German-occupied Poland.*

operations could proceed efficiently and secretly. The *Aktion* depended upon surprise, speed, and deception.

Aktion Reinhard superseded other "territorial" plans for the solution to the "Jewish problem." Those plans had proved inefficient or unrealizable as the Reich expanded and more Jews came under its control. These included the 1939 Nisko—or Lublin—Plan, which called for expelling the Jews to a "reservation" in the Lublin District. After France's fall in June 1940, the Nazis also considered and abandoned a plan to resettle Jews on the remote African island of Madagascar.

The pace of implementation was rapid. In the winter and spring of 1942, the death camps began operations, complete with gas chambers. Jewish property and possessions were confiscated. During that spring and summer, massive deportations began and by mid-1943 almost all the Jews of Poland were dead. These death camps were then closed and dismantled.

Belzec

Belzec was located in southeast German-occupied Poland on the Lublin-Lvov railway line. Between February and December 1942, the German SS and its collaborators killed close to a half-million Jews in its gas chambers.

During its 10 months of operation in 1942, despite being closed for expansion for almost 60 days, Belzec was day-by-day the most lethal of the six Nazi death camps in occupied Poland. The overwhelming number of Jews murdered there came from Galicia, Lublin, and the surrounding areas, as well as from other provinces constituting the heart of Galician Jewry. Victims also included Jews from Austria, Germany, and Czechoslovakia. Belzec operated as a regional death camp, "cleansing" the surrounding ghettos of their Jews and murdering them. Once they were killed, Belzec was dismantled.

There were only two known survivors of Belzec. Rudolph Reder of Lublin was the lone survivor to give extended testimony. A second survivor, Chaim Hirszman, was murdered after his first day of testimony. All we know from him is what he told his wife, who insisted on telling his story.

The staff of Belzec consisted of 14 to 30 SS officials—and some 90 to 120 Ukrainians joined them as guards.

The design of the gas chambers is attributed to *SS-Haupscharführer* (Master Sergeant) Lorenz Hackenholt, who first served as a mechanic operating mobile gas vans. After his experience at Belzec, he constructed the gas chambers at Sobibor and Treblinka.

An intercepted German document puts the number murdered at Belzec at 434,508. Historians have put the figure as high as 500,000 based on prewar population of Jewish communities.

How did the killing work?

Reder's testimony is the most rare of all. He was the only Belzec survivor to bear witness:

About noon the train arrived in Belzec....

The area between Belzec and the camp was surrounded by SS men. No one was allowed in. Civilian people were shot at if they happened to wander in....

Dozens of SS men would open the wagons yelling "Los!" [get out]. With whips and their rifle butts they pushed people out . . . everybody, old and young; many broke their arms and legs falling down. They had to jump down to the ground. The children were mangled in the bedlam. Everybody pouring out—dirty, exhausted, terrified . . .

The sick, the old, and the tiny children—those who could not walk on their own—were put on stretchers and dumped at the edge of huge dug out pits—their graves. There the Gestapo man Irrman shot them and pushed their bodies into the graves with his rifle butt.

Tall, handsome, dark haired, looking like any normal man, he lived in Belzec in a small house next to the station alone—like the others, without a family and without women.

Immediately after the victims were unloaded they were gathered in the courtyard surrounded by armed askars [guards] for Irrman to give a speech. The silence was deadly. He stood close to the crowd. Everyone wanted to hear. Suddenly there was hope—"If they talk to us . . . maybe they want us to live. . . . Maybe there will be work . . . maybe?"

Irrman talked loud and clear: "You are going now to bathe. Later you will be sent to work. That's all."

Everybody was glad, happy that, after all, they will be working. They even applauded.

The men went straight ahead to a building with a sign "Bade und Inhaletionsraeum" ["bath and inhalation rooms"]. The women proceeded 20 meters more to a large barrack . . . to have their head[s] shaved. . . . Silence was everywhere.

Later I learned that after a few minutes they were made to line up and made to sit on wooden stools, eight at a time. When eight Jewish barbers entered and silently like automated figures started to shave off hair completely to the skin with shaving machines, that's when they realized the truth. . . .

Everybody—young and old, children and women—everybody went to certain death. Little girls with long hair were herded into the shaving barracks. Those with short hairs [sic] went to the barracks with the men.

Suddenly, without even a transition from hope to despair—came the realization that there was no hope. People began to scream—women became hysterical, crazed. . . .

I was chosen to be one of the workers. I would stand on the side of the courtyard with my group of gravediggers and looked at my brothers, sister, friends and acquaintances herded toward death.

The killing process:

While the women were rounded up naked and shaved, whipped like cattle into a slaughterhouse, the men were already dying in the gas chambers. It took two hours to shave the women and two hours to murder them. Many SS men using whips and sharp bayonets pushed the women toward the building with the chambers.

Then the askars counted out 750 persons per chamber . . .

I heard the noise of sliding doors, moaning and screaming, desper-

The victims usually arrived by train, and their belongings were immediately taken away. They were then ordered to undress.

ate calls in Polish, Yiddish—blood curdling screams. All that lasted fifteen minutes.

Screams of children, women and finally one common continuous horrible scream. All that lasted fifteen minutes.

The machine ran for twenty minutes and after twenty minutes there was silence.

The askars *pulled open the doors on the opposite sides of the chambers, which led to the outdoors.*

We began our assignment.

We dragged bodies of people who minutes ago were alive. We dragged them—using leather straps—to huge, prepared mass graves. And the orchestra played— played from morning till night.

"How did it feel to work in this atmosphere?" Reder was asked. He responded:

When the barracks were locked for the night and the lights were out one could hear a whisper of prayers for the dead. The Kaddish *[the Jewish mourner's prayer], and then there was silence. We did not complain—we were completely resigned.*

We moved like automated figures, just one large mass of them. We just mechanically worked through our horrible existence.

Every day we died a little bit together with the transports of people, who for a small moment lived and were suffering with delusions.

Only when I heard children calling: "Mommy. Haven't I been good? It's dark." My heart would break.

Later we stopped having feelings.

Sobibor

Sobibor was established in German-occupied Poland, just south of Wlodawa in the General Government. It was located in a wooded area near a small village by the same name in the Lublin District.

In March 1942, the Germans began building the camp in preparation for the mass murder of Polish and other Jews. Jewish slave workers labored on the site. The camp functioned from May 1942 until October 1943, but the largest transport of victims arrived from June through October of 1942, the peak period of killing. Sobibor was used mainly for the murder of Jews from German-occupied eastern Poland and occupied parts of the Soviet Union. Non-Jewish prisoners of war as well as Jews from Czechoslovakia, Austria, Holland, Belgium, and France were also murdered at Sobibor. The total number of victims is estimated at 250,000.

The victims usually arrived by train, and their belongings were immediately taken away. They were then ordered to undress. Women had their hair shorn, and the naked mass of people was forced into five gas chambers, which had a total capacity of 500 persons. The gassing lasted 15 minutes. Various systems for the disposal of the dead were used.

Some of the very few surviving participants of the uprising at the Sobibor death camp; Chelm, Poland, 1944.

At first mass graves were dug, and later the corpses were burned in heaps. In the last stage, the Nazis burned the bodies on disused iron rails. The victims' belongings were carefully sorted and sent, along with the women's hair, to Germany.

The gas chambers were powered by a 200-horsepower engine, which produced carbon monoxide. Special accommodations were made for those too weak to walk; a narrow-gauge railway was used from the station to the gas chambers to take these Jews to their destination. Those who could not manage the final steps, including infants, were shot.

The camp staff consisted of approximately 30 SS men and about 100 Ukrainians under their command.

The killing happened in two stages. The first, from May through July 1942, utilized the gas chambers, which proved inadequate under the strain of massive deportations. Then, as at Belzec, Sobibor camp operations were halted while three more gas chambers were created under the same roof. The capacity was doubled from 600 to 1,200.

Treblinka

Treblinka was about 62 miles northeast of Warsaw, concealed by dense forests. It became the final destination for transports that brought Jews from the ghettos of the General Government and about ten European countries.

After the beginning of mass slaughter in the Belzec and Sobibor camps in March and May 1942, Treblinka II (Treblinka I was a nearby work camp with both Polish and Jewish prisoners) became the third and, in terms of capacity, the largest of the *Aktion* Reinhard death camps. The camp was divided into three sections: the reception area, the killing area, and the living area (used by camp personnel).

The killing center was completed on July 22, 1942. A day later, massive deportations began arriving from the Warsaw ghetto.

The Germans applied the experience gained at Belzec and Sobibor. Deportation trains to Treblinka, consisting of 50 to 60 cattle cars carrying some 6,000 to 7,000 persons, arrived at the nearby station. Twenty cars were brought into the camp, while the remainder waited on the train in the station. Arriving Jews were forced to disembark, and an SS officer announced that they had arrived in a transit camp where they would shower, have their clothes disinfected, and then proceed to various labor camps. After the announcement, the Jews were taken to "Deportation Square." Men and women were then separated, with children accompanying the women. Eventually a fake train station was built to further deceive arriving Jews. Later, a barrack was painted with a huge Red Cross symbol and deceptively called the "infirmary."

Germans confiscated the valuables of prisoners, stripped them naked, shaved their hair, and then killed them in gas chambers. Gold was removed from their teeth, and their bodies were burned in crematoria or open pits.

Three small gas chambers were housed in one building. Ten more large chambers were added in a building erected at a later date. The staff of both sectors consisted of about 30 SS men, 120 Ukrainians, and about 1,000 to 1,500 Jewish prisoners. These Jews frequently became so emaciated that men from new transports replaced them.

The gas chambers were fitted with showerheads to give the false impression that they were showers. Openings in the ceilings were connected to pipes

Brothers in the Bielsko-Biala ghetto; German-occupied Poland, May 1941. Both boys and their parents were killed at the Treblinka death camp.

leading to diesel engines located in annexes. After the engines were started, fumes containing carbon monoxide emanated from the pipes and consumed all the oxygen in the hermetically closed room, causing the suffocation of the people crowded inside. Death in the chambers was calculated to occur within 15 to 20 minutes. However, the process sometimes lasted much longer, especially in the larger chambers and when the engines malfunctioned.

Jews arrived on transports from Theresienstadt, Greece, and Slovakia as well as Poland. Jews from the Bulgarian-occupied zones of Thrace and Macedonia were sent to Treblinka. There were also Jews from Austria, Belgium, France, Germany, and the occupied Soviet Union. Some 2,000 Roma and Sinti (Gypsies) were also deported there to be murdered.

How did the killing work?

The victims were lined up in a row, ready for the "chase," naked and barefoot, even on the worst winter days. Before them stretched a 150-yard path connecting both sectors of the camp, called by the Germans *Schlauch* [tube] or, with dark irony, *Himmelstrasse* (Way to Heaven). The condemned ran between the rows of torturers, who shouted, battered them with their whips, and pricked them with bayonets, forcing the victims into the gas chambers.

Prisoner barracks at the Majdanek death camp.

After the poison gas was given a chance to work, an SS man ascertained, by looking through the peepholes, that all movement had ceased, the trap door was lifted from the outside and a singularly nightmarish scene would be revealed. The corpses "stood" pressed one against the other ("like basalt pillars") appearing to stare with the horror of suffocation. The first corpses had to be pulled out with hoops, and after that they fell out in heaps on the concrete platforms—pale and damp and bathed in perspiration and secretions. In the corridors, the *Sondekommando* (Jewish inmates forced to work in the gas chambers) began cleaning and washing the chambers for the next shift, sprinkling the *Himmelstrasse* with fresh sand. On the side, men began to run with the corpses, under a storm of blows and threat of pistols, toward the enormous graves.

The gravediggers placed corpses in the gigantic cavities head to feet, and feet to head, in order to fit in the maximum number. On the way to the graves stood a squad of "dentists," who extracted gold teeth and dentures from the mouths of the corpses. Another group of specialists checked whether diamonds were hidden in the corpses' rectums or in women's private areas.

Music accompanied the process at Treblinka—at first *klezmerim* (traditional Jewish music bands) from the surrounding villages, and later an excellent chamber orchestra, which played under the direction of Artur Gold (known for his jazz ensemble) from Warsaw. There was also a prisoner-composed marching song and a choir that, every evening, sang the idyllic song *"Gute Nacht, Gute Nacht, schlaft gut bis der Morgen erwacht"* ("Good night, sleep well until you awake in the morning"). None of those musicians survived. During roll call and on their way to work, prisoners were forced to sing the "Anthem of Treblinka."

The greatest number of transports occurred in the late summer and autumn of 1942. From July 22 to September 21, at least 265,000 Jews were transported from the Warsaw ghetto alone. During the winter of 1943, the frequency and number of transports decreased. After the German defeat at Stalingrad, the Nazis cremated the corpses to eliminate the traces of their crimes.

According to original calculations, at least 731,600 persons were murdered at Treblinka. Other sources offer a figure of 870,000 on the basis of German documents discovered later by Jewish researchers.

Majdanek

Majdanek was located in the valley outside of Lublin in proximity to Little Majdan, from which it derived its name. It was in the Polish territory occupied by Germany.

The concentration and death camp served multiple functions. It was the place where the warehouses from *Aktion* Reinhard were located, where the clothing and valuables taken from the prisoners were delivered, sorted, and stored and shipped back to Germany. It was also the headquarters for the destruction of regional ghettos and the place of supervision for the *Aktion* Reinhard camps—Belzec, Sorbibor, and Treblinka.

Majdanek also was used as a prison camp and as a transit camp for those deported elsewhere. It later became a killing center, though that was not its primary purpose. Though the minority of Majdanek's prisoners, the Jews were the vast majority of those murdered there.

Jews were sent to Majdanek from diverse places, including Slovakia, Theresienstadt, and Germany in 1942, and later from the Lublin and Warsaw districts of Poland and from the Bialystok ghetto upon its destruction. From October 1942 to September 1943, the SS built two and possibly three gas chambers at Majdanek. Modeled on the gas chambers that were built but not used at Dachau, they could operate either on carbon monoxide or the deadly insecticide Zyklon B, which was used at Auschwitz.

Historians differ in estimating the number of Jews killed at Majdanek, varying from 59,000 to many times that figure. Part of the confusion arises because after 1942 camp officials stopped recording Jewish deaths, and in 1944 the records of the Majdanek camps were burnt just before its liberation.

Almost one in three Jews were murdered during the so-called *"Erntefest"* ("Harvest Festival") of November 3, 1943, when SS and police units carried out Heinrich Himmler's orders to murder the Lublin District's surviving Jews, including Majdanek's remaining Jewish prisoners. They concentrated 18,000 Jews from various camps and prisons in Lublin, including at least 8,000 Jewish prisoners in Majdanek, and then shot them in large, prepared ditches outside the camp fence near the crematorium. The killing at Majdanek on November 3, 1943, was among the largest single-day, single-location massacres during the Holocaust. Majdanek was captured whole by the Soviet troops in July 1944, before the Germans had time to destroy the camp.

Auschwitz

Auschwitz was the largest of the Nazi death camps. It was actually three types of camp in one, serving three distinct yet

Top: *A warehouse filled with containers of Zyklon B (poison gas pellets) at the Majdanek death camp.* Above: *Shoes confiscated from Jews upon their arrival at Majdanek.*

Hungarian Jews line up on the Selektion ramp at Auschwitz-Birkenau in May 1944.

interrelated functions, bringing together everything the Germans had learned about killing and slave labor.

Auschwitz I was a German prison camp that housed many Polish prisoners. They were incarcerated because of their perceived threat to Nazi domination.

Auschwitz II, also known as Birkenau, was the killing center of the Auschwitz complex.

Auschwitz III, also known as Buna-Monowitz, was the slave-labor complex at Auschwitz. Many of Germany's most prominent firms invested heavily in its infrastructure. German corporations invested 700 million Reichsmarks in Auschwitz in 1942 on the assumption that the camp was built to last and that slave labor would be a permanent part of the German economy.

Auschwitz II and Auschwitz III, Birkenau and Buna-Monowitz, were part of an interrelated killing process. Arriving prisoners were divided upon arrival. When workers were needed, the young and the able-bodied were chosen to work and sent to Buna-Monowitz. Children and the old, women with children, and those who appeared incapable of work were sent to the gas chambers immediately. For the workers, only the first danger had passed. The victims were literally worked to death. The Nazis held frequent inspections (termed *Selektion*), and those

Children and the old, women with children, and those who appeared incapable of work were sent to the gas chambers immediately.

who lost the capacity to work were sent to the gas chambers at Birkenau.

The survivors of Auschwitz described their ordeal...

Arrival

Eva Mozes recalls her arrival:
The cattle car door slid open and this mass of people poured out. We stepped down. My mother grabbed my sister and me by the hand and I was trying to look around to see where on earth we are—what is that place and what does it look like. Everything looked gray, lifeless. Huge barbed wire. The smell.

Walter Thalheimer could never forget that smell:
There was an incredible stench, an odor that I had never ever smelled in my life and I couldn't understand what it was.

Mike Vogel remembered:
Every German guard had a rifle, a German shepherd dog on a leash and either a whip or a cane in his hand and started beating us off the cattle cars, yelling and screaming in German: "All Jews out, out!"

Fritzie Weiss recounted:
When the train stopped in Auschwitz, we didn't know where we were. The train arrived in the middle of the night so we were greeted by very bright lights shining down on us. We were greeted by dogs and whips, by shouting and screaming orders to empty the train, by confusion, and by men in striped uniforms.

One of those men saved her life. He whispered to her in Yiddish. "Remember, you are 15. Fifteen!" So Fritzie lined up with the older children.

Selektion

Norbert Wollheim described his experience:
They ordered us to line up in different groups—men, women with

children, and women. And that was the moment I was separated from my wife and my child.

Fritzie Weiss:
Men went to one side. Babies were taken and put on the truck. Young children and babies were taken out of mothers' arms and the mothers running after them, screaming, "My baby! My baby!" Women and men were separated, as were children. My mother stood in the wrong line. I found out several hours later that her line went directly to the gas chambers.

Joseph Hausner arrived with the massive deportations of Hungarian Jews, more than 430,000 Jews on 147 trains in 54 days. He remembered:

We were lined up five abreast and marched slowly past an SS officer. And he pointed right or left.

When it was Walter Thalheimer's turn:
My father was in front of me. He asked him, "How old are you?" My father answered: "I am 54 years old." I was 18 at the time. He didn't ask me anything, just pointed me to the other side.

Felicia Galas was with her mother:
And he said like this: "You go this way, and you go that way." And I said to him, "She's my mother." He said, "Yes, but she's old."

We have no accounts from the old, from the women and children, or those not able to work. Some 80 percent of arriving Jews were sent directly to their deaths in the gas chambers of Birkenau. When there was no need for workers, everyone was sent directly to the gas chambers.

Processing

Elaine Mortkovic Welbel described what happened next:
We were marched inside a building where we saw the shower stalls. So they asked us to strip naked, take off your clothes and you get the shower.

On the way out from the shower, we saw chairs lined up and behind every chair was a girl with scissors. My hair was so beautiful and they shaved it off and I felt my naked body, my hair slipped down my back.

Lilly Appelbaum was 15 when she arrived from Belgium. She recalled:

I felt that I was not a human person anymore. The men were walking around and laughing and looking at us. And you take a young girl at my age who was never before exposed to a man and you stay there naked. I wanted the ground should open, and I should go in it.

They tattooed me and they told us from now on this is my name. My name is A-5143.

Mike Vogel:
My number is 65,316. There were 65,315 people already tattooed ahead of me.... When the Nazis

The entrance to the main camp of Auschwitz. The gate deceptively reads "Arbeit Macht Frei" ("Work Brings Freedom").

called you towards him, your caps came off, you clapped your hands on your thighs, and you would say in German, "Prisoner 65,316!"

"Life" in Birkenau

Pearl Herskovic recalled life in the Birkenau camp:

It was gray all the time. In the morning, the little bit that we could sleep, [we'd] wake up with that smell of burning flesh and burning bodies.

In the morning and in the evening there were roll calls.

Mike Vogel:

Roll call was a long process. . . . There was always someone missing somewhere. In most cases, they didn't escape. In most cases, they were either dead or dying somewhere in between the barracks.

Fritzie Weiss:

The dead people that would die during the night from starvation or disease, or from killing, from beatings, they too would need to be carried out from the barracks every single morning, and lined up in front of the barracks. They, too, needed to be counted. Every single

body needed to be accounted for. Day in, and day out. We would not get any food until every single person was accounted for.

Edith Stern described the sleeping arrangements:

We slept either seven or eight women, you know, like sardines. When one turned around, we all had to turn around. The latrine was in the middle of the barracks with big pots where you relieved yourself.

Hannah Messinger recalled: "Bunks, no mattresses, no straw, just wooden planks."

Primo Levi, the Italian writer who was interned in Auschwitz in 1944, wrote of the need to understand the language of the *lager* (the camp). Today we use ordinary words and they mean ordinary things. Hunger is when we missed breakfast or lunch. Cold is when we should have brought a sweater. In the *lager,* inmates were in perpetual hunger. They wore ill-fitting shoes and clothes that exposed them to the freezing cold of Eastern Europe in the winter. They possessed few if any blankets to use at night in the overcrowded barracks. They got cold in October and warm again in April or May. Hygiene was almost impossible to maintain, as clothes were not washed and prisoners were forced to exist in their own bodily filth, with open sores and covered with lice.

Fritzie Weiss shared her frustration in describing the reality she lived:

How do I describe the fear? How do I describe hunger to someone who has probably had breakfast and lunch today? Or even if you are dieting or even if you are fasting today. I think hunger is when the pit of your stomach hurts. When you would sell your soul for a potato or a slice of bread. How do I

Hungarian Jewish women, whose hair was shorn shortly after their arrival at Auschwitz-Birkenau; May 1944.

describe the lice in your clothes, on your body?

Where Have All the Others Gone?

Many survivors said that they learned of the killings from the veteran inmates.

Pearl Herskovic:

So we asked this one woman; we said, "When are we going to meet our family—our father and children?... When are we going to see them?" And she took us by our hands. She came out from the barrack and she pointed to the three big chimneys bellowing with fire in it. She says, "See where your father and your sister and the children are?"

Helen Herskovic:
"You see those chimneys? That's where your father is, your sister and the children." And we started screaming.

Fay Scharf:
The sky was red. The chimneys were burning full blast. And the smell of bones and hair was so thick that you couldn't—your eyes were watering.

Elaine Mortkovic:
We were watching those people coming off the train and we knew that they have maybe a couple of hours to live. Their life is coming to an end and they don't know that the direction they are walking they are coming closer to their death.... Soon as we saw that smoke coming through the chimney we knew that those people.... They are already being cremated. We smelt in the air human flesh burning.... We smelt it constantly... around the clock. Those crematoriums never stopped working.

The Killing Process

Sam Itzkowitz, who worked as a *Sonderkommando,* a member of the units that were forced to work in the gas

Forced laborers at Auschwitz work on the construction of a Krupp factory; c. 1943.

chambers and the crematoria, described the process:

The Germans were in charge. In the undressing room they presided. They told the incoming Jews that they were going to the shower and then to work. They instructed them to remember the hook upon which they hung their clothing so that they could retrieve it afterwards. An SS man would drop the gas. A German doctor would come by after the gassing and pronounce the words: "Everything is finished." He would then leave in a Red Cross vehicle.

A doctor would preside because the Germans sought to portray this as a medical process in continuity with the "mercy killings" that had been authorized for the incurably ill. The Red Cross vehicle was an essential part of the deception.

Itzkowitz continued:
First the women had to go in, into the gas chamber. They led them in and packed them as tight as they could. Then the men had to go after that—the chamber was filled to capacity. But they knew it was going to be filled, so they held back a lot of youngsters, boys and girls, and they held them back. As the chamber was filled to the capacity, the Sonderkommando *had to grab kids by their legs and their arms and shove them in on the heads of*

GASSING

In an order backdated to September 1, 1939, to give it the appearance of a wartime measure, Hitler instructed his personal physician and the chief of the Chancellery to put to death those Germans who were considered "life unworthy of living."

What evolved over time was the so-called "euthanasia program" in which mentally retarded, physically infirm, and chronically ill Germans were put to death. At first, passive means were used: starvation and withholding of medicine. Gradually, more active measures were introduced, such as sedatives.

Finally, gas chambers were employed, staffed by physicians and nurses in a process of medical killing. Initially, mobile gas chambers—which had the appearance of ambulances—were used, but they eventually were replaced by stationary gas chambers.

While the T-4 program, named after its headquarters at Tiergarten 4 in Berlin, might seem unrelated to the Holocaust, it was a prefiguration. As the killing centers came on line in 1942, they were staffed by T-4 veterans who, instead of killing thousands and tens of thousands, could employ their skills for the murder of hundreds of thousands and millions.

Mobile gas vans were employed at the death camp of Chelmno as well as in Minsk and in Yugoslavia for the murder of Serbian Jews. In spring 1942, Jewish women and children were incarcerated in Sajmiste within view of Belgrade. They were murdered in mobile gas "vans." The general population understood precisely what was happening because they could see the mobile gas vans.

The major technical design of the gas vans was turned over to auto mechanics. The chief of the motor vehicle administration turned to an automotive specialist to ask his chief mechanic if exhaust gas could be directed into a truck to kill the passengers. Minutes thereafter, five models of these trucks were secured. Furniture delivery vans with storage compartments about 15 feet long and six feet wide were painted steel gray. Within weeks, 40 naked Russians were led into such vehicles and locked in. After 20 minutes, all were dead. A firm was contracted for the conversion of 30 vans.

There were large problems associated with the use of vans, and some significant complaints. The first problem was how they were to be unloaded.

The second was that rear axles broke down when the back of the van suddenly got a tremendous surge of weight; that is, when people inside the trucks pressed against its doors.

The murder of Serbian Jewry was carried out by well-educated and sophisticated organizers and lower-middle-class executioners—the grunts. The gassing that took place was primitive. A hose was connected by one of the drivers, and the exhaust system was reconfigured so that the exhaust gas went right into the truck. Twenty minutes later, the vehicles arrived at a shooting range, where they were received. Bodies were thrown into open graves and buried, a task that took a little bit less than an hour. The gassings became routine: one a day, and on occasion two. The last Jew in Sajmiste was killed on May 8, 1942, and there was no time wasted in reporting the success.

Killing by gas began at Chelmno on December 8, 1941. Jews were assembled in groups and taken to the cellar, where their valuables were confiscated and they were told to undress. To deceive the victims, a sign read: "To the Washroom." They proceeded by ramp to gas vans, whose two rear doors were open. They too were disguised as delivery vans in a clumsy effort to deceive the local population. The doors were shut, and a flexible hose connected the exhaust pipe directly to the rear compartment of the truck. As the passengers gasped for air, the driver drove to nearby Waldlager. Death by gassing took a few minutes; meanwhile, the truck continued to a mass grave in the nearby forest. Following a typhoid epidemic in the district caused by the decaying corpses in the summer of 1942, the Germans constructed two crematoria.

In his masterful documentary, *Shoah*, Claude Lanzmann interviewed Simon Srebnik, who was 13 years old when he entered Chelmno. Srebnik recalled:

There were 80 C in each van. When they arrived, the SS said: "Open the doors." We opened them. The bodies tumbled right out. An SS man said, "Two men inside!" These two men worked the ovens. They were experienced. Another SS man screamed: "Hurry up! The other van's coming!" That's how it went all day long.

the people, of the victims in the gas chamber, and kept poking them... so they would go further, and the scream of the victims that were walked on was horrendous, but the kids had to move further in until they got all of them in, and then they slammed the door, and gave the signal to the SS man upstairs to put the gas in.

He was asked: "Did people know they were going to die?"

Itzkowitz said:

They knew. They knew but couldn't do anything. They were naked, they were one against the other, and nowhere to go and no—you couldn't move an arm or a leg. What can you do?

Eliezer Eisenschmidt tried to allude to the fate that awaited the victims. He tried to warn their leader. Seeing an entire community about to be murdered, he turned to its Rebbe (the rabbinic leader of the community), warning, "Say *viddui* [the final confession in Jewish liturgy] with your congregation." "No!" the Rebbe replied. "God will help us."

Auschwitz was not a place of miracles.

Other *Sonderkommandos* were reticent to tell the prisoners what awaited them.

"I did not say the truth," one *Sonderkommando* recalled. "What could I say, that you are going to die? I am thankful that I did not say the truth; I did not have the heart to say that you are going to die."

Others presumed that they knew.

"Most of them knew they were doomed; there was nothing they could do about it," another *Sonderkommando* said. "And most of them did not believe. Somehow their human instinct is so strong that they see death in the front of them and they tried to wipe it off. No, that cannot be! This cannot happen. But in reality, finally they had to face it."

How did people behave in the moments before their death? Josef Saker, a Greek Jew who arrived in Auschwitz on the eve of Passover 1944, reported:

Children behaved like children looking for their parents' hand. Parents embraced their children. Children didn't know anything.

What did people say inside the gas chambers? Shlomo Dragon, one of two brothers who worked as a *Sonderkommando,* said:

People called one another by name. Mothers called their children, children, their mothers and fathers. Sometimes we could hear "Sh'ma Yisrael." Hear O Israel, the Lord is our God; the Lord is One. [The traditional line recited by Jews at death.]

After the gas was evacuated from the gas chambers, the *Sonderkommandos* entered. They lifted out the bodies one by one and sent them one floor up to the crematoria. Gold was extracted from the teeth; even body cavities were inspected in search of valuables. And then the cremation process began, either in the ovens of Birkenau or, when the pace of killing was too intense, in open fields.

Pearl Herskovic:

There were bodies piled up high, just bodies. They didn't have room in the crematory to burn all the bodies.... Our job was because they needed a lot of space; so he told us to pile them up as high as we can.

Between 1.1 and 1.3 million people were murdered at Auschwitz. Nine out of 10 of them were Jews, murdered from many different countries of Europe to implement the Final Solution. Also killed at Birkenau in the very same gas chambers were the Roma and Sinti (Gypsies), whose family camp was "liquidated" in 1944.

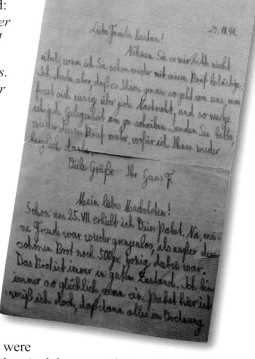

A letter written in German by Hans Finke (John Fink) to his family on July 29, 1944. The letter was smuggled out of Auschwitz. It translates in part: "Dear Kastan family, I already received your package July 25, so my excitement is boundless because next to the letter 500 grams of honey was attached. The bread is always in good condition. I'm always so happy when there is a package here so I know everything is all right."

FRITZIE WEISS FRITZSHALL

1929–

Fritzie Weiss was born in Klucharki, Czechoslovakia, about 12 miles from Munkacs (Mukacevo). It was a close-knit community in which the few Jews mingled freely with non-Jews. Her best friend was a non-Jewish girl. "I stayed at her home and she stayed at mine," Fritzie recalled. "We slept in one bed."

Fritzie's storekeeper father immigrated to the United States when she was young, working at Chicago's Vienna Sausage Company. (He sent half his wages to his wife, two sons, and daughter.) When the war began in 1939, her father sent for his family, but her mother was afraid to travel across the war-stricken Atlantic.

Klucharki came under Hungarian control in November 1938. Jews faced discrimination and persecution, and men were taken to work camps and labor battalions. Following German occupation in March 1944, persecution increased.

When Fritzie arrived at school one morning with her best friend, "she was allowed to walk in but the door was closed to me," Fritzie recalled. She was sent home with her brothers. Fritzie couldn't walk on the sidewalk when German soldiers were patrolling.

Her mother would put food on the table for her three children, but she would not join her young ones. Only later—much later—did Fritzie realize that her mother had starved herself to better feed her family.

Hungary discriminated against its Jews and sent some to forced labor, but it did not kill its own Jews— that is, not until after the Germans invaded in March 1944 and took control, imposing the Final Solution.

Deportation followed. Fritzie's grandparents, aunts, uncles, and all of Klucharki's Jews were loaded onto a train. "We thought we were being relocated," Fritzie recalled. Auschwitz had been operating as a killing center since 1942, and yet word had not reached the Jews of Hungary. "We were not told where we were being taken to," she said.

Fritzie was part of the massive deportation of Hungarian Jews. From May 15 to July 9, 1944, more than 430,000 Jews were taken from their homes and sent primarily to Auschwitz on 147 trains.

What was it like on the train? Fritzie tried to explain:

How do I tell you about a train ride like that? About the dignity that is taken away from you when you need to use a bucket as a toilet in the middle of a compartment on a train, in front of everyone. . . . About the mothers holding on to hungry children. The crying, the stink. The fear. It's strange; fear gives out a certain smell and that mixed with the open bucket.

She rode like that for two and half days and arrived in Birkenau, the death camp at Auschwitz, at night.
. . . we were greeted by very bright lights shining down on us. We were greeted by dogs and whips, by shouting and screaming orders to empty the train, by confusion, and by men in striped uniforms.

One of those men saved her life. He whispered to her in Yiddish. "Remember, you are 15." So Fritzie lined up with the older children.
Men went to one side. Babies were taken and put on the truck. Young children and babies were taken out of mothers' arms and the mothers running after them, screaming, "My baby! My baby!" Women and men were separated as were children. My mother and I stood in the same line. When they called age, I told my mother she was in the wrong

line. *I found out several hours later that the line she went into went directly to the gas chambers.*

Fritzie repressed these memories. She has carried the guilt of telling her mother to move into another line all of her life.

I see the separation. I see the lines. I see the trucks moving. But I do not recall going into the camp. My first memory of camp is sitting in a chair and having my hair shaved, the hair falling and mingling with my tears and a uniform being thrown at me and a pair of clogs.

A lady walked up to me, and kept staring at me. The lady turned out to be my mother's younger sister whose hair was shaved already and who was in uniform.

Only later did Fritzie realize that her mother had starved herself to better feed her family.

Fritzie with her mother; c. 1940.

By the time they took us back to the barracks at night, we could barely crawl, but we needed to show that we could still walk and we were strong enough to give one more day.*

She lived like that at Auschwitz for nine months, and then she faced another *Selektion.*

I was literally in the door of the gas chamber. I will never know the reason why. Six of us were pulled out and put onto another truck with several other women to go to work in a factory.

Fritzie's forced-labor job was to put springs in compasses for German planes. She was the youngest of 600 women chosen for that transport; she had 599 mothers. "If anyone rested, I rested," she said. "I was their hope to survive. I was their hope to carry their message to the world."

Fritzie described what the Nazis termed *Selektion,* when German physicians stood at the ramp and made the ultimate choice who would live and who would die. Those who were selected to die were taken to the gas chambers. Those who were to live—for a time—were branded and sheared. Fritzie still searches for words:

How do I describe the fear? How do I describe hunger to someone who has probably had breakfast and lunch today? Or even if you are dieting or even if you are fasting today. I think hunger is when the pit of your stomach hurts. When you would sell your soul for a potato or a slice of bread. How do I describe the lice in your clothes, on your body?

Fritzie's job was to carry huge rocks from one side to the other. It was exhausting, meaningless work.

Fritzie was ultimately evacuated on a death march, walking from town to town. Liberated by the Russians and nursed back to health, she returned home, where she and other survivors gathered at her grandmother's shattered home. With an uncle and aunt, she went from the Soviet-occupied zone across the German border. In 1947 her father, still in Chicago, provided her with papers that allowed Fritzie to join him.

For four decades, Fritzie could not speak of what had happened. But gradually, under her children's coaxing, she understood that it was time to carry the message of the women with whom she worked to the world. She was active in creating the U.S. Holocaust Memorial Museum and was a leading force in creating the Illinois Holocaust Memorial Museum. As she speaks to students, her testimony is riveting.

FELICIA GALAS BRENNER

1925–2008

Fella Galas, now known as Felicia Brenner, was born in Lodz—Poland's second largest city and its industrial heartland. Her father ran a successful leather-goods business, and her mother lovingly tended to a large family of four boys and three girls. Her family was religious: Her father's store was closed on the Sabbath, when the family table—complete with home-baked challah—was often graced by visitors or students in need of a meal. As a child, Fella felt protected, rarely experiencing antisemitism.

At age 14 in 1939, Fella was on vacation in Cracow, visiting her sister and baby nephew, when the war broke out. She recalled that when she returned to Lodz:

> *The city looked entirely different. Stores were closed; my father was home—my father was never home. It was a working day. And my mother was restless, and I started crying because I expected to be welcomed, and I wasn't.*

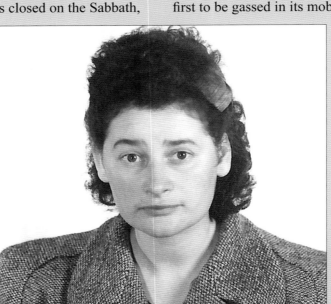

"All of a sudden, I lost my hope that I would ever see my mother."

In 1940 Lodz's Jews were forced to move into a sealed ghetto, where the Galas family shared a small apartment with other families. One family, with a young daughter, lived in the kitchen. When the little girl died, Fell remembered, "they kept the corpse for a couple of weeks, so they could have her food ration."

The Lodz ghetto was separated from the rest of the city. The German-appointed leader of the Jewish Council, Mordecai Rumkowski, enunciated a strategy

for survival. Lodz would become a labor camp producing goods for the German army, and thus position itself to survive the war. Still, the plan was risky.

On December 8, 1941, the death camp at Chelmno began operations and the Jews of Lodz were among the first to be gassed in its mobile gas vans. But that truth was kept from the Jews, who were told that they were being resettled elsewhere. Fella recalled:

> *They would call people to leave—older people, young people—and they would lie so much to us. They [said they] would send you to a farm where we can work, and we would have more to eat.... People were so hungry that they went freely... because they figured they would have more to eat.*

When they sent for her brother, Fella told him to hide in the basement. She went instead, and was forced to sleep on the floor of a large cinema for more than a week. Fella escaped that deportation—she suspected her father had bribed an official—and returned to her family.

When the Germans were "liquidating" the ghetto—the Nazi term for ridding the city of its Jews—in August 1944, Fella hid under a wardrobe:

> *...I don't remember...how long I was lying [there] until I heard some steps—people were coming back. So, absolutely certain that my mother and father were coming back, I ran out. And a few neighbors told me, "You should be*

ashamed of yourself! They took your mother and father."

So ashamed was Fella that she reported to the train and found her mother. They rode together to Auschwitz, where they faced *Selektion*. The SS doctor ordered her to separate from her mother, saying, "She's old. She will need transportation."

For one moment, for one terrible moment . . . I thought, "Maybe he's right. Maybe it's a long distance for her to go. Maybe she should have transportation." I didn't even give my mother a hug or a kiss or anything. And I walked that way. And my mother went through a gate. And I stopped. And I said, "Dear God in heaven. I promised myself never to leave her, not even for a second."

So I turned back to follow. I didn't see her. There were so many. And the guard in the tower—he was waving his arms . . . to me. "Go away! Go away!" And I was being pushed. And I wasn't human anymore. I just turned into some kind of an object. I didn't feel anything. I didn't know anything. All of a sudden, I lost my hope that I would ever see my mother.

At nineteen years old, Fella was alone.

She arrived at Auschwitz in August. In September, the Allies bombed Buna-Monowitz, the slave labor camps at Auschwitz (also known as Auschwitz III), hoping to destroy its synthetic rubber capacity, but the gas chambers at Auschwitz were left untouched.

With the Soviet Army closing in on Auschwitz, Fella was shipped to Bergen-Belsen. Overrun with newly arriving prisoners, the basic systems of Bergen-Belsen broke down. There was no sanitation. Women were forced to use the hollowed trunk of a tree for their bodily needs.

Still, Fella met women who kept track of the Jewish calendar, who observed Jewish holidays even in the hell of a concentration camp. Anticipating the festival of Hanukah, she stole some oil and used a bit of flannel to fashion a wick.

I handed it over to the only mother in our camp. And when she lit the candle and said the prayer over the candle, it became very quiet.

Liberated at age 19, Fella was in disbelief. Another girl found a mirror and, for the first time in nearly a year, she caught a glimpse of herself, shocked to see that a large stripe of her hair had gone gray. Seeking out her family, she met a young man who had been with her brother in Buchenwald. He told her that her brother had died of starvation. Fella married the man after the war, a marriage born in loneliness and isolation.

The couple came to the United States, first to Minneapolis and later to Chicago. Fella worked hard, gave birth to two daughters, divorced, raised her daughters as a single parent, and remarried. Proud of her children and three grandchildren, she remained content with her life, with a few wishes:

For my children and grandchildren to live in a secure world. Such monstrosities should not be repeated. And I would like for the state of Israel to be safe.

Gershon and Felicia Brenner; c. 2000.

CONFRONTING DEATH

How did one live inside the death camps?

Max Epstein said: "I saw only one thing; either you survive or you don't. The rule of survival."

How? "Organize," he was told, meaning: "Steal, trade, and deal."

In ordinary life, Primo Levi said, we enjoy support systems—family, community, even government—to protect us from tumbling to the worst depths. At Auschwitz, there were none. One could fall all the way to the bottom.

Sylvia Fishman spoke from her own experience:

> You had to help yourself. And the one that didn't do that—the one that said I'm going to die anyway—went right away. Right away they went.

Despair was easy: Eva Mozes, one of the twins experimented on by Dr. Mengele, recalled:

> Once the person lost her will to live, you are gone. It didn't take very long to die. Dying was very easy.

Within the camps, there was a word for the walking dead: *Musselman,* or Muslim. This was a symbolic and poetic reference to the Muslim practice of lying prostrate in prayer. Those labeled *Musselman* were avoided by those struggling to survive because the distance between survival and despair was razor thin.

The barbed wire that surrounded each of the sections of Birkenau was electrified. Anyone who touched the wires was electrocuted, and some used the wires as a method of suicide. Hannah Messinger recalled:

> People had made an end to their lives by touching the wires. I wasn't ready for that.

One could not live life thinking about long-term goals. Every hour was a battle for survival. Zev Rogalin recalled that he tried to "prolong life another hour, six hours, a day."

> **"The best way to get any food was to become an organizer. To organize in the Auschwitz language meant stealing from the Germans."**
>
> —Eva Mozes, a prisoner at Auschwitz

The Bielski partisan family camp; Naliboki Forest, German-occupied Poland, 1943.

Struggling to Maintain Humanity

Though all survivors believe they survived merely on luck, it took skill and mutual aid to survive. Eva Mozes recounted:

The best way to get any food was to become an organizer. To organize in the Auschwitz language meant stealing from the Germans, and the best place to organize was to go to the kitchen and steal some potatoes—organize some potatoes. Potatoes seemed to be the miracle food in Auschwitz.

Only a very few inmates could survive alone. Mike Vogel understood that all too well:

You had to have a partner—a partner to take care of you—and you to take care of him. A partner who you could organize food with and would share food with. You had to have someone to help because if you stood by yourself... you couldn't survive. You didn't survive. There were those people who didn't want to share anything. They were always afraid to share a piece of bread. And those were the people who went first.

George Kennedy agreed:
Three of my friends and I decided to live as brothers. Everything, a hundred percent for each other, not as individuals. And we shared everything; we did everything together.

Despite the imposed dehumanization, inmates maintained their humanity through comradeship and helping one another. Some inmates defied the dehumanization by maintaining a code of ethics, others by uniting according to secular political ideologies, including communism, socialism, Bundism, and Zionism. Some religious Jews continued to pray—even to bear homage to their religious leaders.

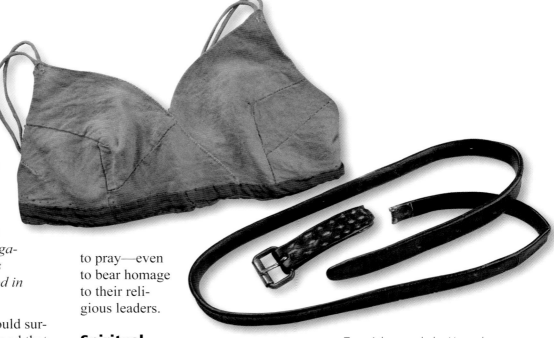

Spiritual Defiance

Spiritual defiance was difficult in the camp, where intense dehumanization was aimed at destroying the spirit. The commandant of Belzec and Treblinka was asked: Why did you dehumanize the people if you were going to kill them anyhow? Franz Stangl answered: "It made it easier."

Alice Lok stood in front of the filthy latrines at Birkenau and remembered:

At this place, I was with my sister, Edith, next to me. And so Edith whispers to me... "It's almost Shabbat. This is Friday. It's almost Shabbat." How we used to celebrate Shabbat in our house—with food and singing and with praying and lighting the candles. I told her, "Why don't we celebrate Shabbat inside the latrine?" We ran back to the end and we started to make our Shabbat ceremony and we started to sing, "Shalom aleichem malachei ha-Shalom malachei elyon" ["Peace be upon you Angels of Peace, Angels on High"]. And as we sang the melody, other children came around us. Somebody was from Poland, somebody was German, somebody was from Hun-

Top: *A bra made by Hannah Messinger from fabric and thread that she stole in the labor camp at Merzdorf, Germany. Maintaining personal dignity, however possible, was essential for a prisoner's morale.* Above: *A leather belt found in the Deblin concentration camp in German-occupied Poland by Szlamek Rzeznik (Sam Harris).*

gary—Czechoslovakia, all thrown together. And suddenly the Hebrew songs, prayers. The Shabbat united us in the latrine of Auschwitz.

How did one pray at Auschwitz? Norbert Wollheim recalled:

I saw that friend of mine... was standing there not far from me praying.... I said, "What are you doing?" He said, "I am praising God." I said, "Are you out of your mind?... What are you thanking God for?" He said, "I'm thanking God for the fact that he didn't make me like the murderers around us."

David Weiss was a young 16-year-old from Sighet (formerly Romania) when he arrived at Birkenau. He was an *illui,* a child prodigy who was already ordained as a rabbi and deeply respected for his learning and piety.

On Rosh Hashanah 5704 (1944), he was at Auschwitz. The themes of the Jewish New Year are God's mercy and God's justice, themes so very difficult to contemplate in a world without mercy and with Nazi justice. David could not address God as the merciful one. And yet, he was able to pray the words of the liturgy in a new and more urgent way:

Our God and God of our fathers, reign in your glory over the whole universe and be exalted by the whole earth, so that whatever has been made may know that You made it, so that whatever has been created may know that You have created it; and so that whatever

Pinchas Neiman gave this prayer book to Abraham Rosenblum in a concentration camp just before he died. Rosenblum carried the book with him throughout the war.

has breath in its nostrils may say: "The Lord God of Israel is King and has dominion over all."

Even within the crematoria, prayers were recited, Yom Kippur was observed, and a Torah was sequestered and read. But as Sam Itzkowitz, who as a *Sonderkommando* worked within the crematoria at Birkenau, described it:

One rabbi, he took it upon himself; he picked up all the infants and all the children when they pulled them from the gas chamber and cradled every one in his hand, kissed it and said the Kaddish [the Jewish mourner's prayer] over every one of them.... He worked like that the whole day and without stop.

In other camps, where conditions were less severe, inmates found other means of survival:

Somebody found a violin for me and that is what saved my life.... I had all kinds in my barracks— Polish people, Russian people, German, Austrian, French, Hungarian—and everybody started to try to get [in] a little bit of better mood because nobody knew what tomorrow brings. So they started singing and I was playing all the folk tunes that I didn't know and that I did know because I was the musician in the barracks.

Psychologists are aware of disassociation, of being in one place and removing oneself from that place, imagining oneself elsewhere. Gerda Weismann recalled how useful it was at Bolkenhain:

There was laughter in the camps... there was joking, there, there were funny stories, there were things that lightened our burden.... We could go on...for hours, spinning the sort of tales which totally blocked out reality, and made the horror around us... disappear. And, I think it was those things which helped enormously, survival.

Each of the uprisings occurred among veteran prisoners who had worked at the camp for some time and had no illusions about the likelihood of their survival.

During the death marches, Gerda recalled, she spent a whole day "wondering whether I would wear a red dress or a blue dress to a party." She had no dresses. There was no party to go to. In fact, she was walking in the snow, seeing other inmates who were so frostbitten that they would "break off their toes like twigs." "Only those with imagination could survive," she said, "only those who could remove themselves from their own condition and imagine themselves elsewhere."

Death Camp Revolts

Spiritual resistance and maintaining one's humanity were not the only forms of resistance in the camps. At Treblinka, Sobibor, and Auschwitz, armed uprisings occurred.

Each of the uprisings occurred among veteran prisoners who had worked at the camp for some time and had no illusions about the systematic nature of the killing or the likelihood of their survival if they did not take action. Each occurred toward the end of the killing process, when the pace of gassings had slowed and there was some time to contemplate what might come next. Each was an act of desperation with the most limited chance of success, the act of desperate yet brave inmates.

The Uprising at Treblinka occurred on August 2, 1943. Inspired by the Warsaw Ghetto Uprising, prisoners clandestinely stole weapons from the camp armory. They had hoped to take control of the camp, but were soon discovered. They understood that it was now or never. They stormed the gates of the camp, running for their lives. The guards fired away from the guard towers. Some 300 prisoners escaped and the Germans

hunted them relentlessly. Immediately thereafter, the order was given to dismantle the camp. Remaining prisoners were forced to dismantle Treblinka, plow it under and plant trees. When their work was complete, they were shot.

Chiel Rajchman recalled:

We wanted to destroy the gas chambers. But we set on fire the garages, the warehouse chambers. Our plan was to get out of there and free the penal camp, but we were not able to do it. It became so chaotic . . . After a few moments, the Germans started shooting and killing. They kept shooting and we were running wild. I was screaming, "People save yourself." Some of them chose not to run and went back to the barracks. I was one of the last to leave. When I left many were lying on the ground, already dead.

The armed revolt at Sobibor took place on October 14, 1943. There were

Abba Kovner (standing, center) poses with members of the Jewish partisan unit Nekama (Vengeance) *in liberated Vilna, Lithuania, in 1944.*

Top: *Aron Dereczunski (Derman), who escaped deportation and joined Jewish partisans, who were fighting in the forest; Poland, c. 1945.* Above: *"Attack," drawn by partisan Alexander Bogen; Narocz Forest, German-occupied Poland, 1943. Art was an important form of documentation and another manifestation of resistance.*

300 Jewish laborers in the camp, but the pace of killing was slowing down. The revolt was led by a Soviet Jewish POW, Alexander Pechersky, and his deputy, Leon Feldhendler, who had been chairman of the *Judenrat* at Zolkiew in Eastern Galicia. Several German supervisors and Ukrainian *Hiwis* (*Hilfswillige*; "volunteers") were coaxed into buildings where they were attacked and their weapons confiscated. They tried to get keys to the arsenal. At the roll call, some attempted to break out of the camp. The German supervisors and the *Hiwis* opened fire on the fleeing Jews and prevented them from reaching the exit of the camp. The Jews then came into the area of barbed wire fences and minefields.

Thomas Blatt recalled:
Though we had planned to detonate the mines with bricks and wood, most of us did not do it and we couldn't wait. We preferred sudden death to a moment more in that hell. People were scrambling for freedom. When I was only halfway through the fence, it crumbled and fell on top of me. I thought it was the end for me. Instead, this probably saved my life; for lying under the wires, trampled by the stampeding crowd, I saw mines exploding and bodies torn.

It was so close. I was behind the last of the fugitives. Each time

I got up and ran further...one hundred yards...fifty yards... twenty-five yards...and at last the forest. Behind us, blood and ashes. In the grayness of the approaching evening, the towers' machine guns shot down the last of their victims.

Some 300 Jews escaped, but most were later killed by the Germans. Some were captured by local Poles and turned over to the Germans. In the end only 50 survived. Immediately after the revolt, Sobibor was closed down and a grove of trees planted over the site.

The Uprising at Auschwitz occurred on October 7, 1944. The *Sonderkommando* expected that they would soon be killed as the Nazis rotated the assignment and never kept one group working in the vicinity of the gas chambers and the crematoria for very long. They had seen too much and were routinely killed after their rotation. On the morrow a new group could be forced into action.

The Jewish inmates were in contact with the Polish Underground cell in the camp and planned on carrying out a coordinated attack with them. Noach Zabludovits—who together with Roza Robota was a member of the *Hashomer Hatzair* Zionist youth movement in Ciechanow, Poland—established the contact and coordinated the plans for the revolt.

Zabludovits recalled:
We knew for certain that in Auschwitz there was an anti-Nazi underground, but there were no Jews in it. We didn't know how to begin. To organize [in cooperation with the Polish Underground] I went to my friend Roza Robota and said, "Comrade Roza, I would like you to contact the women who are working in the Pulverpavilion *[gunpowder room] in the Union [munitions factory], and ask them to smuggle gunpowder into the camp." Roza agreed and organized a group of women who agreed to*

carry tiny amounts of gunpowder [in their clothing] and in match-boxes between their breasts. When they brought it into the camp, Roza placed it under the corpses on wag-ons that went to the crematorium. There the Sonderkommando *took it.*

And then, one day—this hurts ter-ribly—the Germans murdered the Sonderkommando *and changed the guard. The new* Sonderkommando *told me, "Noach, tomorrow we are rising up." I said it was impos-sible, because the command to revolt was supposed to come from the* Armija Krajowa *(Polish Home Army) who were supposed to join the prisoners after the first shot. Dogs! Sons of dogs! Not one came. The Jews were all killed.*

Jewish women working in the nearby munitions factory had been smuggling dynamite to the *Sonderkom-mando* with the hope that the cremato-ria could be blown up and the killing process slowed, perhaps even stopped. Somehow the dynamite did not go off, but the *Sonderkommando* set one crematorium on fire and a mass escape was attempted. Prisoners throughout the camp heard of the uprising, which gave them hope.

On January 6, 1945, four women—Regina Saperstein, Alla Gaertner, Estusia Wajcblum, and Roza Robota—were hanged for their part in smug-gling in the dynamite. Hanging from the gal-lows, Roza shouted, *"Hazak V'Amatz,"* be strong and coura-geous, the Biblical words that Moses had said to Joshua as he assumed leadership.

Confronting Mass Murder in the Ghettos

Even while Jews were being deported to the death camps, many ghettos continued to exist in ever-deteriorating conditions. Rumors from other ghettos of mass shootings and deportations for "resettlement in the East" raised deep concerns about how new German anti-Jewish policy might be developing. But, in contrast to the stark reality that Jews encountered in the death camps, most ghetto Jews continued to be hopeful and maintain their belief in *iberleben,* which is Yiddish for to survive and outlast. Although large numbers of Jews would surely die, the majority opti-

Jewish women working in the nearby munitions factory had been smuggling dynamite to the *Sonderkommando* with the hope that the crematoria could be blown up.

Members of the Hashomer Hatzair *Zionist youth move-ment ride on a hay wagon on their training farm; German-occupied Poland. 1942.*

mistically believed that it was possible for many, especially the productive, to survive. Indeed, for the approximately 60,000 remaining Jews in the Lodz ghetto, this conviction was maintained until the final deportations in August 1944. Moreover, many of those deported from Lodz continued to believe they were being sent to labor camps, where they would continue to work for the German war machine.

Resistance

As noted, Swiss historian Werner Rings described four different types of resistance in each of the European countries under German occupation: *symbolic and personal resistance,* maintaining dignity, identity, and continuity; *polemical resistance,* disseminating information regarding the German crimes; *defensive resistance,* protecting and aiding one's own.

Based on their history of oppression, Jews were practiced in the art of symbolic and spiritual resistance. Initially, they attempted to thwart Nazi intentions by nonviolent means; they stopped short of direct confrontation, as Jews would inevitably be overpowered. Moreover, any attempt at organized escape or armed resistance would result in a brutal collective punishment against the entire Jewish community.

Jews were masters at polemical resistance: Newspapers, diaries, pamphlets, and even major historical enterprises of documentation appeared in almost all of the ghettos. Artists documented the crimes through the tools of their professions; historians, writers, and poets did so by their words; and rabbis resisted through teaching Torah and interpreting Jewish law. But not only professionals were committed to documentation. Children kept diaries, and amateur photographers documented what was happening and kept meticulous records.

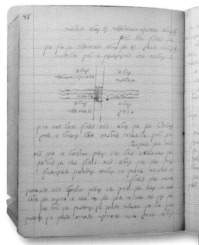

Above: *A diary written in Yiddish by Aron Dereczunski (Derman) while fighting in a partisan unit; Poland, 1941.*
Right: *A zemlyanka—a primitive, camouflaged partisan dugout in the forest. It provided some protection against the elements and could not be detected from afar.*

Leaders did their part. In Kovno, Lithuania, Abraham Tory kept a detailed diary of the daily events of the Jewish Council. Adam Czerniakow, the leader of the Warsaw *Judenrat,* wrote in his own detailed journal until his final hours. Hirsch Kidushin (George Kadish) took photographs in Kovno using a secret camera—as did Mendel Grosman and Henryk Ross in the Lodz ghetto and others elsewhere.

Jews were well schooled in assisting one another. Ghettos had house committees, welfare drives, and soup kitchens. They also pursued other innovative efforts to support each other under the most desperate of conditions and against the most determined of enemies.

But in many places at different times, and to diverse people, it became clear that death could not be evaded by cooperation, negotiation, or forbearance.

Armed resistance was not the only means of expressing personal courage. Janusz Korczak was offered a passage out of the Warsaw ghetto. He was told of Treblinka and the death by gassing that awaited the children at his orphanage. Once it became clear that he could not rescue the children under his care, he led the students in a silent march to the *Umschlagptaz* and boarded the train with them, continuing as their teacher and caregiver unto death. Rabbi Leo Baeck stayed in Berlin as long as Jews could. Offered haven elsewhere, he chose to remain with his community, joining them in Theresienstadt, where he continued to teach and to preach. These were men of courage no less than the young men who fought courageously.

The record is clear: Jews fought in the forests of Eastern Europe; they fought in the armies of the Allies and of the Soviet Union; they fought within resistance groups in France and Russia. Jews fought in Yugoslavia—where the second in command to Tito was a Jew— and in Italy and even Poland, where they battled clandestinely (in resistance units hostile to Jews) and openly (in those welcoming their presence).

They fought in Jewish resistance brigades in Eastern Europe, establishing not only fighting units but also family camps, which were a haven for young warriors, the elderly, and children. These camps served two purposes: resistance and rescue—rescue through resistance.

Lisa Nussbaum described her sense of wonder after escaping the Grodno ghetto and finding Jews in the forest:

We came to the underground and we saw Jewish men and women walking around with arms and free. . . . I said, "[if] only the Jews in the ghetto would know that eight nights away from here Jews live free. They walk around with weapons and they are not afraid of the Nazis."

Miles Lerman, who fought as a resistance fighter in southern Poland, described the price that was paid:

I knew that they would accept me. But not my mother, not my sister and her children.

Only in the family camps, such as the Bielski Brigade, would fighters take in those who were in no position to go on the offense, to confront the all-powerful Germans, derail their trains, sabotage their food supplies, and attack their soldiers.

Each of these contexts presented particular obstacles to Jewish participation:

- Some resistance groups were reluctant to accept Jews as members. Two such groups in Poland were noted for antisemitism, and Jews wishing to fight for them had to do so without revealing their identity. Soviet resistance groups also were antisemitic. They were reticent to receive Jews, believing that Jews would not fight.
- Jews could not blend in with the general population. In most cases,

Below: *Boris Kacel; Berlin, 1945.* Bottom: *Backpack used by Boris Kacel to store carrots and potatoes during his escape from the Buchenwald concentration camp.*

Rifka Grynblat (Renny Kurshenbaum) as a resistance courier, smuggling information for the underground; Warsaw, German-occupied Poland, c. 1943.

local populations supported opposition to the German-occupying authorities, and non-Jewish resistance fighters could find shelter, comfort, assistance, and supplies among the general populace. In many places in Eastern Europe, defiance of the Germans did not yield support for the Jews they were oppressing. Furthermore, many Jews looked different from the local population, and some spoke the native language with a distinctive accent. Only those whose language skills were adequate and who did not look particularly Jewish could blend in. Women could more easily serve as couriers. Jewish men were endangered by their circumcision.

- The Germans responded to resistance with the doctrine of collective responsibility—all were held responsible for the actions of a few—and with swift and disproportionate response. For example in Yugoslavia, 100 people were killed in response to an attack on a German soldier. In Bohemia and Moravia, after the attempted assassination of Reinhard Heydrich, Germans destroyed the entire town of Lidice, which had no complicity. Jews were particularly vulnerable since ghettos were captive cities and their populations could be slaughtered in response to resistance.

- Jews and non-Jews operated on different timetables for resistance. Whether they knew it or not, Jews had a deadline: the moment when deportations to the death camps commenced, when the Final Solution was imposed. As a rule, by the time armed resistance was organized in the non-Jewish population, the Jews were already dead. The Polish

Uprising was in the late summer of 1944, more than a year after April 1943's Warsaw Ghetto Uprising. When the Jews had to fight or die, the Poles were not yet ready to fight. Only in Denmark was the Jewish timetable—their need for rescue—met with bold, swift action by non-Jewish resistance.

Nevertheless, resistance did occur in many places throughout German occupation. French Jewish organizations mobilized numerous resistance groups throughout the country. Armed underground groups operated in more than 90 ghettos in Eastern Europe. However, most ghetto Jews opposed armed revolts; they believed that the uprising would hasten the total destruction of the ghetto. Because of this, many underground members chose to escape the ghetto and join the partisans in the forests.

Ghetto Uprisings

Uprisings took place in many different ghettos, large and small. Warsaw was the most famous, but in Poland there were armed revolts in Bialystok, Bedzin, Sosnowiec, Tarnow, and Czestochowa as well as in smaller ghettos such as Starodubsk, Glembokie, Tatarsk, Tuczyn, Kleck, Lachwa, Luck, and Nieswiez, among others.

An uprising almost always occurred at a particular point in time: when the Jewish population understood that the ghetto was about to be destroyed and that the Jews would be sent to their death. The Warsaw ghetto did not rise in rebellion when the Great *Aktion* took place from July 23 to September 21, 1942. A resistance movement emerged only after the shock that more than 265,000 had been sent to death, after leaders understood that Treblinka was a death camp where Jews were being gassed—that trains were arriving full and leaving empty.

Vladka Meed described her experience in Warsaw:

We had heard the first news about gassing from Chelmno. And at that time we in the shops decided, the illegal youth group, that if they will come to take us, we will stand up.... It was not easy, especially for people like me. I didn't have any idea how a revolver looked or how dynamite looked.

In the areas that the Germans conquered from the Soviet Union, killing occurred before ghettoization. As noted earlier, a small number of political activists—especially the leaders of the Bundist and Zionist youth movements—began to suspect a possible shift of German anti-Jewish policies: Were mass shootings the omens of a totally unprecedented reality, even if they could not yet grasp its dimensions?

Geography was a major factor in the success of uprisings. Some ghettos were near dense forests, to which one could escape. Others were located in urban environments surrounded by the local population, offering few places to hide or escape.

As a rule, resistance groups were led by the young. They were the outgrowth of youth movements: Zionists, Communists, and Bundists. (The ultra-Orthodox did not generally participate in armed resistance.) Resistance required the kind of solidarity, trust, bonding, and sense of shared destiny that youth movements provide. Their young activists were unconstrained by family ties to young children or elderly parents; they could think primarily of themselves. In Warsaw, many were alone, having seen their families deported to Treblinka.

Rumors of impending deportations weren't enough to spur a ghetto uprising. These rumors had to be internalized—and acted upon. In the most famous call to action of the resistance movement, Abba Kovner, the poet fighter of Vilna, proclaimed on January 1, 1942:

A Jewish man crawls out of a bunker that was hidden under the floor. Jews hid in the bunker during the Warsaw Ghetto Uprising in 1943.

Jewish youth, do not believe those that are trying to deceive you. Out of 80,000 Jews of the Jerusalem of Lithuania [the way Jews referred to Vilna], only 20,000 are left. Before our eyes they took away our parents, our brothers and our sisters.... Where are our own brethren from the ghetto?

Those taken through the gate of the ghetto will never return. All the Gestapo roads lead to Ponar and Ponar means death.

Ponar is not a concentration camp. They have all been shot there. Hitler plans to destroy all the Jews of Europe and the Jews of Lithuania have been chosen as the first in line.

We will not be led like sheep to the slaughter. True we are weak and helpless, but the only response to the murders is revolt. Brethren, it is better to die fighting like free men than to live at the mercy of the murderers. Arise, Arise with last breath. Take Courage!

The proclamation tells us much about armed resistance. First, it depended on the perception that the

Armed underground groups operated in more than 90 ghettos throughout Eastern Europe.

A housing block was put to the torch to force resistance fighters to surrender during the Warsaw Ghetto Uprising.

Germans planned to kill *all* Jews. It required seeing through all the measures of deception: German deception, self-deception, promises of hope, and the assurances of Jewish leaders who wanted to keep the ghetto calm.

It insisted on lucidity. Kovner and his colleagues intuited the Final Solution. He grasped that this was German policy, three weeks *before* the Wannsee Conference, the same month that the first death camp came into operation.

Still, Vilna never saw an armed revolt. The Vilna ghetto population never came to share Kovner's intuitions. Hence, the armed underground movement in Vilna, the United Partisan Organization (UPO), reluctantly chose to escape to the forests rather than fight a civil war against their Jewish brethren in the ghetto. The ghetto residents continued to believe in *iberleben,* that rescue and survival for many Jews was still possible. So, the majority of the ghetto's Jews were prompted to vehemently oppose the UPO and the idea of armed resistance.

For the small minority who believed that Germany was instituting total mass murder, this radical realization presented stark choices: revolt and death with dignity. The question was *how* to die, since death, they believed, was inevitable.

Other calls to action were similar, if less nuanced. Resistance fighters acknowledged impending death and expressed anger at those who did not resist. "Know that escape is not to be found walking to your death passively, like sheep to the slaughter," the Jewish Military Underground proclaimed.

"Jews, we are being led to Treblinka! Like mangy animals we will be gassed and cremated. Let us not passively go to the slaughter like sheep," they proclaimed in Bialystok.

In Warsaw, resistance fighters were angry at Jewish leaders, calling them traitors. In Bialystok, they said: "Do not believe that labor will save you, for after the first liquidation, there will be a second and a third." Honor, strength, valor, and war were values espoused by resistance leaders.

How are we to understand the repeated references to "sheep to the slaughter"? Such imagery is harsh, but deliberately so. It was designed to spur action and anger. It is not the judgment of history, not the judgment that can be made by those who were not there, who did not face those circumstances.

Resistance in the ghetto faced a mismatch. It represented a last stand. Resistance fighters had no illusions about prevailing or surviving. Marek Edelman, a commander of the Warsaw Ghetto Uprising, said that "resistance was not a choice between life and death, but a choice as to how to live until you died."

Warsaw's resistance fighters assumed that they would die in the fight and made few plans for escape. Only after they survived more than a week was Simcha Rotem—"Katzik," a street kid who was familiar with the sewers—given the assignment to find a way out.

The Warsaw ghetto arose in rebellion on April 19, 1943, the eve of Hitler's birthday. A *Judenrein* (Jew-free) Warsaw was to be a gift to the *Fuhrer*. For the Jews, it was the night of the Passover seder. On that day, for millennia, Jews had commemorated the exodus from Pharaoh's Egypt.

After the great deportations of the summer of 1942, no resistance arose. The young regretted not putting up a fight. Resistance was organized and a united armed underground was established, the Jewish Fighting Organization (JFO/ZOB) on July 28, 1942. The aim: to fight the next deportation. After the great deportation, the ghetto consisted of young and able-bodied men and women. Few children or elderly people remained. The *Judenrat* and the Jewish police had lost all credibility and authority.

After a deportation began on January 18, 1943, the resistance responded with armed action, and several days later the deportation was stopped. The JFO interpreted this as a great victory. German documents tell a different story: Only a small deportation was planned. But after January, Jews prepared for the next round of deportations.

Barbara Steiner told of the preparations:

We prepared in the bunkers some goods. And we made sure that we have a supply of water. Most of the things we did ourselves. We had Molotov cocktails in the basement.

Ghetto fighters were clearly at a disadvantage. They lacked weapons and were few in number. Great armies had been unable to stand up to the might of the German military. But these young fighters had three factors in their favor: they knew the ghetto, the enemy was not expecting an attack, and they had nothing left to lose. When fighting broke out, small arms and Molotov cocktails forced the Germans to retreat. It is difficult to imagine the joy that the Jews felt at seeing the German forces running for their lives.

Renny Kurshenbaum recalled:
And the mighty Germans—you see them fall dead, really dead, that they can die too.

The Germans returned in force the next day and yet still could not make progress. German Commander Jurgen Stroop ordered that the ghetto be destroyed—block by block, building by

building. Flamethrowers were brought in and the fighting continued. The battle continued for more than three weeks—longer than some armies had held out against the Germans. The Jews refused to yield. On May 16, Stroop blew up the great Tlomackie Street Synagogue in Warsaw and wrote to his superiors: "The Jewish Quarter is no longer." The remaining Jews were either killed or captured and deported to death camps.

And yet something significant had been achieved. The 24-year-old commander, Mordecai Anielewicz, wrote to his colleague on the "Aryan side," Yitzhak Zuckerman, on April 23, 1943:

I have only one expression to describe my feelings and the feelings of my comrades: things have surpassed our boldest dreams: the Germans ran away from the ghetto twice.... The main thing is the dream of my life has come true. I've lived to see a Jewish defense in the ghetto in all its greatness and glory.

Barbara Steiner was less poetic but no less proud. Her sense of history may have been less acute, but her sense of destiny no less intense. "This little Warsaw ghetto," she said, "fought much longer than any country in Europe."

False papers acquired by the Haspel family, and a Madonna and child pendant worn by a Haspel family member. Alina Haspel and her father and sister posed as Polish Catholics throughout the war.

ARON DERMAN

1922–2006

Aron Dereczunski was born in Slonim, Poland, the second of four children (and the only son) of Haim, a businessman, and Merke. The vast majority of Slonim's inhabitants were Jews. The community was well organized, with synagogues and summer camps, a communal fund, a famous *yeshiva,* and a wide variety of Jewish schools. Aron went to a Tarbut school that emphasized Zionism and the Hebrew language more than religion. He saw his future in Palestine, which after 1948 would become the State of Israel.

Though the town was predominately Jewish, Aron lived next to a Muslim household. The two families were so close that the neighbors spoke Yiddish and ate matzah. His family was religious, marking the Jewish holidays with warm family celebrations. Aron, however, slowly moved away from observance. During Sabbath, he rode a bicycle to another town, taking care not to embarrass his father in public with his sacrilege.

When the war began, Soviet troops occupied Slonim. The Jewish population swelled to some 20,000 people as escapees from German-occupied Poland flooded eastward. "We felt for a time like God saved us," Aron recalled. Still his father, a capitalist, couldn't find a job. Aron was trained to operate and repair movie projectors.

In June 1941, the Germans invaded Slonim and the Dereczunski home was burned. Fortunately, Aron's parents had bought another home as a dowry for their daughters. The family moved into that house, in a part of town that soon became the ghetto.

Aron was arrested during the *Aktion* and put in a boxcar. It seemed that his luck had run out.

Aron and his father were taken in the first *Aktion* in November 1941. His father was among the more than 1,100 men killed, but Aron, young and able-bodied, was spared. At 19, he became the head of the household, the lone provider. While working for the Germans, Aron smuggled some weapons into the ghetto. With some friends, he prepared to join the partisans. When his mother learned of his intentions, she begged him not to go. "How can you leave your three sisters?" she asked.

Aron met Lisa Nussbaum, a beautiful woman four years his junior. Amid the uncertainties and dangers of war, they fell in love.

By the time the second *Aktion* began on June 29, 1942, the Jews were prepared. Each had created a hiding place, and none reported as ordered. Aron had indirect contact with the *Einsatzgruppen,* who were arriving for the killing. They needed whiskey as preparation for their slaughters and reward for their rampages. Aron's family was in a hiding place under the floor and Lisa was hiding in the local bakery behind the ovens.

Aron worked with two very different German commanders— both captains. Captain Miller wanted to enrich himself and capture the booty that the Jews were leaving behind. Captain Bauer was "the only German in *my* whole history who was ashamed of what was happening," Aron said. He recalled Bauer saying, "I can't believe that my people can do it." To Miller, Aron made himself useful, telling him: "I can get you what you want." Aron was to appeal to Bauer's humanity when the time arose.

The Germans set the entire ghetto on fire. Aron found Lisa, cut her hair, changed her into boys' clothing, and put her on his work detail. When he suddenly reported to Miller with a five-"man" contingent, Lisa was discovered. He explained to the irate captain that Lisa was his sister.

"This is no place to hide a Jew," Miller replied. Aron then hid Lisa in a storeroom and brought his mother and family to another hiding place. When Lisa's family decided to escape to Grodno, Aron had to make an impossible choice between family and the woman he loved.

I made up my decision. I was going to separate from my family. It was the hardest decision of my life.

In fact, I never saw them again.

Grodno provided only a temporary haven. On November 2, 1942, the Germans initiated a grand *Aktion* there, and Aron fled again. A Polish friend, Tadeus Soroka, offered to take Aron and Lisa to Vilna. Aron was arrested during the *Aktion* and put in a boxcar. It seemed that his luck had run out. Frantically, Aron managed to pry the bars loose from a small window and jump. Losing consciousness, he was again captured and brought to the synagogue to await the next deportation. There, he noticed a side room, where he hid, using safe passage to Vilna as his currency to bargain with the Jew already hiding there. Three would now travel, not two.

A harrowing trip atop a German troop train brought Aron and Lisa to Vilna, where Aron searched for contacts with the Underground. After the arrest of a resistance leader, some resistance fighters—including Lisa and Aron—were sent to the forests to join the partisans. They walked for eight nights, hiding by day.

As a partisan, Aron blew up bridges and derailed trains. Although the Soviets supplied arms, there were deep tensions between Soviet and Jewish partisans. Fighting a common enemy did not inspire agreement on tactics and division of desperately needed arms and food.

Aron and Lisa were liberated by the Soviet army in 1944, and Aron's expertise as a projectionist saved him from being drafted into the Red Army. When the war ended, he and Lisa repatriated to Poland, then departed for Palestine. They escaped into Italy after a difficult and clandestine passage over the Alps, and were married by a rabbi in Rome. Traveling to the United States, where both had family, they planned to stay only briefly, until the State of Israel was established.

Their temporary stay in Chicago lasted a lifetime. Aron established a clothing business, and the couple raised three sons and became active in Jewish life and Holocaust remembrance. They worked hard to find and to honor the man who had saved them. When Lisa died in 2002, Aron assumed her responsibilities as a witness and teacher, and he helped fulfill her pledge to build the Illinois Holocaust Museum and Educational Center.

Lisa and Aron Derman; c. 1990.

LISA NUSSBAUM DERMAN

1926–2002

Lisa Nussbaum was born in 1926 in the Polish city of Raczki, near the German border. She had an older sister and younger brother. Her father, Herschel, was an exporter of geese and lumber to Germany, and her mother ran a textile store. The family lived with Lisa's paternal grandmother in a spacious home. As Lisa remembered, Raczki had some 50 Jewish families—a small but intensely active minority among the 2,000 residents. Nearly all were deeply religious. She recalls little antisemitism.

Lisa attended a public school, but she received Hebrew tutoring and religious education at home. Hers was a comfortable life in a community in which her family had lived for generations. And then...

The Nazis rose to power in Germany. By 1936, her father could no longer conduct business there. Instead of Germany, he exported to Turkey and England.

The German army invaded Poland on September 1, 1939, and about two weeks later the Soviet Union invaded from the east. Both armies made their way to Raczki. Herschel's experience in Nazi Germany convinced him that contrary to historical experience (the Germans had been benign occupiers during World War I), it was better to live under Soviet occupation than under Hitler. Thus, the family left with the Soviet army and fled to Slonim, where they stayed nearly two years.

Her father could not get work, but he had apparently saved enough to get by.

In June 1941, the Germans stormed into Soviet territory, and Slonim was occupied shortly thereafter. A ghetto was established, and on November 13, 1941, the Germans launched an *Aktion* against the Jews of Slonim, killing more than 1,100 men.

The response of Lisa's mother was to flee the ghetto. "We went to the barbed wires and took off yellow stars," Lisa recalled. A former neighbor took in Lisa and her sister. Blonde and blue-eyed, both could pass for non-Jews. Still, when word reached the former neighbor that Jews were being killed, the woman became frightened and would not let the girls stay in her house. Her humane instincts and simple courage had been replaced by fear.

Hiding out in the forest, Lisa and her sister came across the massacres, but they immediately fled after witnessing the screams and blood. A ranger betrayed them as Jews, but he did not take them directly to the pits. Rather, he sent them to the road where Jews were being marched to their deaths. Knowing of the massacres, the girls ran away to the field.

A woman took them in. "You do not have to tell us where you are coming from," the woman said. "I know God brought you to the right house; I will save you."

Recalled Lisa: "I am alive today because somebody cared."

Lisa and her sister returned to the ghetto, where she learned that her mother and an aunt had been killed. Her father and younger brother had survived. It was then, in the aftermath of the destruction, that she met Aron Dereczunski. Dashing and daring, he was also shaken by what had happened.

The Nussbaums lived in the ghetto knowing full well that the Germans were murderers; never knowing when the next *Aktion* would take place. Hiding places were prepared, and everyone understood that the Ger-

Lisa engaged in armed conflict, blowing up trains and sabotaging German supplies.

Lisa and Aron Dereczunski (Derman); c. 1946.

mans were to be avoided. On June 29, 1942, the second *Aktion* took place in the ghetto. Lisa and her family hid behind ovens in a bakery. Entering, the Nazis did not approach the ovens. They departed that evening, leaving behind slaughtered Jews and a burning ghetto.

Somehow, Aron found the family. He cut Lisa's hair, dressed her in boys' clothing, and had her join a work detail clearing a beautiful Jewish home that had been "requisitioned," or stolen, by a German captain.

By September, the remaining Jews were to be killed, and once more the Nussbaums fled. Her father rewarded a woman who would hide them in Grodno. But that ghetto was to be liquidated in November.

Aron tried to bribe a guard, who did not take the bait. Aron therefore had to kill the man with the guard's own rifle—and flee. A Polish non-Jewish friend of Aron's, Tadeus Soroka, arranged for their escape. They rode atop a German troop train all the way to Vilna, where they entered the ghetto and almost immediately joined the resistance.

In Vilna, the notion of armed resistance did not gain widespread support, as in Warsaw. And unlike Warsaw, Vilna had adjacent forests, offering places to hide and mount resistance against the Nazis.

Aron and Lisa fled to the forests. Life was difficult, but at night there was singing and comradeship. Women faced a particular danger, as resistance fighters treated women as reward for their missions *unless* a woman was protected by a man, a fighter perceived to be strong. An unprotected woman could be raped, but Lisa was protected by Aron.

Lisa engaged in armed conflict, blowing up trains and sabotaging German supplies. She, Aron, and her father were liberated in the summer of 1944 by the Soviet army. (Her sister was killed in the roundup, and Lisa left her brother and father behind when she left with Aron.) They returned to Poland and then journeyed to Czechoslovakia and Italy thanks to false papers provided by *Bricha,* a clandestine effort to bring more Jews to Palestine. Lisa and Aron were married in Rome after the war.

Lisa and Aron dreamed of going to Palestine, but both had relatives in the United States. They made a home in Chicago, first on the South Side and later in suburban Skokie, where Aron worked at a variety of jobs and eventually established his own clothing store. All three of their sons became physicians.

Lisa told her story to her children and to her family, to anyone who would listen, but never in public—until her youngest son, Daniel, assigned to write about resistance, brought his mother to class. After that experience, Lisa began teaching in schools and speaking to students, continuing to bear witness until the end of her life. She became the second president of the Illinois Holocaust Foundation. Under her leadership, the Holocaust mandate was passed by the Illinois Legislature and the first plans for the Illinois Holocaust Museum and Education Center were developed. Along with 120 students, Lisa went back to Poland, where she saw the sites of destruction as well as the places where she had lived and fought.

Forty years after her escape to Vilna, Lisa and Aron sought out Tadeus Soroka, their rescuer. They brought him to the United States, took him to schools and churches, and documented his deeds so that he was honored by Yad Vashem (Israel's memorial to the Holocaust) as "Righteous Among the Nations" for his selfless and noble deed.

MATUS STOLOV

1928–

Born in Minsk, Belorussia, now called Belarus, Matus Stolov was the son of Polish Jewish parents who had fled to Russia after the 1917 Revolution to build the socialist utopia in Russia. His father, a pharmacist in Poland, worked as a bookkeeper—perhaps even as an economist—in the Soviet Union. His mother taught German at an advanced level.

Matus's father was one of 13 or 14 children; like his father, his uncles were Bolsheviks/socialists, and they served in the Red Army during the Russian Civil War. Their beliefs underwent a severe test, as four of his father's siblings were arrested in the great Soviet purges of the mid-1930s; one was killed in a Russian gulag in 1943, not by the Germans but by conditions of Soviet rule. One of his uncles, Efraim, married a non-Jewish woman and moved from Minsk to the city of Birobidzhan in the 1930s to participate in the planned Jewish Socialist autonomous republic in the Far East. Efraim became a judge, but he was soon arrested and killed in 1938. His wife was sent to a prison camp. Their daughter, Lena, was sent to Minsk to live with his mother's sister, also named Lena. So the two became known as Big Lena and Little Lena within the Stolov family.

Big Lena was also married to a Jew. This situation was later to become a lifeline for Matus and his mother. Matus had an older brother, who attended a Yiddish school in the 1930s. Under the Soviet constitution, Yiddish was one of the accepted national languages. The Soviet Union was officially not antisemitic. Yiddish-speaking secular schools were operational for a while, but by the time Matus was ready for school, the schools had been disbanded. Matus went to public school, where the language of instruction was Russian and the curriculum ideologically Communist.

Matus remembered secular holidays: May Day (Workers' Day) and the anniversary of the Revolution. Avid Communists, his family did not observe Jewish tradition. Still, the Stolov family was culturally Jewish. Matus's mother participated in a circle of Jewish poets in Minsk, but after 1934–35 there was no Jewish life, at least not openly.

World War II began in Poland in September 1, 1939. Just days before, the Soviet Union and Nazi Germany entered into a hasty alliance, agreeing to divide Poland between Soviet and German zones of occupation. Parts of western Poland were annexed to Germany; other regions were occupied. The Soviet Union occupied eastern Poland, including the Grodno region, where Matus's grandparents and their family lived. They were murdered during the Holocaust.

Matus's brother had just completed his third year of medical school in early 1941. He was an A student and a star athlete, playing for the Belorussian volleyball team. But the Stolovs' lives changed dramatically on June 22, 1941, when the Germans invaded Soviet territories and the Soviet Union's Great Patriotic War began.

Matus's mother and her two sons tried to escape from the advancing German army by moving eastward, farther into Soviet territory. They ran for a train, and the two sons jumped onboard. Their mother could not make the leap, so Matus jumped off the train to stay with her.

Outside was a pile of 60 to 80 corpses from the next house, and large puddles of blood.

After the German capture of Minsk on June 27–28, the city became the district capital. Wilhelm Kube, the German general commissioner of Belorussia, was headquartered in Minsk. In July, a ghetto was established that contained some 100,000 Jews from Minsk and other towns. And from November 1941 to October 1942, more than 35,000 Jews from Germany, Bohemia, and Moravia were deported to the Minsk ghetto. Special gas vans were employed to kill some of the arriving Jews in Maly Trostinets, some eight miles east of Minsk. It was an early use of gas vans—mobile, operational vans that appeared normal but were airtight and equipped as gas chambers.

Matus's mother chose to live near the outer part of the ghetto adjacent to the "Aryan side." They shared one room with members of another family, who were friends of his brother and most especially with their 17-year-old daughter, Esther. When the Germans appeared ready to kill the Jews on November 7, 1941, Matus, his mother, and Esther hid with Big Lena, who was also hiding her Jewish sister-in-law and her half-Jewish niece, Little Lena.

One night in March 1942, the Stolov family hid in a cellar. This time they were separated from Esther, who searched for them. She found them only after the danger had passed. Outside was a pile of 60 to 80 corpses from the next house, and large puddles of blood. On a subsequent *Aktion* on July 28, 1942, they hid in a "Malina," a hiding place created by erecting false walls.

Big Lena had connections with the non-Jewish underground. Knowing of their desperate situation, she arranged for false documents in October-November 1942. Matus became "Arnold." His mother, who was blonde and did not appear obviously Jewish, had an easier time passing as a non-Jew. For several days, they walked at night, avoiding German and local police before eventually reaching the partisans. Seeing the first real Soviet partisan/fighter, they breathed a sigh of relief. Here, with war all around them, they might be killed, but not because they were Jews.

Mother and child were not welcome to join the partisans. The partisans' commander sent them away with a group of partisans and underground fighters across the front line to the Great Land (*Bolshaya Zemlya*, non-occupied Soviet Union). Hiding, and suffering from cold and hunger, and in constant fear of being killed by Nazis or Soviet collaborators, they walked at night and tried to find friendly peasants and food. They traveled for a month to the northeast of Belorussia, crossed the front line under fire, and met Soviet soldiers in their uniforms. It was their liberation to freedom.

Matus with his brother, Boris (left); mother, Fanya; and father, Abram; Minsk, Belorussia, 1935.

They were shipped eastward to Kazan, where Matus's mother joined the faculty of the university, teaching German. But first she had to survive intensive interrogation from the KGB, who feared that because of her fluent German, she was actually a German spy—which, they thought, might explain why she and Matus had not been killed.

After liberation, they returned to Minsk and were happily reunited with Esther. They also learned that Matus's brother had been reported missing in action in December 1942.

Matus's schooling had been interrupted by the war. He had gone through seven years of school and returned three years later, much older than his fellow eighth grade students. Anxious to continue his education, he enrolled in technical school and skipped over his grade. He earned a high school equivalency degree, then studied to be a mechanical engineer. He worked with fossil power plant boilers, turbines, and auxiliary equipment.

In 1950 all the students in his specialty wrote a collective letter to the Soviet government, the Ministry of Education, and other agencies complaining that the plants and positions where the authority was sending them to work were not corresponding to their specialty. Matus was among the five top Jewish students who initiated this letter, and as a result was expelled from the engineering school just short of receiving his degree. Matus was able to advance in his professional work, at least until he was drafted by the army. Discharged in 1953, he resumed his studies and had a successful career in the Soviet Union.

Matus could not advance to the limits of his abilities because he was Jewish. His wife, Victoria, an ophthalmologist, was not allowed to work in hospitals because she was Jewish. His daughter, Irina, after finishing high school with gold medal honors, was not accepted at a university (her specialty was applied math) only because she was Jewish. Through all his life after World War II, Matus witnessed discrimination against his family and others who lived beneath the Soviet government's anitisemitic policies.

When Jews started to leave the Soviet Union in the late 1970s, Matus decided that the family would have a better future by immigrating to the United States. In 1980 the family applied to emigrate, but they were denied for two years. As a *refusenik,* Matus lost his job, and the family did not know if they could ever leave the Soviet Union. After two years of visiting and applying to high-level officials in the Ministry of Internal Affairs of Belorussia, they received permission in December 1982 to leave the country in one month.

The family arrived in Chicago in April 1982 during the second day of Passover. For the first time in their lives, the family celebrated the Passover Seder, doing so at the Chicago apartment of Matus's American cousin, Orah Winograd. They settled in Chicago as part of the great wave of immigration that brought more than a million Jews to lands of freedom, most especially Israel and also the United States. Matus worked in the United States as a mechanical engineer. His daughter has followed in his footsteps, working as an electrical engineer.

Matus with his mother, Fanya; 1945.

GETTING THE WORD OUT

istorians distinguish between knowledge and information. Much *information* was available to government officials and civilians, military commanders and church leaders, perpetrators, bystanders, rescuers, and sometimes even victims—to all those in a position to affect the fate of the Jews. But such information rarely transformed into *knowledge,* which might, finally, have led to an effective response. A significant exception: People who knew what was happening to Europe's Jews found the truth unbearable. They had internalized the unprecedented reality—that *all* Jews were to be killed—and were consumed by it.

Two very young and very great men tried their best, at great personal risk, to get the information out about the Final Solution, to spur action, to plead for rescue—but to no avail. Their failure would torment them to the end of their days.

Gerhart Riegner was a lawyer from Leipzig. In 1933 he fled from Germany to Switzerland, where he became the secretary of the World Jewish Congress, stationed in Geneva. His task was to gather information and facilitate rescue.

On August 8, 1942, Riegner sent two identical telegrams:

> RECEIVED ALARMING REPORT THAT IN FUEHRER'S HEADQUARTERS PLAN DISCUSSED AND UNDER CONSIDERATION ALL JEWS IN COUNTRIES OCCUPIED OR CONTROLLED GERMANY NUMBER THREE AND HALF TO FOUR MILLION SHOULD AFTER DEPORTATION AND CONCENTRATION IN EAST AT ONE BLOW EXTERMINATED TO RESOLVE ONCE FOR ALL JEWISH QUESTION IN EUROPE STOP ACTION REPORTED PLANNED FOR AUTUMN METHODS UNDER DISCUSSION INCLUDING PRUSSIC ACID STOP WE TRANSMIT INFORMATION WITH ALL NECESSARY RESERVATION AS EXACTITUDE CANNOT BE CONFIRMED STOP INFORMANT STATED TO HAVE CLOSE CONNECTIONS WITH HIGHEST GERMAN AUTHORITIES AND HIS REPORTS ENERALLY RELIABLE STOP.

The information was so explosive that Riegner used secure Allied diplomatic mail lines from neutral Switzerland to protect its confidentiality.

But Riegner's "early" telegram

Gerhart Riegner, who said he felt a strong sense of "abandonment, powerlessness, and loneliness" after his telegram was largely ignored by the West.

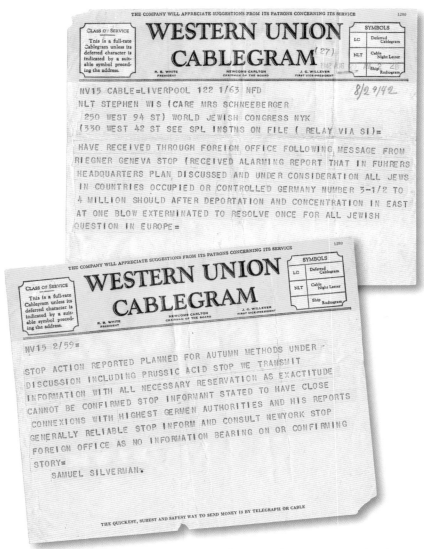

THE COMPANY WILL APPRECIATE SUGGESTIONS FROM ITS PATRONS CONCERNING ITS SERVICE

WESTERN UNION CABLEGRAM

CLASS OF SERVICE
This is a full-rate
Cablegram unless its
deferred character is
indicated by a suit-
able symbol preced-
ing the address.

SYMBOLS
LC Deferred Cablegram
NLT Cable Night Letter
Ship Radiogram

NV15 CABLE=LIVERPOOL 122 1/63 NFD   8/29/42

NLT STEPHEN WIS (CARE MRS SCHNEEBERGER
250 WEST 94 ST) WORLD JEWISH CONGRESS NYK
(330 WEST 42 ST SEE SPL INSTNS ON FILE (RELAY VIA SI)=

HAVE RECEIVED THROUGH FOREIGN OFFICE FOLLOWING MESSAGE FROM
RIEGNER GENEVA STOP (RECEIVED ALARMING REPORT THAT IN FUHRERS
HEADQUARTERS PLAN DISCUSSED AND UNDER CONSIDERATION ALL JEWS
IN COUNTRIES OCCUPIED OR CONTROLLED GERMANY NUMBER 3-1/2 TO
4 MILLION SHOULD AFTER DEPORTATION AND CONCENTRATION IN EAST
AT ONE BLOW EXTERMINATED TO RESOLVE ONCE FOR ALL JEWISH
QUESTION IN EUROPE =

THE COMPANY WILL APPRECIATE SUGGESTIONS FROM ITS PATRONS CONCERNING ITS SERVICE

WESTERN UNION CABLEGRAM

CLASS OF SERVICE
This is a full-rate
Cablegram unless its
deferred character is
indicated by a suit-
able symbol preced-
ing the address.

SYMBOLS
LC Deferred Cablegram
NLT Cable Night Letter
Ship Radiogram

NV15 2/59=

STOP ACTION REPORTED PLANNED FOR AUTUMN METHODS UNDER
DISCUSSION INCLUDING PRUSSIC ACID STOP WE TRANSMIT
INFORMATION WITH ALL NECESSARY RESERVATION AS EXACTITUDE
CANNOT BE CONFIRMED STOP INFORMANT STATED TO HAVE CLOSE
CONNEXIONS WITH HIGHEST GERMEN AUTHORITIES AND HIS REPORTS
GENERALLY RELIABLE STOP INFORM AND CONSULT NEWYORK STOP
FOREIGN OFFICE AS NO INFORMATION BEARING ON OR CONFIRMING
STORY=
SAMUEL SILVERMAN.

THE QUICKEST, SUREST AND SAFEST WAY TO SEND MONEY IS BY TELEGRAPH OR CABLE

The Riegner Telegram, sent by Samuel Silverman, informing Stephen Wise of the Gerhart Riegner telegram. The State Department had refused to deliver the telegram that Riegner had sent directly to Rabbi Wise.

was too late. By then, Germany's plan had already been approved and was operational, a result of the Wannsee Conference that had been held by Nazi functionaries nearly eight months earlier.

Riegner's informant, Eduard Schulte, was general manager of the Georg von Giesche Mining Company, which had extensive holdings near the Nazi death camp at Auschwitz, Poland. He was deeply repulsed by what was happening and made contacts in Switzerland to inform the West of the Germans' intentions. His report was highly reliable—even if it came too late. For a generation, even after Schulte's death, Riegner would not reveal Schulte's name.

Riegner sent one of his telegrams to Rabbi Stephen Wise, president of the American Jewish Congress in New York, via the State Department in Washington. He sent the other to Samuel Silverman, a Jewish member of the British Parliament, via the British Foreign Office. The British delivered the telegram. The Americans did not, as they questioned the accuracy of the contents and did not want to prompt Wise, the leader of American Jewry, to call for action.

However, on August 29, Silverman telegrammed Wise the contents of the August 8 cable. When Wise inquired about his copy, Undersecretary of State Sumner Welles asked him to remain silent until the information it contained could be confirmed.

Welles initiated a series of discreet inquiries to verify the unconfirmed reports. On November 24, Welles told Wise: "I regret to tell you, Dr. Wise, that these confirm and justify your deepest fears. There is no exaggeration."

Wise was freed to share this information with journalists, but when he met with reporters to reveal this explosive information, the State Department would not confirm what it had just told him, so the information appeared in the press as if it were private information of anxious Jewish leaders instead of government-confirmed intelligence based on a significant clandestine source. During World War II, government information was credible, and such important information would have received prominent play—the front pages of major newspapers and news magazine. No similar respect was given to "Jewish sources."

Though Wise had no luck, Jan Karski tried his best to convince the West of the Final Solution.

Jan Karski was a young Polish courier serving the Polish government-in-exile. A diplomat by training, Karski was recruited into the Polish underground by his brother, a ranking Polish security official in Warsaw. Blessed with a photographic memory, Karski was trusted by political forces in

"I regret to tell you, Dr. Wise, that these [reports of mass murder] confirm and justify your deepest fears. There is no exaggeration."

–U.S. undersecretary of state Sumner Welles

Poland. Arrested, he withstood torture, and even attempted suicide to ensure his own silence. Rescued, he resumed his underground activities.

On the eve of what was his last mission abroad—weeks before Rabbi Wise heard back from Welles—Karski was asked to carry information regarding the ghettoized Jews to London. He insisted on meeting with the Jews directly and not through intermediaries, so that his reports in the West would have greater credibility. Thus, he entered the Warsaw ghetto and met with two Jewish leaders, Menachem Kirschenbaum of the General Zionists and Leon Feiner of the Bund (Jewish Socialist Party).

These leaders were the final remnant of what had once been the largest and most influential Jewish community in Europe, Warsaw. More than 265,000 of Warsaw's Jews had been deported to the death camp of Treblinka some 40 miles away in the summer of 1942. Only 50,000 desperate Jews, mostly young men and women without families, remained alive.

These two Jewish leaders from opposing political philosophies were desperate enough to set aside their differences and come together in a plea to the world. They stressed that they were speaking on behalf of all Polish Jews, regardless of political differences. They asked that the Allied governments stop the murder of the Jews, demanding:

- A public announcement that preventing the physical extermination of the Jews was part of the Allied war strategy;
- That all statistics, facts, and data on Jewish ghettos, concentration camps, involved German officials, and methods used be spelled out;
- Public appeals to the German people be made to pressure their government to stop the extermination;
- That the German masses be considered collectively responsible for the genocide if they did not rise up to stop it;
- That if none of the other steps halted the genocide, the Allies would bomb selected sites of German cultural importance and execute Germans in Allied hands who professed loyalty to Hitler after learning of his crimes.

Karski told the men: "It is against international law. I know the British. They will not do it. It is hopeless. It weakens your case."

One leader replied: "Say it. We don't know what is realistic or not realistic. We are dying here."

Karski also boarded a deportation train headed for a place he thought was Belzec. From his description of the camp, we can surmise that it was Izbica, a transit camp near Belzec in southeast Poland. He wore the uniform of a Ukrainian guard. He broke down at what he saw and fled imme-

Polish courier Jan Karski, who went to the United States to inform Allied leaders about Nazi policy in Poland, including the mass murder of Jews.

Kurt Gerstein was a German nationalist and a Christian. To learn more about the Nazis' activities, which he clandestinely opposed, Gerstein joined the Waffen-SS in March 1941 and became an employee at its Hygiene Service. In 1942, as an expert in the use of Zyklon B—a poison gas used prior to WWII for rodent fumigations— Gerstein was sent to the death camps of Belzec and Treblinka. Upon his return to Berlin, Gerstein tried to stop the murders, informing Swedish and Swiss diplomats, representatives of the Vatican, and underground Church groups of his experiences, but despite the accuracy of his reports, he encountered disbelief and indifference. Gerstein continued to play his double role to the end. He delivered Zyklon B shipments to the camps and unsuccessfully attempted to arouse German and foreign awareness of the mass murder operations. Arrested by the French as a suspected war criminal, Gerstein was found hanged in his cell on July 25, 1945, a victim of either suicide or murder.

diately, fearing that his behavior would betray him.

When he arrived in London, Karski transmitted his messages on behalf of the Poles. He spoke to Jewish leaders and Allied leaders, including Anthony Eden, the British foreign secretary in London—but not to Prime Minister Winston Churchill. He met privately with the Jewish representative of the Bund in London, Szmul Zygielbojm.

Karski was then sent to the United States to meet with American leaders. Officially, he sought support for the Polish government-in-exile as well as for an independent Poland after the war. He was also there on his own mission—a mission on behalf of the dying Jews.

To orchestrate a meeting with President Roosevelt, Karski met with three American Jewish government officials, men close to the president: Benjamin Cohen, Roosevelt's advisor; Oscar Cox, assistant solicitor general; and, most importantly, Jewish Supreme Court Justice Felix Frankfurter, who had helped shape the New Deal. At a meeting hosted by the Polish ambassador at his residence, Karski spoke late into the evening. Two men left shaken; Frankfurter lingered, and expressed his inability to believe what Karski had detailed—an inability to internalize the reality of the Final Solution.

But Karski got his meeting with Roosevelt, who had little interest in an independent postwar Poland or in saving the Jews in the middle of a desperate war. Both were peripheral to the global battle against Hitler.

Public exposure in the United States made it impossible for Karski to return to Poland as a courier. He spent the rest of the wartime period writing and lecturing, speaking to more than 200 audiences. He stated after the war:

The Lord assigned me a role to speak and to write during the war—as it seemed to me it might help. It did not.

Furthermore, when the war came to its end I learned that the governments, the leaders, the scholars, the writers did not know what had been happening to the Jews. They were taken by surprise. The murder of six million innocents was a secret.

Then I became a Jew, like the family of my wife . . . so all murdered Jews became my family.

But I am a Christian Jew. I am a practicing Catholic. Although I am not a heretic, still my faith tells me that the second original sin has been committed by humanity: through commission or omission or self-imposed ignorance or insensitivity, or hypocrisy, or heartless rationalization.

This sin will haunt humanity to the end of time.

It does haunt me and I want it to be so.

In 1982 Yad Vashem awarded Karski, on behalf of the Israeli government, the honor of Righteous Among the Nations.

ZYGIELBOJM'S SUICIDE PROTEST

Szmul Zygielbojm was one of the leaders of the Bund, the Jewish Socialist Party in Poland. In 1940 he managed to flee from Poland. Reaching London in 1942, he—as representative of the Polish Jews—joined the National Polish Council, which worked with the Polish government-in-exile. Zygielbojm and others tried desperately to draw the attention of the Allied governments to the fate of the Jews in Poland. When the news of the revolt in the Warsaw ghetto came, and with it the final phase of the extermination, Zygielbojm committed suicide as an act of protest against the indifference of the Allied governments to the fate of his people. Before his death, he addressed to the Polish government the following letter, which was transmitted to the British and American governments:

With these, my last words, I address myself to you, the Polish government, the Polish people, the Allied governments and their peoples, and the conscience of the world.

News recently received from Poland informs us that the Germans are exterminating with unheard-of savagery the remaining Jews in that country. Behind the walls of the ghetto is taking place today the last act of a tragedy that has no parallel in the history of the human race. The responsibility for this crime—the assassination of the Jewish population in Poland—rests above all on the murderers themselves, but falls indirectly upon the whole human race, on the Allies and their governments, who so far have taken no firm steps to put a stop to these crimes. By their indifference to the killing of millions of hapless men, to the massacre of women and children, these countries have become accomplices of the assassins.

Furthermore, I must state that the Polish government, although it has done a great deal to influence world public opinion, has not taken adequate measures to counter this atrocity which is taking place today in Poland.

Of the three and a half million Polish Jews (to whom must be added the 700,000 deported from the other countries) in April 1943, there remained alive not more than 300,000 Jews according to news received from the head of the

Bund organization and supplied by government representatives. And the extermination continues.

I cannot remain silent. I cannot live while the rest of the Jewish people in Poland, whom I represent, continue to be liquidated.

My companions of the Warsaw ghetto fell in a last heroic battle with their weapons in their hands. I did not have the honor to die with them but I belong to them and to their common grave.

Let my death be an energetic cry of protest against the indifference of the world that witnesses the extermination of the Jewish people without taking any steps to prevent it. In our day and age human life is of little value; having failed to achieve success in my life, I hope that my death may jolt the indifference of those who, perhaps even in this extreme moment, could save the Jews who are still alive in Poland.

My life belongs to my people in Poland and that is why I am sacrificing it for them. May the handful of people who will survive out of the millions of Polish Jews achieve liberation in a world of liberty and socialist justice together with the Polish people.

I think that there will be a free Poland and that it is possible to achieve a world of justice. I am certain that the president of the Republic and the head of the government will pass on my words to all concerned. I am sure that the Polish government will hasten to adopt the necessary political measures and will come to the aid of those who are still alive.

I take my leave of all those who have been dear to me and whom I have loved.

Szmul Zygielbojm

WORLD RESPONSE: 1940–45

The Japanese attacked Pearl Harbor on December 7, 1941—"a day that shall live in infamy," as President Franklin Roosevelt described it. Suddenly, the bitter debate over American entry into the war had ended. What was uncertain for quite some time was whether the United States would prevail in either the war in the Atlantic or especially the Pacific, where its situation was precarious. The U.S. fleet had been hit hard by the Japanese attack.

With Allied efforts directed at winning the war, the United States mobilized completely. The military and industrial sectors were fully engaged, and the civilian population was on a war footing. Victory was the No. 1 priority; only then, the Allies felt, could something be done about the refugee problem. This policy of "Rescue through Victory" was logical and generated strong support. The Jewish community was concerned—even perplexed—as to how to assist its Jewish brethren while fully supporting prioritizing the war effort.

Few, if any, perceived that the Germans were conducting two wars—the World War and the War against the Jews. The Allies fought one war—the World War.

Indeed, Western leaders greeted the initial reports of mass murder with skepticism and disbelief. As noted, in Washington, D.C., in July 1943, Felix Frankfurter, a Jewish Supreme Court justice appointed by FDR, met with Jan Karski, the Polish underground's emissary smuggled out of Poland, who personally had witnessed the implementation of the Final Solution. After hearing the gruesome details from Karski, Frankfurter said some complimentary words but concluded: "I can't believe you." Polish Ambassador Jan Ciechanowski then protested and vouched for the authenticity of Karski's report, to which Frankfurter replied: "I did not say this young man is lying. I said I cannot believe him. There is a difference."

Clearly the limits of the human imagination did not allow Frankfurter and other statesmen—both Jewish and non-Jewish—to internalize and believe that such unprecedented horrors were being committed by an advanced and cultured Western nation.

The decision to give sole priority to the war effort and to defer other issues until the war was over was not fundamentally reexamined throughout World War II, even when it ultimately became apparent to at least some leaders that Jews were being murdered by the millions.

Rabbi Stephen Wise addresses the crowd at a D-Day rally outside Madison Square Garden in New York City on June 6, 1944.

President Roosevelt held a critical meeting with Jewish leadership on December 8, 1942, one year into the war and one month after the State Department had confirmed Rabbi Stephen Wise's deepest fears from an August 29 telegram he had received regarding implementation of the Final Solution.

Three young non-Jewish Treasury Department officials submitted an internal memo for Secretary of the Treasury Henry Morgenthau, detailing the inaction and misrepresentation they had uncovered in the State Department.

The president warmly greeted Wise, the delegation's leader. An Orthodox rabbi offered a prayer.

When Roosevelt explained that the government was already acquainted with the facts, no one tried to ascertain from the president what facts he meant.

The president called Hitler insane and then offered to make a condemnatory statement. Roosevelt then asked the delegation for suggestions. They offered but a few, including having neutral parties intercede in Germany on behalf of the Jews. The president then spoke to the delegation for 23 minutes. The meeting, which began at noon, ended promptly at 12:29. Clearly, little was accomplished and an opportunity was lost.

Another chance came with the Bermuda Conference in April 1943. With growing domestic pressure for the government to take action regarding the refugee problem, a public move was needed to placate the Jews and their supporters. The United States and British representatives met on the beautiful, isolated island, shielded from the press and from interested pressure groups, on April 19, 1943—the very date that the Warsaw Ghetto Uprising began—to consider solutions to wartime refugee problems. Again, no significant proposals emerged.

In January 1944, when more than 85 percent of the Jews who were to die in the Holocaust were already dead, the U.S. changed its policy. On January 13, 1944, three young non-Jewish Treasury Department officials submitted an internal memo for Secretary of the Treasury Henry Morgenthau, detailing the inaction and misrepresentation they had uncovered in the State Department. The memo was provocatively titled "On the Acquiescence of This Government in the Murder of the Jews."

Their judgment was harsh. The memo stated:

State Department officials:

have not only failed to use the Governmental machinery at their disposal to rescue Jews from Hitler, but have even gone so far as to use this Governmental machinery to prevent the rescue of these Jews.

Secretary of the Treasury Henry Morgenthau, who strongly advocated that President Roosevelt establish the War Refugee Board.

Secretary of State Cordell Hull (left), Secretary of the Treasury Henry Morgenthau (second from left), and Secretary of War Henry L. Stimson (third from left) meet on March 21, 1944. This was the third meeting of the War Refugee Board.

They have not only failed to cooperate with private organizations . . . but have taken steps designed to prevent these [rescue] programs from being put into effect.

They not only have failed to facilitate the obtaining of information concerning Hitler's plans to exterminate the Jews of Europe but in their official capacity have gone so far as to surreptitiously attempt to stop obtaining of information concerning the murder of the Jewish population of Europe.

They have tried to cover up their guilt by:

(a) concealment and misrepresentation
(b) the giving of false and misleading explanations for their failures to act and their attempts to prevent action; and

(c) the issuance of false and misleading statements

Morgenthau read the memo with alarm. He rewrote the memo, entitling it "Personal Report to the President," and met with Roosevelt that January 16, sharing a copy. Knowing the disclosures could be politically damaging in an election year, Roosevelt asked Morgenthau what he wanted. Within days, FDR signed a presidential order establishing the War Refugee Board. Finally—belatedly, but importantly—the United States was on the side of rescue.

The War Refugee Board (WRB)—consisting of the secretaries of State, Treasury, and War—was to implement an American policy of rescue. It was funded by private Jewish sources.

Headed by John Pehle, a young Treasury Department lawyer who had helped Josiah DuBois and Randolph Paul unravel the State Department cover-up, the WRB tried to find a haven for Jews. It influenced White House policy, pushed for war-crime trials, and pressed to have Auschwitz bombed. Through its European and Asian operatives, including Raoul Wallenberg, the WRB played a crucial role in saving perhaps as many as 200,000 Jews. It also helped the United States legally bypass immigration restrictions to bring nearly 1,000 Jewish refugees from liberated areas to Fort Oswego, New York.

The American Jewish Response

American Jews were faced with the difficult challenge of how to aid their brethren under attack in Europe. Until late 1942, the nature and scope of that attack was not known even to American Jewry's leaders. Those who followed the news understood that the situation was ominous and getting worse, but what precisely that meant, they did not know—or, like Western statesmen, were unable to internalize and believe.

American Jewry was divided. Religious groups were divided by denominations—Orthodox, Conservative, and Reform. Regarding the establishment of a Jewish state in Palestine, Zionists, anti-Zionists, and non-Zionists were divided in their stance. Jews were also divided tactically and strategically. How could they reconcile the requirement to support the war effort, which all did wholeheartedly, with the need to pressure the very government they were supporting to do more to rescue Jews?

The Jewish community had only limited aid to offer to beleaguered Jews. Until the United States entered the war, the American Jewish Joint Distribution Committee (the Joint) could operate by providing vital relief in Eastern Europe for Jews in need. Afterward, it had to abide by stringent government regulations that prohibited sending any funds to areas occupied by the Germans and their allies. Some creative leaders in Eastern Europe borrowed funds in the name of the Joint to continue the relief efforts, and after the war the Joint

would honor these IOUs, but the Joint itself was paralyzed just as the situation became more dire.

Orthodox Rabbis decided to act on their own. They established the *Vaad Hatzalah* (Rescue Committee), with the mission of rescuing the rabbinic elite of Eastern European Jewry, the Torah scholars, and their students, who would preserve Judaism for the next generation. The *Vaad* assisted in the rescue of 650 rabbis and students from Lithuania before the German invasion. Its efforts were hampered by chronic underfunding and also by the reluctance of some Lithuanian Jewish leaders to allow their students to immigrate to Palestine and to the United States, for fear that the cultures would compromise their religiosity. During the war, they attempted to launch rescue efforts and continued to support the rabbis and yeshivas that had found a haven in Shanghai, even when such support limited the resources avail-

In October 1943, several hundred Orthodox Rabbis made a pilgrimage to Washington, where they challenged the U.S. to deliver European Jews from extermination. Here, at the Lincoln Memorial after their trip to the Capitol, Rabbi Isaac Horowitz of Brooklyn leads them in prayer.

able to rescue Jews still under German occupation.

In another effort to effect change, 400 Orthodox rabbis participated in a march on Washington in the days between Rosh Hashanah and Yom Kippur in 1943. They marched on the Lincoln Memorial, met with congressmen and senators on Capitol Hill, and even met with the vice president.

Peter Bergson (aka Hillel Kook), the nephew of the sainted late Chief Rabbi Abraham Isaac Kook of Palestine, came to the United States initially to organize Jewish military units. As the war progressed, he turned his attention to mobilizing the American Jewish community to greater action on behalf of the Jews in Europe. Together with Ben Hecht, the award-winning playwright, he staged a pageant in March 1943 entitled *We Will Never Die.* It played to 40,000 people in New York's Madison Square Garden and toured the country. Featuring major actors, many Jewish, it was widely covered by the media and called attention to the murder of Jews.

A month earlier, Bergson took out full-page advertisements in major newspapers that declared "For Sale to Humanity—70,000 Jews." The established Jewish leadership considered his maverick actions reckless and infuriating. Other Zionist groups opposed him because of his politics on Palestine, and

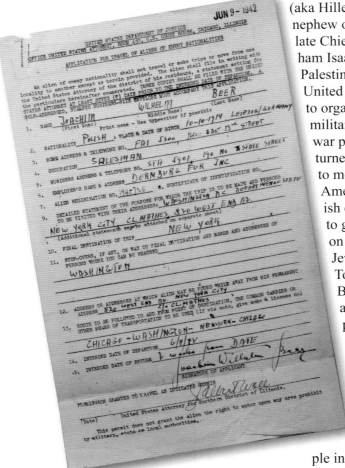

A "United States Department of Justice Application for Travel of Aliens or Enemy Nationalities." The application is for Joachim Wilhelm Beer, a German Jewish immigrant to Chicago.

Jewish organizations were reticent to establish a common front. However, Bergson pushed on and pressured, offering bold suggestions, demanding that something—anything—be done.

The American Jewish establishment tried to use its influence, but it preferred to use the back channels of power in Washington rather than overt demonstrations. They approached congressmen and political appointees and sought to use those who had access to the president and the State Department. Their effectiveness was limited. But even those who condemned the Jewish establishment were ultimately dependent on them. The *Vaad Hatzalah* could not operate on its own and required the help of the Joint, as did the WRB, which received only limited financial support from the government.

The American Jewish community has come to regard its efforts as inadequate to the task of rescue—too timid when it should have been bold; too complacent when it should have been engaged; and too trusting when it should have been skeptical and militant. This self-perceived failure has underscored many of its postwar activities on behalf of Israel and for the rescue of Soviet Jewry.

The legacy of American Jewry and its response to the Holocaust was best stated by a rabbi who studied the American Jewish press and the Holocaust. Haskel Lookstein said:

> The Final Solution may have been unstoppable by American Jewry, but it should have been unbearable for them and it wasn't. That is important, not alone for our understanding of the past, but for our sense of responsibility in the future.

The American Press

Readers of U.S. newspapers could have learned some details of what was happening to the Jews if they had read the back pages of the papers, but not their

The Scorn of Generations to Come

Atrocious Crimes Against Civilization

GERMANY

A political cartoon entitled "Doomed," by Chicago Tribune cartoonist Maxfield Frederick Parrish; April 21, 1945.

at a time when U.S. government information was regarded as critical.

Even the Jewish press was not willing to give it major attention. *The Jewish Frontier,* a national Jewish periodical, published the news of the mass murders on the last of its 12-page newspaper.

headlines. Simply put, the American press was interested in the World War, which drew banner headlines and was covered by radio and in newsreels. The fate of the Jews and the humanitarian issues of the refugees and of the Nazis' victims were clearly not even a secondary issue but a tertiary issue. They were well behind the war news, domestic politics, and—at the height of the World Series—behind even sports news.

On November 24, 1942, Rabbi Stephen Wise held a news conference after the State Department confirmed his deepest fears regarding the news he had received in the Riegner telegram about the systematic murder of Jews. He literally announced the Final Solution as operative German policy. The State Department would neither confirm nor deny in public what it had just confirmed to him in private. Hence, his groundbreaking news was relegated to the back pages and treated as a special pleading of one Jew for another, instead of confirmed government information—

Years later, its editor, Marie Syrkin, described her own action as "moral lunacy." Though understandable at the time, it was incomprehensible to future generations.

In the 1980s, A. M. Rosenthal, who was a young reporter at *The New York Times* during World War II and later its editor, commissioned a study of how the national "newspaper of record" covered the Holocaust. His conclusion was simple but stark: "We blew the story." Laurel Leff entitled her study of the *Times* coverage *Buried by the Times,* and Walter Laqueur entitled his pioneering study *The Terrible Secret: Suppression of the Truth about Hitler's "Final Solution."*

Deborah Lipstadt explored the gap between knowledge of facts and believing in them in *Beyond Belief,* her study of the American press and the Holocaust. She argued that the press did not—could not—believe it was happening.

We cannot know for sure what could have been done. We do know that very little was done.

The American press was interested in the World War. The fate of the Jews and the humanitarian issues of the refugees and of the Nazis' victims were clearly not even a secondary issue but a tertiary issue.

SHOULD AUSCHWITZ HAVE BEEN BOMBED?

The question "Why wasn't Auschwitz bombed?" is not only historical. It has become a moral question emblematic of the overall Allied response to the plight of the Jews during the Holocaust.

First to the historical issues: The question of bombing Auschwitz arose only in the summer of 1944, more than two years after the gassing of Jews had begun, by which time more than 90 percent of the Jews who would be murdered in the Holocaust were already dead. It could not have arisen earlier because not enough was known specifically about the camp, and Allied bombers were not in range to bomb the camps before the spring of 1944. Only when the Allies captured Italian air bases could the issue be raised. By July 1944, information regarding the nature of Auschwitz and its function was available—or could have been made available—to those undertaking such a mission. German air defenses were weakened, and the accuracy of Allied bombing was increasing. All that was required was the political will to effectuate the bombing.

That March, Germany had invaded Hungary. In April, Jews were ghettoized. From May to July, more than 430,000 Jews were deported on 147 trains from Hungary to Birkenau (*pictured*), the death camp of Auschwitz. Any interruption in the killing process might possibly have saved thousands of lives.

Yet bombing a death camp filled with an innocent, unjustly imprisoned civilian population also posed a moral dilemma to the most well meaning of the Allies. To be willing to sacrifice innocent civilians, one had to accurately perceive conditions in the camp and presume that the sacrifices of those killed in Allied bombings were worthwhile in order to interrupt the killing process. In short, one had to accept the fact that those in the camps were destined to die regardless. Such information was not available until the spring of 1944, when a full report on the camp complex was written by Alfred Wetzler and Rudolph Vrba (aka Walter Rosenberg), two men who had escaped from Auschwitz on April 7, 1944. Their testimony was later confirmed in May by two other escapees, Rosin and Mordowicz.

It is generally assumed that antisemitism or indifference to the plight of the Jews was the primary cause of the refusal to support bombing. In fact, the issue is more complex. On June 11, the Jewish Agency Executive Committee (JAE), meeting in Jerusalem, refused to call for the bombing of Auschwitz. David Ben-Gurion, chairman of the executive committee, said: "We do not know the true situation in Poland." He added, "We cannot take responsibility for a bombing that might cause the death of a single Jew." Rabbi Fishman concurred, which means that the religious/secular division did not apply in this case. The JAE soon reversed its June 11 decision, however. Yitzhak Gruenbaum, who headed the JAE's Rescue Committee, cabled committee representatives

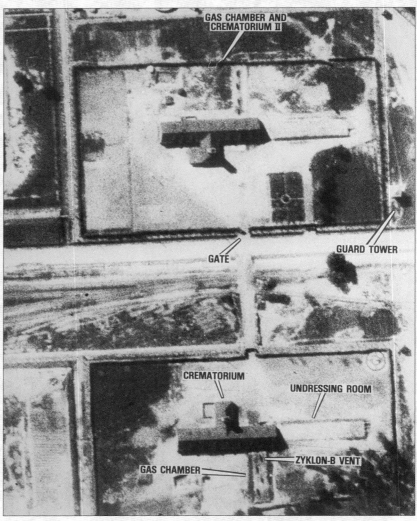

GAS CHAMBER AND CREMATORIUM II

GATE

GUARD TOWER

CREMATORIUM

UNDRESSING ROOM

GAS CHAMBER

ZYKLON-B VENT

in London on June 27, 1944, to demand Allied bombings immediately. By June 30, officials of the Jewish Agency in London were forcefully calling for the bombing.

By then, we can presume that the heads of the Jewish community in Palestine, like the Allied representatives—but not Allied leaders—had seen the report known as the Auschwitz Protocols, filed by Vrba and Wetzler. Vrba, who escaped on April 7, had worked at the Ramp in Birkenau. He revealed that the Germans had built a spur, specifically, it seemed, to receive Hungarian Jews. Anyone who had read the Vrba-Wetzler Report could perceive what was happening in the Auschwitz complex and would therefore be much more willing to risk Jewish lives on the ground rather than permit the gassing to proceed unimpeded. Hence, action was urgent.

What we know for certain is that Moshe Shertok (later Sharett), head of the Jewish Agency's Political Department, and Chaim Weizmann, president of the World Zionist Organization, appealed to British foreign secretary Anthony Eden, who took the issue to prime minister Winston Churchill. Churchill told Eden on July 7, "Get anything out of the Royal Air Force you can and invoke my name if necessary." Yet the British never carried through on the bombing. They turned it over to the Americans, who did nothing.

Requests were also made to American officials to bomb Auschwitz. In an August 14, 1944, letter from John J. McCloy, assistant secretary of war, to Leon Kubowitzki of the World Jewish Congress, the Americans gave several reasons for their refusal:

- Military resources could not be diverted from the war effort, which was reaching its crescendo in the post D-Day battles.
- Bombing Auschwitz might prove ineffective.
- Bombing might provoke even more vindictive German action.

Nowhere did the Americans claim that Auschwitz was not within range of American bombers. In fact, as early as May 1944, the U.S. Air Corps had the capability to strike Auschwitz at will. The rail lines from Hungary were also well within range, though for rail line bombing to be effective it had

The British never carried through on the bombing. They turned it over to the Americans, who did nothing.

to be sustained. On July 7, 1944, American bombers flew over the railway lines to Auschwitz. On August 20, 127 B-17 Flying Fortresses dropped 1,336 500-pound bombs on the I.G. Farben synthetic oil factory fewer than five miles east of Birkenau. The death camp remained untouched. Military conditions imposed some restrictions on the efforts to bomb Auschwitz. For the bombing to be feasible, it had to be undertaken by day in good weather and from July to October 1944.

For three decades, the issue of bombing Auschwitz was a minor sidebar to the war and to the Holocaust. But in 1978, American historian David Wyman wrote an article in *Commentary* entitled "Why Auschwitz Wasn't Bombed."

The impact of that piece was reinforced by the startling photographs that were published shortly thereafter by two leading CIA photo interpreters, Dino Brugioni and Robert Poirier. Developed in 1978 with technology unavailable in 1944, these images gave a vivid demonstration of what American intelligence could have known about Birkenau, if only it had been interested in data not directly related to military targets. One photograph shows bombs dropping over the camp. Because the pilot released the bombs early, it appears that bombs targeted for the I.G. Farben plant were dropped on Birkenau. Another photo shows Jews on the way to the gas chambers.

Historians are uncomfortable with the eternal question: "What if . . . ?" But such is the debate over bombing Auschwitz.

We know that in the end, the pessimists won. They argued that nothing could be done—and nothing was done. Proposals of the optimists were not even considered; Auschwitz was not put on the Allied list of possible targets. Given the reality of what happened in Birkenau during the summer of 1944, the failure to bomb has become a symbol of inaction due to misplaced priorities, which relegated humanitarian concerns (specifically, the fate of the Jews) to a relatively low priority. Inaction helped the Germans achieve their goals and left the victims with little power to defend themselves. What has angered many is that bombing was not offered even as a gesture of protest.

COLLABORATION

In every nation throughout German-occupied Europe, many individuals—too many—collaborated with the Nazis in the implementation of the Final Solution. However odious their behavior, they were the least of dangers. Institutions, industries, and entire nations also collaborated. The horrifying eradication of the Jews was planned and organized by Germany, yet the Nazis could never have carried out their deadly scheme without accomplices. No description of the scope of collaboration can be exhaustive—merely representative.

In Norway, the collaboration of the government of Vidkun Quisling was so complete that the word *quisling* has become synonymous with collaboration.

Romanian soldiers participated in the activities of the *Einsatzgruppen,* slaughtering Jews in areas of the occupied Soviet Union with such cruelty and barbarity that they aroused protest even from the *Wehrmacht,* the German army.

Bulgaria, which eventually refused to deport its own Jews after extensive protest from its population, inititally delivered the Jews of Thrace and Macedonia to the Germans for deportation.

Holland had received much admiration for its February 1941 general strike against German occupation as well as solidarity with its 140,000 persecuted Jews. But it used the Dutch bureaucracy to process "Aryanization" forms that led to the removal of all Jews from the civil service, including its Jewish Supreme Court president, L. E. Visser, in November 1940. Its police participated in the roundup of Jews.

The French police rounded up Jews for deportation. Postwar trials emphasized for the French people that collaboration could not be swept under the rug. Among the targets: Klaus Barbie, known as the butcher of Lyon, and Maurice Papon, who served as a senior police official in the collaborationist Vichy regime. He regularly cooperated with Nazi Germany's SS Corps, which was responsible for the murder of Jews. These acts, including the independent anti-Jewish initiatives of the Vichy regime, forced the French to grapple with their record of collaboration rather than merely celebrate their much-vaunted resistance.

Ukrainian nationalists such as Stefan Bandera and Andrei Melnyk openly collaborated, as did the anti-Soviet Russian army of General Andrei Vlasov.

Slovakia, led by a Roman Catholic priest, Father Josef Tiso, was unique. Not only did Slovakia hand over Jews to the Germans for deportation to death, but it actually paid the Germans—Jew by Jew—for taking the Jews off its hands.

As a rule in politics, the enemy of your enemy is not necessarily a friend, but it is at least an ally.

Such a rule should have applied in Poland, where Jews and Polish non-Jews opposed German occupation. The Germans targeted Polish Jews and Pol-

An officer salutes Hajj Amin al-Husseini during the Jerusalem mufti's inspection of SS Muslim troops in Bosnia, Yugoslavia; c. 1943.

ish Christians, aiming to annihilate the Jews in the Final Solution and to decimate the Christians' leaders—priests and political and intellectual leaders. Moreover, they aimed to make the general Polish population permanently subservient. Even the racially elite among Polish children were kidnapped for "Aryanization," a euphemism for forced adoption by a German family and a life in Germany.

Still, Polish resistance and Jewish resistance had great difficulty cooperating. They had to fight separate fights against a common enemy. The Polish underground army (NSZ) was openly antisemitic. While fighting the Germans, the NSZ also fought the Jews and cooperated in the Final Solution. The *Armia Krajowa* (Home Army; AK) was rife with antisemitism and did not come to the aid of the Jews, even while the Polish government-in-exile, to which it was loyal, tried to assist them. Jews who fought with the AK could not do so openly for fear of betrayal. In Jedwabne, a small Polish town, the presence of Germans in the vicinity following the Russian retreat in June 1941 was sufficient to give license to local Poles to murder the town's 1,600 Jews, so that Poles—and not the Germans—could make good use of the booty.

The Jedwabne massacre in Poland was not an isolated case. In Lithuania, local armed units participated in the mass shootings of Jews carried out by the *Einsatzgruppen.* In Kaunas (Kovno), with the retreat of the Soviet forces from the city, local mobs attacked Jews with such cruelty and barbarity that the arriving German army was forced to curtail the brutal pogrom. Recent archaeological digs at the sites of mass murder in Ukraine have uncovered the weapons used in each of the killing fields. One can now distinguish between the weapons of the *Wehrmacht*—the German army, which collaborated with the SS in the killing process—and the bullets and rifles of the SS, of local gendarmerie or organized antisemitic units, and of the

An antisemitic poster in France. Au secours! *translates to* Help!

home ammunition of the native population in each region of killing.

The SS did not operate alone. Three thousand men were assigned to the *Einsatzgruppen.* They could not kill more than a million Jews on their own—nor did they have to. They received active help from many different levels of the population, from officials to ordinary men and women.

The SS did not staff the death camps wholly on its own. Treblinka, where more than 750,000 Jews were killed, had a staff of only 30 SS men. Ninety other positions were filled by former Soviet prisoners of war and Ukrainians who voluntarily joined their captors in implementing the Final Solution. In Belzec, where 500,000 Jews were killed within 10 months in 1942, only one in seven guards was an SS man; the others were Ukrainians.

Deportations were initiated by the Nazis, but very often Latvians, Lithuanians, and Ukrainians provided the personnel necessary to implement so massive an *Aktion.*

The German railroad, staffed by ordinary railroad workers, became—wittingly and unwittingly—the most important tool in implementing the Final Solution. Railroad schedules were met. Trains were available for deportation, one of the many tasks they had to

The *Einsatzgruppen* received active help from many different levels of the population, from officials to ordinary men and women.

Right: *Adolf Hitler greets Ante Pavelic, leader of the Croatian puppet state, upon the latter's arrival for a state visit; Berchtesgaden, Germany, June 9, 1941.* Below: *A poster advertising the antisemitic propaganda film* Der Ewige Jude *(The Eternal Jew) hangs on the side of a Dutch building; Amsterdam, German-occupied Netherlands, 1942.*

perform during wartime. And railway workers were aware that trains traveled in one direction overcrowded with passengers and returned empty.

German businesses were active participants in the killing process. Some of the major business firms invested heavily in the slave labor camp at Auschwitz III, known as Buna-Monowitz. They read as a Who's Who of German corporate life: Frick, I.G. Farben, BMW, Siemens, Messerschmitt, Daimler-Benz-Mercedes, and Krupp. Participation in exploiting slave labor was voluntary. The decisions were made not necessarily by Nazis but often by corporate executives who worked at a distance from the camps—men who followed

sound economic principles and sought maximal profits. Ovens designed and guaranteed by Topf and Company were built for cremations at Birkenau and other camps. Architects and engineers designed the crematoria. Mechanics at first tinkered with simple trucks that were used for mobile gassing. Stationary gas chambers replete with crematoria were more sophisticated operations; they were the work of highly trained professionals.

Some countries had their own Nazi-like party. Members were no less enthusiastic but perhaps less skillful and disciplined than the Germans in implementing the Final Solution. Austria had its own Nazi Party, which modeled itself on its German neighbor; Romania had its Iron Guard; Hungary, the Arrow Cross. The Slovak People's Party was enthusiastic in its support. The *Ustasa* in Croatia, which operated its own concentration camps and persecuted native Jews as well as Serbs, was the lone Nazi-like party that remained in power throughout the war.

Historian Eli Tzur distinguished among four main types of collaboration:
  • Accommodation
  • Administrative collaboration
  • Economic cooperation
  • Ideological collaboration

Accommodation meant seeking a way of operating with the victors, under the assumption that German rule would continue. It is important to keep in mind that, other than Vichy France, no occupied European country signed a peace treaty with Germany. Accommodation was found throughout Europe in varying degrees, especially when Germany seemed invincible in the early days of the war. Jews, such as Mordecai Chaim Rumkowski of Lodz, who clearly was not a collaborator, believed that a modus operandi could be found with the Germans. The Jews were eventually sorely disappointed. Despite Jewish labor's utility to the German army and the war efforts, these were clearly secondary considerations when it came time for the Final Solution.

Administrative collaboration was essential to German rule. In every country that the Germans conquered, they had to find a means to govern. In some cases, they found an allied administration such as in Vichy—quasi-independent France. In others there was what Tzur defined as supervised administration; major tasks were performed by the native government under German supervision. In other areas, governmental administration was in German hands, and only local officials openly and unquestionably loyal to the Nazis were allowed to function. And the most extreme form was colonial administration, where Germany ruled without local governmental cooperation.

Economic cooperation was the means by which the local population sustained itself throughout German domination. A thin but still perceptible line demarked economic cooperation and eco-nomic collaboration. Some sought to exploit the German labor shortage caused by the massive need for personnel during the war for survival; others sought to exploit it for massive profiteering, regardless of the assistance they provided to the war effort.

Ideological cooperation was the embrace of a shared agenda, a common goal, a partnership of the willing. Some notable examples include Croatia, Slovakia, and at different periods Romania, Hungary, and Vichy France.

Every Jew who hid was afraid of collaborators, those individuals who would turn in Jews to the police for financial or political reward or for its own sake—for the joy of being rid of one more Jew. Unlike many victims in occupied countries, Jews could not be sure that the local population would not betray them. That hampered Jews' ability to resist and made it exceedingly dangerous to hide. The willingness of captive people to betray Jews in hiding meant that the Germans had an army of people willing to assist in the capture of Jews.

In a Jew's effort to hide, even a neighbor's indifference would have been of assistance.

A round-up of Jews by French police and German officers; Paris, German-occupied France, August 20, 1941.

JEWS IN GREECE AND YUGOSLAVIA

On April 6, 1941, Germany invaded Greece in what is now considered a prelude to the invasion of the Soviet Union that was to follow in June.

Unable to resist the German and Axis onslaught, Greece was divided into three zones of occupation. Bulgaria controlled Thrace. Italy occupied central and southern Greece as well as the capital, Athens. The Germans held the region around Salonika, the main Jewish population center in northern Greece, as well as the western and central parts of Crete. The Jews in Salonika were overwhelmingly Sephardic, tracing their origins to Spain. They spoke Ladino, a Judeo-Spanish hybrid used among the Sephardic. Eastern European Jews spoke Yiddish.

The fate of Jews in Greece differed by region of occupation. In general, Jews under Italian occupation were far better off than their counterparts. The Italians in all territories they occupied refused to implement the Final Solution and even gave refuge to Jews who fled to their territories. In March 1943, Bulgaria consented to the deportations of Jews to Treblinka from the regions they occupied. They provided the boxcars for transport and played a direct role in the deportations. At home, Bulgarian Jews were persecuted, but due to popular opposition, they were not deported for death.

In Salonika, an area under direct German control, the Final Solution followed a familiar course, including the mandatory wearing of the Yellow Star. In mid-July 1942, 9,000 Jewish men aged 18 to 45 were publicly humiliated and physically terrorized, and some 2,000 were sent into forced labor. They were ransomed for large sums of money raised by the Jewish community. In February 1943, the Jews of Salonika were concentrated in two ghettos, one in the East and one in the western Baron de Hirsch section of the city, near the railroad station. Adolf Eichmann's deputies, Dieter Wisliceny and Alois Brunner, were dispatched to arrange for the deportations. And when the train transport was in place, more than 45,000 Jews were sent (from March to August) to Auschwitz-Birkenau. Three in four were gassed upon arrival. Those remaining were utilized for slave labor. Jews holding Spanish citizenship living in Salonika (and later in Athens) were deported to Bergen-Belsen—not Auschwitz.

Italy's armistice with the Allies on September 8, 1943, required that Italy give up its zones of occupation. Thus, the way to the Final Solution was clear in the regions Italy had formerly occupied. In Athens, Jewish property was confiscated on October 7, 1943. In March 1944, the Germans used the ruse of the distribution of matzah (unleavened bread required to observe Passover) to arrest some

A deportation of Jews from Dhidhimotikhon in German-occupied Greece in 1943.

800 Jews in Athens. On March 24–25, the first days of Passover, Jews were arrested and shipped to Auschwitz. Some 500 additional Jews were arrested in their homes, and some Jews from outside of Athens were also rounded up. Other Athenian Jews went into hiding.

Germany then continued to round up the Jews of the islands, including 2,000 Jews of Corfu, who were arrested in June 1944 (of those, only 200 returned) and the 1,800 Jews of Rhodes, who had a similar fate and were deported in 1944. In Rhodes, some 50 Turkish Jews or Jews who could demonstrate links to Turkey, however tenuous, were not deported, thanks to the efforts of Turkish Consul Selahattin Ulkumen.

Upon arrival at Auschwitz, Greek Jews who were not gassed immediately faced one additional significant hurdle: Most had no language in common with their Eastern European brethren, the Yiddish-speaking Ashkenazi Jews. They could neither pick up the immediate clues that Hungarian Jews—who arrived at the same time—received from veteran prisoners nor could they understand SS orders. Because they could speak only with one another, other survivors recall the Ashkenazis' clannishness and solidarity. Some Greek survivor accounts of their arrival and stay at Auschwitz are more visual because they could not understand much of what was being said.

In the end, the Nazis killed almost 90 percent of Greece's 80,000 Jews. Of those who escaped death, many joined the partisans and were hidden in the mountains, which were a stronghold of Greek resistance. A small number were sent to neutral Turkey and onward to Palestine.

Yugoslavia

Germany, along with military units from Bulgaria, Italy, and Hungary, invaded Yugoslavia in April 1941. The Jewish population was approximately 80,000, of which some 40 percent were of Sephardic origin.

Germany occupied northwest Yugoslavia, and the puppet pro-German state of Croatia was established. Hungary received Backa, and Bulgaria got Macedonia. Italy occupied the coastal region. The country was divided, and the fate of each sector was dependent on the anti-Jewish policies of the occupying power.

In German-occupied Serbia, Jews were interned in concentration camps. Most Serbian Jewish men were shot by German army firing squads in the fall of 1941. Women and children were initially spared but interned in the Sajmiste concentration camp, where in spring 1942 mobile gas vans were used to kill them within view and with the knowledge of the local population.

In independent Croatia, two-thirds of the Jews were imprisoned by the end of 1941. More than 20,000 Jews were killed in the concentration camp of Jasenovac on the territory of independent Croatia. They were killed by the *Ustasa* Croats (right-wing nationalists and extreme antisemites and anti-Serbs), not by Germans. An additional 7,000 Jews were deported to Auschwitz-Birkenau.

Bulgaria deported the Jews of Macedonia, with the Bulgarian police and military forces assembling the Jews and turning them over to the Germans once they left Macedonia.

Hungarian authorities murdered several thousand Jews and Serbs in Novi Sad in January 1942, but they refrained from full deportation until the Germans invaded Hungary and toppled its government in March 1944. Only Jews in the Italian zone of Yugoslavia escaped deportation— at least until September 1943, when the Germans took control.

Approximately 65,000 Jews of Yugoslavia were killed in the Holocaust.

> **The Nazis killed almost 85 percent of Greece's 80,000 Jews. Of those who escaped death, many joined the partisans.**

Gypsies are led to their execution in Yugoslavia; c. 1942.

JEWS IN NORTH AFRICA

Students sit outside a primary school in the Jewish quarter of Casablanca, Morocco.

Vichy France's anti-Jewish laws were also applied to French colonies in North Africa. In October 1940, Jews were defined by race based on the religion of their grandparents. They were excluded from civil service and from working for businesses with public contracts, and they could teach only in Jewish schools. On October 7, the French revoked the citizenship of Algeria's 120,000 Jews. In June 1941, they moved against the Jews' economic status, excluding Jews from finance, managing businesses, and working for the media. Jewish property was "Aryanized"—transferred to non-Jewish ownership.

The application of the anti-Jewish statutes in Tunisia and Morocco differed. Few of Tunisia's 85,000 Jews

Morocco established more than 30 forced-labor and detention camps, where Jews were made to work in the difficult desert climate.

were French citizens, so for most there was no change in legal status. A sympathetic French official was less than rigorous in implementing the law, and an Italian official looked after Tunisia's Italian citizens who were Jews.

Morocco, with some 200,000 Jews as well as many Jewish refugees who had fled Europe, established more than 30 forced-labor and detention camps, where Jews were made to work in the difficult desert climate. Even after the liberation of Morocco by American forces in November 1942, it took several months to annul all anti-Jewish laws and to release the Jews from the camps.

In Algiers, a predominantly Jewish underground group—angered by the persecution of Algerian Jews—took over the city and held it for more than 24 hours until the U.S. Army arrived in November 1942. Even then, Algerian Jews had to wait until mid-1943, when the Vichy forces were ousted by General Charles de Gaulle, to regain their citizenship. Algerian Jews living in France were stateless and thus subject to deportation to Auschwitz.

During the brief German occupation of Tunisia, a Jewish Council was appointed and required to supply forced labor. Jewish property was confiscated, and the president of the Jewish community was arrested. Though some Muslims sheltered Jews against German designs, the Germans raided the Jewish neighborhoods of Tunis, arrested prominent Jews, and deported 20 Jewish activists to death camps in Europe. The Germans also demanded that Jewish workers be supplied for forced labor. Some 5,000 Tunisian men were detained. Conditions in the camps run by the Germans were especially difficult. In certain areas, Jews were forced

to wear the Yellow Star. The oppression continued as long as the Germans occupied Tunisia (until May 1943). As its military situation weakened, Germany garnered less and less support from the local population.

The early liberation of North Africa by Allied forces prevented the implementation of the Final Solution and the destruction of the Jewish community.

Libya

The fate of Jews in Libya was directly linked to Italy, which ruled the country until 1943. Marshal Italo Balbo, the ranking Italian authority, was friendly to the Jews and did much to prevent anti-Jewish laws enacted in Rome from being enforced in Libya. Only Jews of Italian citizenship employed by the civil service were affected by these laws. Balbo died in a plane crash in June 1940.

Early British victories over Italian forces in North Africa persuaded Hitler to send in the German army, and when these territories were recaptured, Italian authorities accused Jews of collaborating with the British. Some 300 Jews with British citizenship were deported to Italy and interned in concentration camps. In 1944 these Libyan-British Jews were deported to the Bergen-Belsen concentration camp in Germany.

As the battles went, so went the fate of the Jews. When Germany drove the British out, Libyan Jews were utilized in several labor camps—notably Giado, Tigrinna, and Gharyan. Jewish men aged 18 to 45 were drafted for forced labor and kept in forced-labor camps, where many died from exhaustion and disease. Anti-Jewish laws were decreed but never enforced. The British liberated Libya on January 23, 1943.

GERMAN ALLIES AND THE JEWS

In the years before it became an ally of Germany in November 1940, Romania was coerced by its neighbors to cede about 30 percent of its territory and population. The Soviet Union received Bessarabia and northern Bukovina. Transylvania and its vast Jewish population were given to Hungary, and Bulgaria was given part of southern Romania.

In September 1940, Romania's King Carol II was forced to abdicate, and a new radical right-wing dictatorship under General Ion Antonescu and the Iron Guard, an extremist nationalist and antisemitic political party, came to power. Jews in Bucharest were immediately attacked, and restrictive measures were imposed. In one particularly brutal episode in Bucharest on January 21, 1941, amid the rebellion of the Iron Guard against the regime, its members hanged dozens of Jews on meat hooks in a Bucharest slaughterhouse. They mutilated their victims to mimic "kosher slaughtering."

On the night of June 28–29, 1941, Iasi exploded with one of the most savage pogroms in Romanian history.

Romanian troops stormed Jewish homes and attacked and murdered the inhabitants indiscriminately. On Sunday, June 29, 5,000 to 6,000 Jews from Iasi were marched by German and Romanian troops to police headquarters, where they were attacked and spat upon by civilian spectators as they were dragged into a courtyard. Once in the courtyard, they were massacred by German soldiers and Romanian policemen.

Under Antonescu, Romania joined the Axis and participated actively in the German invasion of the Soviet Union. They also joined the *Einsatzgruppen* in the mass shootings of Jews. Even the German army, not known for its sensitivity to the treatment of Jews, complained about the brutality of Romania troops:

> *The way in which the Romanians are dealing with the Jews lacks any method. No objections could be raised against the numerous executions of Jews, but the technical preparations and the executions themselves were totally inadequate. The Romanians usually left the victims' bodies where they were shot, without trying to bury them.*

Romanian police examine the bodies of Jews removed from the Iasi–Calarasi death train; Targu Frumos, Romania, July 1, 1941

After their push eastward into the Soviet Union in the summer of 1941, the Germans returned to Romania the areas that it had lost to the Soviets.

Antonescu did not have a consistent policy for Jews. He called for the murder of the Jews of Bukovina and Bessarabia but not the Jews of the Regat (Old Romania). In the areas controlled by Romania between the Dniester and Bug rivers known as Transnistria, there were massacres, ghettos, and concentration camps. In December 1941, Romanian troops aided by Ukrainian auxiliaries murdered most of the Jews in one of these camps, Bogdanovka. At other concentration camps that were established, the survival rate was exceedingly low. The Romanians even deported their Jews on railroad cars. However, unlike the Germans, who had a precise destination—death camps—the Romanians had none. They kept the prisoners on board until they died, and buried them in mass graves in the Romanian countryside.

Between 150,000 and 250,000 Romanian and Ukrainians Jews were killed in Transnistria or en route to there, victims of murder or because of conditions that caused them to die. In all, more than 270,000 Romanian Jews were killed or died from the conditions under which they lived—most at Romanian hands.

In 1942 Antonescu sensed that Germany would not win the war and refused to go along with previously approved plans for the deportation of nearly 300,000 Jews to Belzec. Instead, he offered to exchange 70,000 Jews for ransom, an idea to which the Germans would not consent. Antonescu himself was overthrown in August 1944 (he would be executed in 1946), and Romania withdrew from the war.

Italy

Although Italy had been under the Fascist rule of Benito Mussolini since 1922, the Italians had little inclination to participate in the Final Solution. Jews had

Italian Jewish forced laborers toil at a lumber mill in Gorizia, Italy, in September 1942.

lived in Rome since before the destruction of the Second Temple in Jerusalem in the year 70 C.E., since before St. Peter was Bishop of Rome. In September 1938, Mussolini's government did enact antisemitic laws, and foreign Jews were ordered to leave Italy.

Italy entered the war in June 1940, as a German ally. As recompense, it received territory in Yugoslavia, Greece, and southeast France. Wherever Italians occupied territory, Jews were better off; they were not subject to killing, and Italy often allowed refugees a haven. In Italy itself, foreign Jews who had not left the country were confined to concentration camps, but in contrast to German-run camps, conditions were livable.

As the war turned against Germany in 1943, Mussolini was overthrown and the Italians switched sides. The Germans responded quickly by invading northern and central Italy (the Allies were already in the South) and reinstating Mussolini, who this time was in no condition to resist participation in the Final Solution. Germany also took over Italian-occupied lands in France and Yugoslavia.

From September 1943 until liberation in April 1945, Jews were rounded up in the major cities under German control—including Rome, under the very windows of the Pope. As in the

West, they were interned in German-run transit camps—such as San Sabo, Fossoli di Carpi, and Bolzano—and from there deported to Auschwitz.

Of the 8,000 deported from Italy to Auschwitz and other camps, some 7,600 were murdered there. Still, in Italy, more than 40,000 Jews survived, mostly because the Italians were unwilling to impose the Final Solution in a fanatical or systematic way.

Bulgaria

In October 1940, a pro-German Bulgarian government enacted the country's first anti-Jewish laws. The public cried out against these laws, but the parliament passed them nonetheless.

Bulgaria became a German ally, joining the Axis in March 1941 in return for the promise of territory. After participating in the attack on Yugoslavia and Greece, Bulgaria regained Macedonia and Thrace.

When the Germans pressed the Bulgarian government to deport Jews in 1943, it agreed secretly that at first only the Jews of Thrace and Macedonia would be deported. Later, Bulgarian Jews would be targeted. In March, 12,000 Jews from Thrace, Macedonia,

and eastern Serbia were sent to Treblinka. Bulgarian police participated actively in the deportation. So the hands of the Bulgarian government were not clean.

But the attempt to deport Bulgarian Jews met with stiff resistance. Writers and artists, jurists and parliamentarians protested. Even the Jewish community felt secure enough to hold public demonstrations. The government, mindful of public opinion and the collapsing German war effort, postponed the deportation.

Still, persecution of Jews intensified. The Jews of Sofia were expelled to the provinces, and Jewish men between the ages of 20 and 60 were sent to slave-labor camps. However, there were no deportations to death camps. At the end of the war, almost all of the prewar 50,000 Bulgarian Jews remained alive.

Why were Bulgarian Jews saved? The reasons are still obscure. Seemingly, it was the combination of nationalistic sensibilities, the absence of antisemitism among many Bulgarians, and the sentiment of the population. Timing may have played a part as well. By 1943, when Germany pressed Bulgaria to deport its Jews, Hitler's victory was at best uncertain. This may have stiffened Bulgaria's resistance to cooperate with the Final Solution.

Slovakia

Between World War I and World War II, Slovakia was part of Czechoslovakia, an uneasy binational state. In 1938 Slovakia became an autonomous national region. In March 1939, as the Germans occupied Czech Bohemia and Moravia, Slovakia became a puppet state under the leadership of Father Josef Tiso, a pro-Nazi Roman Catholic priest who led the antisemitic Slovakian People's Party. Anti-Jewish legislation was introduced, and Dieter Wisliceny—a German expert on Jewish affairs who worked with Adolf Eichmann—became an "adviser to the

Europe's Borders at the Height of Nazi Domination: By 1942 Germany had occupied most of Northern Europe, while most Southern European countries were ruled by pro-Nazi regimes. In the East, German forces advanced deep into the Soviet Union. In the second half of 1942, the Soviets began to push the Germans back.

ATLANTIC OCEAN
N
NORWAY
FINLAND
SOVIET UNION
Leningrad
Farthest German Army Advance
SWEDEN
North Sea
Moscow
IRELAND
GREAT BRITAIN
DENMARK
REICHSKOMMISSARIAT OSTLAND
NETHERLANDS
Berlin
London
GREATER GERMANY
Warsaw
BELGIUM
LUXEMBOURG
GENERAL-GOUVERNEMENT
UKRAINE
Paris
FRANCE
PROTECTORATE OF BOHEMIA & MORAVIA
SLOVAKIA
SWITZERLAND
Budapest
HUNGARY
Unoccupied Zone
ITALY
CROATIA
ROMANIA
SERBIA
SPAIN
Rome
BULGARIA
YUGOSLAVIA
Mediterranean Sea
ALBANIA
TURKEY
GREECE
AFRICA

Greater Germany & Occupied Territories
German Allies or Dependent States
Neutral
Allies
0   400 miles
0   700 kilometers

government on Jewish Affairs." According to census figures, 88,951 Jews were in Slovakia in December 1940.

In the fall of 1941, a few months after the German invasion of the Soviet Union, Slovakia entered the war on Germany's side. Anti-Jewish legislation intensified, with laws modeled on the German Nuremberg Laws, which defined, impoverished, and isolated Jews. Slovakia's Jews were forced to wear a badge with the Jewish star.

In March 1942, Slovakia became the first Axis government to consent to the deportation of its Jews under the Final Solution. Deportations began immediately. Slovakian forces sent Jews to labor and transit camps, brought them to the border, and turned them over to the Germans for deportation and death. Slovakia paid the Germans for taking the Jews off their hands. Between March and October 1942, about 58,000 Slovakian Jews were deported to the Auschwitz and Majdanek death camps and to the Lublin district, once conceived of as a Jewish reservation. Reports reached the Vatican of these deportations and of the role of Tiso.

Father Tiso hesitated, for reasons still unclear, in the deportation of the remaining 23,000 Jews.

In desperation, the Slovakian underground Working Group, led by Orthodox Rabbi Michael Dov Weissmandel, and a Zionist woman leader, Gisi Fleischmann, tried bribing Wisliceny, hoping to halt the deportations by dangling before him a multimillion-dollar bribe (money they did not have) if deportations were halted. They tried to negotiate the Europa Plan—an attempt to halt the deportations of all Jews in Europe in exchange for $2–3 million from Jews in the West—and even helped the government establish three Slovakian labor camps where Slovak Jews would be worked harshly but not killed.

In the summer of 1944, with the fronts collapsing against Germany, a popular national uprising tried to overthrow the pro-Nazi government. By October, the Germans crushed the revolt, arresting and deporting another 13,000 Jews.

The role of the priest-president of Slovakia caused considerable embarrassment to the Vatican—then as now.

Slovak officials (Nazi collaborators) check off the names of local Jews who are about to be deported at an assembly point in Zilina, Slovakia.

Slovakian forces sent Jews to labor and transit camps, brought them to the border, and turned them over to the Germans for deportation and death.

RESCUERS

In every nation throughout German-occupied Europe, including Germany, a few individuals came to the rescue of Jews. They offered shelter, assistance, or even a place to hide, however briefly, often at the risk of their own freedom and, especially in Poland, at the risk of their lives and their family's lives.

Almost no one survived without assistance, active or passive. In the years since the Holocaust, the Jewish people, through Yad Vashem—Israel's National Memorial to the Holocaust—have honored more than 20,000 rescuers, naming them "Righteous Among the Nations."

Students of the Holocaust are somewhat familiar with the famous rescue stories: the Danish people; the village of Le Chambon in France; Raoul Wallenberg in Hungary; Oskar Schindler in Poland. Some may be familiar with less-known instances of rescue diplomats, such as Chiune (Sempo) Sugihara and Jan Zwartendijk. But most rescuers were not national leaders, distinguished diplomats, or successful businessmen. Many were motivated not by religious conviction but by more simple virtues: right versus wrong, respect for all human beings without regard to religion or race, or simply care for a friend or compassion for a child.

Denmark

Though many individuals, a few diplomats, and some institutions saved Jews, there was only one nation that rescued its Jewish population: Denmark. Germany respected Danes as kindred souls, and the occupation of Denmark was particularly light. Its governing institutions remained in place as did its king—who, contrary to legend, did not wear the Yellow Star in protest (since Danish Jews were not required to wear the Star). When Germans raised the issue of the "Jewish question" in Denmark, Danish leadership replied: "We have no Jewish question." Jews were accepted as citizens of Denmark, nothing less and nothing more.

Germany was reticent to push for the Final Solution in Denmark. The deportation of Danish Jews was not set until the fall of 1943—well after its implementation in other countries and despite the objection of some German diplomats in Denmark, who were less concerned about the Jews than about alienating the Danish population.

The situation of Danish Jews was unique in two other ways:

- Deportation occurred after the German defeat in Stalingrad, when the tide of the war was changing.
- Neutral Sweden, which had offered to receive Scandinavian Jews, was only miles across the sea.

Denmark's Jews also received the most unexpected of help: German naval attache G. F. Duckwitz warned Hans Hedtoft, the leader of the Social Democratic Party in Denmark, that a German *Aktion* was underway. "Your poor fellow citizens are going to be deported to an unknown destination," Duckwitz said.

Jewish escapees aided by the Danish underground are ferried out of Denmark aboard fishing boats in 1943. They are bound for neutral Sweden.

The Danish people sprang into action. Ministers opened their churches. Fishermen ferried Jews by boat. Communities along the seacoast sheltered Jews who awaited their escape to freedom.

Danish Jews escape deportation aboard Danish fishing boats that are bound for neutral Sweden; Denmark, 1943.

The day of deportation was to be October 1, 1943—the second day of Rosh Hashanah, the Jewish New Year. When Hedtoft told C. B. Henriques, the chairman of the Jewish community, of the pending deportation, his response was as swift as it was surprising: "You lie!... It can't be true.... I don't believe it." He used the words uttered by so many other victims and bystanders when they first learned of the Final Solution. But Henriques was soon persuaded of the seriousness of the warning and the accuracy of the information.

Jews believed the warning and prepared to go underground. Synagogues stood empty on Rosh Hashanah, as Jews fled Copenhagen for the seacoast, the lone escape route.

The Danish people sprang into action. Ministers opened their churches. Fishermen ferried Jews by boat. Communities along the seacoast sheltered Jews who awaited their escape to freedom. Ambulances served to bring Jews to the sea and from the sea to the harbor. German patrol boats were hoisted up for repair and therefore unable to chase the fleeing population. Unlike the situation in other countries, Danish church leadership condemned the treatment of Jews.

Bishop Hans Fuglsang-Damgaard of the Danish Lutheran Church sent a letter of protest to the German government, which was read in every church in Denmark on October 3, 1943:

Race and religion can never be in themselves a reason for depriving a man of his rights, freedom or property.... We shall therefore struggle to ensure the continued guarantee to our Jewish brothers and sisters [of] the same freedom which we ourselves treasure more than life.

We are obliged by our conscience to maintain the law and to protest against any violation of human rights. Therefore, we desire to declare unanimously our allegiance to the work. We must obey God rather than man.

In the end, some 7,200 of Denmark's Jews were ferried to freedom. Of the remaining Jews, 464 were arrested and deported to Theresienstadt. But the government of Denmark continued to inquire of their fate, which led to a Red Cross inspection of the "model ghetto" and transit camp. Nine out of 10 Jews of Denmark were saved. When Yad Vashem wanted to honor individuals, Denmark insisted that only the "people of Denmark" be honored.

The Village of Le Chambon

Le Chambon is a village of Huguenots, Protestants in an overwhelmingly Catholic France. Le Chambon's efforts were led by Pastor Andre Trocme, who preached a simple Gospel. Characteristically, he ended his sermons with the following scriptural verses: "Love the Lord your God with all your heart, with all your soul and with all your strength" and "Love your neighbor as yourself." Then he would add, "Go practice it."

And practice it they did. Villagers in Le Chambon and in nearby communities opened their homes and institutions to Jewish children and served as a haven for some 5,000 Jews, whom they rescued. When asked to describe the goodness of their deeds, a villager demurred:

How can you call us "good"? We were doing what had to be done. Who else could help them? And what has all this to do with goodness? Things had to be done, and we happened to be there to do them. You must understand that it was the most natural thing in the world to help these people.

Raoul Wallenberg

Raoul Wallenberg was an American-educated architect, the scion of an aristocratic Swedish family. The Wallenbergs were the Rockefellers of Sweden.

Wallenberg was recruited in 1944 by the American War Refugee Board and financed by the Joint (AJDC). In 1944 he was sent on a perilous undercover assignment as a Swedish diplomat to save as many Jews in Hungary as possible. He arrived in Budapest on July 9 at a critical juncture. From May to July, more than 430,000 Hungarian Jews were deported, primarily to Auschwitz, and the Jews of Budapest were among the last Jews in Europe. Through his ingenuity, Wallenberg arranged for Swedish "protective passports" for Jews. These passes entitled them to the protection of the neutral Swedish government. They also allowed safe houses flying the Swedish flag to house Budapest Jews.

Wallenberg worked with neutral ambassadors—Charles Lutz of Switzerland, in particular—as well as with Giorgio Perlasca, an Italian businessman who passed himself off as a Spanish diplomat. Even the Vatican's help was enlisted to protect the last Jews of Hungary. Wallenberg was personally threatened by the Germans: "Even diplomats can have accidents." He is credited with saving tens of thousands of Jews.

Wallenberg was last seen by his colleagues on January 18, 1945, in Soviet custody. He had presented the Soviet liberators with a plan to restore the Jews of Budapest. It is known that he was arrested and sent to a Gulag, where, according to Soviet and even post-Soviet testimony, he died two years later. However, there were a number of reports from former Soviet prisoners of a Swedish prisoner still in custody, years after Wallenberg was reported to have died. His fate remains unknown.

Sugihara and Zwartendijk

Chiune (Sempo) Sugihara and Jan Zwartendijk were diplomats living in Kaunus (Kovno), the prewar capital of Lithuania during the brief period of Lithuanian independence. Sugihara represented Japan and Zwartendijk the Netherlands. They were co-conspirators in a plan to rescue Jews, working at the most pivotal of moments.

Zwartendijk discovered that no visa was required for entry to the Dutch-

Below: *Raoul Wallenberg in his office at the Swedish legation; Budapest, German-occupied Hungary, November 26, 1944.* Bottom: *A group of Jews saved from deportation by Raoul Wallenberg; Budapest, November 28, 1944.*

controlled Caribbean island of Curacao. He understood that an ink stamp, though seemingly meaningless, could make the difference between life and death for a refugee. So he had a stamp made: "Valid for entry in Curacao." That enabled the Japanese Consul to issue a transit visa for Jews to travel via Japan to Curacao. (Although Japan was unwilling to accept Jews seeking refuge, it would allow those with valid visas to travel via Japan to another destination.)

Working until the final moments of his stay in Kaunas, Sugihara issued hundreds of transit visas for Jews, including Talmudic students at the famed *Mir Yeshiva*. They ultimately found refuge in Shanghai, China (then under Japanese occupation), which previously had a small but influential Jewish community. That community grew to some 20,000 during the war.

Nathan Lewin was a small child when he and his family escaped. He recalled:

> My parents escaped Poland, smuggling across the border to what was still independent Lithuania with my maternal grandmother and my uncle in the middle of the night. I was three years old, and they warned me to keep absolutely silent while the smuggler led us through

the forest because, they said, wolves would come out from between the trees if I made a sound. Miraculously, I kept still and we made it to Vilna. My mother then invoked her former Dutch citizenship to obtain an endorsement on our travel document from Jan Zwartendijk, the Dutch Consul in Kovno. And this endorsement—declaring that we needed no visa to enter the Dutch colonies of Surinam and Curacao—was the basis for the issuance of a transit visa by a Japanese Consul named Chiune Sugihara. That visa enabled us to travel across Russia, through Japan, and then to the United States.

Sugihara was reprimanded by the Japanese Foreign Office for his efforts. His diplomatic career ended. Zwartendijk was under unique pressure as the Netherlands was already under German occupation. Both he and Sugihara are now on Yad Vashem's honor roll of Righteous Among the Nations, as are the village of Le Chambon and Raoul Wallenberg.

Oskar Schindler

Oskar Schindler was an unexpected German rescuer. A member of the Party and

Top left: *Chiune (Sempo) Sugihara.* Top right: *Samuel Iwry, Zorach Wahrhaftig, Leon Ilutowicz, and Samuel Graudenz (left to right); Kovno, Lithuania, c. 1940. These Jews met with Sugihara to obtain visas.* Above: *A Japanese transit visa issued by Sugihara to Rabbi Morduch, Zlata Malkaz Ginzburg, and their daughter, Esther; Kovno, August 6, 1940.*

Top: *Oskar Schindler (second from left) with his Jewish employees at the Emalia enamelworks; Krakow, German-occupied Poland, 1940.* Above: *Schindler (second from left) at a party with friends and a German army officer; Krakow, April 28, 1942. Schindler often used such contacts to learn of impending deportations so that he could save his workers.*

a highly visible Nazi, he sought to exploit his contacts in order to make a fortune during the war years in Krakow, under German occupation. Using Jewish capital, he established an enamel-works factory outside of the ghetto and employed the cheapest labor he could find: Jews.

There is little evidence that he began his efforts seeking to save Jews; at first, he protected them only out of self-interest: They were making him rich. Over time, as he came to understand the Nazi Final Solution to the "Jewish question," he became a staunch but clandestine opponent, protecting his workers even at the expense of his profits.

He added Jews to his "list," the one made famous by Steven Spielberg's brilliant 1993 film *Schindler's List.* He even rescued some of his female workers from within Auschwitz by using his connections and bribing appropriate officials. As the slave-labor camp of

Plazsow and the ghetto of Krakow—his two main sources of labor—were being emptied, he moved his factory to Brunnlitz in his native Sudetenland. There he pretended to manufacture essential items for the German army. While promising much and delivering little, he expended a fortune to protect his Jews.

Schindler's case is an anomaly. A womanizer and war profiteer, he can hardly be called "righteous." His motivations were at first not pure. But over time, he became fierce in his opposition to the Nazis and in his determination to protect Jews. He did what he could do, and he defied the notion that nothing could be done.

In the end, Schindler and his wife, Emilie, saved some 1,200 Jews from the gas chambers of German-occupied Poland and were honored by Yad Vashem.

Irena Sendler

Irena Sendler was a Polish social worker who provided false documents and assistance to Jewish children in the Warsaw ghetto during World War II. Working with Zegota, the underground Polish council that aided Jews, she headed its children's department. Because of her work in social welfare, she had a permit allowing her to enter the ghetto and check for typhus. The Germans permitted Poles to do these inspections, as typhus did not distinguish between Jew and "Aryan."

Sendler wore the Jewish star in the ghetto, perhaps as a gesture of solidarity, perhaps also to avoid calling attention to herself. She smuggled hundreds of Jewish children out of the ghetto in ambulances, on trams, in suitcases, and in boxes. The children were placed with Polish families or in Roman Catholic orphanages. She hid the original names of the children and their locations in a jar because Zegota, which funded the operation, was committed to returning these children to their Jewish families after the war.

Arrested in 1943, Sendler was sentenced to death. She was on her way to her execution when a bribed German official left her to die in the woods, her arms and legs broken. She survived, and spent the rest of the war in hiding while continuing to save Jewish children.

Sendler was recognized in 1965 by Yad Vashem as a Righteous Among the Nations. In 2003 she was honored by a personal letter from Pope John Paul II, himself a Pole who lived under German occupation during World War II. Sendler also received the "White Eagle," the highest civilian honor the Polish government bestows.

In 2007 she was among those nominated for the Nobel Peace Prize. She died in 2008 in her 98th year.

The Rescued

Those that were rescued also have a story to tell. Chicagoan Irene Poll found refuge in France from her native Germany. She was given a warning: "One day, I got a phone call . . . the Gestapo is after me." She was taken to the home of a French priest, Father Raymond Vancourt.

Sometime later, she recounted:
I took ill. . . . What I didn't realize, and that I learned gradually, Father Vancourt had given me his bedroom . . . and on the mantel piece, there was a little head of Christ, but I noticed that there was a spot on the wall above that where there was a crucifix before,

but the crucifix was taken down out of respect for me. . . .

One day I felt rather down spirits, and I said to him, "If I were converted, if you baptized me, then I wouldn't be a Jew here." Well, we didn't even enter into a discussion. He took both my hands, and he said, "Look, I love you as a human being, and I respect you as a Jew, so don't you ever ask anything like that."

. . . Father Vancourt had students come to the house every day. . . . I thought they were students. . . . What I didn't know, and I found out the day of the liberation, is that he was a member of the French underground. . . .

Recently when I asked Raymond, "Why did you do what you did?," he said, "Well, you needed help. . . . "I mean, no ifs or buts. . . . "Wouldn't that be what everybody would do?"

Ever since I knew Father Vancourt, my life has changed. . . . I asked him point blank. . . . "How can I ever thank you for saving my life?". . . . He said, "Just enjoy it."

Marie Catherine Rossi, a French Catholic, rescued three children. When asked about her motivation, she said:
. . . I did what I had to do. . . . What would you do with the children? Let them die? No, you wouldn't do it either.

In almost every case, the rescuers were not motivated by complex values or complicated calculations but by the simple recognition that the Jews were people like themselves—people entitled to basic human rights, worthy of being treated with elemental human decency. We cannot let the precarious circumstances under which they lived overshadow the simplicity of their deeds, nor can we allow the simplicity of their deeds to obscure their nobility.

Schindler's motivations were at first not pure. But over time, he became fierce in his opposition to the Nazis and in his determination to protect Jews.

Father Raymond Vancourt, a priest and a professor of theology and philosophy, who hid Irene Poll in the French city of Lille until liberation.

KATE ROSSI LIPNER

1925–

Kate Rossi Lipner was born Marie Catherine Rossi in Nice, France. The oldest of two children, she had a sister, Nanette, just 15 months her junior. Her father worked in construction as a laborer. Her mother was the caretaker for an apartment building—a job that provided the Rossis with a rent-free apartment.

As the oldest child, Marie had many responsibilities. She was blamed for everything, or at least that is how she felt. Big and strong beyond her years, she would protect her sister, and her mother insisted that she perform arduous chores. Resentful at the time, she eventually would come to appreciate the expectations placed upon her.

Like many people raised in southern France, her parents had spent their entire lives within 20 miles of home. The Rossis were Catholic, but Marie was comfortable among the many Jews who were neighbors and friends. She went to convent school, where the strict discipline and unyielding ways brought out the rebel within her—and alienated her from her family's faith.

When France declared war on Germany after the German invasion of Poland in September 1939, the Rossi family stocked up on basic food—flour, sugar, and baking oil. They knew shortages were ahead. Marie went to work for a Jewish family as a nanny, taking care of a boy named Robert, whose mother had died. Marie learned to love him as her own.

When the Germans invaded France in May 1940, France was divided into two parts: a German-occupied zone and, in the South, a collaborationist Vichy regime, which was subservient to the Nazis. Drawn to the underground, Marie plastered dissenting posters on town walls and distributed pamphlets against the Nazis. Henri, young Robert's father, knew that she was anti-Nazi. He learned to trust Marie as pro-Jewish as well.

Recalling the danger, Marie said: "We were young and never thought I would get caught. We had the connections to get food and distribute it to those in need." She also served as a guide for Jewish families fleeing to Switzerland. After her mother died suddenly of a cerebral hemorrhage in 1942, Marie could no longer serve as a guide. She was responsible for Nanette. By the age of 17, she had lived a lifetime.

Marie decided to hide Robert and his father, Henri. Another family joined them—a mother named Dora and her two children, Maurice and Ellen. When Dora fled

Marie and her younger sister, Nanette; c. 1940.

to Spain—a dangerous journey over the Pyrenees—she entrusted her two children to Marie. Marie became enamored with Henri and they soon were lovers. He was decades her senior, and she was the only one he saw as he lived in hiding.

Marie was arrested twice and the Nazis tried to intimidate her, but to no avail. One evening, when she found a Gestapo man in her hallway, she shot him. Her neighbors, who were not collaborators, protected her and cleaned up for her. Fortunately for Marie, Allied bombs had left parts of Nice ablaze and parts in rubble; Germans had taken to shelters rather than patrolling the streets.

Marie did not know other people who hid Jews. Typical of resistance movements everywhere, the French worked in cells, so Marie had but limited knowledge of any other operatives or their activities.

One would imagine that Marie would reap the rewards of her heroism, but liberation proved difficult and painful. She had grown to love Maurice and Ellen, so when their mother sent for them after the war, the "parting was awful," recalled Marie. "I was not needed anymore." Henri had met another woman, and at 19 Marie was crushed.

She met a young American solider and went on a date. Within two days, he proposed. Marie was candid: "I don't love you very much," she told him. "I love you for both of us," replied Lawrence Benashiak, a Polish

One evening, when she found a Gestapo man in her hallway, she shot him.

American from Chicago. Two days later, they were married. Marie came to America in January 1946.

Lawrence suffered a stroke in 1966 and died three years later. Marie, who changed her name to Kate, married Philip Lipner in a civil ceremony. He was Jewish and Kate was nominally Catholic. It seemed her tumultuous life would finally enter a period of stability. But Philip died shortly after their marriage. Her son, Paul, was so taken with Philip that years later he named his first son after his stepfather. And Kate was so touched by her relationship with Philip and the world it represented that she later converted to Judaism.

Over the years, Kate stayed in touch with the children she had saved, especially Maurice and Robert. She and Maurice were reunited in France, and then Maurice undertook all the requisite steps to see that Kate was honored by Yad Vashem, Israel's memorial to the Holocaust, as a Righteous Among the Nations for saving the life of a Jew, without recompense and at risk to her own life.

Even her moment of honor in 1995 was, like so much of her life, bittersweet. On the day she was honored, Robert, the child she had rescued, died of AIDS in his father's arms in France.

Asked what gave her the special strength to do what she did, Kate explained: "My mother. She made me stronger. Now I know she made me what I am."

VICTOR AITAY

1921–

Victor Aitay was born in Budapest, Hungary's capital and largest city, to an upper-middle-class family. His father, Sigmund Gigot, owned a large apartment house that was home to some 40 families, but his real passion was the violin. Each evening, Sigmund played music for the family, and young Victor soon picked up his father's interest. As was common among Budapest's assimilated Jews, Victor's parents were of different faiths. Sigmund was Jewish; his wife Irma was not.

Victor's early life was centered around music, and he entered Budapest's respected Academy of Music. The school had a quota for Jewish students, but it was willing to accept applicants of exceptional talent. Victor warmly remembers his teachers as well as the opportunities even young students had to attend concerts and opera, where they heard some of the greatest musicians of their time. His routine was intense: ordinary schooling, musical training, evening concerts, and up to eight hours of practice every day. But when playing the violin, Victor experienced the joy of mastery rather than the burden of a difficult training regimen.

Victor always knew that he was Jewish, but it was of little concern and rarely discussed. His father went from time to time to the famed Dohány Synagogue in Budapest, the country's largest.

Hungary was an ally of Nazi Germany, and as such it could pursue its own anti-Jewish policies without regard to the Final Solution, according to its own timing and national interest—at least for a time. It was difficult for Jews to find employment and more difficult still for a young artist just beginning a career. Budapest's Jewish community did provide opportunities for musicians,

actors, and other performers by renting a beautiful hall and staging performances. So Victor had the opportunity to play, if not in the grand concert halls of which he had dreamed.

Despite antisemitism in Hungary and some violence, the guards at the academy protected Jewish students from outside attack. Victor underestimated the difficulties that were to follow. "We did not believe it would be as severe as it turned out to be," he said. "We couldn't believe somebody could go back to the Middle Ages and behave in such a barbarian manner."

Victor was sent to a labor camp in 1942, when young Jews were conscripted for forced labor battalions. Hungarian Jews were subject to discrimination, persecution, violence, and forced labor. Victor was sent to Bereck, near the Romanian border. Three themes dominated all discussions among the prisoners: food, how to preserve one's life, and how to escape. For the first time since the age of five, Victor was separated from his violin.

Victor tried twice to escape. The first time he was caught and brought to judgment. He could have been killed, but his life was spared—perhaps because he stated that his profession was a violinist, or perhaps because the military officer was a musician. The second time, Victor—dressed as a priest—successfully escaped back to Budapest in the summer of 1944.

A brief review of history puts Victor's experience in context: By 1944 Germany was losing the war, and there was some talk of Hungary shifting sides. Hitler summoned Admiral Horthy, Hungary's leader, to a meeting, where the ultimatum was given regarding the Final Solution. In March 1944, Germany invaded Hungary. In April and May, Jews were forced to wear the Yellow Star and many were ghettoized. From May 15 through early July, Jews outside of Budapest were deported to death camps. By July 9, Budapest—home of Hungary's last living Jewish community—was on the edge of annihilation. Swedish diplomat Raoul Wallenberg, with the help of some neutral consulates, arrived to save the Jews of Budapest.

By the time Victor returned to Budapest, Wallenberg had made the Swedish Embassy a haven for Jews. He also rented buildings that flew the Swedish flag and declared them sovereign Swedish territory, protected by diplomatic law. Victor found a place in the Swedish Embassy. One of his musician friends recognized him, and Wallenberg allowed the 23-year-old prodigy to stay. Still without his violin, Victor worked as the embassy's telephone operator.

"We couldn't believe somebody could go back to the Middle Ages and behave in such a barbarian manner."

Victor recalled the Swedish rescuer: "He was always in motion; everyone wanted something from him and he tried to satisfy each and every person."

Victor did not witness first-hand Wallenberg's heroic escapades. He did, however, see their consequences. One day the pro-Nazi Hungarian Arrow Cross invaded the Swedish Embassy and took some 120 people to the river, ostensibly to drown them or shoot them. Victor had been given a secret number to call, and within hours they were returned.

The Soviet Army liberated Budapest in January 1945, the last time that anyone saw Raoul Wallenberg as a free man. He was arrested by the Soviets; their motivation and Wallenberg's fate are still unknown.

Victor returned home to his parents. Irma, who as a non-Jew was not subject to arrest or persecution, had hidden her husband. Victor's violin was still at home, awaiting his return, and he played a Brahms concerto in celebration.

Victor's father had grown weaker during the war, and his heart failed him shortly after liberation. Victor soon sought a haven in the West, where as a musician he could travel and perform. He married Eva Kellner in the fall of 1945. Her uncle provided affidavits to bring the young couple to the United States. They settled first in New York, where Victor became concertmaster of the Metropolitan Opera from 1948 to 1954. They relocated to Chicago, where they established a home and a family. Over time, Victor's mother and his sister and her family joined Victor in Chicago.

Victor became assistant concertmaster of the Chicago Symphony Orchestra in 1954, and he was elevated to concertmaster in 1967. Through music, Victor plays a special tribute to the man who saved his life, Raoul Wallenberg.

Victor, shortly after his arrival in the United States; c. 1950.

DEATH MARCHES

Inmates from Dachau are led on a death march; Gruenwald, Germany, April 29, 1945.

Elaine Mortkovic described her last night at Auschwitz, in 1945:

It was January 18. We were asleep. One of these Nazi women came up and yelled: "Up, up, up, everybody!" We didn't know what happened. "Get dressed! Don't turn on the lights. We have to leave in a hurry!"

Then we understood that something was wrong because that never happened before. So okay we felt if this is coming to an end, thank God.

We noticed the Nazis were burning documents. Big fires. "Line up! You are going to receive food for the road."

So we started marching and we marched day and night. People marched before us and people

marched behind us. On the same road, men were marching in separate groups, women marching in separate groups. . . . And every one of us had Nazi security; soldiers on the sides with their rifles with their German shepherds making sure nobody is going to run away from the line.

We marched in the middle of the road. Then we noticed bodies lying in those pits on the side of the road. Dead bodies! So we found out that those people who couldn't walk any longer were just killed. They would leave them behind. . . .

The more we watched the more bodies we saw. If they killed half of us, I don't even know to this day. But many, many of us were killed on this death march. . . .

My feet were so soaking wet to the bone that [when] we sat down for a couple of hours my feet froze to the ground. We kept walking. One night we slept inside the woods. Just on snow. They loaded us on cattle cars until we arrived at Ravensbruck.

Ralph Bell, another death-march survivor, described his ordeal:
We walked and we walked and we walked.

And God wasn't very merciful. He gave us the biggest freezes, the coldest nights, the coldest days during the time when we walked in the light cotton clothing with torn shoes and without socks.

Helen and Pearl Herskovic, twin sisters—Mengele twins (twins experimented on by the infamous Dr. Mengele at Auschwitz)—left Auschwitz on their 24th birthday, January 18, 1945. Helen said she survived in part because she was not alone. She had to walk beyond all human endurance. For her, the death marches were an inner battle between life and death.
I don't know how we walked—I just know some inner spirit or will to live, because every time I got sick I said to [Pearl], "Let me die in peace." And she said "No. If you die, I will die. So we better try to be well."

By the winter of 1944–45, German defeat was all but certain. The Soviet Union was moving toward Berlin; the Allies had long since liberated Paris and Brussels, and were advancing to the Rhine River. Germany would be defeated, but would its Jewish victims live to see that day?

What would happen to those in death camps? As the final part of their well-practiced plans of deception, Germany wanted to erase all evidence of the crime.

No evidence—no crime!

The Red Army had captured the death camp of Majdanek in July 1944. Its massive collection of shoes and uniforms and its operative gas chambers bore witness to what had occurred in the valley just outside of Lublin.

The Germans wanted no repetition of the capture of a death camp and its eyewitnesses.

Gas chambers were shut down even at Auschwitz, where the last gassing occurred in November 1944. As Soviet troops advanced toward Auschwitz, the SS decided to hastily evacuate and destroy the camp. On January 17, 1945, roll call was taken at Auschwitz for the last time.

German officers fled. Josef Mengele, the SS physician who had performed cruel "medical" experiments on Auschwitz inmates, left with his notes, still believing that they would be his key to academic prominence in the world beyond the camp. Other guards took with them the treasures that they had looted from the storehouses or from bribes they had taken from inmates.

More than 60,000 Auschwitz prisoners began a long winter march westward without food, without a place to sleep, and without even a chance to pause for biological functions. It was the final stage of killing.

Those who remained behind were too ill to make the journey. They assumed that they would be executed immediately. But they were not. For 10 days they lived in limbo, not knowing what the morning would bring—death or liberation.

The SS blew up the crematoria and gas chambers and tried to destroy the camp, but the time was too short, the task too massive. When Soviet troops entered Auschwitz on January 27, 1945, they encountered compelling evidence: 836,255 women's dresses; 348,000 men's suits; 38,000 pairs of men's shoes; 14,000 pounds of human hair. And former prisoners who were ready to talk.

The death marches were the antithesis of the deportations, which for almost three years had brought Jews to centralized killing centers. In contrast,

Many Jews who began this journey as walking skeletons soon became corpses. They were literally walked to death.

Inmates from Dachau are led on a death march toward Wolfratshausen, Germany; April 1945.

this dispersion sent them off in various directions toward Germany, which was receiving back the Jews it had once so ferociously expelled.

The technological, industrialized, assembly-line process at the death camps gave way to a much more primitive struggle: to march or to be shot. Many Jews who began this journey as walking skeletons soon became corpses. These individuals were literally walked to death.

Some prisoners were sent from one concentration camp to another, as the Nazis searched for a place that could handle the extra burden.

Ralph Bell described his experience at Mauthausen:

If Auschwitz was bad, Mauthausen was worse. We had to go into a swimming pool [more likely a cess-pool], which consisted of human waste. Many died right there. From the 9,000 people who started the march, there were 3,000 left. People were just falling like flies.

The concentration camps in Germany and Austria to which Jews were sent simply could not handle the load. The German infrastructure had collapsed. There could be no deliveries of food and no collection, burial, or cremation of the dead.

Others prisoners were simply marched around and around, going seemingly nowhere, until they died or until the war came to its end. Elaine Mortkovic left Auschwitz in January 1945. Her ordeal on foot continued until May.

The German tactic of forced evacuation was not new. In 1941 hundreds of thousands of Soviet prisoners of war had been marched along the highways of newly captured Soviet territory. In November 1944, Adolf Eichmann marched tens of thousands of Hungarian Jews from Budapest to the Austrian border. He would not wait until railway transports were ready.

The response of the civilian population to the sight of these walking skeletons varied from town to town and country to country. Of the Czechs, Norbert Wollheim said: "Whatever they had, they gave us." In Austria, he recalled, there was "nobody to help us anymore."

Rabbi Menachem Rubin, a prominent Hasidic master, described his ordeal by interpreting Psalm 118 in a radically new way. He said: "The Lord has punished me severely, but has not given me to death. The most severe of all the punishments we received is that we did not die."

HELEN RAPPAPORT

1921–

Helen Herskovic was born in Cinadovo, Czechoslovakia; her twin sister, Pearl, was but an hour older. At birth, Helen was as "tiny as a teaspoon," she said. The midwife told her mother that she would not survive.

Her mother's immediate response: "As long as God gave her to me, I want her to live."

When the babies started walking, they were considered as cute as twin poodles. Her father worked making custom-tailored suits, and their much-older sister was a dressmaker, so the twins were always dressed alike. Once grown, Pearl attended a teachers college while Helen opted for business school and technical training.

In 1939 Germany turned over its region of Czechoslovakia to Hungary, which introduced laws persecuting its Jews. As a German ally, Hungary could set its own policies toward the Jews. Until the March 1944 invasion, the Jews of Hungary were allowed to live.

Immediately after the German invasion, Jews were singled out and their property was confiscated. And just after Passover, Cinadovo's Jews were sent to a ghetto in neighboring Munkacs.

"First they took my father and my brother-in-law. My sister and I remained," Helen recalled.

But soon, the pair was taken to the brickyard that was the site of the ghetto. After several days, they

Helen and twin sister Pearl, 1923.

were deported along with more than 430,000 Hungarian Jews who were sent to Auschwitz from May to July.

When they arrived in Auschwitz-Birkenau, they faced *Selektion*. Remembered Helen:

My niece Nancy was 13. . . . She went to the right. Smaller kids with [my] father went to the left. We still didn't know [of] the atrocities [of] the chimney.

All of a sudden we hear this handsome son-of-a . . . is walking toward—looks like Clark Gable, Mengele even handsomer, just with shiny boots. And he is hollering, "Twins step out!" I'm looking at my sister; she looks at me. [Pearl] says, "We have to step out." And we didn't know if it was good or bad; whatever, we'll be with each other. So we stepped out.

How did they learn of the fate of other prisoners? A *Kapo* [prisoner foreman] told them.

"You see those chimneys? That's where your father is—your sister and the children. The fire you see, the ashes falling on you. That's from your family." We were like in a daze. That was the first evening.

The twins were taken to a special barracks. They were tattooed, which, they were told, was a good sign. "That means you are going to live," they heard. Unlike other arriving prisoners, their heads were not shaved.

After waiting and then waiting some more in the barracks, Pearl and Helen volunteered to work one day. They were taken to a large morgue and told to move bodies from one side to another of the room and to disinfect the area. They were stunned. "Let's pretend it is potatoes or onions, a sack," Helen suggested. How did they adjust? Helen spoke of numbness: "We got like a robot, like a stone. We never got used to it."

Josef Mengele, who was both an M.D. and a Ph.D., called the twins *mein kinder* (my children). They were taken to a laboratory and told to undress. The hair on their eyelashes was counted, strand by strand. Their earlobes were measured and compared. Blood was taken every day. And each day they were given injections. Mengele, an enthusiastic young eugenicist, wanted to study twins with the idea of breeding a "master race."

"We saw twins disappearing—always less and less," Helen recalled. She soon learned that if a twin died for any reason, the second one was murdered, dissected, and measured. Helen herself nearly died. She was struck with tuberculosis and was on the brink of death, but somehow she survived.

January 18, 1945, the twins' 24th birthday, was also when they began the death marches. They were two of more than 60,000 prisoners hastily evacuated from Auschwitz.

We were walking about three weeks without food, without water—nothing. Just marching and sleeping in the snow. We ate up the snow. All around us there were bombs falling all over when we were marching. We begged God throw one [a bomb] and finish [us]. Let's get finished.

As January pushed into February and March, the struggle became one of time and energy. Would Helen and Pearl run out of strength, or would Allied troops liberate them? "The SS were

"Shoot me. Get it over with."
—Helen Rappaport to an SS officer

Helen (left) and Pearl; 1946.

slowly disappearing and putting on civilian clothes and pretending to be part of the native population, who protected them," Helen remembered.

Desperate and at the end of her strength, Helen approached an SS officer. "Shoot me. Get it over with," she said.

"I didn't get the order, so I cannot do it," he told her.

The twins lived to see liberation with the arrival of Americans: "We hugged them and they hugged us," she said. Slowly, Helen was nursed back to life. She became a dressmaker, creating clothes out of parachute cloth for her sister and for herself as well as for other survivors.

Pearl and Helen returned home to find their town virtually without Jews. Their next-door neighbor took Helen in. Immediately, Helen noticed something: The bedspreads had come from her home; the children were dressed in her clothes. "As soon as they took us away, there was looting . . . ," Helen remembered. "Our house was ransacked." Helen was able to find her brother and a niece.

A Russian Jewish soldier gave them advice: "If you want to be free, go to the United States." Pearl and Helen had the address of their older sister, who had emigrated in 1939. They began the process of getting affidavits for immigration. In the interim, Helen fell in love and married Herman Rappaport, who then escaped Hungary for Israel. Helen visited him in Palestine as he awaited his visa to America. They then immigrated to the United States. They settled in Chicago and later relocated to Evanston, where they raised their two daughters.

Helen never learned what injections she had received. However, like many of Mengele's twins, she and Pearl suffered from kidney diseases in their adult lives.

LIBERATION

In the final days of World War II, as Allied troops pushed across Germany toward Berlin, American soldiers came upon the concentration camps of Ohrdruf, Mauthausen, Nordhausen, Buchenwald, and Dachau. British forces entered other concentration camps, foremost among them Bergen-Belsen, in which they encountered stacks of corpses and an advanced typhus epidemic. Thirteen thousand people were to die after liberation despite the valiant efforts of British medics.

Allied troops had not intended to liberate the camps but to conquer a country to defeat the enemy. The encounter with the camps was as accidental as it was decisive. And the camps they entered were not the worst of the Nazi concentration camps.

In July 1944, the Soviet army captured the death camp of Majdanek, which was described on the front page of *The New York Times*. H. W. Lawrence wrote: "I have just seen the most terrible place on earth." Soviet correspondents were equally graphic, but their powerful writing had limited impact since the West was suspicious of Soviet reportage.

The Germans had abandoned Auschwitz on January 18, 1945, burning down the crematoria and the gas chambers and hastily destroying records and documents before they ran for their lives. Only a few thousand prisoners, many too ill to walk, were left behind. The Nazis had destroyed Treblinka, Belzec, and Sobibor in 1943 as their work—the destruction of Polish Jewry—had been virtually completed.

Still, what awaited the Western Allies was gruesome. Prisoners arriving from forced evacuation ("death marches") from concentration camps in the German-occupied East, stumbled into these camps, which were collapsing under the weight of their prisoner population just as the Allied armies entered.

Even to battle-weary veterans, the conditions encountered were unimaginable. Lieutenant Colonel Richard Seibel recalled getting on the radio after entering Mauthausen. "We've come across this big camp, we don't know what it is," he said. "People are dying everywhere.... People don't do this to people."

Help was needed urgently: medics to handle the sick and the dying; chaplains to deal with the dead and the living; engineers to purify the water; sanitation crews to deal with the filth. Military reinforcements were required to continue the fight.

Food was needed desperately. In the days preceding liberation, systems in the concentration camps had broken down. Many in the camps could not remember when they had eaten their last meals. They were weak and in many cases just days, or even hours, from death. Bodies of the dead had not been buried for days, perhaps even weeks.

The stench in the camps was horrific, and the images in them frightening. One GI recalled: "Before I left the camp that evening, I saw death reduced

Recently liberated prisoners at the Dachau concentration camp; Dachau, Germany, spring 1945.

Help was needed urgently: medics to handle the sick and the dying; chaplains to deal with the dead and the living; engineers to purify the water; sanitation crews to deal with the filth.

to such ordinariness that it left me with nothing, not even sickness in my stomach."

Fred Friendly, a young Jewish GI who later achieved prominence as a CBS executive, wrote home to his mother:

I saw their emaciated bodies in piles like cords of wood. I saw the living skeletons, some of whom, regardless of our medical corps work, will die. I saw where they lived; I saw where the sick died, three and four in a bed, no toilets, no nothing. I saw the look in their eyes.

Anticipating his mother's disbelief, he wrote:

This was no movie, no printed page. Your son saw this with his own eyes and in doing this aged ten years.

William Levine, a Jewish GI from Chicago, recalled his first encounter:

You can't describe in any language that scene. . . . They were not only dirty, filthy, but how the men—the condition they were in—they were actually skin and bone. . . . It's just an impossible thing to look at. The hollow— their eyes were into their heads. They weren't just eyes that were on the surface. The skin was tight against their skull and a sallow complexion—everything told you that they had to be miserable for a long time.

How did the soldiers react? Levine explained:

Many of the men just threw up. Some cried. Some vented their spleen by firing into the guards that were still present.

American soldiers wanted to feed the emaciated prisoners, thinking it was an act of kindness. Zev Rogalin recalled:

K rations started to fly from the tanks. People saw these K rations. If I saw once in my life falling over food—this was the time. But that was also the downfall. People lived through that whole misery—that whole devastation and died a couple days later.

Again Levine remembers:
They couldn't handle that food. It was too rich for them.

Survivor Herman Roth recalled:
Every drop of bread was like if I had 20 needles in my gums.

Another American GI, Philip Drell, remembered that the Army brought in more easily digestible food:

Eventually there were huge truckloads of soft bread that they brought in, and they served cans of some kind of a soup. I think it was potato soup. . . . And after everybody was served, and the cans were still standing there, the survivors would come over, and they would shove each other to get close to the cans.

U.S. Army soldiers walk through the entrance gate of the Buchenwald, Germany, concentration camp in 1945.

Among those who entered the camps soon after liberation were two unique groups of American soldiers: African Americans who were serving in a segregated army—blacks and whites were restricted to separate units—and Japanese Americans, also in separate units, and whose parents were incarcerated in American detention camps back home. Blacks were often assigned to sanitation crews, and this was surely a cleanup operation.

Leon Bass, an African American soldier, recalled:

Something happened when I walked through the gates. My blinders came off. My tunnel vision dissipated. And I began to realize that human suffering is not just delegated to me and mine. Human suffering touches everybody.

On April 12, 1945, hours before they learned of President Franklin Roosevelt's death, generals Dwight Eisenhower, Omar Bradley, and George Patton visited the Ohrdruf concentration camp. Eisenhower turned white with rage at the scene, but insisted on seeing the entire camp. "We are told that the American soldier does not know what he was fighting for," he said. "Now, at least he will know what he is fighting against."

Eisenhower soon wrote to the U.S. Army's chief of staff, General George Marshall:

The things I saw beggar description. The visual evidence and the verbal testimony of starvation, cruelty, and bestiality were so overpowering. I made the visit deliberately, in order to be in position to give first-hand evidence of these things if ever, in the future, there develops a tendency to charge these allegations to propaganda.

General Bradley later wrote about the day: "The smell of death overwhelmed us." George Patton was overcome. He refused to enter a room where

the bodies of naked men who had starved to death were piled, saying he would get sick if he did so. But he was also outraged, and he ordered that all of Weimar's residents be marched through Buchenwald, a concentration camp just four miles from the town's center. A film of the visit shows the Germans entering the camps smiling, as if on a pleasant excursion. Minutes later, they emerge from the barracks, ashen-faced. Other American officers followed Patton's lead as Germans were marched through the camp and recruited to dig the mass graves in which the dead would be buried. Many locals claimed that they had not known what was happening in their own backyard.

Eisenhower, after deciding to call attention to the concentration camps, summoned the press and a congressional delegation. Photographers, including *Life* magazine's Margaret Bourke-White, were present in the camps. Joseph Pulitzer expected to find that the reports of the camp were exaggerations.

Top: *American soldiers inspect the crematorium after liberation of the Dachau concentration camp in the spring of 1945.* Bottom: *American GI Jerry Glass of Chicago at the Mauthausen concentration camp; Mauthausen, Austria, May 1945.*

Instead he found them to be understatements.

Bittersweet Moments

For survivors, liberation was bittersweet. Hadassah Bimko, who had lost her husband and son at Auschwitz, recalled:

For the greatest part of the liberated Jews of Bergen-Belsen, there was no ecstasy, no joy at our liberation. We had lost our families, our homes. We had no place to go to, nobody to hug. Nobody was waiting for us anywhere. We had been liberated from death and from the fear of death, but we were not free from our fear of life.

For the first time, survivors could permit themselves a moment of feeling that overcame their numbness, which was essential to their survival. Margaret Oppenheimer recounted her emotions:

That's when I broke down. I cried. . . . And I said, "What am I going to do now? I have nowhere to go. I have no place—I have no one to go with. What am I going to do?"

At Buchenwald, one of the Americans mounted the stand and said in German, "You are free!" He recalled that the "people bellowed. It wasn't a shout of joy; it was an animal outcry."

American chaplain Herschel Schachter remembered the moment:

I stood there. I didn't know what to say, I didn't know what to do. Impulsively I shouted out in Yiddish. "Sholom Aleichem yidn, ihr zeit frei." (Peace be with you. You are free.") Continuing in Yiddish with "The war is over. I am an American, I'm a rabbi, you are free."

Primo Levi, a chronicler of Auschwitz, wrote:

24 January [1945] Liberty. The breach in the barbed wire gave us a concrete image of it. To anyone who stopped to think, it signified no more Germans, no more selections, no blows, no roll calls, and perhaps, later, the return.

But we had to make an effort to convince ourselves of it and no one had time to enjoy the thought. All around us lay destruction and death.

American editors and publishers are shown the corpses of prisoners during an inspection of the Dachau concentration camp; spring 1945.

AARON ELSTER
1932–

How does a young boy survive alone in isolation? Cast away by his mother, he is saved by an antisemite.

Aaron Elster was born in Sokolow Podlaski, a Polish town northeast of Warsaw. The town was home to some 5,000 Jews, a third of the general population. According to Aaron, they lived in two separate worlds: "their world and our world."

His father, Chaim Sruel, and his mother, Cywia, spanned both worlds, running a non-kosher meat market that served a mostly gentile clientele. He had two sisters, Ita (Irene), who was three years older, and Sara Rivka, four years younger. His parents showered the children with affection; the relationship between his parents was reserved. The family lived in a two-story apartment building that was also home to Aaron's uncle, a rabbi, and Aaron's *cheder,* the Hebrew school.

Sokolow's Jewish community supported two synagogues, a *yeshiva,* and a theater—even a Jewish newspaper. Aaron experienced some antisemitism: He was called a "Christ killer" at an age when he did not know who Jesus Christ was. He denied being alive when Jesus was crucified.

Aaron was seven when the Germans invaded in September 1939. They destroyed the synagogue and later forced the Jews into a ghetto that Aaron would later remember as full of human waste, foul smells, disease, hunger, and dead bodies.

His parents sometimes sent Irene—who could pass for a non-Jew—to the "Aryan" side for food and to sell possessions for money. As the situation grew dire, death became a daily reality, and rumors of murder became prevalent. Irene was smuggled out of the ghetto and placed with a Polish couple by the name of Gorski. Because of her non-Jewish appearance and her fluent language skills, she had a greater chance for survival on the "Aryan" side.

The final deportations from Sokolow and killings in Treblinka began on the morning after Yom Kippur, Judaism's most sacred day, in late September 1942.

With a number of other families, Aaron and his family had been hiding behind a false wall on the second floor of their apartment building. As the Germans and Ukrainian police searched for Jews, Aaron quivered and a young baby cried. The mother held the child close, putting her hand over the infant's mouth in a desperate attempt to silence the baby. Tragically, the child was smothered to death.

As the town's Jews were forcibly gathered in the marketplace, awaiting resettlement, Aaron's father insisted that Aaron run and try to save himself. His father kept Sara, his younger daughter, at his side for a journey to the unknown. (They were indeed sent to Treblinka, where Chaim Sruel and Sara were murdered upon arrival.)

Alone, Aaron tried to remain inconspicuous, unseen. He crawled on his hands and knees through the sewer along the road, in hopes that he would not be found and shot. He made his way to an uncle's home, where he found an aunt and a cousin hiding in the cellar.

The next morning, a woman outside of the ghetto motioned him to come. Crawling under the barbed wire, ripping his pants and cutting his leg, Aaron escaped to the "Aryan" side and approached a restaurateur, a customer of his father's, who gave him bread, then pushed him away. His presence was just too dangerous; German soldiers were eating inside.

With no place to stay, Aaron returned to the now-empty ghetto. There he came across his mother, who had been allowed to stay as part of a work detail. She was now accompanied by a German-Jewish refugee, Gedalia. The three escaped to the forests, where they

Aaron crawled on his hands and knees through the sewer along the road, in hopes that he would not be found and shot.

hid by day, scavenged at night, and begged food from farmers. Aaron's mother told him that they must separate. "Go to the Gorskis," she said, referring to prewar family friends. Aaron recalled:

Deep down I hated my mother for making me leave. I would not look back and give them the satisfaction. I decided that I have to care for myself. I cannot trust or depend on anyone else.

A farmer sheltered 10-year-old Aaron in his cellar. He wanted to help but feared being discovered by the Nazis. The farmer told Aaron to give himself up, as "there was no longer any future for people like me," Aaron recalled. But Aaron was determined to survive. He went to the Gorskis, who let him stay in the attic. He remembered Mrs. Gorski saying:

Your mother is a shrew, a Jewish shrew, who talked me into taking your sister and jeopardizing my safety as well as my husband's. You two are a curse to me.

It was the first that Aaron had heard that his sister Irene was alive.

He was alone in the attic, day and night, with straw to sleep on and a bucket for bodily functions. He was given food each evening, but not enough to satisfy his hunger and barely enough to survive. To survive mentally, he took his mind to another place and another time. Occasionally Irene would visit, briefly easing his loneliness. In her absence, it only intensified. He lived like that for more than a year and a half.

As the Russians bombed the town and attacked German soldiers, the Gorskis sought shelter in their basement, forcing Irene to join her brother in the attic. The Gorskis did not want to die with Jews.

One day, Aaron and Irene were found by retreating Ukrainians and understood that the war had ended for them. Malnourished, both he and his sister could barely

walk. Aaron became a street kid. He joined the other Jewish survivors of Sokolow: 29 men, women, and children in all; 29 of 5,000.

Aaron learned that his mother and Gedalia had been betrayed only three months before the Russians arrived. He was told that his mother had been pregnant. He was forced to testify on behalf of the man who turned in his mother, to sign a document exonerating him.

Aaron was reunited with his uncle Sam. They moved to Lodz, Poland, where Aaron stayed in an orphanage before being smuggled with Sam to Czechoslovakia and then to Germany, where Aaron was placed in a displaced-persons camp. With help from the Hebrew Immigrant Aid Society (HIAS), and a Chicago relative's affidavit, he sailed to America in 1947 and settled in Chicago. Just shy of 15, he began life anew.

Aaron at the Neu Freimann DP camp.

Aaron served in the Korean War and eventually worked for Metropolitan Life Insurance. He married and had children and grandchildren. Once he retired, he began to lecture on the Holocaust, sharing his experience and bearing witness.

By listening to my story, young people have the responsibility to create a better world. They are the future decision-makers, and the world—for better or worse—is in their hands and hearts. I ask that they never be a bystander. I pray that they be careful how they use words, to be more tolerant, accepting, and to make a difference.

JUSTICE?

The United States and its allies insisted on nothing less than unconditional surrender by Germany. They flatly turned down all overtures, including a suspicious offer made in 1944 during the height of the killing of Hungarian Jews. The German offer aimed to separate the United States and Great Britain from its wartime ally, the Soviet Union, by offering one million Jews in exchange for 10,000 trucks that would be used solely on the eastern front against the Soviets.

With Germany's unconditional surrender came responsibilities for the Allies, including occupation and planning the next steps for Germany and Europe.

The question facing the Allies was: How do we rebuild from the ashes? For the survivor there is, as we have seen, one journey: returning to life and finding a place to live in freedom. For the world, there is another: rebuilding society and restoring justice.

On December 17, 1942, the combined Allied governments declared their commitment to prosecute Nazi leaders for war crimes against Jews and other civilian populations. In November 1943, as victory appeared possible but certainly not assured, the Allies—U.S. president Franklin D. Roosevelt, British prime minister Winston Churchill, and Soviet leader Joseph Stalin—issued the Moscow Declaration, which again pledged to bring Nazi leaders to justice.

After the war, this cry to bring the guilty to justice became ever more urgent as the public grasped the scope of what Germany had done. Harry Truman, who had ascended to the presidency after the death of Roosevelt, honored the commitment to joint trials by the three Allied countries and France. Such trials required not only justice but also the appearance of justice. They had to be given a unique stature.

Truman took the bold step of asking a Supreme Court justice, Robert Jackson, to take leave from the court and head the prosecution team. The city of Nuremberg was chosen. Nuremberg had been the site of Nazi Party rallies, the place where the infamous Nuremberg Laws had been promulgated. While the site was chosen because the core of the city was still intact, it was nonetheless appropriately symbolic.

The indictment of the defendants did not speak of the Holocaust or the Final Solution; specific crimes against Jews had been deleted in internal discussions preceding the indictment. Four crimes were specified:

- Crimes against peace: Planning, preparation, initiation, or waging of a war of aggression.
- War crimes: Violations of laws and customs of war, such as the murder, ill-treatment, or deportation of slave labor or for any other purpose of civilian populations . . . killing of hostages, prisoners of war, plunder of private property, destruction of towns and cities.
- Crimes against humanity: Murder, extermination, enslavement, deportation . . . against any civilian population . . . persecution on political, racial, or religious grounds . . . whether or not in violation of domestic laws of the country where perpetrated.
- Conspiracy to commit such crimes.

Chief American prosecutor Robert Jackson, a U.S. Supreme Court justice, delivers the opening speech of the American prosecution at the International Military Tribunal Trial of Major War Criminals; Nuremberg, Germany, November 21, 1945.

The combined Allied governments declared their commitment to prosecute Nazi leaders for war crimes and for crimes against humanity.

Surviving leaders of Nazi Germany, civilian and military, listen to the proceedings at the International Military Tribunal Trial of Major War Criminals at Nuremberg.

with the philosophies they conceived and with the forces they directed that any tenderness to them is a victory and an encouragement to all the evils which are attached to their names. Civilization can afford no compromise with the social forces which would gain renewed strength if we deal ambiguously or indecisively with the men in whom those forces now precariously survive.

The International Military Tribunal began on October 18, 1945, and concluded on October 1, 1946. Of the 22 men, 12 were sentenced to death, three were found not guilty, and the remainder were sent to prison. The Nazi Party leadership, the SS, the SA, and the Gestapo were condemned as criminal organizations. The Cabinet, the High Command, and the Army General Staff were not.

Clearly, not all who participated in the crimes could be tried—nor would even the entire leadership be tried. Instead, visible leaders who stood as representatives of the whole were tried.

Robert Jackson indicated what was at stake in the trial:

> *In the prisoners' dock sit twenty-odd broken men. . . . It is hard now to perceive in these miserable men as captives the power by which as Nazi leaders they once dominated much of the world and terrified most of it. Merely as individuals, their fate is of little consequence to the world.*
>
> *What makes this inquest significant is that these prisoners represent sinister influences that will lurk in the world long after their bodies have returned to dust. They are living symbols of racial hatreds, of terrorism and violence, and of the arrogance and cruelty of power. They are symbols of fierce nationalisms and of militarism, of intrigue and war-making. . . . They have so identified themselves*

What did these trials achieve? David Cesarani, a distinguished British historian, argued:

- They generated a massive record of the Nazi regime and accumulated the documents that would provide the basis of a history of the regime.
- They held the political echelon accountable in an international court, sitting before the court of world opinion, for the crimes committed in the planning and conduct of war.
- Obedience to superiors' orders was not accepted as an excuse, so both soldiers and civilians had to accept individual responsibility for carrying out the orders they were given.
- They satisfied the need for retribution, however inadequate and symbolic, and they preserved the facade of justice, the skeleton of civilization.

- In retrospect, but only in retrospect, Nuremberg was a useful model as to what to do in the aftermath of mass murder and genocide.
- Above all, they firmly established the concept of crimes against humanity.

After the first trial was concluded in 1946, a second series of trials at Nuremberg commenced in October 1946 and lasted until April 1949, with 177 defendants divided into 12 groups.

In the Doctors' Trial, physicians were tried for their participation in *Selektion,* murder, and medical experimentation. The medical experimentation received great attention—far more than participation of physicians in the so-called "euthanasia" program, which had resulted in the murder by 1941 of more than 70,000 Germans who had been deemed "life unworthy of living."

The trials of other professionals proved less groundbreaking, but still important. Judges were tried for their roles in the Nazi regime. They had preserved the facade of legality as a cloak for inhumanity. Some argued that they were merely enforcing the law without regard to the law that they were enforcing.

Otto Ohlendorf, the highly gifted economist, faced the docket. In riveting testimony, he described his role in the mobile killing units. Generals who led the armies that attacked civilians and disturbed the peace were held accountable. Rudolph Hoess, commandant of Auschwitz, was tried by a Polish court for the systematic murder that occurred in the camps under his watch. On April 16, 1947, he was hanged on a gallows erected adjacent to the gas chamber at Auschwitz I.

Proximity to the crime was a measure of one's responsibility. Officers of the *Einsatzgruppen,* concentration camp commandants, and doctors who presided over experiments were regarded as more culpable than those in the corporate and industrial structure that made their activities possible. The officers, commandants, and doctors were held accountable, whereas the architects who designed the camps, the engineers who modified the crematoria, and the chemists who made the gas were not. Industrialists were given lighter sentences. Thirty-five defendants were acquitted.

In the midst of the trials, international attention shifted to the Cold War—the struggle between the United States and the Soviet Union, capitalism and communism. To most Germans, these trials were victors' justice. The American government was eager to win over the Germans to their side because Germany was the most critical front in the Cold War—even more so after the Russians initiated the Berlin blockade of 1948. The trials soon became a nuisance, seen as the activities of idealist do-gooders after a difficult war. Not long after the trials ended, clemency boards were introduced, sentences were reduced, pardons were granted, and time off was given for good behavior.

By 1951 the high commissioner for Germany, John J. McCloy, who as U.S. assistant secretary of war had pushed for the war crimes trials in 1944, commuted death sentences and freed 77 Nazi officials, including the leading industrialists.

The trials touched only a few of those who perpetrated the crime—mostly top leaders whose roles were immediately visible. However, some trials continued.

- Trials were held in nearly every country in which the Holocaust occurred.
- War Crimes trials were conducted in the British Zone from 1945 to 1949, including trials of personnel of Bergen-Belsen, the concentration camp liberated by the British.
- French trials centered on what happened in France. After liberation, kangaroo courts gave way to actual trials over a nine-year period. The complicity of the Vichy regime was not addressed until decades later, when elderly leaders were brought to justice.

"Civilization can afford no compromise with the social forces which would gain renewed strength if we deal ambiguously or indecisively with the men in whom those forces now precariously survive."
—Robert Jackson, prosecutor at the Nuremberg Trials

- From 1949 to 1986, approximately 100,000 people were indicted in Germany on charges related to the Holocaust. Approximately 13,000 were tried, and about half were convicted. The most famous cases were of the death camp guards at Treblinka, Majdanek, and Auschwitz as well as the commandant of Sobibor and Belzec, Franz Stangl.

Israel, a country that did not exist when the crimes occurred, conducted two major trials on behalf of the Jewish people. The first was the Adolf Eichmann trial of 1961, which brought to the docket the effective Nazi bureaucrat responsible for the deportation of Jews and for the implementation of Nazi anti-Jewish policies. The proceedings took place in Jerusalem, where survivors were brought face to face with their tormentors. The testimony was riveting, and its impact on Israeli society was enormous. Widely covered in the press and with live radio broadcasts in Israel as well as internationally televised broadcasts, it also was a major element in the establishment of a worldwide consciousness of the Holocaust in the early 1960s.

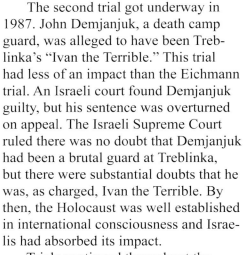

A film is screened as evidence during the trial of Adolf Eichmann, the SS official in charge of deporting Jews to their death; Jerusalem, Israel, June 8, 1961. Many survivors testified at and attended the trial.

The second trial got underway in 1987. John Demjanjuk, a death camp guard, was alleged to have been Treblinka's "Ivan the Terrible." This trial had less of an impact than the Eichmann trial. An Israeli court found Demjanjuk guilty, but his sentence was overturned on appeal. The Israeli Supreme Court ruled there was no doubt that Demjanjuk had been a brutal guard at Treblinka, but there were substantial doubts that he was, as charged, Ivan the Terrible. By then, the Holocaust was well established in international consciousness and Israelis had absorbed its impact.

Trials continued throughout the 20th century and into the first decade of the 21st. Yet most of those responsible escaped judgment.

Some Nazi officials established new identities in Germany and Austria. Others fled to South America. Some Nazi leaders sought refuge in the Middle East among the enemies of Israel. Still others availed themselves of Vatican help. It is estimated that 10,000 Nazi war criminals fled to the United States. Heralded as anti-Communists, they arrived through the front door with their papers in order.

The initial flurry of trials led to early actions by the United Nations. A Convention for the Preventions of Crimes of Genocide was adopted by the United Nations on December 9, 1948. A Universal Declaration of Human Rights followed the next day. Fearful of a loss of national sovereignty, the United States postponed the ratification of the Genocide Convention. Almost four decades after its adoption, the convention was finally ratified by the U.S. Senate in 1988, just months before President Ronald Reagan left office.

LEMKIN DEFINES "GENOCIDE"

Raphael Lemkin was a Jewish international lawyer educated in Poland, Germany, and France. Born in 1900, he was named secretary of the Court of Appeals in Warsaw in 1927 and participated in the Madrid Conference for the unification of penal law in 1933. Under increasing antisemitic pressure, he was forced to give up his official position. Most of his family was murdered in Warsaw, but Lemkin, who joined the Polish Underground, escaped.

Lemkin managed to secure a position at the University of Stockholm, where he lectured on international law. He began to assemble the legal decrees that the Nazis issued in each of the countries they occupied. In compiling these laws, he hoped to demonstrate the sinister ways in which law could be used to propagate hate and incite murder.

In April 1941, Lemkin arrived in the United States, where he immediately began to campaign to save the Jews of Europe. Combining his knowledge of international law, his aim of preventing atrocity, and his long-standing interest in language, Lemkin began searching for a name commensurate with the truth of his experience and that of millions. He would be the one to give the ultimate crime a name.

This name had to chill its listeners and invite immediate condemnation. It would be the rare term that carried in it society's revulsion and indignation. It would be what Lemkin called an "index of civilization."

The word he settled on was a hybrid that combined the Greek *geno,* meaning race or tribe, together with the Latin derivative *cide,* meaning killing. *Genocide* was short, it was novel, and because of the word's lasting association with Hitler's horrors, it would also send shudders down the spines of those who heard it.

In 1944 Lemkin published his book *Axis Rule in Occupied Europe: Laws of Occupation, Analysis of Government Proposals for Redress,* in which he first systematized the material under the new term *genocide.*

In 1946 Lemkin succeeded in mobilizing sufficient support to have genocide put on the agenda of the United Nations General Assembly. The Economic and Social Council invited him to present a draft convention. Assisted by Herbert V. Evatt, the Australian president of the General Assembly, Lemkin campaigned for its adoption by the UN, which unani-

Raphael Lemkin

mously accepted it on December 9, 1948. Genocide was defined as follows.

Any of the following acts committed with intent to destroy, in whole or in part, a national, ethnical, racial, or religious group, as such:

- *Killing members of the group;*
- *Causing serious bodily or mental harm to members of the group;*
- *Deliberately inflicting on the group conditions of life, calculated to bring about its physical destruction in whole or in part;*
- *Imposing measures intended to prevent births within the group;*
- *Forcibly transferring children of the group to another group.*

Lemkin overoptimistically assumed that the major powers were ready both to apply the word and oppose the deed. He described the pact as an "epitaph on his mother's grave" and as a recognition "that she and many millions did not die in vain."

Yet four decades would pass before the United States would ratify the convention, and 50 years would elapse before the international community would convict anyone of genocide.

DISPLACED PERSONS

Allied military leaders, who controlled the zones of occupation, were slow to understand the unique plight of the Jews.

A U.S. Army chaplain marries Ruth (Gold) Rontal and Cantor Moishe Rontal in Stuttgart, Germany in 1946.

As the war ended, Allied armies found millions of people displaced by the war from their countries of origin. Most returned home: Their communities and families were still intact; their homelands still welcomed them.

Many of those who remained could not return home. Some non-Jews— Poles, Estonians, Latvians, Lithuanians, Ukrainians, and Yugoslavs—feared political repercussions for their wartime activities. Some had collaborated; they had grown close to the Nazis, and now there was hell to pay. Some were fiercely anti-Communist and did not want to—or could not safely—live under Soviet rule.

The Jews' situation was different. Their communities had been destroyed, left desolate. Their homes, their businesses, their schools, and their synagogues had been either ravaged or occupied by others.

Many returned home briefly to search for surviving relatives. The reunions were heart-wrenching. Joyful to see those few who were alive, survivors also became even more mindful of those who had been killed.

Barbara Zyskind Steiner described her return to Warsaw:

I found no one. Nothing was left. Everything was gone. I couldn't find one person who knew me from before the war. I was a broken person, consumed with survivor's guilt, not wanting to live.

Pertle and Helen Herskovic, twin sisters from Czechoslovakia, returned home to discover who had survived. Their town was without Jews. A next-door neighbor took them in. Immediately, Helen noticed something familiar: The bedspreads had come from her home; the children were dressed in her clothes. "As soon as they took us away, there was looting. You know, even the best [looted]. Our house was ransacked." She did meet her brother, who survived, and her niece, then 14, who had pretended to be much older in order to survive.

A Russian Jewish soldier warned: "If you want to be free, go!"

They took his advice.

With nowhere to go, Jews fled to displaced-persons (DP) camps in the Western zone. Many others were forced to stay in camps adjacent to the sites of their liberation. Despondent, they had nothing except the clothes they were wearing. Few Jews could imagine living for an extended time within Germany, the very country that had sought to annihilate them.

Allied military leaders, who controlled the zones of occupation, were slow to understand the unique plight of the Jews. At first, Jewish DPs were quartered together with their non-Jewish countrymen, many of whom had collaborated in the murder of Jews. Army commanders seeking to solve the DP problem quickly through repatriation were frustrated by the Jewish survivors' fervent refusal to return to their former countries, which were drenched in Jewish blood. They could not understand

the anger and bitterness, or the physical condition, of the dispossessed Jews they encountered. As those who had fought against the Germans and liberated the camps were rotated home, new recruits came to take their places. They often found the Germans an attractive and cultured people and the survivors distrustful and alienating.

Moreover, what could the army do about the overwhelming immediate problems—food, sanitation, housing, and survivors' burning desire to discover the fates of their loved ones? Military officials had even less patience for the issues of psychological and physical recuperation or the question foremost in survivors' minds: What to do with their future. Where to go? How to get there? And how to survive in the world they would now encounter?

The Harrison Report

In the summer of 1945, President Harry Truman dispatched Earl Harrison, dean of the University of Pennsylvania Law School, to report on the Jewish DPs in the American zone of occupation. Harrison's report was harsh, perhaps even overstated: "As matters now stand, [we] appear to be treating Jews as the Nazis treated them, except that we do not exterminate them."

His recommendations were equally dramatic:

- Jews must be recognized as a distinct national group.
- They should be evacuated from Germany quickly.
- One hundred thousand Jews should be admitted to Palestine.

President Truman endorsed the report and rebuked the army—writing personally to General Dwight Eisenhower, the supreme Allied commander—and intensified pressure on Britain. He authorized DP immigration to America, within the existing quotas.

Meanwhile, former Jewish partisans and ghetto fighters in Eastern Europe operated *Brichah* (Flight), a clandes-

tine organization whose goal was to organize "illegal" immigration to Palestine. Led by Abba Kovner, they understood that the only hope for survival was in a Jewish homeland—in Palestine.

Survivors were desperate to resume their interrupted lives. Many were willing to undertake the dangerous journey to Palestine, which was closed to Jewish refugees, traveling clandestinely over mountains and seeking to elude the British navy at sea. *Brichah,* working with Palestinian soldiers of the Jewish Brigade, led the refugees to coastal areas where they embarked on ships supplied by a Zionist organization known as *Mossad Aliyah Bet,* (literally, Ascent to Israel B). Its counterpart, *Aliya Alef* (Ascent A) utilized legal means. Ascent B tried everything else.

In 1946 the Soviets allowed some 175,000 Jews who had fled to the Soviet Union to return to Poland. Like Jews liberated from the Nazi camps, these survivors quickly understood that nothing remained of the Jewish communities they had left behind. They realized that

Top: *Jewish survivors rest in the transit camp at the Rothschild Hospital in Vienna, Austria, in 1946. They were brought there by the* Brichah *(Flight) underground movement.* Above: *A Talmud printed for DPs by the* Vaad Hatzala *(Rescue Committee) and the U.S. Army; 1948.*

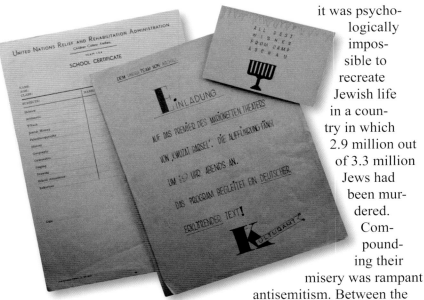

Above: *A school certificate, an invitation, and a Hanukah card from Dr. Gertrude Pollitt, who directed Camp Aschau (near Muhldorf, Germany), a displaced-persons camp that housed many Jewish children and teenagers; c. 1946.* Below: *Jewish demonstrators at the Bergen-Belsen, Germany, DP camp demand immigration to British-controlled Palestine; September 8, 1947.*

it was psychologically impossible to recreate Jewish life in a country in which 2.9 million out of 3.3 million Jews had been murdered. Compounding their misery was rampant antisemitism. Between the end of the war and the summer of 1946, hundreds of Jews were murdered throughout Poland. On July 4, 1946, a pogrom in Kielce claimed the lives of 42 Jews who had returned after the war.

The Kielce Pogrom resulted in a mass flight of some 100,000 Jews from Poland and neighboring countries. Organized by *Brichah,* and aided by sympathetic Jewish chaplains and by the U.S. Army's decision to receive them, they flooded the American and British zones of occupation. Yehuda Bauer, the noted Israeli Holocaust historian, concluded: "A total of 250,000 Holocaust survivors were moved by *Brichah* into Germany, Austria, and Italy with the aim of ultimately arriving at the coasts—the largest organized, illegal mass movement in the twentieth century."

Jews within the DP camps immediately organized themselves under the Hebrew name *She'erit Hapletah,* a biblical term meaning Surviving Remnant. With the establishment of separate Jewish DP camps following the Harrison Report, the Surviving Remnant took responsibility for running them. Committees in each camp looked after sanitation, hygiene, cultural activities, education, and religious life. More than 70 newspapers and journals were published. Commemoration and research projects on the Holocaust—then called *Churban* (Destruction)—were initiated, and a network of theaters and orchestras was established.

American Jewish chaplains—rabbis who were officers in the U.S. Army— used their good offices to assist the DPs. They cut through Army red tape and appealed to officers and enlisted men alike to provide for the survivors. Many were doing double duty: working for the U.S. Army and serving the GIs while working for their fellow Jews. The Army even assisted in the publication of a special edition of the Talmud to spur religious learning and boost Jewish morale.

The American Jewish community, which had been powerless during the war since it could not operate behind enemy lines, stepped in with full force. The American Jewish Joint Distribution Committee raised huge sums of money and sent enormous quantities of supplies and dedicated staff to work with the newly liberated Jews. ORT (Occupation, Rehabilitation, and Training), which had long worked with Jews who needed a fresh chance, operated in ways that fulfilled its original mission on a grand scale. The Jewish Brigade—Palestinian Jews who had enlisted in the British Army during World War II—brought the survivors hope and a new image of the Jew as a fighter. Together with emissaries sent from Palestine by the Jewish Agency, they organized youth organiza-

tions and Zionist movements in the DP camps. They taught Hebrew and skills needed for settlement in the Jewish homeland.

Zionism offered survivors a political ideology. Even if many were not to make the Jewish homeland their own home, they embraced its establishment as their cause.

In October 1945, David Ben-Gurion, the leader of the effort to build a Jewish state in Palestine, visited the displaced-persons camps. Major Irving Heymont, the commander of Landsberg, described the visit to his wife: "To the people of the camp, he is a god.... Never had I seen such energy displayed in the camps."

Rabbi Herbert Friedman, a U.S. Army chaplain, reported Ben-Gurion's words: "I come to you with empty pockets. I have no certificates [for entry into Palestine] for you. I can only tell you that you are not abandoned. You are not alone. You will not live endlessly in camps like this. All of you who want to come to Palestine will be brought there as soon as is humanly possible."

Hoping to influence the struggle to create a Jewish state, DPs organized mass demonstrations and created political movements to control their own lives and influence Allied policy.

In response to growing international pressure, the British called for an Anglo-American Commission of Inquiry, which consisted of six American and six British commissioners. Its members were deeply shocked by conditions in the camps and impressed by the DPs' desire to go to Palestine. They, too, recommended that 100,000 Jews be admitted immediately to Palestine. The British government demurred. Foreign Minister Ernest Bevin wryly commented: "The Americans wanted 100,000 Jews in Palestine because they didn't want them in New York."

Noar Zioni, *a Zionist youth group, marches during a Purim parade in the Landsberg, Germany, DP camp, in 1947.*

The British continued to impede immigration by seizing "illegal immigrant" ships. Passengers on captured ships bound for Palestine were interned in detention camps on Cyprus. The most controversial of these vessels was the *Exodus,* whose passengers were forcibly returned to Germany.

On December 22, 1945, President Truman authorized preferential treatment to DPs to immigrate to the United States. Within 18 months, 22,950 DPs were admitted to the U.S., 15,478 of them Jews.

Most DPs, however, wanted to live in the Jewish homeland. The United Nations voted on November 29, 1947, to support the creation of the Jewish state, and after the establishment of the State of Israel in May 1948, two-thirds of the DPs arrived in Israel. It took three years from the war's end, but finally the bulk of the survivors living in Germany were able to move elsewhere to begin new lives.

The Return to Life

Contrary to the prevalent image of them as "broken vessels," the Surviving Remnant was determined to rebuild Jewish life. Many quickly married, and there was an unprecedented baby boom. Romana Strochlitz Primus explained the mystery of her origin:

"You are not alone. You will not live endlessly in camps like this. All of you who want to come to Palestine will be brought there as soon as is humanly possible."

—David Ben-Gurion, addressing survivors in a displaced-persons camp

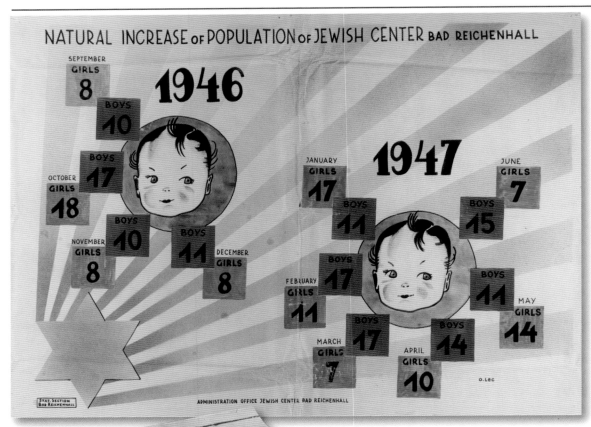

NATURAL INCREASE of POPULATION of JEWISH CENTER BAD REICHENHALL

1946

SEPTEMBER GIRLS 8
BOYS 10
BOYS 17
OCTOBER GIRLS 18
BOYS 10
NOVEMBER GIRLS 8
BOYS 11
DECEMBER GIRLS 8

1947

JANUARY GIRLS 17
BOYS 11
FEBRUARY GIRLS 11
BOYS 17
MARCH GIRLS 7
BOYS 17
APRIL GIRLS 10
BOYS 14
MAY GIRLS 14
BOYS 11
JUNE GIRLS 7
BOYS 15

STAT. SECTION BAD REICHENHALL

ADMINISTRATION OFFICE JEWISH CENTER BAD REICHENHALL

o.lec

Top: A poster illustrating the Jewish "baby boom" in the Bad Reichenhall, Germany, DP camp. Above: A Jewish New Year's card from Glika and Noah Scheinabum, who are pictured with their son, Leibel; Bergen-Belsen, Germany, 1947.

My parents, who had met briefly in Birkenau, were both liberated in Bergen-Belsen. My mother weighed 78 pounds and was delirious with typhus; she barely understood that she was liberated. My father weighed 88 pounds. They had lost their families, their communities, their way of life. And yet, I was born in a Bergen-Belsen DP camp less than 15 months after the liberation.

There was an intense need to begin life again. All alone without parents or siblings, many married quickly. Felicia Brenner described her marriage.

One man I met.... He was with my brother almost all the time. And

he helped me. And he said to me that my brother died of starvation at Buchenwald toward the end of the war. That was very hard....

And young couples were getting married, you know. And so, the Jewish boy and I—we got married. It was the first wedding done by a rabbi— the first wedding after the war.

For the fortunate, love followed the wedding. For most, the ties of desperation bound the couple together indelibly. Friends became family. In one DP camp, a parachute was made into a wedding dress. It was passed from bride to bride. Months later, children were born, boys were named for their murdered grandfathers or even for the brothers they were never to know. Girls were named for dead mothers or sisters that they, too, were never to know. Many boys were called Menachem (one who brings consolation) and girls Nechma (consolation), symbols of rebirth.

While some had learned from the war to hide their Jewishness and assimilate completely—even changing their religion and not even telling their children of their origin—most Jews openly embraced their past. Arnold Weider was a *Mohel*, a ritual circumciser. Together with his father, he traveled from DP camp to DP camp to circumcise newborn sons, and also boys born during the war, when the mark of circumcision would have been a death sentence.

SAMUEL R. HARRIS
1935–

How did a Polish Jewish child survive the Holocaust? By luck. By accident. Because of the help of so many. And because of the determination of but one person.

Szlamek Rzeznik (later known as Samuel R. Harris), the youngest of seven children, was born in Deblin, Poland. Sammy's father, Shmuel, was a scribe who penned Torah scrolls and created other Jewish ritual objects. His was a profession entrusted to pious and respected men.

Sammy's mother, Sheva, was the second of his father's wives—sister to his father's late first wife. Sammy's sister Sara, one and a half years older, was the closest in age. Older siblings David and Rosa were to play a central role in his survival.

As a child, Sammy suffered from polio, which afflicted his eyes, forcing him to spend many hours in darkness, often alone. Ironically, this affliction would help him survive. His illness strengthened the bond between his care-giving mother and her youngest son.

Sammy would often spend Sabbaths at his maternal grandparents' village home in Cholna, Poland, enjoying his large extended family. It was a life full of love—"love that carried me through," he recalled.

When the Germans invaded Poland on September 1, 1939, he was four—too young to understand the danger. The airplanes seemed wondrous until their bombs began to fall. Sammy saw tanks and soldiers, heard German songs, and witnessed beatings. Then came confinement, hunger, Jewish stars. Sister Rosa returned from Warsaw to join the family.

In late 1941, the Nazis started building the infrastructure for killing Jews—the death camps. In 1942, en route to the train that would bring ghettoized Jews to their deaths, his father pushed him out of line to run away with his sister Sara.

They found shelter on a Polish farm—in an outhouse, then a barn—before returning home to witness a gruesome sight: bodies piled in the street, stacked like cordwood. There had been no time—or effort—to bury the Jews who had been killed. Sammy saw movement in one pile and heard a child begin to cry. The boy had been trapped by the adults who had fallen upon him; the bullet had missed him. Sammy helped the boy climb out.

Sammy's sister Rosa gave the children to a Polish friend, who bravely protected them at the risk of her life. The woman's husband, however, objected and threatened to turn the children over to the Nazis. Sara and Sammy had to be split up, and Sammy was hidden with other Jews in a potato cellar. He found safety, but only for a short time.

With nowhere to hide, he was taken back to the Jewish quarter of Demblin, now more a concentration camp than a ghetto. Sammy slept on bunks with adults, but the anxiety so affected him that he was afraid to go out at night, and began wetting his bed. He was uncomfortable and ashamed. By day, when others worked, Sammy hid.

In Demblin, his sister Rosa fell in love with a Viennese Jew, Walter, whose ability to speak German greatly enhanced his odds of survival, because the Germans needed translators. All the while, trains passed Demblin—trains filled with Jews en route to their deaths.

With the front collapsing in the fall of 1944, the remaining Jews of Demblin were transported to Czestochowa. Facing selection, Sammy stood on his tiptoes. But since he was only nine, he was not needed in a work camp. Upon arrival, Sammy was separated from his older sister and taken away to be killed along with four other children. Among them was the child of a man who was well connected with the Germans and able to garner his child's release. The father upped the ante: all the children or none. The German officer shrugged, and Sammy was saved from death.

Sammy was able to go into the Czestochowa concentration camp, where he was passed from prisoner to prisoner, many of whom had lost their own children. Few of them had held a child for many months, if not years. Because of his size and his ability to appear inconspicuous, Sammy was useful to the inmates: He could crawl into small places and steal potatoes.

It was from Czestochowa that he was liberated.

With Walter and his sisters, he returned home to Demblin, but the town felt unsafe. So they returned to Walter's home in Vienna, where Sammy was placed in an orphanage with Sara while Walter and Rosa tried to reestablish their lives. The young couple struggled to raise the children as their own, but they reluctantly concluded that the children would be better off in the United States—where they were sent for adoption.

Arriving in New York, Sammy was sent to Chicago, where he was adopted by Dr. Ellis Harris, a respected Northbrook pediatrician, and his wife, Harriet Golden

Harris. (Sara was also adopted by a Chicago family.) Sammy attended Crestwood Elementary School in Northbrook and New Trier High School in Winnetka. He was a Boy Scout and athlete, diligent in his studies, intense in athletic competition. High school was followed by college and a career, marriage and fatherhood. He had put his past behind him—or so he thought.

Sammy's wife, Dede, understood that something was missing. Samuel R. Harris had constructed his identity apart from the story of Szlamek Rzeznik, the Sammy he once was.

The World Gathering of Jewish Holocaust Survivors, a 1981 reunion of 5,000 survivors in Jerusalem, enabled him to reconnect with many with whom he shared painful memories—and to experience pride as a survivor.

A pilgrimage home to Demblin, to Czestochowa, and to his grandfather's village again allowed him to reconnect. He joined the Illinois Holocaust Museum and began to speak of his past. He is now the president of the museum, and it has been under his leadership that the new building has been created and the new exhibition launched.

Szlamek and Samuel feel connected; the life is one. The journey is now whole as Sammy's past speaks to the present and the present to the future.

> ## Sammy was separated from his older sister and taken away to be killed along with four other children.

Szlamek (Harris) (front row, far right) with boys at his orphanage; Lublin, Poland, c. 1946.

NEW HOMES: ISRAEL AND NORTH AMERICA

"**N**ow what?" was the question on the minds of nearly all survivors.

They had survived. Many quickly learned of their loved ones' fates, but others would not learn what had happened until years had passed. Of those, a few very lucky survivors would learn, decades later, that someone who they had presumed had died—including the closest of relatives—had in fact survived.

They had begun a long process of physical recovery: eating again, gaining weight, recapturing their health, and restoring their vitality. Then came the even longer process of psychological recovery. Essential to that recovery was finding answers to several questions:

"Where shall I go?"

"What shall I do?"

"With whom will I share my future?"

For child survivors, there was catching up to do. Their education had been interrupted. Teenagers had last been in school in third or fourth grade; some 10- or 11-year-olds had never been to school. Adult survivors who had lost years urgently wanted to make up for lost time.

Survivors felt a particular urgency to decide where they would live, for it was clear to most Eastern European Jews that they could not return home. Their communities had been destroyed and their homes inhabited by others who did not welcome their return.

Lucine Horn described her situation: "We did not want to stay in Poland too long. I felt that every stone had blood on it and every wall had memories for me."

It didn't matter to Aaron Elster where he went. "I wanted to go any-place. I wanted to go to America. I wanted to go to Israel. I mean I would go anyplace."

Joseph Hausner said of his native country of Hungary: "I felt that my former home country of which I was a loyal citizen betrayed me. . . . Instead of defending me, [it] handed me over to the enemy for annihilation. So it broke the contract. So I was under no obligation to go back and I didn't."

Sergeant William Best greets 19-year-old relative Joseph Guttman, a survivor of Buchenwald; New York City December 24, 1948.

They would not stay in Germany, living among their tormentors, the killers of their families, in the land of their oppression.

They would not stay in Germany, living among their tormentors, the killers of their families, in the land of their oppression.

Walter Thalheimer, a native of Germany, whose father had been deeply patriotic, told it simply: "We decided that we would never go back to Germany after what the Germans did to us."

Most survivors wanted to go to one of two places: Palestine, which in 1948 became the independent state of Israel, or the United States, primarily for family and financial reasons.

The United States held little ideological pull but great psychological

The Aliyah Bet *refugee ship* Exodus, *bound for Palestine in 1947.*

attraction. Many chose the United States because they had relatives there already. Moreover, in the land of opportunity, they could live in freedom and comfort, resume their lives, and—in time, they hoped—prosper.

Israel

Palestine, on the other hand, was ideologically attractive. The events of World War II had given added impetus to the Zionist analysis of the Jewish condition. Jews were a distinct people. They sought normality, not as a minority within majority cultures that would tolerate their existence—or, more positively, respect and accept it—but in their own land, where Jews could be a majority and enjoy freedom, democracy, and independence. Theodore Herzl, the 19th century founder of political Zionism, sought to make the Jewish people a nation like any other nation—with its own language, flag, and land, protected by an army of its own.

In their postwar German captivity—or German exile, as they described it—Jews in displaced-persons camps had prepared themselves for life in Palestine. Jews originally from urban areas learned how to farm and their children learned Hebrew. They held political demonstrations on behalf of the Jewish state. And survivors were willing to risk their freedom once again in order to immigrate to Palestine.

Brichah (Flight) was a Zionist group established by survivors. It was aided by the Jewish Brigade, which had fought with the British against Germany, as well as by operatives from Palestine and European Jews yearning to move there. As Jews arrived in Germany's American and British sectors from Soviet-occupied territory, *Brichah* organized their mass migration to Palestine—especially after the July 1946 Kielce pogrom made it evident how precarious life would be in Poland.

The *Mossad,* the forerunner of Israel's secret intelligence agency, organized clandestine sea voyages to Palestine. Its members sought to escape detection by the British Navy, which would arrest passengers and crew and incarcerate them in nearby Cyprus or return them to Europe. *Mossad Aliyah Bet* (Ascent B) employed extralegal means because the British, who controlled Palestine at the time, were unwilling to allow mass Jewish migration to Palestine.

Zev Rogalin, a Lithuanian Jew, described his experience:

We went to their place to be organized and they brought us to Santa Tazzaria and we stayed there as a school and as a preparatory time until we left for Israel. And the idea that we leave Italy to Israel as a group, and settle in Israel as a group, creating a new settlement, it sounded for us just as ideal as it could be.

The time we spent in Santa Tazzaria was spent between teaching the Hebrew language to a lot of youngsters that survived. . . . I was among the oldest among this group, and they made me right away a madrich, *a counselor.*

On November 29, 1947, the United Nations voted to end the British mandate over Palestine. On May 14, 1948, David Ben-Gurion proclaimed the State of Israel. In its Declaration of Independence, the newly founded State of Israel saw itself neither as consolation for the *Churban* (the great destruction, now called the Shoah), nor as compensation by the world for the destruction of two out of three European Jews, but as an opportunity to create conditions Jews had not known. In part, the declaration asserted:

The catastrophe which recently befell the Jewish people—the massacre of millions of Jews in

The refugee ship Exodus after its capture at sea by British forces in the Haifa port. These survivor passengers were forcibly returned to Europe; July 18, 1947.

Europe—was another clear demonstration of the urgency of solving the problem of its homelessness by reestablishing in Eretz-Israel [the historic land of Israel] the Jewish State, which would open the gates of the homeland wide to every Jew and confer upon the Jewish people the status of a fully privileged member of the comity of nations.

The Surviving Remnant of the Nazi Holocaust in Europe, as well as Jews from other parts of the world, continued to migrate to Eretz-Israel, undaunted by difficulties, restrictions, and dangers. They never ceased to assert their right to a life of dignity, freedom, and honest toil in their national homeland.

From 1934 to 1948, some 130,000 Jews—nearly one in four immigrants—came to Palestine in violation of British law. Some 104,000 of these immigrants arrived on 136 boats, and the remainder took difficult land routes. From 1939 onward, when Jews were most desperate for a place to go, the British government issued a White Paper that restricted Jewish immigration to 15,000 per year.

From the moment of Israel's independence, all restrictions on Jewish immigration ended. In a few days, two ships, the *State of Israel* and *To Victory,* arrived, filled with Holocaust survivors now coming to a state that was being attacked by its neighbors. Within days, the newly established government began the evacuation of the camps in Cyprus and the DP camps in Europe. It also began an intensive recruitment effort for the Israel Defense Forces (IDF) among the young and able-bodied survivors, some of whom had fought in the Allied armies or as partisans. Resistance fighters from Warsaw and Vilna soon fought in Jerusalem and the Negev. About two-thirds of the displaced persons, some 200,000, immigrated to Israel.

In 1950 Israel passed the Law of Return, granting Jews immediate citizenship upon their arrival. Once unwanted everywhere, Jews now had a country willing to open its borders to them. Israel offered itself as a haven to Jews fleeing persecution. Under the Law of Return, Jews fleeing Khomeini's Iran, starvation in Ethiopia, political instability in Argentina, and persecution in the Soviet Union would find freedom in Israel.

Some survivors were unwilling to come to Israel. They did not want to go from one war to another. Many others saw the urgency and viewed this new battle in historical terms. Max Epstein—a survivor of the Lodz ghetto, of Auschwitz, and of the death marches—was studying at the *Technion,* Israel's Israel's Institue of Technology, when

Zev Rogalin (right) and his friend as members of the Israeli Army; Israel, 1949.

he was recruited to join the *Haganah,* Israel's pre-state underground defense force.

Max understood, as did others around him, that this was a historic event, to change the powerlessness of the Jewish people by establishing a secure and independent Jewish state. For Max, it was a turning point: "We were participating in an event that happens once in 2,000 years." The Jewish people had last been independent in the year 70 C.E., some 2,000 years before.

Arrival and New Challenges

Eva Mozes (Kor), who had been a Mengele twin—the subject of medical experiments by Dr. Mengele in Auschwitz—described her arrival:

The ship pulled up into Haifa early morning. People started singing Hatikvah ["The Hope," the Zionist anthem] and the sun rising, it was just the most beautiful thing that I can remember. It was just like welcoming us. Many people got off the ship and kissed the ground, crying.

Moshe Shamir also recalled being overwhelmed by coming to Israel:

When we arrived in Israel—how shall I describe to you the feeling, my feeling, and the feelings of most of us, to see the Carmel Mountains? No sooner did we disembark that we saw for the first time a Jewish policeman.... A policeman who said "Shalom."

Elaine Mortkovic Welbel remembered how she felt when she arrived in Palestine: "I finally reached the Holy Land. It was sand; I had landed on a beach. I bent down and kissed the ground. It felt good."

She had arrived in Palestine from Naples after a harrowing 10-day trip on a small fishing boat overloaded with 180 passengers. She had to stay below deck in the August heat because the ship feared detection by the British Navy blockade. Traveling with her husband, she became separated from him briefly upon arrival. He went to a cousin's home and she was sent to a family. She remembered: "Right away dinner and a hot shower and a bed, clean white sheets. My God, I hadn't seen a bed for many, many years." Reunited with her husband, she then found her sister:

Can it be this lady is my sister? I haven't seen her for many years. I was a little girl when she left. But I say: "Sounds like my sister." So then I answer: "Rose."

She hears me and she says, "Are you my sister?"

"Yes, Rose, that's me, that's me."

We hugged, we kissed, we cried and then she tells me: "Tell me! Tell me about you. What happened?"

"They killed everybody. Nobody's alive, I am the only one."

For many Jews, the birth of the State of Israel just three years after the Holocaust was—and remains—the most significant positive consequence of the Holocaust, a moment of consolation that gave rise to the hope that the Jewish future would be different.

Historians believe that the Jewish state would have been born eventually because of the efforts of Jewish nationalism to return the Jewish people to the historic land of Israel. Clearly, survivors in DP camps increased worldwide support and sympathy for the Jewish state and hastened its formation. Yet Israel is not an answer to the Holocaust. Its formation could not undo the horror of the death camps. To assign Israel such a role places an unbearable burden on the Israelis, whose very conduct and continued survival must redeem the irredeemable evil of the Holocaust.

Ruth Rontal speaks at a community celebration for Israel's birth; Chicago, 1948.

The United States

Lisa and Aron Derman were young Zionists who wanted to go to Palestine, but they were unwilling to wait to resettle. They intended on staying in the United States temporarily for the most simple of reasons. Each had relatives here—the only family they had. Their temporary stay in Chicago lasted a lifetime.

Fritzie Fritzshall's father had immigrated to Chicago before the war. Like many Eastern European immigrants, he had come in anticipation of bringing his family and had sent for them just before the war. Fritzie's mother could not imagine what was to happen. She was hesitant to cross the dangerous Atlantic Ocean when ships were being shot at. Her mother and siblings were killed in Auschwitz. Her father sent papers as soon as he discovered that she was alive.

Zora Goldberger's experience was very different:

Before we came, you had to have an affidavit because they didn't let us go otherwise. So, my husband found a telephone book, and he took all Goldbergers. He wrote about . . . a hundred letters . . . all

Once unwanted everywhere, Jews now had a country willing to open its borders to them. Israel offered itself as a haven to Jews fleeing persecution.

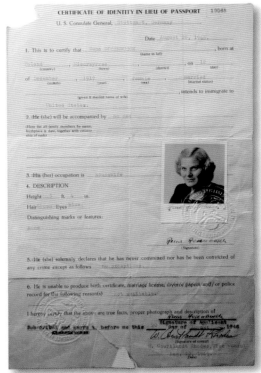

A Certificate of Identity in Lieu of Passport. This was issued to Rena Rosenbusch by the U.S. Consulate General in Stuttgart, Germany; August 20, 1946.

over the United States. And we got some replies. Sorry, but they don't have any relatives in Europe.... But one family from Chicago, Alfred Goldberger, wrote us. It was a beautiful letter. He says: "We are not related, because our grandparents were born in the United States. But from this day, we consider you like a relative, and we are going to be happy to help you...."

The United States was not especially welcoming for new immigrants. The 1924 quota system was still in place, restricting immigrants on the basis of the 1890 census. Though there were labor shortages during World War II, no one could know how the American economy would perform with millions of young soldiers returning home and entering the workforce.

As noted, President Harry Truman did what he could within the limits of the immigration laws. On December 22, 1945, he granted preferential treatment to displaced persons. Over the next 18 months, 22,950 DPs were admitted; two out of three were Jews. The problem of the Surviving Remnant could not be solved by tinkering with the quota system, and there was little support in the public even for doing that. Even the staunchly pro-immigrant American Friends Service Committee (Quakers) was hesitant to press. One of its leaders said:

> Now that immigration to this country is not a matter of actual rescue from persecution or danger... we feel that plans for immigration should be given careful consideration and weighed against all possible alternatives of return to the native country, remaining in the country of current residence, or possible migration to other countries.

The refugee situation got even more difficult in 1946, when the Soviet Union allowed Polish Jews who had found refuge in the Soviet Union to be repatriated, and after the pogrom in Kielce, Poland, when President Truman and American military officials allowed Jews escaping from Soviet-occupied zones into American and British zones of occupation. These Jews lingered in DP camps.

There was an intense political struggle to admit more DPs. Even some within the Jewish community opposed the idea, believing that the presence of displaced Jews on European soil would only increase support for the establishment of a Jewish state in Palestine that was willing to receive these refugees. The British demurred. One British leader commented sarcastically on an American proposal to open Palestine to 100,000 Jews, saying "100,000 Jews in Palestine means 100,000 less Jews on the streets of New York or Paris."

In 1948 Congress passed a bill that provided for the admission of 205,000 refugees over two years. Truman called it "flagrantly discriminatory against Jews." In 1950 the act was amended to make it slightly less discriminatory. But by then most Jewish DPs had gone to Palestine.

Arrival in the United States

What was it like for the new arrivals?

Adam Starkopf arrived with his wife and young daughter. They had escaped from the Warsaw ghetto and had passed themselves off as non-Jews in Poland. He recalled:

> Joanne, our daughter, was holding onto my wife's, Pella's, skirt or dress. "Mommy, Mommy, are they killing here? Are they killing here people, too? Are they killing people?" So she said, "No, darling, this is a free country. They

don't kill anybody here. You see the Statue of Liberty here?"

Sam Harris was a young orphan who arrived in the United States. He remembered:

I knew what the Statue of Liberty was. I couldn't speak English well. I did learn on the ship three words. And they were "Yes," "No," and "Coca-Cola."...And I remember leaning on the railing, slowly approaching, seeing in the distance, this lady of freedom...and just...approaching a new world with tall buildings, lots of water and land.

Frank Shurman described his arrival in the United States, speaking perhaps literally as well as metaphorically: "After complete blackout and darkness, we came to this city of light and light and light."

New York of 1946 was so very different than the Europe he had left:

I had never seen a skyscraper. And here were these skyscrapers and thousands of cars riding up and down. And people fast talking; all somehow seemed to have a goal in life, and I was arriving, and I didn't know which way to turn. I didn't have any mishpucha *[family].*

To Talk but Not to Be Heard

Many survivors remember that although they were prepared to tell of their experiences, Americans were not prepared to listen. Irene Poll, who had been rescued in France, recalled:

When I came here, and I wanted to talk about what I saw there, nobody wanted to listen. Everybody just said, "You're here now. You're safe. Have a good time." I

Meyer Rubinstein (center,, his wife, Esther (right), their son, Harry, and an unidentified employee in front of the Rubinsteins' family grocery store at 357 S. Pulaski; Chicago, 1956.

didn't even know what a good time was.

Ernest Katz concurs:
They didn't want to hear about our plights, what happened in Europe. They kept saying, "Forget about it. Forget about it. Don't talk about it anymore. It's gone. You have to forget about that."

Other survivors are less charitable in their recollection. Roman Kent, a survivor of Lodz and Auschwitz, remembers that when he started to speak of the camps, he would be silenced. "We suffered plenty during the war," he was told. "We couldn't get meat, and gasoline was rationed."

New Challenges

Each survivor faced a brand new challenge. Sam Harris remembered:
I was taken to a foster home in Chicago, 7730 Marquette Street.... And I went to school. And started to learn English, started to learn how to catch a ...

baseball. [We never] had a baseball in Europe. And no one had soccer here. So, I learned—tried to learn—all the customs, the food, the language.

Helen Rappaport described her efforts to learn English:
I never stopped reading. Everybody said only that way you will learn how to spell and to read and to talk a little bit if you will read a newspaper. Every day I was commuting from Gary to Chicago; and the paper was always in my hands. And to this day I have to have the paper every single day.

Irene Poll did not realize how difficult it was to recover:
When my children were small and went to nursery school, my nursery school teacher said, "I have a problem with your children." And she came to the house, and we talked for a while, and she said, "I have the answer." And I said, "What was the problem?" She said, "Your children do not smile." I had not smiled. I had forgotten to smile. I put myself in front of the mirror, and I actually learned to smile. I knew how to laugh, but not smile. So that was something I had to teach myself again.

In Poland, Leo Malamed had spoken Yiddish at home and Polish to non-Jews in the streets. As a child refugee in Shanghai in Japanese-occupied China, he heard Chinese spoken in the streets and Yiddish spoken at home. He came to Chicago after the war and again lived in two worlds, speaking two languages:
I became a Chicago resident, living my life as a child growing up

U.S. Certificates of Naturalization. These were issued to Holocaust survivors who made their new homes in Chicago.

in the inner city of Chicago at first. I was a refugee, and it was a little difficult, but by the time I hit high school, I lost my accent. I was one of the guys. And I grew up as anybody having been born to Chicago without any real difference. No one cared. I certainly didn't wear it on my shoulder. . . . [But] in the house, I was very much different. I was in the Yiddish world. My parents remained in the Yiddish world. I recited Yiddish poetry. I grew up with Yiddish culture and Yiddish organizations and remain so to this day. I was in the theater. I was a Yiddish actor. . . . I was on radio. But outside of the home and outside of that circle, I was no different. In fact, no one even knew of my Yiddish existence.

Americanization

Lala Fishman recalled what the process of becoming American was like for her:

The first thing everybody asked: "How do you like America?. . . I was trying to put the bad memories, whatever I went through, the nightmare, I was trying to put it in the back of my mind. And I was trying to become Americanized. . . . I had my children, I brought them up here.

For some, America was a land of dreams, dreams that could sometimes overtake nightmares. Margaret Oppenheimer remembered:

This is what kept me alive. All the while I was in camp, I said, "I want to be a nurse.". . . And my dream was fulfilled. I worked 25 lovely years in the hospital here. It was the time of my life. My dream.

Survivors were determined, ambitious. They had to make up for lost time. Lucine Horn said:

We decided that this is our country, we are going to live here, there's no going back, there's no

complaining; we have to become American citizens. We have to take the opportunity that this country has given us.

Rabbi Herman Roth told of his first job interview:

I went for the first interview as a rabbi in a small town called Woodbine, New Jersey. It's about a hundred miles from New York. A small town: The rabbi had to be chief, cook, and bottle washer. I had to be a teacher also. But we have to be with the youth group to play baseball. [They asked:] "Do you know how to play baseball?" I said, "No. I don't know how to play baseball." So I didn't get the job.

Rabbi Herman Schaalman remembers the moment he felt at home in his new home:

The adjustment to America became ever more natural. There was a moment when I dreamt in English. And I knew I now belonged here.

Top: Holocaust survivor Rabbi Tzvi Hirsch Meisels (center) stands under a chuppah (Jewish bridal canopy) during the wedding of Yetta Abramovitz and Shaya Abramovitz; Chicago, 1969. Above: A Division of Americanization First Certificate for Thekla Koch, a German Jewish survivor; Chicago, June 18, 1952.

MAX EPSTEIN

1925–

Max Epstein was born in Lodz, Poland, an industrial textile center known as the Manchester of Eastern Europe. His father, Israel Epstein, owned a lumberyard. Max's mother, Dola Grad, was born in Grodno, in Belorussia.

An ardent Zionist, Israel Epstein enrolled Max in an expensive, private high school that blended instruction in general studies with Hebrew-language study of the Bible and Jewish history and religion. Had they not been Jewish, many of his highly educated teachers would have qualified for faculty positions at universities.

The depression of the 1930s brought Israel Epstein from comfortable prosperity to near poverty. Just after returning from summer camp in 1939, Max found himself in a city occupied by Germany. Beginning on September 9, 1939, everything changed. Students and teachers began to disappear—due to escape, deportation, or "liquidation."

On May 1, 1940, Lodz's ghetto was sealed. Schools remained open but with a decreasing number of students and teachers—absences now were caused by death from hunger and disease or, periodically, because of deportations. In September 1941, the schools closed and everybody joined the labor-force ghetto factories. A German organization managed the ghetto and offered only starvation rations.

Max worked first in a leather factory, then in a statistical office and eventually in a plant for the production and repair of telephones. He read voraciously to escape reality, educating himself in the process.

The ghetto's *Judenrat* (Jewish Council) was chaired by Mordecai Chaim Rumkowski, who early on assumed dictatorial powers. Ghetto currency was printed with his image on it. Rumkowski believed that by turning the ghetto into an effective work camp to serve vital German interests, he could save many (though surely not all) of the Jews. He made the tortuous decision to agree to deport the so-called "unproductive": the elderly and, in September 1942, all children under 14. Without children, Max recalled, the ghetto lost any semblance of normality. It felt like a labor camp.

Unable to reconcile with the world around him, Israel Epstein, then in his 50s, simply closed the shutters; he didn't want to see out. He worked for a while in a lumberyard in the ghetto, then—after the trauma of September 1942—fell ill, dying of hunger and disease in January 1943. Max's mother, considerably younger, worked in a kitchen from the inception of the ghetto, but she was so afraid of being caught stealing food that she had to watch her husband die of hunger. All of Max's uncles, aunts, and cousins died of hunger and disease or were deported.

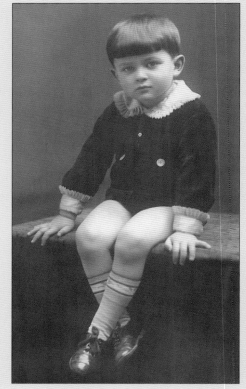

Rumkowski's gamble almost paid off, as the Lodz ghetto—among the first to be established in Poland—became the last to be destroyed. "Liquidated" was the term the Nazis used. The ghetto fell in August 1944, almost two years after most of Poland's other ghettos. The remaining Jews of Lodz were deported, primarily to Auschwitz. On August 19, 1944, Max and his mother were sent by cattle car to Auschwitz, where they were separated. During the three-day journey, they went without food and water in unbearable August heat.

Max was sent from Auschwitz to Sachsenhausen and several other camps. He was liberated at the end of the war while on a transport through Czechoslovakia. He lived and worked in Prague until the late summer of 1945. In early May, he traveled for a few days to Lodz seeking his mother, but without success.

After wiring two uncles in the United States, he learned that his mother had survived. She was liberated from a concentration camp in Austria and transferred by the members of the Jewish Brigade in the British army to Italy for the purpose of illegal immigration to Palestine.

After a month's journey through Germany, Austria, and Italy, Max was reunited with his mother in Italy on September 15, 1945. That December, they left Italy on an "illegal" ship to Palestine. A fishing boat built for 50, the ship contained 950 passengers, mostly survivors (Max was the only one with a mother). For two weeks, everyone had to hide below deck for fear of being discovered by British planes. Eventually the British navy intercepted the ship. The passengers were interned briefly and then allowed to enter the country.

First settling on a kibbutz, they left in 1947 for the city of Haifa. Max began his studies at the Technion, the MIT of Israel.

First in the *Haganah* (a Jewish underground military organization in British Palestine) and then in the newly established Israeli army, Max participated in Israel's War of Independence—an experience he would consider the most significant in his life.

They gave me a gun and they let me participate in a war as a soldier in a free country. While you may think it strange that is I am thanking a society for sending me to war, in effect, they did the best thing they could have done for me psychologically. In my quest for normalcy, this was the most effective catharsis.

Max participated in Israel's War of Independence—an experience he would consider the most significant in his life.

Max as a member of the Israeli Army; Israel, 1948.

Max understood, as did others around him, that this was a historic event, to change the fate of the Jewish people and to establish and secure an independent Jewish state. For Max it was a turning point: "We were participating in an event that happens once in 2,000 years."

With the reopening of the universities, Max continued his studies at the Technion and graduated in 1952. That autumn, he immigrated with his mother to the United States. Max continued graduate studies at the Illinois Institute of Technology (IIT) in Chicago, where he worked as an instructor and research engineer. He completed his studies in 1958 and received his doctorate in 1963. He continued to work at the IIT Research Institute until 1967, when he joined the faculty of Northwestern University and remained there as professor of electrical and biomedical engineering.

MARGOT WIND SCHLESINGER

1918–

Maria Miriam (Margot) Wind was born in Berlin. Though her deeply religious father, Jacob, wanted his four sons to be educated, he was indifferent to the education of his two daughters. Jacob studied Talmud at a daily *shiur* (lesson) and was well respected as a *talmid chacham,* a master of Jewish religious tradition. Margot's mother, Sabine Sima, was "a bit more modern," recalled Margot, pushing for her daughters to receive an education as well.

Margot graduated from the eighth grade at age 14, just before the Nazis came to power in 1933. Unable to continue in school, she had to find a job in a Jewish company—and got one as a cutter in a firm that designed lingerie and beachwear.

Athletic, Margot swam and played all sorts of sports. She also loved attending the theater and frequenting coffeehouses. Just as her teenage years were coming to an end, she was forced to give up many of these "luxuries." German theaters were closed to Jews; so were non-Jewish sports clubs. In response, Jews organized their own theaters throughout Germany, and Jewish sports clubs played against each other. Teams mixing Jews and "Aryans," if not yet illegal, were no longer comfortable. One day, her brother came home with a bloody nose; he avoided a worse fate only because one German had stood up for him: "Stop, he's my friend."

Margot lost her job in November 1938, when laws forced Jews to sell their businesses at distressed prices to "Aryan" owners. Her family dispersed in the late 1930s, just before the war. One brother went to Palestine, two immigrated to the United States, and the last went to Shanghai, China, then under Japanese occupation and a haven that would draw some 17,000 Jewish refugees.

Margot's Polish-born father was expelled from Germany along with his remaining children, who—though born in Germany—were not citizens. The Winds were caught in no-man's land: Their German papers were no longer valid, and Poland did not welcome back its Jewish citizens. Finally, they were able to get to Tarnow, Poland.

There Margot met young Chaskel Schlesinger, a successful businessman. While living under German occupation, Chaskel registered as a locksmith, believing that specific skills would make his life less dispensable and increase his chances to live.

When the deportations began in June 1942, Chaskel—smitten with Margot—warned the Wind family to hide. Margot's father would not hear of it, but Margot hid for several days. To secure her safety upon her return to Tarnow, Chaskel boldly forged documents stating she was his wife— in the hope that his own papers would protect her.

When Margot came back to Tarnow, her parents' home was sealed and she went to stay with Chaskel and his brother Chaim. New, smaller ghetto boundaries were established, placing the Schlesingers' apartment outside the ghetto but the Wind apartment inside. The Schlesinger brothers and Margot lived with four other people in increasingly crowded and desperate conditions.

Chaskel got a break. Through a friend employed by a German clothing firm, he was asked to organize a branch of the firm in Tarnow. His new position enabled him to go outside the ghetto and thus, with money—and by daring—he was able to secure food. In July 1942,

Margot and Chaskel were formally married by a rabbi. They worked for the German firm from August 1942 to September 1943, the most intense time in the murders of Polish Jews. Six death camps were in operation, some killing as many as 50,000 Jews a month.

As the final deportations from Tarnow were about to begin, Chaskel built a false wall and hid 72 people. But he could not elude capture. Margot, Chaskel, and Chaim were deported to Plaszow, the labor camp near Krakow under the boot of notorious commandant Amon Goeth. They remained there from September 1943 to October 1944.

Through connections, Chaskel was able to secure a place for himself, Margot, and Chaim on "Schindler's List." Oskar Schindler was a Sudeten German war profiteer who became increasingly hostile to the Nazi treatment of the Jews. He eventually saved the lives of some 1,200 Jews who worked for him. His motive was not simple altruism, at least at the beginning. He wanted to secure skilled workers from Plaszow and thus expand his business. Margot was number 233 on the list.

When Margot and other women were taken to Auschwitz, Schindler followed them into the death camp and secured their release so that they could continue to work for him. He moved his enamelworks to Brunnlitz, in his native Sudetenland (formerly Czechoslovakia), now operating it as an armaments factory.

When Margot and other women were taken to Auschwitz, Schindler followed them into the death camp and secured their release so that they could continue to work for him.

Margot and Chaskel Schlesinger; 1946.

Margot remembered with fond admiration Schindler's wife, Emilie, whom she described as beautiful and gentle.

Chaskel, Margot, and Chaim worked in Brunnlitz until May 9, 1945, when a Russian arriving on horseback announced their liberation. They moved in with a German woman who wanted the young Jews as protection. Margot made herself a blouse and skirt and once again felt human.

The group went back to Tarnow, but Margot could not find many people she knew from before the war. Chaskel and Margot returned to Krakow, and in September 1945 they arrived in France. They obtained visas to America to join Margot's relatives. They journeyed to Chicago, settling in East Rogers Park. Their three children attended Jewish day schools and received an intensive Jewish education.

For many years, Margot did not share her experience. But in 1982, after her rabbi expressed interest in Thomas Keneally's book on Schindler (a decade before Steven Spielberg's famous film), Margot began to speak. She was interviewed by her own daughter, who worked for the radio station WBBM, and made presentations in the Chicago public schools for the Facing History and Ourselves Program.

"I cannot forgive, but to hate will only eat me up—and life is too short to hate because it makes yourself sick," she said. "As long as you are alive and you are a person, you have hope."

THE PLANNED NAZI MARCH ON SKOKIE

In October 1976, Frank Collin, the leader of a Nazi group called the National Socialist Party of America (NSPA), requested permission to march in Skokie. Earlier, the Chicago Park District had denied his request to march in Marquette Park. After searching for alternatives, he chose Skokie because it was home to a large number of Jews. Among its 70,000 residents, some 40,000 were Jews—7,000 of them Holocaust survivors. Lacking much money or support, he hoped to garner free media publicity by demonstrating there.

Skokie was a quiet residential neighborhood in the near-north suburbs of Chicago, the type of place in which little happened that was controversial or momentous. It had been 31 years since the survivors' liberation from the camps—decades since they had resettled in the United States, struggling to adjust to their new home.

Collin circulated pamphlets titled "We Are Coming!" that stated, "... our successful opposition to the Black invasion of Southwest Chicago will now be turned on the culprits who started it all: the Jews!"

In an interview with a Chicago journalist, Collin said, "I hope they're terrified. I hope they're shocked. Because we're coming to get them again.... The unfortunate thing is not that there were six million Jews who died. The unfortunate thing is that there were so many Jewish survivors."

Generally, American city officials, police, the media, and citizens groups—including Jewish organizations fighting antisemitism and bigotry—had reacted to such extremist groups by quarantine: denying them controversy and starving them of publicity.

The *Chicago Tribune* editorialized: "More people should learn that the best weapon against extremist exhibitionism is a protracted yawn."

At first, the Skokie Village Council felt that if the demonstration were allowed and ignored, the Nazis would be deprived of the publicity they wanted. But the local Jewish community, led by Holocaust survivors and Jewish World War II veterans, adamantly rejected this advice in testimony to traditional community-relations agencies such as the Anti-Defamation League (ADL). This was far from a theoretical debate to them. In their youth, survivors had witnessed small Nazi marches blossom into massive movements of hatred. They had seen Nazis use the freedoms of a democratic society to destroy German democracy.

Skokie's mayor, Albert Smith, agreed, and the Skokie Village Board denied the request to march.

Firmly committed to the Constitution's guarantee of free speech—no matter how offensive the

A Neo-Nazi rally held at Northwestern University; Evanston, Illinois, October 1980.

speech—the American Civil Liberties Union, or ACLU, stepped in to defend the Nazis' right to march. The controversy gained national attention while the issue played itself out in the courtroom for two long years.

Ultimately, three court cases surrounded the proposed demonstration in Skokie. After an extended legal struggle, the Nazis' right to free speech prevailed and the courts ruled that they be allowed to demonstrate.

The village of Skokie reluctantly issued a parade permit to NSPA for Sunday, June 25, 1978. Tensions ran high as the day approached. Community and religious leaders planned a counterdemonstration, which was quickly supported by hundreds of national organizations. The police and National Guard were on alert.

Three days before the march, Collin canceled. A judge had ruled that Chicago had to give the NSPA permission to demonstrate in the city. Claiming a victory in the courts, the neo-Nazis decided to avoid Skokie. On July 9, Collin and about 20 supporters showed up at the Federal Building Plaza in Chicago. Meanwhile, several thousand Americans—Jews, Catholics, Protestants, African Americans, Polish Americans, and others—turned out to protest.

For many in Skokie, the threatened demonstration in their community was a reminder of the horrors they had survived. For others, it brought to light hatred and racism in their own backyard. As events unfolded, however, it also became a study in America's democratic ideals and the judicial process.

The Jewish Community: United and Divided

While the Jewish community was united in its outrage at the thought of Nazis demonstrating in downtown Skokie, there were differing opinions about how to handle the situation.

Previously, the ADL had recommended ignoring such demonstrations completely and thus limiting media

CASE #1:
VILLAGE OF SKOKIE V. NATIONAL SOCIALIST PARTY OF AMERICA

In April 1977, the village of Skokie filed suit to obtain a court order to prevent the proposed demonstration at Skokie Village Hall by the National Socialist Party of America (NSPA). Frank Collin of the NSPA sought the assistance of the American Civil Liberties Union (ACLU), and the Chicago office agreed to represent him.

On April 29, 1977, the Circuit Court of Cook County barred the NSPA from marching in uniform, displaying the swastika, or distributing pamphlets that might incite or promote hatred against Jews or other groups. The NSPA—with the help of the ACLU—appealed immediately, first to the Illinois Appellate Court and then the Illinois Supreme Court.

When these Courts declined to halt the lower court's order, Collin's attorneys appealed to the U.S. Supreme Court. On June 14, 1977, the Supreme Court ruled that an Illinois appellate court must review this restraint on speech. If the courts did not grant this review, the court ruled that the State must allow a stay.

In the summer of 1977, the Illinois Appellate Court modified the original Circuit Court injunction, but left in place an injunction prohibiting the intentional display of the swastika in the course of a march.

Collin's ACLU attorneys appealed the Illinois Appellate Court judgment to the Illinois Supreme Court. On January 27, 1978, the Illinois Supreme Court reversed the Appellate Court judgment prohibiting the display of the swastika. The village of Skokie did not seek review of the judgment of the Illinois Supreme Court, ending the state court proceedings.

coverage. As Abbot Rosen, then ADL's Midwest leader said, "The less publicity you give these clowns the less likely they are to grow."

But Skokie turned out to be a special case. After hearing the agonized testimony of Holocaust survivors in the community, the ADL agreed that a Nazi march targeted at this particular location, with its significant number of Holocaust survivors, constituted a "psychic assault."

The American Jewish Congress proposed a compromise: that the NSPA be allowed to march through Skokie, but without uniforms or any Nazi insignia.

CASE #2:
COLLIN *V.* SMITH

On May 2, 1977, while the state court order barring the NSPA demonstration remained in effect, the village of Skokie passed three ordinances to govern speech and assembly in Skokie. The first ordinance, a permit system for all large public gatherings, required applicants to provide $300,000 in liability insurance and $50,000 in property-damage insurance. The second and third ordinances prohibited dissemination of material that incites racial or religious hatred and demonstrations by members of political parties while wearing military-style uniforms.

Collin applied for a permit to conduct his demonstration at the Village Hall. The village manager denied the permit because of the group's intent to wear military-style uniforms. Collin and his party filed suit in the United States District Court, seeking to have the ordinances declared unconstitutional, in violation of the First Amendment.

On February 23, 1978, the District Court declared all three ordinances unconstitutional. Skokie appealed, and on May 22, 1978, the U.S. Court of Appeals for the Seventh Circuit affirmed the District Court's judgment. The village of Skokie sought review by the U.S. Supreme Court; their petition was denied on October 16, 1978.

A poster made by the Jewish Defense League for the 1978 Neo-Nazi march in Skokie.

They argued that a march without swastikas or uniforms "would not infringe on the right of the Nazis. It would not prohibit them from marching or parading in the city of Skokie. It would merely prohibit them from marching with swastikas or uniforms which are an abusive, insulting affront to every Jew and particularly to that section of the Skokie population who are concentration camp survivors." And so the Anti-Defamation League decided to file a class-action lawsuit asking the court to bar Collin from Skokie "while wearing or displaying Nazi insignia."

The Nazis were not a symbolic threat to Skokie's survivors. Sol Goldstein, one of the survivor leaders testified: "[The swastika] reminds me [of] my closest family who were sent to death by the swastika, and it reminds me [of] a threat that I am not safe with my life. It reminds me that my children are not safe with their lives."

Still, some survivors differed. They felt confident as Americans in a free society. The *Chicago Tribune* quoted one such survivor: "Years ago, in Europe, when the Nazis marched we stayed in our houses, afraid. Now I am not afraid. I want to face them.... This time they will not put us in gas chambers."

Some even advocated violence. Daniel Fagin said: "I'm against violence. I'm not a violent man. I couldn't do any harm. But if I see a swastika in my backyard—and my backyard is Skokie—I will resist." The militant Jewish Defense League (JDL) wanted the Nazis to feel afraid to enter a Jewish neighborhood, and argued that they should not leave unharmed.

Skokie Took the Legal Offensive

Lawyers for the village of Skokie argued that the government has a responsibility to protect vulnerable citizens, and that by permitting hate speech, it is implicitly endorsing it.

In the spring of 1977, the Skokie Village Board passed ordinances that prohibited the NSPA from parading in uniform. The lower court agreed with Skokie and issued an injunction barring the Nazis from displaying the swastika or any materials that would promote hatred against Jews.

In reaction, the NSPA appealed for its right to march and sought the ACLU's assistance. A lengthy legal battle ensued, and three separate court cases developed. Ultimately, the Illinois Supreme Court decided that the county court's ruling violated the First Amendment and that the NSPA would be allowed to march in uniform.

The American Civil Liberties Union

The ACLU took a principled and unpopular position: Freedom of speech is protected for all views, even abhorrent ones, they argued. Ira Glasser, who headed the ACLU, said: "We defend the First Amendment for everybody because there is no other way to defend it for ourselves. . . ."

The ACLU paid a price for its participation in the lawsuit: In 1977 it lost approximately 30,000 members, or 15 percent of its membership. The dip in membership and funding cuts amounted to a $500,000 loss (equivalent to about $1.8 million today). The Illinois affiliate estimated that it lost approximately 30 percent of its annual funding.

Holocaust Education and Museums

Previously, Skokie's Holocaust survivors had mostly tried to keep their painful memories to themselves, but the NSPA's threat to march provoked them to action. In 1981 Chicago-area survivors formed the Holocaust Memorial Foundation of Illinois and began an endeavor to educate people about the horrors they had encountered. The survivors raised funds to establish a small Holocaust museum in Skokie, which opened in 1984. It focused on educational outreach to Midwest schools.

In remembrance of the Holocaust and the survivors who lived in Skokie, a statue was unveiled in the village's square on May 31, 1987. It depicts a small group of individuals: a Jewish freedom fighter, a grandfather standing with his grandson, and a mother holding her lifeless child.

In 1990 Illinois's legislature passed the Holocaust Education Mandate, which required that the state's elementary and secondary schools include the Holocaust in their curricula. In 2005 the Holocaust Memorial Foundation was influential in expanding this mandate to require that schools teach about all genocides.

Fay Waldman at a protest rally; Skokie, c. 1978.

In 2009 the Illinois Holocaust Museum and Education Center opened. It will ensure that generations to come will remember the Holocaust and continue to fight intolerance and genocide.

Perhaps most importantly, survivors felt that it was time for them to stand up and speak out, not to have others talk for them. They assumed the leadership of this effort, and they have remained at the forefront for three decades.

"The Planned Nazi March on Skokie" was written by Benjamin Avishai.

CASE #3:
GOLDSTEIN *V.* COLLIN

The final case was a suit brought by Sol Goldstein, a Holocaust survivor living in Skokie. In conjunction with the Midwest office of the Anti-Defamation League (ADL) and assisted by the Chicago Jewish Federation's public affairs committee, he brought a class-action suit on behalf of Skokie's Holocaust survivors.

The suit argued that Nazis marching in uniform in Skokie would be a deliberate attempt to inflict severe emotional and mental distress on survivors. The suit was ordered dismissed by the Illinois Supreme Court on January 27, 1977, the same day as the decision in *Village of Skokie* v. *National Socialist Party of America.* On October 16, 1978, the U.S. Supreme Court declined to hear the case.

LEGACY OF THE HOLOCAUST

If the Holocaust were simply a "story" and not actual history, we might now be ready for the concluding chapter, which might be based on John Lennon's song "Imagine."

Imagine if...
...following Raphael Lemkin's lead, the United Nations defined and outlawed genocide—and the world was so horrified by the evil of the Holocaust that no genocide ever again occurred.

Imagine if...
...after most survivors had rebuilt their lives in their lands of freedom, despite their own emotional scars, they could take satisfaction in knowing that no other people would be victimized by genocide. Their suffering had not been in vain.

Imagine if...
...journalists had learned a lesson in reporting on mass murders in different corners of the world. They had followed the example of Jan Karski and Gerhard Riegner that information was needed urgently and that attention to genocide can save lives. Journalists firmly demanded that once a country was clearly attempting genocide, international action be taken—prevention, sanctions, alleviation, rescue, rehabilitation, even military intervention followed by prosecution of the perpetrators.

Imagine if...
...after the State of Israel had risen from the ashes, Jews now had an independent country living securely and comfortably in their historic homeland, among the family of nations. Thereby they had achieved an end to Jewish statelessness and vulnerability. They had acted on the conviction that powerlessness often invites victimization and thus an empowered Jewish people would not—and could not—be persecuted or victimized as Israelis or as Jews living in other countries.

But if fables come to happy endings, simple and just conclusions, history is messy and difficult. History is complex and offers few neat resolutions. History continues, often in baffling ways.

World War II affected world Jewry profoundly and cannot be compared with other cataclysmic events in Jewish history. The world's Jewish population fell from 17 million to 11 million. Even now, more than six decades after the Holocaust, the world's Jewish population is smaller than it was in 1933. Jewish religious life suffered enormously, as close to half of the six million victims were Orthodox Jews. Many Hasidic dynasties were wiped out completely. Renowned *yeshivot* were destroyed. The Nazis and their collaborators also decimated Jewish material culture and monuments. Synagogues, cemeteries, and entire Jewish neighborhoods were reduced to rubble.

In June 1981, some 6,000 Holocaust survivors from around the world gathered in Jerusalem at the Western Wall to transmit their legacy to the Second Generation.

The Holocaust nearly destroyed Yiddish as a daily and vibrant language, as well as the diverse expressions of Yiddish culture. The age-old Jewish village—the *shtetl*—was destroyed. Europe was no longer the center of Jewish leadership and learning. Judaism in Poland, which served as the biological and spiritual center of Jewish life, was destroyed, while other old European Jewish centers suffered deeply. Jewish Vienna, Jewish Berlin, Jewish Prague, Jewish Amsterdam, and Jewish Salonika were no more.

The Nazis' defeat ended their war against the Jews. However, it did not end threats to Jewish liberty, lives, and observance—even after the establishment of Israel. The short history of Israel has been punctuated by recurring wars with its Arab neighbors. Even today Israel continues to face terror and threats of destruction. However, as a sovereign state with its own army, it continues to thwart its enemies while paying a high price in lives lost on the battlefield and in terrorist acts perpetrated against innocent civilians.

The end of Jewish powerlessness also means that Israel can act independently. It means that the nation can take concrete actions to aid and give refuge when discrimination and calamity threaten Jews anywhere on the globe. Across much of the Middle East and North Africa and in Ethiopia, Jews have been endangered repeatedly in the postwar period by persecution, violence, and hostile governments.

After World War II, renewed antisemitism threatened the 2.5 million Jews of the Soviet Union. Throughout Soviet-controlled Eastern Europe, millions of Jews were denied the freedom to openly practice their beliefs. By the 1960s, many were demanding the right to emigrate. Israel's remarkable victory in the 1967 Six Day War helped boost their Jewish pride and Zionist convictions, strengthening the desire of many to move to Israel.

The great majority of threatened Jews from Muslim countries, Ethiopia,

A man sobs at the site of the Treblinka death camp during a ceremony for the 50th anniversary of the Warsaw Ghetto Uprising; 1993.

and the former Soviet Union eventually found haven in Israel. Some immigrated to the United States and other Western nations. This clearly reflects the new reality of the post-Holocaust era: Israel, along with empowered Jewish communities throughout the world, can intercede and protect Jews under distress and danger.

Survivors thus proclaimed a simple message: *Never Again.* It was the proud cry of an anguished people saying that no one—Jews or others—should have to suffer as they had suffered.

And yet since 1945, genocide has been committed again and again. We know the names of the places. We even have images committed to memory:

- Cambodia
- Biafra
- Rwanda
- Serbia /Srebrenica/Kosovo (former Yugoslavia)
- Darfur

Television brings these genocides into our living rooms. At one time we said, "If only people knew, the world would never permit it to happen." Yet in an age of CNN, the Internet, and satellite phones, we cannot repeat the simple declarations of the past—at least not with conviction and confidence. More importantly, we cannot act as if we do not know.

Survivors thus proclaimed a simple message: *Never Again.* It was the proud cry of an anguished people saying that no one—Jews or others—should have to suffer as they had suffered.

Again and again and again the world has failed to confront genocide.

In Rwanda, the armies of Belgium and France left the country prior to the genocide. American Marines came ashore to bring Americans to safety. They did nothing to stop the genocide conducted by machete-wielding Hutus against their Tutsi neighbors. The United Nations, which had piously outlawed genocide in 1948, confined its troops to base in 1994 while the slaughter in Rwanda continued.

In Sudan's Darfur region, Secretary of State Colin Powell declared that the killing there constituted genocide. His position was reinforced by President George W. Bush. The United Nations declared the situation dire, and world attention has been focused on Darfur for years, yet the killing continues.

There is reason for despair and more than ample justification for outrage and disappointment.

And yet there are small but genuine signs that the remembrance of the Holocaust has slowed the progress of genocide. Consider two political examples:

In 1979 Vice President Walter Mondale began the International Conference on the Boat People—refugees from Communist-controlled Vietnam—by

French Justice Minister Rachida Dati examines portraits in the "Hall of Names" in the Yad Vashem Holocaust Memorial Museum; Jerusalem, September 21, 2008.

invoking the failure of the Evian Conference:

"The boat people." "The land people." The phrases are new, but unfortunately their precedent in the annals of shame is not. Forty-one years ago this very week, another international conference on Lake Geneva concluded its deliberations. Thirty-two "nations of asylum" convened at Evian to save the doomed Jews of Nazi Germany and Austria. On the eve of the conference, Hitler flung the challenge in the world's face. He said: "I can only hope that the world, which has such deep sympathy for these criminals, will be generous enough to convert this sympathy into 'practical aid.'" We have each heard similar arguments about the plight of the refugees in Indochina.

At Evian, they began with high hopes. But they failed the test of civilization. Let us not reenact their error. Let us not be the heirs to their shame.

The United States took the lead, and the boat people were brought to these shores and to countries throughout the world—including Israel, where they rebuilt their lives. An elemental lesson of the Holocaust had seemingly been learned—at least for a time.

In Kosovo, President Bill Clinton, who had failed to act in Rwanda, initiated bombing runs to to stop ethnic cleansing. Days of bombing turned into weeks and then months before the bombings had their intended impact. That enabled Clinton to call all the parties to a conference at which U.S. ambassador to the United Nations Richard Holbroke—whose grandparents and mother had fled Nazi

Germany—fashioned the 1995 Dayton Accords. The agreement did not bring peace, but it did halt ethnic cleansing. It also led to the removal of Serbian president Slobodan Milosevic from office.

In terms of law, the aftermath of the Holocaust has had a lasting effect. The precedent of the Nuremberg Trials, for instance, led to trials for later genocides. Milosovic was put on trial at the International Court in The Hague. So, too, were participants in the Rwandan genocide. Justice was imperfect, as it was at Nuremberg a half-century earlier—imperfect, but still essential.

On the religious front there has been progress. Following the long reign of Pope Pius XII, Archbishop Roncalli was named Pope John XXIII in 1958. Already an old man, he was expected to serve only briefly, chiefly focusing on continuity. Instead, he transformed Vatican teaching and in particular Church teaching toward the Jews. He studied the origins of antisemitism with French historian Julius Isaac and changed the teaching of the Church—termed the "Teaching of Contempt"—regarding the Jews. The process he initiated led to the historic Vatican Council statement *Nostra Aetate* (In Our Time), which Pope Paul VI proclaimed in October 1965. It renounced a centuries-old libel and absolved the Jews of blame for the cru-

cifixion of Jesus. It also changed Roman Catholic liturgy so that the words "perfidious Jews" were not recited on Good Friday.

Under his later successor, Polish-born John Paul II, who experienced the Holocaust first-hand in Krakow, the Vatican went even further. As Bishop of Rome, Pope John Paul II worshipped in the Main Synagogue of Rome, treating Chief Rabbi Elio Toaff as his spiritual colleague and addressing Jews as older brothers. On a trip to Israel in 2000, he apologized for the antisemitism of Christians and placed a note of apology and a prayer in the Western Wall, the most enduring link of Jews with the ancient Temple of Jerusalem. He condemned antisemitism as anti-Christian at Yad Vashem, Israel's Memorial to the Holocaust. He even visited the Chief Rabbinate, a gesture of respect never before accorded to Jews and Judaism.

These remarkable gestures of healing and transformations of teaching vastly helped to improve Jewish-Catholic relations. French bishops went even further in their condemnation of the Holocaust. Other churches reexamined their own teachings. The American Lutheran Church, for example, renounced the teachings of Martin Luther on the Jews, lest they perpetuate antisemitism.

"The Catholic Church … is deeply saddened by the hatred, acts of persecution, and displays of antisemitism directed against the Jews by Christians at any time and in any place."

—Pope John Paul II while visiting Yad Vashem in Jerusalem

Over time, survivors found meaning in how they lived their lives in the aftermath— how they bore witness and transmitted the legacy.

On a local level, Chicagoans enjoyed the leadership of Joseph Cardinal Bernadine and understood how papal leadership was followed up with local initiative. And outside of the formal lines of the Church hierarchy, Father John Pawlikowski, a professor at the Chicago Theological Union, became an internationally influential figure in Jewish-Catholic relations, and a recognized authority on antisemitism.

Still, tensions and concerns persist. The Vatican still has not opened Holocaust-linked archives to all scholars, thus blocking unfettered access to documents that would enable understanding of the Vatican's role during the Holocaust. From time to time, efforts arise to elevate the wartime pope, Pius XII, to sainthood—a controversial issue considering Pius's neutrality during the war. Moreover, some voices within the Church advocate undoing significant changes of Vatican II.

Scholars of every discipline have studied the Holocaust at universities, seeking to understand its importance and to identify its stages in the hopes that knowledge can lead to prevention. One distinguished scholar, Gregory H. Stanton, has developed a "process model" of the stages of genocide. They will be all too familiar to visitors of the Museum

and readers of *Memory and Legacy.* Stanton's eight stages are:
- Classification (us vs. them)
- Symbolization
- Dehumanization
- Organization (hate groups)
- Polarization
- Preparation (identification, expropriation, concentration, transportation)
- Extermination
- Denial

Stanton's model is designed so that policymakers can recognize what may likely follow a process of dehumanization. (One hopes it can inform those who resist genocide rather than provide guidance for its perpetrators.)

Pulitzer Prize-winning *New York Times* columnist Nicholas Kristof has decried genocide in Darfur, writing column after column to call attention to the problem, pleading for action and for press coverage. Though critics complain that he has become obsessed and repetitive, his admirers understand that speaking out is an indispensable tool if there is to be a response to genocide.

A classic Hasidic expression summarizes Kristof's dilemma: Sometimes, you scream at the world to change the world, and sometimes you scream to make sure that the world—and its indifference— does not change you.

Perhaps a glimmer of hope, a small measure of consolation, can be found in the achievements of the survivor generation, which— six decades after liberation—is nearing its biological end. Survivors can look back on their collective activities on behalf of remembrance with a sense of achievement.

Under the leadership of survivors:

The groundbreaking for the Holocaust Memorial Monument in Skokie, Illinois; 1986.

- The Shoah has been moved into the forefront of contemporary political and ethical consciousness. It has become the negative absolute, a cornerstone for consideration of values.
- Museums and memorials teaching and commemorating the Holocaust have been created throughout the world.
- Holocaust remembrance has become a basic part of the Jewish calendar and increasingly a part of the calendars of many nations affected by the Holocaust, including the United States, Germany, Poland, and Great Britain—as well as the United Nations. Because of Holocaust denial and antisemitism, nations have intensified the emphasis on Holocaust commemoration.
- The International Task Force on Holocaust Education has led a large-scale effort to teach tolerance; to promote pluralism, respect for human rights, and dignity; and to remember the past in order to transform the future.
- Testimony has been gathered on an unprecedented scale, in the most contemporary technologies. In addition, many memoirs have been written. Both of these forms will provide living voices of their witness far beyond their lifetimes. Their stories will form cornerstones for films and educational programs for generations.

Holocaust survivors, who were a small minority of the victims, were faced with the question of what to do with the random "accident" of their survival: "Why did I survive?" Over time, they found meaning in how they lived their lives in the aftermath—how they bore witness and transmitted the legacy.

Because they have faced death, many have learned what is most important in life: life itself, love, family, and community. They have found value even in what survivor Gerda Klein called "a boring evening at home."

For most Holocaust survivors, the survival of the Jewish people and Israel's security became paramount. The final statement of Jewish history and Jewish memory must be about life and not death, no matter how pervasive that death. Survival required Jewish empowerment; that process was accelerated by the creation of the State of Israel and its armed forces.

Holocaust survivors responded to survival in the most biblical of ways possible: by remembering evil and suffering to deepen conscience, by enlarging memory and broadening responsibility. It is thus that the Ancient Israelites responded to slavery and the Exodus. It is thus that its survivors responded to the Shoah.

They transformed victimization into witness, dehumanization into a plea to deepen our humanity.

The survivors leave the rest of us who are not survivors or descendants of survivors with an important legacy with significant responsibilities.

We were not witnesses. We have lived in the presence of witnesses.

We *can* become witnesses to the witnesses, taking forth from the Museum and from this book what we have learned and what we have seen and transforming it into action to better the world, to prevent genocide, and to alleviate the world's suffering and help heal its victims.

The challenge is ours. The responsibility is ours.

It is the most fervent hope of survivors that their memory might become our legacy.

The Holocaust Memorial Monument in Skokie, Illinois.

THE HOLOCAUST: A CHRONOLOGY

Blue text signifies the range of Jewish responses both under German domination and in the free world.

1932

July 31, 1932: The National Socialist Party (Nazis) receives 37.3 percent of the vote. They now have 230 of 608 seats and are largest party in the *Reichstag* (Germany's parliament). Socialists have 133 representatives and Communists have 89, reflecting extreme polarization between the radical right and left.

August 13, 1932: Adolf Hitler declines an offer by German President Paul von Hindenburg to become vice chancellor.

November 6, 1932: In the new election, the percentage of votes for the Nazis declines to 33.1 percent and the number seats in the *Reichstag* is reduced to 196.

December 3, 1932: Conservative leader General Kurt von Schleicher is named chancellor of Germany.

1933

January 28, 1933: General Schleicher resigns after serving only 55 days.

January 30, 1933: German President Hindenburg appoints Hitler as chancellor (prime minister); Franz von Papen is named vice chancellor. The Nazis are a minority in the new government, with only three ministers.

February 2, 1933: Political demonstrations are banned in Germany.

February 27, 1933: The *Reichstag* is set on fire. Communists are blamed for the blaze.

February 28, 1933: Using a provision of the Weimar Constitution, President Hindenburg grants Hitler emergency powers, and civil liberties and constitutional protections are suspended.

March 4, 1933: Franklin Delano Roosevelt is inaugurated as president of the United States.

March 5, 1933: In elections called by the Nazis to eliminate Communist opposition and their right-wing allies who constituted a majority in the cabinet, the Nazis gain 288 of the 647 seats in parliament. This constitutes more than 17 million voters and nearly 44 percent of all votes. The Socialists win 120 seats and the Communist Party takes 81 seats.

March 22, 1933: The first concentration camp is opened at Dachau, near Munich.

March 23, 1933: German parliament passes the Enabling Act. The new law removes the power of legislation from parliament and gives it to the Nazi-controlled government, creating a legally declared dictatorship.

March 26, 1933: In a telegram to the American Jewish Congress, German Jewish leaders strongly oppose planned protests against Germany. They believe that anti-German demonstrations would further harm German Jews.

March 27, 1933: The American Jewish Congress organizes a mass protest against the Nazis at Madison Square Garden in New York, and in other American cities. A boycott of German goods is threatened if Germany makes good on its promise to boycott Jewish goods in Germany.

April 1, 1933: The German government institutes a boycott of Jewish stores and businesses. Expected to last several days, it is suspended after one.

April 4, 1933: Robert Weltsch, editor of a Zionist weekly newspaper in Germany, publishes his editorial "Wear the Yellow Badge with Pride," urging German Jews to take pride in their Judaism and reject the Nazi attempts to defame them.

April 7, 1933: The Law for the Restoration of Professional Civil Service bans Jews from government. Those excluded include doctors working for the national health organization, lawyers, university professors, and government workers.

April 13, 1933: The Central Committee of German Jews for Help and Reconstruction is established to coordinate economic and social assistance, initially for Jews who have lost their jobs or business following anti-Jewish legislation. Actions undertaken include legal suits against government offices to have "illegal" dismissals reversed, and compliance of legally stipulated compensation benefits.

April 21, 1933: The German government prohibits *shehitah*, the ritual slaughter of animals required by Jewish dietary law. Some German Jews evade the law and continue to perform kosher slaughtering clandestinely, despite the threat of severe punishment. Others pay the higher prices for kosher meat imported into Germany.

April 25, 1933: The Law Preventing Overcrowding of School and Schools of Higher Education restricts Jewish enrollment in German schools. The Jewish community responds by creating new Jewish schools and expanding existing schools.

May 10, 1933: German students and their professors remove and burn "un-Germanic" books from libraries and bookstores throughout Germany. More than 20,000 books are burned opposite a university in Berlin. Authors include Jews, opponents of Nazism, and others defined as un-Germanic.

May 12, 1933: Franz Bernheim, backed by Jewish organizations, files a complaint against the German government in the League of Nations. The Bernheim Petition challenges the legality of Nazi anti-Jewish laws within the areas of former Poland that had been annexed to Germany. Remarkably, the League, which supervises this area, will uphold the grievance. Germany will be forced to retract its laws and, until 1937, stop discriminating against Jews in Upper Silesia.

May 14, 1933: The American League for the Defense of Jewish Rights calls for an economic boycott of Germany.

June 16, 1933: The Jewish Cultural Association (*Kulturbund*) is created. It allows Jewish artists and audiences who had been excluded from public cultural life to continue their cultural activities in newly organized theaters and orchestras throughout Germany.

July 14, 1933: The National Socialist Party is made Germany's only legal party. • Eastern European Jews living in Germany are stripped of their citizenship, if obtained after 1914. • Laws are enacted that permit the sterilization of "unfit" parents and so-called "euthanasia of "defective and useless eaters," those who are deemed "life unworthy of living."

July 20, 1933: The Vatican signs a concordat with Germany, negotiated by Cardinal Eugenio Pacelli, the future Pope Pius XII. The concordat grants Hitler much needed political recognition and in return seemingly protects the rights of Catholics in Germany.

August 25, 1933: The *Haavara* (Transfer) Agreement is signed between the German government and the Zionist Organization. It enables Jews to leave Germany and transfer some of their holdings to Palestine, thereby allowing them to enter Palestine under the unrestricted "capitalist" quota. Some 20,000 German Jews will immigrate to Palestine by means of "capitalist" certificates.

September 8, 1933: Jewish organizations meeting in Geneva call for a worldwide boycott of German products.

September 17, 1933: The Central Organization of German Jews (*Reichsvertretung der deutschen Juden*), led by Rabbi Leo Baeck, is founded. Uniting the often-conflicting ideological groups under a single umbrella organization, it will serve as a much-needed liaison with the hostile German government as well as a source of material aid, education, and emigration assistance for its Jewish constituents.

September 22, 1933: Jews are banned from journalism, theater, music, art, literature, and broadcasting in order to eradicate Jewish influence on German society.

September 29, 1933: Jews are banned from farming in Germany.

October 4, 1933: The German Orthodox Jewish community sends a petition to Adolf Hitler protesting the anti-Jewish laws, including laws banning *shehitah*, the ritual slaughter of animals required by Jewish dietary law. They consider their situation "wholly intolerable, both as regards their legal position, their economic existence, and also as regards their public standing and their freedom of religious action."

October 19, 1933: The Reich Union of Jewish Frontline Soldiers sends a letter to German authorities, proclaiming their loyalty to Germany and readiness to serve the Fatherland.

October 29–November 1, 1933: In London, major Jewish organizations meet at an International Jewish Conference to aid German Jews. Attended by representatives of the American Jewish Joint Distribution Committee (the Joint), the Jewish Colonization Association (ICA/JCA), the Central British Fund for German Jewry, the Jewish Agency for Palestine, and others, the conference resolves to oppose the emigration of elderly German Jews from Germany.

November 12, 1933: The Nazi Party, now the only party permitted to run in the elections, wins 93 percent of the vote for the *Reichstag*.

Nazis write on the window of a Jewish business in Germany on April 1, 1933.

December 31, 1933: Approximately 37,000 Jews left Germany in 1933. Most are political leaders targeted by the Nazis, cultural figures barred from their fields, and young people.

1934

January 26, 1934: Germany and Poland sign a 10-year nonaggression pact.

February 19, 1934: The first Youth Aliya (Youth Immigration) group arrives in Palestine. The organization was created in late 1932 by Recha Freier, the wife of a Berlin rabbi, to rescue endangered Jewish youth in Germany, and eventually from throughout Europe, by sending them to Palestine. Immigrating without their parents, more than 5,000 children will arrive in Palestine before the outbreak of World War II. They will live on kibbutzim and in well-established youth villages funded by the Youth Aliya Office, under the leadership of American Zionist and Hadassah leader Henrietta Szold.

April l, 1934: Germany establishes a "People's Court" to try enemies of the state. The right to a trial by jury or to appeal the verdict is canceled.

May 1934: The Center for Adult Jewish Education is established, with branches throughout Germany. Its mission is to combat anti-Jewish propaganda and raise Jewish morale. Its director, philosopher Martin Buber, speaks of learning about Jewish heritage, holding fast, and preserving the spark of Jewish traditions.

May 17, 1934: The German-American Bund organizes a pro-Nazi rally at Madison Square Garden in New York City.

June 30, 1934: In the "Night of the Long Knives," Hitler loyalists purge the Nazi Party of hundreds of enemies—real or imagined—including high-ranking SA officers and veteran Hitler associate Ernst Rohm, the SA's chief, who was gay. Persecution of German male homosexuals will intensify.

July 4, 1934: Theodor Eicke heads the newly established Inspectorate of Concentration Camps.

July 25, 1934: Austrian Chancellor Engelbert Dollfuss is assassinated. The Nazis try but fail to seize power in Austria.

August 2, 1934: German President Paul von Hindenburg dies in office. Hitler fills the vacuum, combining the roles of president and chancellor to become commander-in-chief of Germany's armed forces. Soldiers will now take a personal oath of allegiance to Hitler, not to the state or the Constitution.

August 19, 1934: German voters overwhelmingly (89.9 percent) approve of Hitler's new powers.

December 31, 1934: Some 23,000 Jews emigrated from Germany in 1934. The first wave of refugees fled to neighboring countries, many hoping to return to Germany when the situation improved. By early 1935, some 10,000 Jews will return to Germany; Jewish refugees in neighboring countries were sliding into poverty and often felt culturally alienated.

1935

January 13, 1935: A plebiscite under the League of Nations brings the Saar region into Germany.

March 1, 1935: Germany retakes the Saarland.

March 16, 1935: Germany initiates the draft in direct defiance of the Treaty of Versailles. France, England, and the United States decide not to confront Germany.

April 1, 1935: Anti-Jewish legislation is passed in the Saar region.

May 12, 1935: Polish leader Jozef Pilsudski dies, ending an era of relative tolerance toward the Jews in Poland.

May 31, 1935: Jews are banned from the German armed forces.

June 26, 1935: The Law for the Prevention of Offspring with Hereditary Diseases provides for compulsory abortions in certain instances.

September 15, 1935: The Nuremberg Laws are enacted. The Reich Citizenship Law deprives Jews of their citizenship. The Law for the Protection of German Blood and Honor prohibits Jews from marrying non-Jews and from employing German women under the age of 45. Under its provisions, Jews are defined biologically based on the religion of their grandparents and not by the identity they affirm or the religion they practice.

Yom Kippur, 1935: Rabbi Leo Baeck, head of the Central Organization of German Jews (*Reichsvertretung der deutschen Juden*), has composed a prayer of defiance, "The *Reichsvertretung* Speaks to Us," to be read in synagogues throughout Germany on Yom Kippur. The prayer directly challenges Nazi antisemitic ideology, calling it a lie and a slander. When the Gestapo discovers the prayer, it forces the *Reichsvertretung* to send telegrams forbidding the prayer to be read, and it arrests Rabbi Baeck.

November 1935: The Jewish Winter Relief (*Winterhilfe*) is established in response to Jews being excluded from the general relief programs following the Nuremberg Laws. It aids and supports many impoverished Jews who, for the first time, need to receive welfare.

November 14, 1935: In regulations clarifying the Nuremberg Laws, a Jew is defined as anyone with two Jewish grandparents who is a member of the Jewish community or anyone with three or more Jewish grandparents. *Mischlinge* ("hybrid") is specified as anyone with Jewish blood. Marriage between Jews and second-degree *mischlinge* is prohibited.

November 15, 1935: German churches provide records to the government indicating who is a Christian and who is not.

December 31, 1935: The remaining Jews in Germany's civil service are dismissed. • About 21,000 Jews fled Germany in 1935. Jews stopped returning in 1935, following Nazi threats of internment in concentration camps for returnees.

1936

February 4, 1936: David Frankfurter, a 27-year-old medical student born in Daruvar, Croatia, and the son of an Orthodox rabbi, assassinates the head of the Swiss Nazi Party, Wilhelm Gustloff, in the Alpine resort town of Davos, Switzerland. In response to the Nuremberg Laws and other anti-Jewish acts, Frankfurter, who studied medicine in Germany prior to moving to Switzerland in 1934, acted to protest Nazi antisemitism and attract world attention to the desperate plight of Germany's Jews. He will be tried by the Swiss and sentenced to 18 years in jail. Pardoned after the war, he will die in Israel in 1982.

March 3, 1936: Jewish doctors are denied the right to practice medicine in German government hospitals.

March 7, 1936: German troops occupy the Rhineland in defiance of the Treaty of Versailles. The United States, Britain, and France denounce the move but do not respond actively.

March 15, 1936: The Council for German Jewry is established. The council is a unified organization of major American and British Jewish philanthropic bodies together with representatives of German Jewry and the Jewish Agency for Palestine. Based in London, the council aspires to organize a massive and rapid emigration of German Jewry, especially the young. A rare example of a unified international Jewish endeavor, the council at this time is the only major Jewish organization in the world to advocate total emigration of Jews from Germany.

March 29, 1936: The SS guard formation is named SS Death's Head Units. It will provide guards for concentration camps.

June 17, 1936: Heinrich Himmler is appointed chief of German police.

June 19, 1936: Boxer Max Schmeling defeats future world heavyweight champion Joe Louis. It is a propaganda victory for the Nazis, who claim that it confirms German racial dominance.

June 26, 1936: Heinrich Himmler appoints Reinhard Heydrich as head of the SD (Security Forces).

July 1936: The Spanish Civil War begins.

August 1–16, 1936: The Olympics are held in Berlin. For weeks prior to the games, antisemitic posters, including "Jews Are Not Wanted Here" signs, are removed and antisemitic discourse is diminished. African American runner Jesse Owens wins four gold medals and is slighted by Hitler, who leaves the Olympic Stadium rather than present the medals. Two American Jewish runners, Marty Glickman and Sam Stoller, are forced not to run the 400-meter relay by Avery Brundage, head of the American Olympic Committee, lest Hitler be embarrassed further. Because of their absence, Owens is chosen to run the final lap and wins his fourth medal.

September 7, 1936: All Jewish property is taxed by 25 percent.

The Wollman sisters; Germany, 1936.

September 23, 1936: The Sachsenhausen concentration camp opens.

October 1, 1936: Criminal court judges must swear an oath of allegiance to Hitler, not to the Constitution or the state.

October 25, 1936: Hitler and Italian leader Benito Mussolini sign a treaty forming the Berlin-Rome Axis.

November 18, 1936: Germany's volunteer Condor Legion leaves for combat on the side of Francisco Franco's troops in Spain.

November 25, 1936: Germany and Japan sign the Anti-Comintern Pact in order to block Soviet activities abroad.

December 27, 1936: Great Britain and France agree not to intervene in the Spanish Civil War.

December 31, 1936: Some 25,000 Jews left Germany in 1936.

1937

January 1937: Half of Germany's 1,600 Jewish communities disappear or are on the verge of disappearing, as rural Jews seek safety and economic aid from Jewish welfare bodies in the cities.

March 14, 1937: Pope Pius XI condemns the use of racist laws against baptized (converted) Jews in a papal letter, *"Mit brennender Sorge"* ("With Burning Concern"). However, he does not denounce Nazi antisemitism and does describe the Jews as deicides, those who killed Christ.

March 15, 1937: The Joint Boycott Council stages a mass anti-Nazi rally in New York City.

July 1937: A "Degenerate Art" exhibition, featuring the work of Jewish and other "unacceptable" artists, opens in Munich.

July 1, 1937: Pastor Martin Niemoller, an antisemitic yet anti-Nazi German pastor, is arrested because of his opposition to Hitler.

July 15, 1937: The Buchenwald concentration camp is opened.

September 7, 1937: Hitler declares the Treaty of Versailles invalid.

October 12, 1937: The SS takes control of Grafeneck, an institution for crippled children in Wurttemberg, and starts transforming it into a "euthanasia center."

December 31, 1937: Nearly 130,000 Jews (including 37,000 in 1937) have fled Germany since 1933—about one-quarter of Germany's Jewish population.

1938

Early 1938: In Britain, the Chief Rabbi's Religious Emergency Council is created by Rabbi Solomon Schonfeld to bring Orthodox rabbis and teachers to England. A total of some 3,700 Jews are granted entry permits to England as a result of the council's efforts.

January 21, 1938: The Romanian government strips Romanian Jews of their citizenship.

March 12, 1938: The German army enters Vienna, Austria, which is annexed by Germany. Antisemitic laws enacted in Germany from 1933 to 1938 are immediately imposed in Austria.

March 28, 1938: Jewish community organizations lose governmental recognition in Germany.

April 5, 1938: Anti-Jewish riots rage throughout Poland.

April 21, 1938: Jews are eliminated from Germany's economy; Jewish assets may be seized.

April 23, 1938: Jews in Vienna are rounded up and forced to eat grass by the Nazis on their Sabbath.

April 26, 1938: The German government mandates the registration of all Jewish property and other holdings in excess of 5,000 Marks. Expropriation follows; "Aryanization" intensifies, meaning the process of transferring Jewish-held property into non-Jewish German possessions.

May 3, 1938: The Flossenberg concentration camp is opened.

June 9, 1938: The main synagogue in Munich is set on fire.

June 14, 1938: All Jewish businesses that have not been registered must now do so.

June 15, 1938: German officials arrest 1,500 Jews for minor violations—including traffic violations—and intern them in concentration camps.

June 22, 1938: Joe Louis knocks out Max Schmeling in a heavyweight championship fight, avenging his 1936 defeat.

June 25, 1938: It is ruled that German Jewish doctors may treat only Jewish patients.

July 6–14, 1938: An international conference, called by U.S. President Franklin Roosevelt, is held at Evian-les-Bains, France, to consider the "refugee problem," a euphemism for Jews. Thirty-two nations attend. To assuage British concerns, Palestine is not on the agenda. No country is asked to change its law or increase it budget for refugees. The results are limited and incommensurate with the growing needs of refugees; i.e., Jews.

July 14, 1938: In response to Evian, a German newspaper is published with the banner headline: "JEWS FOR SALE AT BARGAIN PRICE: WHO WANTS THEM? NO ONE."

August 8, 1938: A concentration camp is opened at Mauthausen in German-occupied Austria. It is the first of several camps established on formerly Austrian soil.

August 10, 1938: The Great Synagogue in Nuremberg is destroyed.

August 17, 1938: A law is passed requiring that by January 1, 1939, all Jewish men in Germany must assume the middle name of Israel and all Jewish women must assume the middle name of Sarah.

August 26, 1938: Adolf Eichmann establishes the Central Office for Jewish Emigration in Vienna to hasten the departure of the Jews. This will become the model for a nationwide program six months later.

September 15, 1938: British Prime Minister Neville Chamberlain meets with Hitler to discuss the Sudeten crisis. Hitler demands that Sudetenland, heavily populated by ethnic Germans, be ceded to Germany.

September 26, 1938: Hitler promises that Sudetenland will be his last territorial demand in Europe.

September 27, 1938: Jews are barred from practicing law in Germany.

September 29–30, 1938: The Munich Conference is held in Munich, Germany. Attendees include Chamberlain, Hitler, French Premier Edouard Daladier, and Italian leader Benito Mussolini. France and Britain settle on a policy of appeasement. Hitler is given Sudetenland, and Chamberlain will declare "peace in our time."

October 1938: The Polish government revokes the passports of all Jews who have lived outside of Poland for more than five years.

October 5, 1938: Germany complies with a Swiss federal police request that all German passports held by Jews be marked with the letter *J* (to prevent Jews passing into Switzerland).

October 28, 1938: Germany expels 17,000 Jews with Polish citizenship. Poland refuses to accept these deportees and Germany refuses their reentry to Germany, so they languish in no-man's land. Many are stranded in Zbaszyn, Poland. Jewish communal leaders Emanuel Ringelblum and Yitzhak Gitterman arrive from Warsaw to set up relief services.

November 1938: Father Bernhard Lichtenberg, a Berlin-based Roman Catholic, condemns Germany's assault on the Jews.

November 2, 1938: Sections of Slovakia and the Transcarpathian Mountains are annexed by Hungary.

November 7, 1938: Herschel Grynszpan, distraught because his family is caught in Zbaszyn, goes to the German Embassy in Paris and mortally wounds Ernst vom Rath, the third secretary.

November 9–10, 1938: The November pogroms, known as *Kristallnacht* (Night of Broken Glass), erupt in Germany. Throughout Germany (including newly annexed Austria), some 1,400 synagogues are attacked and many are burnt and desecrated. Jewish stores are looted, and 30,000 Jewish men, ages 16 to 60, are arrested and sent to concentration camps.

November 9, 1938: In Hamburg, Germany, Dr. Seligmann Bamberger and other synagogue leaders risk their lives to save the Torah scrolls, housed in the holy ark, from the burning Bornplatz Synagogue. Similar acts transpire throughout Germany and Austria.

November 12, 1938: Herman Goring convenes a meeting to consider the results of *Kristallnacht*. The Jewish community is fined one billion Marks ($400 million in 1938 dollars). Jews must repair their property, and Jews residing in Germany cannot collect insurance payments. All Jews are to be removed from the German economy, culture, and society.

November 15, 1938: In protest of *Kristallnacht*, the United States calls home its ambassador to Germany. • All remaining Jewish students are expelled from German schools.

November 21, 1938: British Home Secretary Sir Samuel Hoare announces his support for the *Kindertransport*, resulting in the formation of the Movement for the Care of Children from Germany in December. Working together with Jewish organizations in Germany, Austria, and former Czechoslovakia—who set up the procedures and arranged for the children's journey to England—the British organization will arrange for the rescue of

nearly 10,000 children (90 percent Jews) by September 1939.

December 3, 1938: The German government decrees that all Jewish businesses must be forcibly "Aryanized."

December 31, 1938: With increasing persecution in 1938, an additional 40,000 Jews escape Germany this year.

1939

January 1939: The *Mossad Le'aliyah Bet* is created by the Jewish Agency for Palestine. The organization will organize ships of "illegal" immigrants to Palestine in direct defiance of the British mandate's strict restrictions on Jewish immigration.

January 30, 1939: On Hitler's sixth anniversary as chancellor, he addresses the *Reichstag* and issues a threat against the Jews. He warns that if a world war is to break out, the result will be the destruction of the Jews. Three years later, the warning will be self-described as a prophecy.

February 10, 1939: Pope Pius XI dies. On his night table is an unpublished encyclical on racism and anti-semitism.

February–June 1939: Senator Robert Wagner and Representative Edith Nourse Rogers introduce the Child Refugee Bill to permit the entry of 20,000 children from Germany over a two-year period. Despite press support, the bill dies in committee, leaving restrictive 1924 quotas in force.

March 2, 1939: Cardinal Eugenio Pacelli is elected as Pope Pius XII.

March 15, 1939: German troops enter Czechoslovakia and occupy its capital, Prague. Germany annexes Bohemia and Moravia into the Reich, now known as the Protectorate. Slovakia becomes a German puppet satellite under Catholic priest Father Josef Tiso.

March 25, 1939: About 20,000 people march in a "Stop Hitler" parade in New York. An additional half-million view the demonstration.

March 31, 1939: Prime Minister Neville Chamberlain announces that Britain and France will protect Polish sovereignty.

April 30, 1939: A German directive allows German landlords to evict Jews. They will force many Jews to move into specially marked "Jewish Houses."

May 3, 1939: Joseph Stalin replaces Jewish Commisar for Foreign Affairs Maksim Litvinov with Viacheslav Molotov.

May 15, 1939: The German luxury ship SS *St. Louis*, filled with some 1,000 Jewish refugees, leaves Hamburg en route to Cuba. Although the Jews have entry permits to Cuba, they are refused entry into Cuba as well as the United States. The *St. Louis* returns to Europe, and its passengers are dispersed to England, Belgium, France, and Holland.

May 17, 1939: The British government issues a White Paper, which limits Jewish immigration to Palestine to 15,000 per year for five years. Jewish land purchases in Palestine are also restricted.

May 18, 1939: Inmates begin to arrive at the first women's concentration camp, established at Ravensbrueck.

July 4, 1939: The German government dissolves the independent Central Organization of German Jews and replaces it with a new association supervised and controlled by the Gestapo.

August 2, 1939: Jewish physicist Albert Einstein, self-exiled from Germany in the U.S., writes to President Roosevelt about developing an American atom bomb.

August 22, 1939: In a speech to his generals on the eve of the invasion of Poland, Hitler urges the liquidation of Poles in order to gain *Lebensraum* (living space) for the Germans.

August 23, 1939: The Ribbentrop-Molotov (German-Soviet) Nonaggression Pact is signed. A secret provision calls for the division of Poland between Germany and the Soviet Union.

August 25, 1939: Great Britain and France declare themselves ready to defend their ally, Poland, if it is attacked.

September 1939: RELICO, the Relief Committee for the War-Stricken Jewish Population, is established in Geneva, by Dr. Abraham Silberschein. Funded primarily by the World Jewish Congress,

it provides assistance for Jewish refugees who are desperately trying to flee. During the war, RELICO will coordinate its refugee activities with other international agencies. In addition to gathering and transmitting information, they will try to deliver packages of food and medicine to ghettos and concentration camps. • Italian Jewish community leaders establish the Delegation for the Assistance of Jewish Immigrants (DELASEM) to aid Jewish refugees in Italy.

September 1, 1939: World War II begins with the German invasion of Poland.

September 3, 1939: Great Britain and France declare war on Germany.

September 6, 1939: German forces occupy Krakow, Poland.

September 8, 1939: More than 6,400 of the 7,000 Jews in Ostrow Mazowiecka, Poland, near Warsaw, join the flood of Jewish refugees fleeing east toward Soviet-controlled territories.

September 17, 1939: The Soviet Union invades eastern Poland.

September 19, 1939: The coordinating committee for Jewish Self-Help in Warsaw is established. It unites the various Jewish welfare and aid organizations.

September 21, 1939: Reinhard Heydrich, SS security chief, orders the creation of Jewish Councils (*Judenraete*), consisting of 24 Jewish men, to be responsible for implementing German orders in each ghetto. All Jewish communities in Poland and Greater Germany (which includes annexed parts of Poland) with populations of less than 500 are dissolved.

September 22, 1939: The Germans establish the Reich Security Main Office (RSHA).

September 27, 1939: German troops capture Warsaw, a city with 375,000 Jews—the largest Jewish population in Europe.

September 28, 1939: Poland surrenders and is partitioned. Germany absorbs parts of Poland and occupies central Poland, an area it calls the General

Government. The Soviet Union annexes eastern Poland.

October 1939: Emanuel Ringelblum begins his secret Warsaw ghetto documentation project, which evolves into the underground *Oyneg Shabbes* archives. • Jews in Palestine volunteer to join the British army. Zionist leader David Ben-Gurion declares, "We will fight the War as if there were no White Paper, and we will fight the White Paper as if there were no War." Ultimately, some 30,000 men and women enlist.

October–December 1939: More than 200,000 Jews escape from German-occupied Poland to Soviet-held territories in eastern Poland. Among the escapees are a majority of the national leaders of Polish Jewry from all sectors of political life. They feared they would be the first targets of Nazi purges.

October 1, 1939: With Poland under German domination, a Polish government-in-exile is established in France.

October 4, 1939: A triumphant Hitler tours Warsaw.

October 8, 1939: The restriction of Jews to Nazi-enforced ghettos begins at Piotrkow Trybunalski, Poland.

October 12, 1939: Jews from Austria and Moravia are deported to ghetttos in Poland.

Mid-October 1939: Hitler signs an order (backdated to September 1, 1939, to give the appearance of a wartime measure) that authorizes Reich leader Philip Bouhler and Dr. Brandt to expand "the authority of physicians, to be designated by name, to the end that patients considered incurable according to the best available human judgment of their state of health, can be granted a mercy killing."

October 18–27, 1939: The Germans begin the deportation of 78,000 Jews to a planned reservation in the Lublin-Nisko region. The Germans consider this a territorial solution to the "Jewish problem."

October 24, 1939: Jews in Wloclawek, Poland, are required to wear the Yellow Star.

October 26, 1939: A German decree in occupied Poland subjects Jewish males, ages 14 to 60, to forced labor. Women will be included three months later.

November 1939: The *Vaad Hatzalah* (Rescue Committee) of the American Orthodox Rabbis is established. It aims to rescue major rabbinical figures, especially the faculties and students of the *Yeshivot* (Talmudic Academies) of Eastern Europe.

November 7, 1939: The deportation of Jews from western Poland begins.

November 12, 1939: Jews from the Warthegau province of Poland are ordered deported to clear the way for resettlement by ethnic Germans.

November 15–17, 1939: The synagogues of Lodz are destroyed.

November 23, 1939: Germans order Jews across occupied Poland to wear Yellow Stars or armbands with the Star of David.

November 30, 1939: The Soviet Union invades Finland.

December 5–6, 1939: Jewish property in Poland is confiscated, further impoverishing the increasingly desperate Polish Jews.

December 9, 1939: The Dominican Republic Settlement Association (DORSA) is founded by the AJDC (Joint). Following the Evian Conference of July 1938, the Dominican Republic's dictator, Rafael Trujillo, expressed willingness to accept 100,000 Jewish refugees. Realizing this figure to be unrealistic, Jewish organizations decided to create a pilot agricultural community at Sosua. In March 1940, the first of 500 Jews will arrive in Sosua.

December 31, 1939: Despite monumental obstacles, 78,000 Jews escaped from Germany in 1939. By October 1941, emigration from Germany will be banned, but 8,500 Jews will leave from 1942 to 1945. All told, nearly 60 percent of German Jews will flee Germany.

1940

January 6, 1940: Jews in Warsaw are forced to burn Jewish books for heat.

January–February 1940: Jewish youth movements in occupied Poland initiate clandestine underground activities.

February 8, 1940: A Jewish ghetto is established in Lodz, Poland. The ghetto will be sealed on April 30.

April 1940: Germany invades Denmark and Norway.

April 1, 1940: Shanghai, China, which is controlled by the Japanese, continues to accept Jewish refugees.

April 5, 1940: Mordecai Chaim Rumkowski, head of the Lodz *Judenrat,* initiates a master plan to make the ghetto residents an essential workforce: "My plan is to solve the problems of life in the ghetto. There are 8,000–10,000 skilled workers in various trades.... The work would be done in the ghetto.... I would turn the finished products over to the authorities in return for payment in cash or in food that I would distribute to the entire ghetto population...."

April 8–11, 1940: Soviet troops massacre 26,000 Polish officers at Katyn.

May 10, 1940: In a multifront attack, Germany invades Holland, Belgium, Luxembourg, and France.

May 11, 1940: The Jewish Council in Lodz allocates agricultural plots in the Marysin area of the ghetto. More than 1,300 youth, from among the thousands of ghetto youth who were active in youth movements, live and work in the training farms established in Marysin.

May 16, 1940: Germany intensifies its anti-Slavic policies by launching a "pacification operation" to eliminate Polish intellectuals and priests.

May 18, 1940: Germany deports 2,800 Gypsies to the Lublin region. In November 1941, 5,000 Gypsies will be sent to the Lodz ghetto.

May 20, 1940: The Auschwitz concentration camp begins functioning. Initial prisoners are Polish.

May 28, 1940: Belgium surrenders to Germany.

June 14, 1940: Paris falls to the Germans.

June 15, 1940: Amelot, a Jewish welfare association, is established in Paris to provide aid and relief to Jews in France.

Amelot will support refugee families, send food packages to Jews interned in camps, and feed thousands of Jews in its soup kitchens.

June 22, 1940: France signs an armistice with Germany.

June 26, 1940: The Hebrew Immigrant Aid Society (HIAS/HICEM) transfers its European headquarters from France to Lisbon, Portugal, to continue aiding Jews escaping from the Nazis. Portugal's western-leaning neutrality—unlike Spain's—as well as Lisbon's port with its worldwide shipping connections, make it the natural choice for both Jewish and non-Jewish rescue organizations to establish their European base of operations there. This includes the AJDC (Joint), the AFSC (Quakers), and the Unitarian Service Committee. Some 90,000 Jews who flee the Nazis are rescued via Lisbon.

Summer 1940: The French Jewish Scouts moves its base of operations south to the unoccupied Vichy zone of France, but continues to operate illegally in Paris. Its children's homes begin to care for the children of Jews imprisoned in Nazi camps. • The first clandestine newspapers of the diverse Jewish underground movements (Bund, Zionists, etc.) appear in Warsaw. During the war, additional Jewish underground newspapers appear in various cities, and there are more than 100 clandestine newspapers in Poland. Underground Jewish newspapers are also printed in German-occupied Belgium, France, and Lithuania.

July 3, 1940: The German Foreign Office proposes turning the island of Madagascar into a Jewish ghetto—another articulation of the territorial solution to the "Jewish problem."

July 10, 1940: The Battle of Britain begins.

August 1940: The Union of Jews for Resistance and Mutual Aid is formed by Jewish Communists in Paris.

September 1, 1940: Soviet officials order Japanese Consul Sempo Sugihara to leave Kovno. He has issued thousands of exit visas for Jews who have an end visa elsewhere to travel via Japan and Japanese-controlled Shanghai. Together with Dutch Consul Jan Zwartendijk, who provided an end visa to Curaçao (which required no visa), he is responsible for saving thousands of Jewish lives.

September 15, 1940: The German *Luftwaffe* (Air Force) suffers major losses in the Battle of Britain. Britain gains the upper hand.

September 23, 1940: Heinrich Himmler establishes a special *Reichsbank* account for gold, silver, money, and jewelry taken from Jews.

September 27, 1940: Japan joins the Axis by signing a treaty with Germany and Italy.

October 1940: Germany deports 7,500 Jews from southern Germany to internment camps in France.

October 3, 1940: Vichy France passes antisemitic legislation that excludes Jews from civil service, schools, the army, media, and other professions.

October 11, 1940: After persuading German authorities, Mordecai Chaim Rumkowski, head of the Lodz *Judenrat*, announces Saturday as the official day of rest for the ghetto. The Germans also permit public prayer services in synagogues. In October 1941, the Germans will revoke the arrangement; Jews will be forced to work on the Sabbath and to pray clandestinely.

October 12, 1940: Yom Kippur is chosen as the occasion to announce the formation of a ghetto in Warsaw.

October 14, 1940: Non-Jews are evacuated from the area that will become the Warsaw ghetto.

Late October 1940: The Jewish Society for Social Help (ZETOS), a "front" organization, is created in Warsaw. Headed by Emanuel Ringelblum, it secretly represents the banned Jewish political parties. ZETOS will organize public kitchens and support children's homes, hospitals, and health clinics. Its main achievement will be the promotion of the House Committees to aid families living in shared courtyards. House Committees, often operating in opposition to the *Judenrat*, help the poor, care for children, and promote cultural life. By early 1942, there will be 1,108 House Committees with

7,500 committee members. They provide at least some welfare relief and contribute to the spiritual survival of the Warsaw ghetto population.

November 15, 1940: The Warsaw ghetto is sealed. Historian Emanuel Ringelblum and his colleagues decide to continue their secretly buried archive of Jewish life, code-naming it *Oyneg Shabbes* (The Joy of Sabbath). • Under German pressure, Holland suspends all Jews from the civil service, including its Jewish Supreme Court president, L. E. Visser.

November 17, 1940: The Lodz ghetto archives are established by the *Judenrat*. It oversees the collection of documentary material, such as posters, that informs the population of various directives as well as announcements pertaining to food distribution, religious services, etc. The archives include images from several photographers, notably Mendel Grossman and Henryk Ross, who take thousands of photographs, including numerous "unofficial" images. The photos document the brutality of Jewish life as well as the ways in which Jews resist dehumanization.

November 20–24, 1940: Hungary, Slovakia, and Romania ally themselves with Nazi Germany. Each already have passed anti-Jewish laws.

November 28, 1940: German filmmaker Fritz Hippler's "documentary," *The Eternal Jew*, premieres in Berlin.

December 1940: The Vatican condemns the "mercy killing" of unfit Aryans.

1941

January 12, 1941: The Chronicle of the Lodz Ghetto is initiated. Under the direction of the ghetto archives, it will be prepared daily and without interruption until July 30, 1944. The daily entries generally include a weather report; statistics on births and deaths; a list of food distribution; data on health conditions; and official announcements. Also included are reports on places where Jews are employed and reports on raids, expulsions, and executions. • Lodz *Judenrat* head Mordecai Chaim Rumkowski orders most of the training farms in Marysin dismantled. The youth movements' members will return home to continue their

activities clandestinely in small groups. They will play a critical role in sustaining and nurturing ghetto youth, both physically through mutual aid and spiritually through their educational and social initiatives.

January 21, 1941: The Romanian Iron Guard launches a *coup d'etat,* during which 120 Jews are killed and thousands are beaten.

January 22, 1941: The Law for the Defense of the Nation is imposed in Bulgaria. It excludes Jews from public service, taxes Jewish businesses, and dismisses Jewish doctors, lawyers, and professionals.

January 30, 1941: On his eighth anniversary as chancellor, Hitler reiterates his 1939 statement in which he threatened the destruction of Jews in Europe.

February 12, 1941: The Germans create a Jewish Council in Amsterdam, the first of many used to control Jews in Western Europe.

February 15, 1941: The Germans begin to deport 1,000 Jews per week from Vienna to ghettos in Kielce and Lublin in German-occupied Poland.

February 25, 1941: Dutch citizens stage a general strike to protest the deportation of Jews from Holland.

March 1941: A cultural center opens in the Lodz ghetto. *Judenrat*-sponsored events include concerts by the ghetto orchestra, lectures, and theatrical plays. Previously, cultural events took place in the soup kitchens of the political parties.

March 1, 1941: Bulgaria becomes an ally of Germany. German troops will enter Bulgaria the next day.

March 26, 1941: The German army's high command approves the tasks of the *Einsatzgruppen* in anticipation of the planned German invasion of the Soviet Union.

March 29, 1941: The Vichy France collaborationist government forms an Office for Jewish Affairs to coordinate anti-Jewish policies and laws in occupied and unoccupied France.

The walling off of the Krakow ghetto, which was formally established on March 3, 1941.

April 6, 1941: German and Italian forces invade Greece and Yugoslavia; the danger to Jews is immediate.

April 18, 1941: Yugoslavia surrenders. Serbia is occupied, and Germany creates a puppet state in Croatia.

Spring 1941: Following ghettoization in March, a Jewish underground is created in Krakow. Led by Zionist youth movements, it focuses on mutual aid and educational activities to maintain morale. It also publishes an underground newspaper, *Hechalutz Halochem* (*The Fighting Pioneer*).

May 1941: The ousting of Heinrich Schwartz as head of the Jewish Council in Slovakia results in the pursuit of alternative Jewish leadership. This develops into the Working Group, a Jewish underground organization intent on rescuing Jews. It is led by Gisi Fleischmann, a leading prewar Zionist activist.

May 22, 1941: Jews in Croatia must now wear the Yellow Star.

June 6, 1941: The Commissar Order is issued. All Soviet officials are to be "liquidated" (murdered).

June 17, 1941: Reinhard Heydrich briefs the *Einsatzgruppen* (mobile killing units) commanders.

June 22, 1941: The German army invades Soviet Union in Operation Barbarossa. Germany is now involved in a two-front war. *Einsatzgruppen*, with the assistance of local gendarmerie and native antisemites as well as the *Wehrmacht*, begin killing Jews immediately.

June 24, 1941: Kovno, Lithuania, is occupied by German troops. Arriving German troops are forced to halt the locals who had initiated brutal massacres of Kovno's Jews. Eventually, the SS will recruit many locals to assist their killing units.

June 25, 1941: The French Jewish underground issues the first edition of its clandestine newspaper, *Unser Vort* (*Our Word*).

June 26, 1941: Croatia, a Nazi puppet state, orders 40,000 Croatian Jews to concentration camps. Ultimately, two-thirds will be imprisoned and killed. • Hundreds of Jews are shot outside of Kovno.

June 29–July 1941: Romanian soldiers and local police begin a pogrom in Iasi. Thousands of Jews are brutally murdered, and 4,000 are deported on trains to the countryside (less than half will survive the journey). A few months later, Romania will initiate the deportation of 150,000 Jews to camps in Transnistria (today Ukraine), where most will die.

Summer 1941: Following the German invasion of the Soviet Union, members of the Union of Jews for Resistance and Mutual Aid, in France, begin sabotaging German industry. It is part of the decision by the French Communists to initiate armed resistance.

Mid-1941: The Amelot Jewish welfare organization expands its activities to aid arrested Jews in France. It also provides aid and relief for Jews who escaped deportation. Additional clandestine activities include securing and maintaining hiding places for children and providing forged documentation and material support for Jews in hiding. More than 1,000 children will be rescued.

July 1, 1941: Rioting erupts against the Jews in Lvov, German-occupied Poland. • The murder of 150,000 Jews (over a period of two months) by *Einsatzgruppen*, the *Wehrmacht*, and a special Romanian unit begins in Bessarabia.

July 3, 1941: Some 3,500 Jews are killed at Zloczow.

July 4, 1941: The murder of 5,000 Jews in Tarnopol, Ukraine, begins. It will last a week.

July 8, 1941: Jews in the Baltic states must now wear the Yellow Star.

July 10, 1941: Some 1,600 Jews of Jedwabne are murdered by their Polish neighbors. The mere presence of German troops in the area is sufficient to spur the massacre, which will be blamed on the Germans for the next six decades.

July 25–26, 1941: Approximately 3,800 Jews are killed in a pogrom in Kovno.

July 31, 1941: Hermann Goring instructs Reinhard Heydrich to evacuate and eliminate all Jews currently in German-held territories, to implement what the Germans call the Final Solution, the systematic mass murder of Jews.

August 2, 1941: Four thousand Jews are killed at Ponary, the killing field adjacent to Vilna, Lithuania.

August 5, 1941: The murder of 11,000 Jews in Pinsk begins. It will conclude on the 8th.

August 17, 1941: A Jewish underground group is formed in the Minsk ghetto, Belorussia. Led by Hersh Smolar, the nearly 450 members will plan to escape and fight with the partisans. While waiting for the partisan movement to establish themselves in the forests, the underground will be active in the ghetto. It will develop a clandestine network that gathers and spreads news about the war's progress, organizes a printing press, establishes contact with the non-Jewish inhabitants of Minsk, and gathers weapons. Following the *Aktion* in March 1942, the underground will escape to the forests, where Minsk Jews will form seven partisan units.

August 20–21, 1941: Approximately 4,300 Jews are deported from Paris to the Drancy transit camp—the first of 70,000 Jews to be interned in Drancy. Many will be deported from there to Auschwitz.

August 21, 1941: A concentration camp opens in Jasenovac, Croatia.

August 27, 1941: Some 25,000 Hungarian Jews in forced-labor battalions are shot near Kamenets-Podolski. The killing takes two days.

August 29, 1941: Germany restricts Belgian Jews to residing in four cities, setting a pattern in the west in which Jews are segregated yet not sealed in ghettos, as in Poland.

September 1, 1941: Jews in Germany, which now includes Austria, Bohemia, and Moravia, must wear the Yellow Star.

September 3, 1941: The first gassing at Auschwitz occurs. Some 600 Soviet prisoners of war and 300 Jews are murdered. These "experiments" in the use of gas as a method of mass killing, will prove significant to the evolution of Auschwitz into a death camp.

September 6, 1941: In the Lodz ghetto, a student named Noach Flug graduates from high school. In the ghetto, some 15,000 children study in the 47 schools run by the Jewish Council's education department, ranging from kindergarten to high school. The school system operates with few disruptions for two years, and provides the children with medical attention and a daily meal. These schools serve as a ray of light in a sea of darkness, and they are an attempt to maintain continuity and normalcy. Formal educational activities will be suspended in autumn 1941, and henceforth children over 10 years will be forced to work. Some workshops will maintain clandestine classes.

September 13, 1941: Eleven members of the *Judenrat* of Piotrkow, German-occupied Poland, who had cooperated with the Jewish underground, are executed after torture.

September 15, 1941: Eighteen thousand Jews are murdered in Berdichev.

September 16, 1941: Some 24,000 Jews from Uman, Ukraine, are murdered at the airport.

September 22, 1941: Ukrainian militiamen massacre 28,000 Jews at Vinnitsa.

September 27, 1941: In Ejszyszki, Lithuania, 3,200 Jews are executed.

September 29–30, 1941: At Babi Yar, a ravine adjacent to Kiev, 33,771 Jews are shot.

October 2, 1941: Three thousand Jews from Vilna, arrested on the sacred day of Yom Kippur, are killed at Ponary.

October 13, 1941: Fifteen thousand Jews are executed at Dnepropetrovsk in German-occupied Soviet Union.

October 28, 1941: One-third of 27,000 Jews in Kovno are selected to be killed in the Ninth Fort. This group includes the elderly and the infirm as well as children.

November 1, 1941: Construction of the death camp at Belzec begins.

November 7, 1941: Some 17,000 Jews are forced from Rovno, Ukraine, in German-occupied Poland, and murdered in the Sosenki Forest nearby.

November 23, 1941: Thirty thousand Jews are murdered at Odessa.

November 24, 1941: A "model ghetto"/transit camp/concentration camp is established at Theresienstadt in German-occupied Czechoslovakia. Czech Jews will be relocated to Theresienstadt, which the Germans will use to deceive the world that they are treating Jews well.

November 27, 1941: Some 10,600 Jews are murdered at Riga, Latvia.

December 1, 1941: The commander of *Einsatzgruppe* 3 reports that 85 percent of Lithuania's Jews are dead.

December 7, 1941: Japan attacks the U.S. naval base at Pearl Harbor, Hawaii.

December 8, 1941: Gassing by mobile gas vans commences at Chelmno in German-occupied Poland. • The United States, Great Britain, Australia, and New Zealand declare war on Japan.

December 11, 1941: The United States declares war on Germany and Italy. Germany and Italy declare war on the United States.

December 21–30, 1941: More than 40,000 Jews are murdered at Bogdanovka in Transnistria.

December 31, 1941: Jewish underground leader Abba Kovner of Lithuania calls for armed resistance against the Germans. He perceives that the Germans aim to kill all the Jews of Europe, and that the Jews of Lithuania are first in line. "Jewish youth, do not believe those who are trying to deceive you. Out of 80,000 Jews of Vilna only 20,000 are left.... All the Gestapo roads lead to Ponary and Ponary means death.... Brethren, it is better to die fighting like free men than to live at the mercy of the murderers. To defend oneself to the last breath."

1942

January 1942: At the beginning of 1942, four out of five of the people who will die in the Holocaust are still alive. A mere 15 months later, the numbers will be reversed. • The *Armee Juive* (Jewish Army; AJ), a French Jewish resistance organization, is established. Founded by Zionist activists Abraham Polonski and Lucien Lublin in Toulouse in southern France, they decide to create a Jewish militia in response to the German occupation. Acting in total secrecy, its members swear their loyalty to the AJ. Recruits begin training to fight even before the AJ has acquired arms. • In the Kovno ghetto, Chaim Yellin establishes, with fellow Communists, the underground Anti-Fascist Organization. In 1943 Yellin's group will merge with the Zionist underground to form the General Jewish Fighting Organization, which will succeed in organizing the escape of some 350 fighters to the partisans.

January 7, 1942: Germans murder by gassing the 5,000 Gypsies who were sent to Chelmno from the Lodz ghetto.

January 19, 1942: Jacob Grojanowski escapes from the Chelmno death camp. He eventually will reach the Warsaw ghetto, where he will supply details of the systematic murder operation to the underground *Oyneg Shabbes* archives. The Grojanowski Report will be delivered to the Polish underground, which will smuggle it out to the Polish government-in-exile in London in June 1942.

January 20, 1942: The Wannsee Conference is held in Berlin, bringing together top Nazi leaders of the party, the German state, and the occupied territories. Their task is to coordinate and implement under SS leadership the Final Solution to the "Jewish problem"—the Nazi euphemism for the murder of European Jews.

January 21, 1942: The *Fareynegte Partizaner Organizatsye* (United Partisan Organization; UPO), a Jewish armed underground organization uniting various Zionist youth movements with the Communists, and eventually the Bund, is established in the Vilna ghetto. Its commander is Itzik Wittenberg (of the Communists), and its deputy commanders (from the Zionists) are Abba Kovner and Jozef Glazman. UPO members will blow up railroad tracks used by German forces, sabotage weapons and equipment in German factories, forge documents, and desperately attempt to obtain weapons from the local population. They also will assemble primitive explosives inside the ghetto. The UPO will establish contact with nearby ghettos to inform them about the mass murders in Vilna and other locations in Lithuania, hoping to spread the idea of armed revolt and resistance.

January 22, 1942: In an attempt to camouflage the clandestine gathering of documentation gathered for the *Oyneg Shabbes* underground archives in the Warsaw ghetto, an essay competition is announced. Ghetto residents are offered prizes for essays (to be submitted to the archives) dealing with various themes on "Jewish Life During the War."

January 30, 1942: In a speech to the *Reichstag*, Hitler reiterates his pledge to destroy the Jews of Europe: "Those who were laughing at my prophecy are not laughing now."

Early 1942: A Jewish underground organization is established in the Grodno ghetto in eastern Poland, uniting various Zionist youth movements, the Bund, and

Communists. There are disagreements regarding tactics. The Zionists aspire to give the struggle a Jewish character via an armed revolt in the ghetto, while the Communists seek to join the partisans and thereby help in the Soviet struggle against the Nazis.

February 15, 1942: The first mass gassing of Jews begins at Auschwitz-Birkenau.

February 22, 1942: Ten thousand Jews are deported from the Lodz ghetto to the Chelmno killing center, where they are gassed.

February 24, 1942: The SS *Struma*, carrying 769 Romanian Jewish refugees, is sunk by a Soviet submarine in the waters off Turkey. David Stoliar is the lone survivor. The engine on the ship did not work, and its passengers were not permitted to disembark in Turkey or to enter British-controlled Palestine.

March 1942: Rabbi Michael Dov Weissmandel, a leader of the ultra-Orthodox Agudath Israel movement, joins the Working Group together with his Zionist relative, Gisi Fleischmann. It is a rare combination of Zionists and ultra-Orthodox Jews, a secular woman and devout rabbi working together in a Slovak Jewish underground. They lead the group in its daring clandestine activities to save Jews, which will include the successful bribing of a senior Nazi official to stop deportations from Slovakia for two years. These negotiations will evolve into the Europa Plan, which aspires to halt depor-

Jews in the Warsaw ghetto. In summer 1942, more than 250,000 Warsaw Jews were sent to Treblinka.

tations throughout Europe. The Working Group also facilitates the escape of some 10,000 Jews from Slovakia and Poland into Hungary, and it aids Slovak Jews deported to Poland. The group maintains clandestine contacts with Jewish organizations outside Slovakia, seeking funds to bribe Nazi officials and also inform the world about the fate of the Jews.

March 17, 1942: The deportation of 30,000 Jews from Lublin begins. This deportation lasts four weeks.

March 17–July 23, 1942: Germany completes a network of six death camps, all located in occupied-Poland. In addition to Chelmno and Auschwitz, these include Belzec, Sobibor, Treblinka, and Majdanek.

March 24, 1942: The first deportation of Western European Jews to Belzec begins.

March 27, 1942: The first deportation of French Jews to Auschwitz begins.

Late March 1942: The Anti-Fascist Bloc, the first organized Jewish fighting organization in the Warsaw ghetto, is founded. Despite their inherently different agendas, the PPR (Communists) and various leftist Zionist youth movements establish a united body. The PPR insists on organizing groups to fight in the distant forests, while the Zionists, who seek an armed uprising in the ghetto, reluctantly agree.

April 1942: Soviet authorities in Moscow announce the formation of the Jewish Anti-Fascist Committee. Led by renowned actor Shlomo Michoels and poet Itzik Fefer, they will travel to America and England in 1943 to enlist active Jewish support for the Soviet war effort. While the war is still being fought, the committee will be one of the first institutions to document the atrocities of the German assault against the Jews and acts of Jewish resistance. Two prominent Soviet Jewish writers, Ilya Ehrenburg and Vasily Grossman, will prepare the manuscript for *The Black Book of Soviet Jewry*, only segments of which will be published due to Soviet censorship.

April 11, 1942: Hungary sends 50,000 Jews in forced-labor battalions to the Soviet front. Lacking proper clothing and often starved, many will die while some will escape.

April 18, 1942: The "Night of Blood" unfolds in the Warsaw ghetto. German forces raid the ghetto with prepared lists of underground activists. Many are shot on the ghetto streets. A total of 52 persons are murdered, including Bund and Zionist underground leaders.

April 29, 1942: In Holland, Germany further isolates the Jews by ordering them to wear a Yellow Star of David.

Early 1942: Following the May 1941 arrest of French Jews, the Union of Jews for Resistance and Mutual Aid creates the National Movement Against Racism, hoping to enlist the support of the non-Jewish population.

May 1942: Poland's Jewish labor Bund, in a report issued after 11 months of clandestinely gathering firsthand accounts, concludes that Germany plans to "annihilate all the Jews of Europe." The report reaches the free world, which doubts the accuracy of the report. Newspaper articles of the detailed report are relegated to the back pages.

May 4, 1942: More than 10,000 Jews are deported from Lodz to Chelmno for gassing. The operation takes 12 days.

May 8, 1942: Tuvia Bielski and his brothers encourage entire families to escape from ghettos and join his armed fighters in the dense forests of Belorussia in eastern Poland. His "Family Camp" ultimately rescues some 1,200 men, women, and children.

May 15, 1942: The first issue of *Der Ruf* (*The Call*), the underground newspaper of the Anti-Fascist Bloc, is published in the Warsaw ghetto. It calls on the Jewish masses to join in an armed struggle against the Nazi oppressor.

May 18, 1942: Herbert and Marianne Baum's Communist underground group— mostly Jewish men and women—sets fire to a Nazi anti-Soviet propaganda exhibit in Berlin. Most are caught and executed.

May 27, 1942: Two Czech underground fighters sent from Britain attack Reinhard Heydrich's car, severely wounding him. He will die from his injuries a week later.

June 1–6, 1942: Seven thousand Jews from Krakow are gassed at Belzec.

June 2, 1942: Based on the Bund Report, the BBC reports that 700,000 Jews have been murdered.

June 5, 1942: The SS reports that 97,000 persons have been "processed" in mobile gas vans.

June 9, 1942: More than 190 men and boys are killed in Lidice in German-occupied Czechoslovakia in response to the assassination of Reinhard Heydrich. The residents of Lidice were not involved with the attack on Heydrich.

June 11, 1942: Ten thousand Jews from Tarnow are deported to Belzec for gassing.

June 12, 1942: An armed uprising erupts in the Druja ghetto in the Vilna district of Poland.

June 20, 1942: The deportation of 13,776 Viennese Jews to Theresienstadt begins.

June 30, 1942: A second gas chamber is opened at Auschwitz-Birkenau.
• *The London Daily Telegraph* reports more than one million Jews have been killed.

July 6, 1942: Anne Frank and her family go into hiding in Amsterdam after Anne's sister, Margot, receives orders to report for "resettlement in the East."

July 8, 1942: Seven thousand Jews from Lvov are killed in the adjacent Janowska labor camp.

July 14, 1942: Thousands of Dutch Jews are arrested and deported to transit camps. Auschwitz is their ultimate destination.

July 16–17, 1942: In Paris, some 13,000 Jews are rounded up by French police. About 7,000 Jews will be packed into the *Velodrome d'Hiver* sports complex for days, without food, water, or toilets. Many thousands will be deported to the Drancy transit camp outside Paris, from where they will be shipped to the death camps in occupied Poland. In southern France in 1942, the Vichy authorities deport Jews in their zone.

July 17, 1942: Heinrich Himmler visits Auschwitz and observes the gassings.

July 19, 1942: A planned armed uprising by the Jewish underground in Baranowicze, in eastern Poland, is postponed due to opposition from the ghetto population, who believe that a revolt would result in the ghetto's total liquidation. The underground will escape to the forest and use their weapons to fight with the partisans.

July 21, 1942: Armed revolt in the Nieswiez ghetto in eastern Poland erupts when German forces come to destroy the ghetto. The underground sets the ghetto ablaze, and most of the nearly 600 Jews are killed after inflicting 40 casualties on the Germans. About 25 fighters escape and join the Soviet partisans in the forests. • Armed resistance occurs in the Kleck ghetto in eastern Poland.

July 22, 1942: Mass deportations from Warsaw begin. By September 21, 1942, 265,000 Jews will be deported to the Treblinka death camp.

July 23, 1942: Adam Czerniakow, chairman of the Warsaw Jewish Council, commits suicide. "They have asked me to kill the children with my own hands," he stated. "This I cannot do."

July 28, 1942: The Jewish Fighting Organization (JFO; ZOB) is established in the Warsaw ghetto. The despair over the inability of the Anti-Fascist Bloc to respond with arms during the deportations results in the establishment of the JFO, which by October will include most Zionist youth movements and, significantly, the anti-Zionist Bund and Communists. Commanded by Mordecai Anilewicz, the JFO will become the dominant authority in the ghetto and will be supported by the masses that no longer respect the Jewish Council and Jewish Police. • Four days of killing begins in Minsk; 30,000 Jews will be murdered.

July 30, 1942: German industrialist Eduard Schulte tells a Swiss colleague of the decision to kill the Jews and to use prussic acid for gassing. Information will soon reach Gerhard Riegner of the World Jewish Congress in Geneva.

July 31, 1942: A Jewish resistance group burns the population files from Belgium's Jewish Council to sabotage deportations.

Summer 1942: Following the mass deportations of French Jews, the Union of Jews for Resistance and Mutual Aid forms partisan combat groups. Their underground press publicizes the Nazi program for mass murder and urges Jews not to report for "resettlement." It calls for the Jews to hide and join them in armed resistance. By the end of the war, the organization will have saved 900 Jewish children. • The *Eclaireurs Israelites de France* (French Jewish Scouts) establishes social services that evolve into a rescue organization. It supplies Jewish children with forged documents, places them in safe homes, and organizes dangerous escapes from France across German-patrolled borders.

August 1942: The Jewish Defense Committee is created. It unites all Jewish resistance organizations in France, including the Communists.

August 3, 1942: Twelve thousand Jews from Prezemysl, in German-occupied Poland, are deported to Belzec.

August 4, 1942: The first deportations of Belgium Jews to Auschwitz begins.

August 5, 1942: Dr. Janusz Korczak—who refused offers to go into hiding—and the staff of his Warsaw ghetto orphanage accompany the children to the deportation train that takes them to the Treblinka death camp. Nahum Remba observes the procession: "It was not a march to the trains; it was an organized protest against the brutality of the oppressors. All the children were standing four in a row, Korczak at the head with raised eyes, holding two children by the hand, leading the children into the train."

SS troops prepare to kill their captives in the Palmiry Forest outside of Warsaw.

August 6, 1942: Armed resistance occurs in the Zdzieciol ghetto in eastern Poland.

August 6–17, 1942: Twenty thousand Jews from Radom are murdered at Treblinka.

August 10, 1942: Jewish partisans, led by Dr. Yehiel Atlas, attack a German garrison at Drechin, in the Belorussian area of Poland, executing 44 German policemen.

August 10–30, 1942: Fifty thousand Jews from Lvov, Poland, are murdered.

August 20–24, 1942: Amid the deportations from Warsaw, 19,000 Jews from Kielce arrive in Treblinka, where they are gassed.

August 29, 1942: Rabbi Stephen Wise, president of the World Jewish Congress (WJC), receives a cable from Gerhard Riegner, a WJC representative in Geneva, informing him "that there has been and is being considered in Hitler's headquarters a plan to exterminate all Jews from Germany and German-controlled areas in Europe after they have been concentrated in the east. The numbers involved is said to be between three and a half and four million and the object to permanently settle the Jewish question in Europe." Wise is asked by the U.S. State Department, which had previously received the cable through secret channels, to keep silent until information is verified.

Early September 1942: The Committee for the Defense of Jews (CDJ) is established in Brussels, Belgium. Also, local Jewish resistance groups are established in Antwerp, Charleroi, and Liege. The CDJ will be active in communal aid while producing forged documents, publishing clandestine newspapers, and supplying the armed Jewish partisans who operate in the cities. A major achievement is the hiding and rescue of some 4,000 children. CDJ members will contact Yvonne Nevejean, who chairs the National Agency for Children (ONE), to help them find homes and institutions to hide Jewish children. The Jewish underground will finance the rescue operation, but when funds run out, Nevejean will supply funding.

Rosh Hashanah, 1942: Rabbi Ephraim Oshry responds affirmatively to the question of whether a cracked *shofar* (ram's horn used for High Holy Days prayers) may be used. Rabbi Oshry, an authority on Jewish law who is confined to the Kovno ghetto, is often sought out by ghetto residents regarding questions of Jewish law. He will bury the thousands of questions and responses and publish them after the war. He sees it as testimony to the Jewish devotion to the practice of their faith, even in the dreadful circumstances of the Holocaust.

September 3, 1942: The Jewish Council of Lachwa, in the Belorussian area of Poland, leads a revolt against the German forces who came to liquidate the ghetto. Some 600 Jews escape.

September 4–12, 1942: Lodz Jewish Council Chairman Mordecai Chaim Rumkowski reluctantly agrees to the deportation of children and old people. He says: "Brothers and sisters, hand them over to me; fathers and mothers, give me your children." His justification: Only some Jews can be saved, and it is better to save some than to risk total destruction. Fifteen thousand are deported. He describes himself as a "broken Jew."

September 21, 1942: Bodies of previously gassed Jews are dug up at Auschwitz and burned in open pits to prevent contamination of local ground water.

September 22, 1942: Forty thousand Jews of Czestochowa are deported to Treblinka. • Jews attack guards during a roundup of Jews in the Baranowicze ghetto in eastern Poland. A Latvian officer is stabbed to death, and a barber named Zubak uses his razor to cut the throat of a Belorussian policeman.

September 23–24, 1942: An armed revolt is staged in the Tuczyn ghetto in eastern Poland. After hearing of the annihilation of the Jews in nearby Rovno, the Jewish leaders of Tuczyn decided to resist. German and Ukrainian troops are shot upon as they enter, and the ghetto is set ablaze. Of the 3,000 Jews in the ghetto, some 2,000 escape to the forests, while the rest are killed in the revolt, which lasts two days. About half of those who reach the forests are soon caught, and 300 women with babies, unable to withstand the conditions in the forest, return to Tuczyn, where they are shot.

September 25, 1942: Jews of Korets, Ukraine, escape to the woods while others set the ghetto ablaze rather than submit to deportation.

September 30, 1942: Slovakia agrees to pay Germany a bounty of 500 Marks per Jew to deport all Slovakian Jews.

October 1942: The Jewish Fighting Organization (JFO) is created in the Krakow ghetto. Due to the limited area of operations in the ghetto, the JFO decides to carry out armed attacks outside the ghetto. The most famous will happen on December 22, 1942, in downtown Krakow at the Cyganeria Cafe, where German officers frequently gather. This attack will result in the killing of 11 Germans, with 13 more wounded.

October 4, 1942: All Jews in concentration camps in Germany are ordered to be sent to Auschwitz.

October 11–12, 1942: Eleven thousand Jews from Ostrowiec Swietokrzyski are killed at Treblinka.

October 15, 1942: Approximately 25,000 Jews of Brest-Litovsk are murdered.

October 21, 1942: Some 22,000 Jews of Piotrkow Trybunalski are deported to Treblinka.

October 28, 1942: The first transport of Jews from Theresienstadt to Auschwitz begins. By war's end, more than 88,000 will be deported from Theresienstadt to Auschwitz.

November 8, 1942: A predominantly Jewish resistance group helps liberate Algiers during the Allied advance that frees North Africa from German rule.

November 13, 1942: Sixty-nine Jews with Palestinian passports arrive in Palestine from occupied Europe. They were exchanged for German nationals residing in Palestine. Based on their firsthand and reliable information regarding Nazi

atrocities, the Jews in Palestine declare a week of national mourning. Its leadership is stimulated into action on behalf of Jews in occupied countries. They will make passionate appeals to the Allies to implement rescue operations.

November 24, 1942: Rabbi Stephen Wise goes public with information regarding the Final Solution. A State Department official told him: "I can confirm your deepest fears." But when pressed, the State Department will not confirm Wise's report. Thus, it appears in the press as a Jewish statement rather than government information, and the impact of the information is limited. The report that two million Jews have been murdered is, in fact, an understatement.

Late fall 1942: The Jewish Military Union (JMU; ZZW), an armed underground group in the Warsaw ghetto, is organized by *Betar*, the youth movement of the Revisionist Zionist Movement. The JMU will succeed in procuring weapons as a result of its ties with the underground Polish Home Army (AK).

December 1942: An operations office of the Rescue Committee of the Jewish Agency for Palestine is established in Istanbul, Turkey. Operating until 1944, the committee will maintain contact with Jewish communities in occupied Europe. It also will organize aid and rescue operations, working together with Zionist representatives in Switzerland.

December 5, 1942: A senior Nazi official asks SS chief Heinrich Himmler to ensure that the army use of rail lines does not interrupt transports to death camps.

December 6, 1942: Germans order Jewish leaders in Tunisia to provide Jews for forced labor. Eventually, 5,000 Jews will be deported to 30 labor camps.

December 12, 1942: Armed resistance occurs in the Luck labor camp in Volhynia, German-occupied Poland.

December 17, 1942: The United States, Great Britain, Soviet Union, and other Allied nations condemn Nazi "extermination of the Jewish People in Europe."

1943

Early 1943: The Relief and Rescue Committee of Budapest is established.

Led by Otto Komoly and Rezso Kasztner, it is composed of representatives of the various Hungarian Zionist groups. The committee will engage in the clandestine smuggling of Jews from Poland and Slovakia into relatively safe Hungary. It also will aid refugees in Hungary and prepare for the self-defense of Hungarian Jewry. • Rabbi Leon Pessah, a graduate of Salonika's rabbinical seminary, escapes with his family from German roundups in Trikala, Greece, and joins the Greek partisans. Fluent in Italian, French, and other languages and dialects of the area, Rabbi Pessah operates as a courier to relay messages among the various groups of partisans.

January 3, 1943: Polish President Wladyslaw Raczkiewicz requests that Pope Pius XII denounce German attacks on Jews. The pope will remain silent.

January 4, 1943: The SS instructs concentration camp commandants to send human hair taken from Jewish women to Germany for processing. • The first act of Jewish armed resistance in the Czestochowa ghetto occurs. Ordered to gather for deportation, resistance fighter Fiszlewicz shoots a German officer with his pistol. His comrade, Feiner, attacks another officer with his knife.

January 10, 1943: Armed resistance occurs in the Minsk Mazowiecki labor camp, near Warsaw, as Germans enter to liquidate the camp. There are no Jewish survivors.

January 12, 1943: The deportation of 20,000 Jews from Zambrow, in German-occupied Poland, begins. The operation will continue for 10 days.

January 15, 1943: A coded letter in Hebrew is clandestinely sent by courier from Rabbi Michael Dov Weissmandel, a leader of the underground Working Group in Slovakia, to Jewish Agency representatives in neutral Switzerland. As per earlier letters, Rabbi Weissmandel focuses on the negotiations to bribe Nazi officials to halt deportations: "As we are dealing with matters of life and death, we must blind them [Germans] with at least a $100,000 deposit from our allies. Three paragraphs have already been negotiated with E [code for Eichmann] and he has agreed to them: (1) Cancellation of deportations to Poland from all occupied countries; (2) Deportations will not be cancelled from [Greater] Germany, or Poland; (3) Assistance by legal means, such as sending limited packages, money, and letters to the deported [Jews]...."

January 18, 1943: Germans resume Warsaw ghetto deportations. Jews respond with resistance, and street fighting erupts. Over a period of four days, 5,000 Jews will be deported to Treblinka from Warsaw. The halt of deportations is perceived by the resistance as a victory. From then onward, Jews remaining in the ghetto will support the idea of armed resistance.

February 2, 1943: The German Sixth Army surrenders to the Soviets at Stalingrad, a momentous event that demonstrates that the Germans can be defeated.

February 10, 1943: The State Department sends a cable to the American legation in Bern, stating that secure government lines cannot be used for the transmission of information to private individuals. Given the cable's reference to previous communications on the fate of Jews, the implications are unmistakable: Shut down information coming in about the Jews.

February 12, 1943: Hayim Greenberg, a Zionist leader in the United States, publishes a harsh critique of American Jewish organizations' failure to effectively act on behalf of those Jews who are under Nazi domination. His editorial, entitled "Bankrupt," appears in the Yiddish newspaper *Der Yiddisher Kempfer*: "It will never be possible to explain why the chief organizations of American Jewry... could not in this dire hour, unequalled even in Jewish history, unite... to save those who *perhaps* can still be saved."

February 16, 1943: A Jewish activist group in the United States, headed by Peter Bergson, places a full-page *New York Times* advertisement: "For Sale to Humanity—70,000 Jews/Guaranteed Human Beings at $50 a Piece."

February 20, 1943: Crematoria II is completed at Birkenau, the death camp at Auschwitz.

February 24, 1943: A ghetto is established in Salonika in German-occupied Greece.

אין די וועלדער

ביערות

Members of the Lenin Brigade, a resistance group.

February 26, 1943: The first Gypsies arrive in Auschwitz, where they are interned in a special section known as the Gypsy Camp.

Early 1943: The French Jewish Scouts establish a fighting unit, which will participate in the liberation of southwest France in 1944.

March 1943: The *Tiyul* (Hike) Committee is established by Joel Brand and Zionist youth movements in Hungary to clandestinely smuggle some 9,000 Jews into Hungary from Poland and Slovakia. The committee dispatches professional smugglers across borders to help fleeing Jewish refugees, or work from addresses supplied by escapees to locate Jews in hiding. The youth movements also establish an underground workshop to produce large quantities of forged documents, which will be used by tens of thousands of people. • In Berlin, Yitzhak Schwersenz and Edith Wolff establish *Chug sChalutzi* (Zionist Circle), a resistance group composed of religious Zionist youth. In addition to maintaining clandestine contacts with the Zionist movement in Switzerland, the group focuses on eluding deportation, smuggling young persons out of Germany, and sustaining the spirits of those who remain. Meeting secretly for prayer and study activities, the members are assigned safe houses at sympathetic Germans' homes. They are provided with ration cards and false documents. *Chug Chalutzi* will be active

until the end of the war and will succeed in saving many of its members. • The German government demands the deportation of Bulgarian Jews, but Bulgaria, which had previously consented to the deportation of Jews from the annexed areas of Thrace and Macedonia, refuses in the face of unexpectedly stiff domestic opposition from intellectual, cultural, and religious leaders. Nevertheless, Jews from those regions will be deported to the Treblinka death camp in early March.

March 9, 1943: The Bergson Group presents the pageant "We Will Never Die" in New York City.

March 15, 1943: Deportations of Jews from Salonika begins. By mid-August, some 56,000 Greek Jews will be deported to Auschwitz.

March 22, 1943: Crematorium IV opens at Auschwitz-Birkenau.

April 19, 1943: The Warsaw Ghetto Uprising begins. The fighting will continue openly until May 16, 1943, when SS General Jurgen Stroop will report to his superiors, "The Jewish quarter is no longer." • Jewish resistance fighters at Tirlemont, Belgium, attack a deportation train transporting Belgian Jews to Auschwitz, freeing 200 Jews. • The Bermuda Conference of Great Britain and the United States is held to consider the plight of Jewish refugees in Europe. Access to the island of Bermuda is restricted, and the public pressure on the delegations is therefore lessened. Representatives at the conference fail to decide on any significant rescue options.

April 20, 1943: Germans respond to the Warsaw Ghetto Uprising by setting the ghetto on fire, building by building, block by block.

May 8, 1943: German troops reach Mila 18, resistance headquarters in the Warsaw ghetto, where Mordecai Anielewicz and his comrades either commit suicide or are killed.

May 12, 1943: Szmul Zygielbojm, a member of the Polish National Council, commits suicide in London as a protest against Allied failure to stop mass murder after the Nazis kill Warsaw's last Jews, which include Zygielbojm's wife and son.

May 16, 1943: The main synagogue in Warsaw is destroyed; General Stroop reports the end of the uprising, though some Jews remain in hiding.

June 1943: *Unser Kampf* (*Our Struggle*), the underground Yiddish newspaper of Jewish Communists in Belgium, warns Jews not to report for "resettlement" but to rise up and take revenge. • The publication *Jeune Combat* (*Youth Fights*), the Communist underground newspaper of the Organization of Jewish Youth Fighting Hitler, begins publication. The paper agitates for the Liberation of France, and the group also engages in armed resistance. It ultimately will be responsible for two-thirds of the anti-Nazi attacks in Paris from July 1942 to 1943.

June 1, 1943: Armed resistance breaks out during the liquidation of the Sosnowiec (Poland) ghetto.

June 21, 1943: Himmler orders the liquidation of all Jewish ghettos in the Soviet Union.

June 25, 1943: In German-occupied Poland, armed Jewish resistance breaks out in Lvov, and the Czestochowa ghetto.

July 16, 1943: A crisis hits Vilna's United Partisan Organization when the group's leader, Itzik Wittenberg, is captured by the police. He will subsequently be freed by his fighters but, lacking the general support of the ghetto population, will choose to surrender to prevent the ghetto's destruction. Wittenberg takes his own life in prison.

July 20, 1943: An armed uprising hits the Kleck ghetto, in the Nowogrodek district of eastern Poland. With the onset of a final *Aktion*, the underground sets the ghetto on fire. Four hundred Jews attempt to escape in the chaos, and only a few dozen reach the cover of the forests. About 25 will fight with partisans and survive the war.

July 25, 1943: Italian dictator Benito Mussolini resigns and is arrested by Italian partisans.

July 28, 1943: Jan Karski, a young Polish Catholic underground courier, arrives in the United States to meet with American government and civic leaders. Among his assignments is to relate the plight of Europe's Jews.

August 2, 1943: Armed resistance at the Treblinka death camp, which is undertaken with stolen SS arms, allows for the escape of 350 to 400 inmates. All but 100 will be recaptured.

August 3, 1943: An armed uprising rips the Bedzin ghetto in German-occupied Poland. After digging underground bunkers and gathering arms, the resistance fighters will hold out for two weeks. Among the casualties is Frumka Plotnicka, a female courier and revolt organizer sent by the Jewish Fighting Organization in Warsaw in September 1942.

August 16, 1943: Germans enter the Bialystok, Poland, ghetto and are met with armed resistance, led by Mordecai Tenenbaum, who was sent by the JFO in Warsaw. Five thousand Jews are killed on the spot, and 25,000 are deported to death camps.

August 20, 1943: An armed uprising occurs in the Glembokie ghetto in Poland's Vilna district.

September 1943: DELASEM, an Italian Jewish aid organization originally established to help Jewish refugees who flee to Italy, begins organizing hiding places and clandestine assistance networks for refugees and Italian Jews in Rome. Working with priests and local non-Jews, they provide forged documents, food, and money for Jews hiding in churches, convents, and apartments. Until the June 1944 liberation of Rome, some 2,500 Italian Jews and 1,500 refugees will be helped by DELASEM.

September 2, 1943: Armed resisters rise in the Tarnow ghetto in German-occupied Poland.

September 3, 1943: The Allies invade Italy. Italy will surrender within six days and sign an armistice.

Fall 1943: The *Armee Juive* (Jewish Army; AJ) begins daring escape operations from France. They will head over the Pyrenees mountains into neutral Spain. From there they plan to travel to Palestine and join the Jewish units of the British army. Braving brutal conditions, some 300 AJ members, including 80 members of the Dutch *HeHalutz Zion-* *ist* youth movement, who clandestinely entered France, will make it to Spain.

September 26, 1943: In Novogrudok, Belorussia, 220 Jews escape to the forests through a 250-yard tunnel excavated under the ghetto courthouse. Many are quickly recaptured, but some 100 will manage to get away, most of them joining Tuvia Bielski's family camp.

October 1943: The Danish people help rescue more than 7,000 Danish Jews, who they send by boat to nearby Sweden. Five hundred Jews are arrested in Denmark and deported, but the Danish government will inquire about their fate.

October 4, 1943: In a speech to SS officers at Posen, Heinrich Himmler acknowledges the men's pride in their work: "Most of you know what it means to see a hundred corpses lie side by side, or five hundred, or a thousand. To have stuck this out and—excepting cases of human weakness—to have kept our integrity, this is what has made us hard."

October 8, 1943: *Hechalutz Halochem* (*Fighting Pioneer*), the underground newspaper of the Jewish Fighting Organization in the Krakow ghetto, reports on the escape to the forests: "Our young people stole away quietly from the ghetto. For the first time in their lives they were holding weapons.... They were never to return to the ghetto, never to unite with their brethren, and only in the far away forest would they fight in the name of freedom against the bloody enemy."

October 14, 1943: Leon Feldhendler and Jewish Soviet POW Aleksandr Pechersky lead an armed revolt at the Sobibor death camp. Eleven Germans are killed and 300 Jews escape. Only 50 of those will survive the war. Two days later, Himmler will order the camp destroyed.

October 16, 1943: Germans deport Jews of Rome to Auschwitz. Although the Vatican shelters a few hundred Jews, and monasteries hide a few thousand, some 8,300 are deported. The pope issues no public protest.

October 17, 1943: A coded letter secretly sent by Gisi Fleischmann, a leader of the underground Working Group in Slovakia, to Jewish Agency representatives in neutral Switzerland reads: "We thank you *chaverim* [comrades] for providing greater *emtza'im* [funds] for *hatzalat pleitah* [rescue of refugees]. We will take [money] out of the *shloshim elef* [$30,000] intended for *Willy* [code name for Dieter Wisliceny, Eichmann's deputy in Slovakia in charge of deportations]. Please replace it through the *shaliach* [courier]. We expect your *ezrah* [assistance] so that we can send *shlichim* [couriers] to where ever they find *yehudim* [Jews] and bring them here. There are still possibilities, but it is terribly difficult to get to the *megorashim* [deportees in Poland] because they are hermetically isolated."

October 20, 1943: The United Nations War Crimes Commission is established.

November 3, 1943: During the German (*Erntefest*) "Harvest Festival," Jews are murdered in three camps in the Lublin, Poland, area.

November 19, 1943: Jewish prisoners in *Sonderkommando 1005* revolt at the Janowska camp in Lvov. Their task had been to dig up bodies and burn them, using bone crushers to get rid of all evidence of murder.

December 1943: The British army begins training of 37 Jewish parachutists in Palestine for secret missions behind enemy lines. Despite Jewish Agency requests to train hundreds of operatives, the British severely limit the number of parachutists trained.

December 16, 1943: Josiah DuBois meets with Donald Hiss at the U.S. State Department and begins to unravel a State Department cover-up of inaction and false representations that hampered the rescue of Jews.

1944

January 13, 1944: U.S. Treasury officials Josiah DuBois, Randolph Paul, and John Pehle present a "Report to the Secretary on the Acquiescence of This Government to the Murder of the Jews," which accuses the State Department of preventing action from being taken to rescue Jews.

January 16, 1944: Secretary of Treasury Henry Morgenthau meets with President Roosevelt and presents a "Personal Report to the President," a condensed and milder version of the report he received. Within days, the War Refugee Board is created.

March 8, 1944: Filip Mueller, a Jewish inmate working in the gassing facilities at Auschwitz-Birkenau, describes the last moments of Czechoslovakian Jews from the family camp: "Suddenly a voice began to sing. Others joined in and the sound swelled into a mighty choir. They sang first the Czechoslovak national anthem and then the Hebrew song '*Hatikva*' [Zionist anthem]. And all this time the SS men never stopped their brutal beatings. It was as if they [the SS] regarded the singing as a last kind of protest which they were determined to stifle if they could."

March 13, 1944: Four Palestinian Jewish parachutists—Abba Berdichev, Reuven Dafni, Yonah Rosen, and Hannah Senesh—are dropped by British planes behind enemy lines in Yugoslavia for clandestine missions in Hungary. Hannah Senesh will be captured and executed by a firing squad in Budapest on November 7. Her body will later be interred in Israel with full military honors.

March 19, 1944: Germans take control of Hungary and its more than 700,000 Jews. They will implement tried and true practices of definition, confiscation of property, ghettoization, and deportation to death camps. The implementation of the Final Solution in Hungary will be complete in fewer than four months.

March 22, 1944: A large group of Jewish internees with two handguns escapes from the Koldyczewo labor camp, in eastern Poland, after poisoning the watchdogs. Twenty-five are killed by pursuing Germans as the prisoners flee to the forests, but hundreds get away, most joining the Bielski family camp.

March 24, 1944: The Gestapo deports 800 Greek Jews, deceiving them with claims that Passover matzah flour will be distributed at the Athens Synagogue.

April 4, 1944: United States aircraft take air-reconnaissance photographs of Auschwitz.

April 7, 1944: Two Slovakian Jews, Alfred Wetzler and Rudolph Vrba (Walter Rosenberg), escape from Auschwitz. They will soon provide the Allies, the Jewish community, and the *Yishuv* (Jewish community in Palestine) with detailed reports of Auschwitz killings. Known as the Auschwitz Protocol, the information will be smuggled to the West by the Working Group, the Jewish underground group in Slovakia.

April 15, 1944: The ghettoization of Hungary's Jews begins.

May 15, 1944: Germany begins the deportation of Hungarian Jews, primarily to Auschwitz. A German document will note that 437,402 were deported on 147 trains. Between this date and July 8, 1944, most of them will be sent to Auschwitz, where a rail spur will lead directly to the Birkenau death camp.

May 19, 1944: In order to buy time and because they are under the illusion that it might actually work, the Germans send Jewish relief leader Joel Brand to Turkey with a proposal of one million Jews for goods. In a second mission by Brand's companion, Bandi Grosz, Germany seeks a separate peace with the West. It hopes to divorce the United States and Great Britain from the Soviet Union and thus enable the Third Reich to survive.

June 2, 1944: Yitzhak Gruenbaum, chairman of the Rescue Committee of the Jewish Agency, requests that Allied aircraft bomb rail lines to Auschwitz.

Partisan Boris Jochai shows how he planted dynamite on tracks; Vilna, Lithuania, 1944.

June 4, 1944: The Allies liberate Rome.

June 6, 1944: Nearly 1,800 Jews on the Greek island of Corfu are deported by boat and rail to Auschwitz. • Allied forces land on French beaches at Normandy on D-Day.

June 9, 1944: Clandestine radio listeners operating in the Lodz ghetto report the Allied invasion of France, causing hope and excitement among the ghetto residents. When German authorities become aware of the ghetto's elevated mood, a group of radio listeners, including Chaim Widawski, is arrested. Rather than expose his comrades, Widawski takes poison.

June 10, 1944: Germans kill 642 residents of Oradour-sur-Glane in revenge for the killing of an SS officer.

June 11, 1944: The Jewish Agency Executive, chaired by David Ben-Gurion, meets in Jerusalem to consider whether to request that Auschwitz be bombed. Ben-Gurion states: "We do not know the truth concerning the entire situation in Poland, and it seems that we are unable to propose anything concerning this matter." Dr. Schmorak concurs: "It is forbidden for us to take responsibility for a bombing that could very well cause the death of even one Jew." The Jewish Agency initially decides not to take any action but will ultimately reconsider.

Summer 1944: *Sonderkommando* (Jewish inmates forced to work at the gas chambers and crematoria) snap clandestine photographs of the murder process and the burning of corpses on an outside pyre at Auschwitz-Birkenau. The photos are smuggled out of the camp by the Polish underground, which hopes that the images will motivate the Allies to action.

June 23, 1944: Red Cross inspectors visit the Theresienstadt ghetto/concentration camp in Czechoslovakia. The Germans clean up Theresienstadt and plant gardens, hand out fresh clothing and bedding, and establish a soccer field in an elaborate setup designed to deceive their visitors.

June 24, 1944: The air arm of the U.S. Army declares any bombing of Auschwitz as an "impracticable" idea requiring the diversion of considerable air support needed elsewhere.

July 1944: Gestapo agents arrest 25 *Armee Juive* (Jewish Army) fighters in Paris. The prisoners are tortured and then shipped to the Drancy, France, transit camp. They will be deported eastward on August 17. En route, 14 fighters will escape by jumping from the moving train.

July 7, 1944: British Prime Minister Winston Churchill tells Anthony Eden, Britain's foreign secretary, that he is in favor of bombing Auschwitz. Eden is told to approach the Royal Air Force and to "invoke my [Churchill's] name, if necessary." Churchill's decision has been spurred by Eden's report of a visit from Chaim Weizmann, president of the World Zionist Organization, and Moshe Shertok of the Jewish Agency.

July 8, 1944: Facing international pressure and a deteriorating war situation, Hungary informs Berlin that Hungarian deportation of Jews will end.

July 9, 1944: Swedish diplomat Raoul Wallenberg arrives in Budapest to do what he can to rescue Hungarian Jews there.

July 16, 1944: Tuvia Bielski leads the 1,230 Jews of his family camp into Novogrudok, Belorussia, as Soviet forces liberate the town.

July 23, 1944: Russian troops enter the Majdanek death camp. H. W. Lawrence, a correspondent for *The New York Times*, writes: "I have just seen the most terrible place on earth." Newspaper reports are met with suspicion of Soviet propaganda.

August 1944: The *Armee Juive* (Jewish Army) is active in the French revolt against the Germans and in the liberation of Toulouse, Lyons, and Paris. Previously, armed Jewish Army units acted in southern France against collaborators and Gestapo agents. In Nice, they broke up a deadly group of collaborators who were often able to spot Jews by their appearance.

August 1, 1944: The Red Army liberates Kovno.

August 2, 1944: Some 2,800 Gypsies are gassed at Auschwitz. • The final deportations of Jews from the Lodz ghetto, the last ghetto in Poland, occur. Over the next three weeks, 60,000 Jews will be deported, including *Judenrat* chairman

Mordecai Chaim Rumkowski. The Lodz ghetto has lasted longer than any other in Poland, yet Rumkowski's strategy of "rescue through work" fails in the end.

August 14, 1944: In a letter to A. Leon Kubowitzski of the World Jewish Congress, Assistant Secretary of War John J. McCloy turns down Kubowitzski's request that Auschwitz be bombed. His reasoning: "Such an operation could only be accomplished by the diversion of considerable air support essential to the success of forces now engaged in decisive operations and would in any case be of such doubtful efficacy that it would not warrant the use of our resources. There is considerable opinion to the effect that such an effort even if practicable might provoke even more vindictive action by the Germans."

August 20, 1944: The U.S. Army Air Force bombs Buna Monowitz, the work camp at Auschwitz, also known as Auschwitz III. The death camp at Birkenau (Auschwitz II)—and its gas chambers— is untouched.

August 23, 1944: Marshall Ion Antonescu is overthrown in Romania, and that nation joins the Allies.

August 25, 1944: German forces surrender in Paris. • Adolf Eichmann and his staff leave Hungary, seemingly ending the deportation of Hungarian Jews.

August 28–29, 1944: Czech and Slovak partisans lead a national uprising in Slovakia. Nearly 10 percent of the male and female partisans—more than 1,500 fighters—are Jews.

September 3, 1944: Brussels, Belgium, is liberated by the Allies. • Anne Frank is among the Dutch Jews deported to Auschwitz from the Westerbork transit camp.

September 12, 1944: Haviva Reik, a female Jewish parachutist from Palestine, is dropped into Slovakia to join the three Palestinian parachutists who landed a week earlier. Reik's mission is to connect with the Working Group, the Jewish underground organization in Slovakia, and aid in rescue operations. Caught up in the events surrounding the Slovak National Uprising, they will be captured by German troops and executed on November 20.

September 16, 1944: Following a Communist coup, Bulgaria declares war on Germany.

October 6, 1944: The Soviet Army enters Hungary.

October 6–7 1944: *Sonderkommando* workers using smuggled explosives stage an uprising at Auschwitz-Birkenau. One of the four crematoria is set on fire.

October 13, 1944: Soviet troops enter Riga, Latvia.

October 17, 1944: Adolf Eichmann returns to Budapest.

October 18, 1944: Oskar Schindler arranges to have 300 women transferred from Auschwitz to his factory.

October 20, 1944: Some 22,000 Hungarian Jews are put on trains headed to Auschwitz.

October 30, 1944: The last deportation train leaves Theresienstadt for Auschwitz. Approximately 88,000 Jews have been sent from that camp to Auschwitz.

November 6, 1944: Hungary's fascistic Arrow Cross forces some 30,000 Hungarian Jews to the old Austrian border.

November 8, 1944: Germans begin a death march of captive Jews from Budapest.

November 25, 1944: The Germans' demolition of Crematorium II begins at Auschwitz-Birkenau.

1945
January 1945: Abba Kovner and other former partisans establish *Brichah* (Flight), a secret organization that smuggles Jewish survivors into Palestine.

January 6, 1945: Germans hang four Jewish women in Auschwitz for having smuggled explosives used in the camp revolt of October 6–7, 1944.

January 17, 1945: The Red Army enters Budapest. • A final roll call is held at Auschwitz. • Soviet officials arrest Raoul Wallenberg.

January 18, 1945: Forced "death march" evacuations begin at Auschwitz. Prisoners are forced to walk toward Germany rather than be captured alive by advancing Soviet troops, reversing the long process of making Germany Jew-free. Many will die on these marches from cold and the absence of shelter, hunger, fatigue, and despair.

Prisoners of the concentration camp in Dachau, Germany, celebrate after liberation.

• Josef Mengele leaves Auschwitz, taking with him the records of his medical experiments.

January 27, 1945: Soviet troops enter Auschwitz and find 7,000 prisoners alive.

February 3, 1945: A forced march of prisoners begins from Gross Rosen to Flossenberg.

February 4, 1945: An Allied Conference at Yalta establishes a postwar division of Europe. This will be the last conference attended by President Roosevelt.

March 5, 1945: The U.S. Ninth Army reaches the Rhine River in Germany.

March 30, 1945: Soviet troops enter Austria.

April 11, 1945: American troops liberate the concentration camp at Buchenwald, Germany; 21,000 inmates are still alive.

April 12, 1945: Generals Dwight David Eisenhower, George Patton, and Omar Bradley visit the concentration camp at Ohrdruf, Germany. Eisenhower reports: "The things I saw beggar the imagination. The visual evidence and the verbal testimony were so overpowering.... I have reported what I saw and heard, but only part of it. For most of it, I have no words." He summons the press and political leaders. • President Franklin Delano Roosevelt dies in Warm Springs, Georgia. Vice President Harry Truman is sworn in as president.

April 14, 1945: Swedish Count Folke Bernadotte negotiates the release of 423 Danish Jews from Theresienstadt.

April 15, 1945: British troops enter Bergen-Belsen, where the situation is so grave that 13,000 Jews will die after liberation.

April 23, 1945: The Nazi concentration camp at Flossenberg, Germany, is liberated by U.S. troops.

April 29, 1945: Hitler's will instructs Germans to continue the War Against the Jews. • American troops enter Dachau.

April 30, 1945: Hitler and his new bride, Eva Braun, commit suicide inside the *Fuhrerbunker* in Berlin. • Germany's *Reichstag* building is captured by the Soviet army.

May 2, 1945: German forces in Berlin surrender.

May 5, 1945: The Mauthausen concentration camp is liberated by American troops.

May 7, 1945: Germany signs an unconditional surrender.

May 8, 1945: VE (Victory in Europe) Day is celebrated in Allied countries.

August 6, 1945: An American B-29 drops an atomic bomb on Hiroshima, Japan.

August 9, 1945: In another bombing run, an American B-29 drops an A-bomb on Nagasaki, Japan.

August 11, 1945: Anti-Jewish riots hit Krakow, Poland.

September 2, 1945: Japan surrenders, ending World War II.

September 17, 1945: The trial of Bergen-Belsen personnel begins.

October 25, 1945: Jews are attacked in Sosnowiec, Poland.

November 15, 1945: The trial of Dachau camp administrators begins.

November 19, 1945: Anti-Jewish riots hit Lublin.

November 20, 1945: The Allies' First International Military Tribunal gets underway at Nuremberg, Germany. Of the 22 defendants, most are high-ranking Nazi leaders and officials.

1946

May 1, 1946: The Anglo-American Commission recommends the admission of 100,000 Jews to Palestine. Britain, which holds the mandate on Palestine, refuses.

July 4, 1946: An anti-Jewish pogrom in Kielce, Poland, follows the disappearance of a non-Jewish child. In the violence, 42 Jews are killed. Over the next year, 100,000 Jews will flee Eastern Europe to American and British zones called *Brichah* (Flight).

September 18, 1946: One part of Emanuel Ringelblum's collection of documents from the *Oyneg Shabbes* archive is discovered buried beneath the rubble of Warsaw.

October 1, 1946: Initial verdicts are reached in the first of the Nuremberg Trials. Of the 22 defendants, three are acquitted. The rest receive penalties ranging from 10 years imprisonment to death.

October 15, 1946: Hermann Goring, the former head of the *Luftwaffe* and Hitler's

designated successor, takes his own life with hidden poison hours before he is to be executed.

October 25, 1946: At Nuremberg, the United States indicts 20 German doctors and three medical assistants on four counts, including war crimes and crimes against humanity, in response to bizarre medical experiments on living human subjects.

1947

January 13, 1947: Eighteen Nazi judges are brought to trial at Nuremberg.

February 8, 1947: Six German industrialists are brought to trial at Nuremberg.

March 29, 1947: Former Auschwitz commandant Rudolf Hoess is sentenced to death at his Warsaw Trial.

April 16, 1947: Hoess is hanged at Auschwitz, outside the gas chamber at Auschwitz I.

May 8, 1947: The trial of 24 board members of manufacturing giant I.G. Farben begins.

May 10, 1947: The trial of 12 former *Wehrmacht* officers begins.

July 1, 1947: Fourteen former SS leaders sit for trial.

August 16, 1947: The trial of 12 executives of arms giant Krupp begins.

August 20, 1947: The so-called "Doctors' Trial" concludes with the court's statement of Medical and Research Conduct, which includes the concepts of informed consent and the right to stop treatment at any time.

November 4, 1947: Twenty-one former senior German diplomats are put on trial.

December 1947: The trial of 40 former Auschwitz administrators begins. These trials are an attempt, symbolic and inadequate as they are, to purge Germany of its Nazi leadership and hold them accountable for their crimes. Interest in the trials will wane, most especially after the Berlin Blockade of 1948 and the need to enlist German support for the West in the Cold War.

1948 and Beyond

May 14, 1948: The State of Israel is proclaimed; its borders are opened to all Jews.

December 9, 1948: The Convention for the Prevention of Crimes of Genocide is adopted by the United Nations to specifically outlaw many of the crimes associated with the Holocaust. The Universal Declaration of Human Rights will follow the next day. The United States will not ratify the convention until 1988.

1949: The Ghetto Fighters' House (Itzhak Katzenelson Holocaust and Jewish Resistance Heritage Museum) is founded in western Galilee, Israel, by a community of Holocaust survivors. In 1995 the *Yad Layeled,* The Living Memorial to the Children of the Holocaust, will open on this site.

May 23, 1949: The Federal Republic of Germany (West Germany) is established.

October 7, 1949: The Democratic Republic of Germany (East Germany) is established.

June 1950: The Displaced Persons Act of 1948 is amended to allow equitable Jewish immigration to the United States.

December 1, 1950: A second portion of Emanuel Ringelblum's *Oyneg Shabbes* archive is discovered in milk cans buried beneath Warsaw. (To date, the third and final portion is still to be recovered.)

April 12, 1951: *Yom Hashoah V'hagevurah* (Holocaust and Heroism Remembrance Day) is established by Israel's *Knesset* (parliament).

September 27, 1951: West German Chancellor Konrad Adenauer apologizes to the Jewish people and offers reparations.

September 10, 1952: Israel and West Germany agree on German payment of reparations to Israel and to Jewish organizations.

May 27, 1953: The cornerstone ceremony is held in Jerusalem for the Yad Vashem Memorial. In 1957 the first buildings at Yad Vashem will open to the public. They include the *Ohel Yizkor* (Hall of Remembrance) as well as the archives and library building.

May 23, 1960: David Ben-Gurion, Israel's prime minister, announces the capture and removal to Israel (for trial) of former SS functionary Adolf Eichmann.

April 11–August 14, 1961: The trial of Adolf Eichmann unfolds in Jerusalem. Eichmann is found guilty and sentenced to death.

May 31, 1962: Adolf Eichmann is hanged and his ashes are scattered at sea, beyond Israeli territorial waters. (To date, Eichmann is the only person ever executed in Israel.)

December 20, 1963: The trial of SS officers posted to Auschwitz is held in Frankfurt am Main. The proceedings will last until August 1965.

April 1978: NBC broadcasts the docudrama *The Holocaust* over four consecutive nights, bringing the event to the attention of tens of millions of viewers.

May 14, 1978: President Jimmy Carter announces his intention to establish the President's Commission on the Holocaust to recommend an appropriate national memorial to its victims.

January 1979: The President's Commission on the Holocaust begins its deliberations, with Elie Wiesel as chair.

September 4, 1979: The Office of Special Investigations (OSI) is established in Washington to investigate Nazi war criminals who have come to the United States.

October 1980: The U.S. Holocaust Memorial Council is established by a unanimous act of Congress to plan and build the U.S. Holocaust Memorial Museum.

June 1981: More than 6,000 survivors gather at the Western Wall in Jerusalem for the first World Gathering of Jewish Holocaust Survivors.

April 1983: More than 20,000 American Jewish Holocaust survivors gather in Washington for the American Gathering of Jewish Holocaust Survivors. Among the speakers are President Ronald Reagan, Vice President George H. W. Bush, and Speaker of the House Tip O'Neill.

1985: French movie director Claude Lanzmann releases *Shoah*, a 9½-hour documentary on the Holocaust.

May 5–7, 1985: U.S. President Ronald Reagan's ceremonial visit to a Bitburg, Germany, cemetery where *Waffen-SS* troops are buried provokes an international controversy.

December 1986: Elie Wiesel is awarded the Nobel Peace Prize for his role as Holocaust Witness and his efforts for human rights and human dignity.

February 1993: The *Beit Hashoah* Museum of Tolerance opens in Los Angeles.

April 22, 1993: The United States Holocaust Memorial Museum opens in Washington, D.C.

October 1993: *Schindler's List*, a film directed by Steven Spielberg, opens in U.S. theaters, where it is seen by tens of millions of Americans. It will win seven Academy Awards.

Late 1993: Citing insufficient evidence identifying him as Ivan the Terrible, while confirming his role as a brutal guard at Treblinka, the Israeli Supreme Court releases John Demjanjuk, who was convicted in 1988 by a Jerusalem court of war crimes.

1994: With the profits from *Schindler's List*, Steven Spielberg establishes the Survivors of the Shoah Visual History Foundation to record on videotape the personal testimonies of 50,000 Holocaust survivors. Within five years, 52,000 testimonies will be taken in 32 languages in 57 countries.

May 1996: Swiss bankers and the World Jewish Congress decide to look into the misappropriation of Jewish funds during and after the Holocaust.

October 23, 1996: Peter Hug, a Swiss historian, shows how Switzerland used funds of Holocaust victims to settle claims by Poland and Hungary.

September 1997: The Museum of Jewish Heritage—A Living Memorial to the Holocaust opens in New York City.

October 1997: Accused former Nazi collaborator Maurice Papon goes on trial in France for the deportations of Jews from France, including children.

August 1998: Swiss banks agree to pay $1.25 billion to compensate Holocaust victims for stolen assets.

August 19, 1998: The Italian insurance group Assicurazioni Generali agrees to pay $100 million to Holocaust victims as compensation for previously unpaid insurance.

December 3, 1998: At a meeting in Washington, D.C., 44 nations agree to return fine art looted from victims of the Nazis.

February 16, 1999: Germany establishes a $1.7 billion Remembrance, Responsibility and the Future Fund. It is financed by the German government and major German corporations that had profited from forced labor during the Nazi era.

May 26, 1999: Germany agrees to compensate Polish slave laborers.

January 2000: The prime minister of Sweden convenes an international conference of 21 heads of state and delegations representing 46 countries to implement Holocaust education.

March 2000: Pope John Paul II visits Yad Vashem in Jerusalem, where he condemns antisemitism as anti-Christian. At the Holocaust memorial and, even more strikingly, in a note inserted into the Western Wall, he apologizes for antisemitic actions by Christians.

April 2000: In a British court, Holocaust denier David Irving loses the libel suit that he brought against historian Deborah Lipstadt. The court finds that Irving did indeed falsify the historical record, and that he is an antisemite and a racist. Because Irving has been the most erudite and visible proponent of the denial movement, this is a major defeat for groups and individuals who have followed his lead.

January 27, 2006: The United Nations observes the first International Day of Commemoration to honor the Victims of the Holocaust. Israeli scholar Yehuda Bauer is the guest speaker. January 27 is the anniversary of the liberation of Auschwitz by Soviet forces.

LEGACY OF ABSENCE COLLECTION

The historical period that covers what we know today as the Holocaust lasted 12 years: from 1933, when the Nazis came to power in Germany, to 1945, when the Allies accepted Germany's unconditional surrender. During those years, the unimaginable not only became real, it became German national policy. Whatever else might be said about the Nazis, they were not careless, and they proceeded along a path in which total war and mass murder were choices deliberately made. In this deliberation, this malignant act of choice, the Nazis produced a legacy that still echoes through the global community.

Before 1933, what the Nazis would do could not be imagined. By 1945, what they had done could not be ignored.

The Nazis had made the act of genocide into what philosopher Berel Lang called "a world-inheritance." Those born afterward, he wrote, "do not remember the world" without the Holocaust in it. They have been born into a *post-Holocaust* world, one in which the Holocaust is both a historical fact and a turning point of imagination.

Evolving over more than seven decades now, these dual elements comprise the preeminent character of the post-Holocaust period. It looks back at history, and forward to the future. The Holocaust has come to influence how societies remember and commemorate the past.

Acts of remembrance honor victims of past crimes, but acts of remembrance are also acts of imagination, ways of

Samuel Bak, Final Movement; *1998.*

expressing hope for a future in which such terrible things will not recur.

Historian Yehuda Bauer explains the contemporary resonance of what happened during the Holocaust:

> [T]here is a growing realization that something unprecedented happened in the genocide of the Jews, something that is both so extraordinary and yet so indicative of the human condition in general, that a vague feeling exists that that is a matter that a person living in our generation has to know something about. It is something that if we are not careful could happen to all of us, not in the same way, not in similar circumstances, but possessed of the same quality, perhaps, and bringing similar dangers to all.

Underscoring the importance of understanding the Holocaust to "our generation," Bauer has made an important distinction. It seems obvious why survivors of the Holocaust—or of any other crime of mass violence—would strive to remember their experience, and to share it with those who were not there. Identifying the character and consequences of the crime is, at least, a first step toward preventing its recurrence.

But concern with a deeply traumatic past does not end, as Bauer suggests, with the generation that was directly involved. Younger generations, what might be called "successor generations," are also drawn toward the past—even a past that was not theirs. Media and educational exposure account for some of this engagement. But there is a deeper aspect to the succession. The survivors of the Holocaust and other mass traumas of the 20th century are passing from the scene. Much of their ordeal has been admirably documented, but the living voice of authority will pass with them.

Successor generations, then, will have to engage differently with the past. Necessarily, this engagement will be a step removed from the experiences of survivors, instead focused on the absence created within a society when the final living link to the past has been cut. This loss is inevitable, a moment of moral succession across generations.

The history of the 20th century provides any number of such transitional moments. The loss of the living authority of survivors forces a step back from the particulars of specific historical traumas. With this step back, the aftermath of a trauma comes into fuller view; we can now see not only what happened in the past, but the depth of its meaning for the present. From this sense of aftermath, we can begin to discern a different kind of moral authority. Based on a continued reckoning with history, this authority emerges from the recognition by successor generations that what they share is a common sense of loss. This loss may be rooted in history and geography, but it extends beyond them into a collective legacy of absence.

The collection explores how this aspect of remembrance appears in modern and contemporary art. The many artists who were moved by the Holocaust to try to remember the past were forced to confront the most salient fact of the world after the Holocaust: the absence of vast numbers of people and communities—all gone because of mass murder. The scale of loss was so vast that traditional artistic approaches to remembrance could not succeed; an artist would never have enough time to commemorate the victims individually. A new visual vocabulary was needed, one that would illuminate what was no longer there by finding ways to depict its absence.

The Legacy of Absence Collection reflects the different ways in which artists have taken on the challenge of remembering. The collection explores how this visual vocabulary has been used in a range of works that commemorate the Holocaust and other episodes of historic, mass violence: Cambodia, Rwanda, the Soviet Gulags, and many others. The link among these wide-ranging works is not historical. Rather, it is the artists' development of a vocabulary focused on

The survivors of the Holocaust are passing from the scene. Much of their ordeal has been admirably documented, but the living voice of authority will pass with them.

absence and loss, the defining qualities of the post-Holocaust perspective.

As time passes, *The Legacy of Absence Collection* reveals another aspect of the continuing impact of the Holocaust on the contemporary world. Memory of the Holocaust has reshaped the ways in which many societies now commemorate their own losses, by remembering the most disturbing and enduring effect of these losses: the vast absences that follow mass violence.

* * *

Memory does not have a time limit. It may flare briefly and disappear. Or it may arc toward the horizon, illuminating each new day. The length of this arc is determined by how deeply we need to remember. Each day, memory may fade or it may flourish. The length and depth of memory—how far it extends—depends on the commitment of those who remember.

As times passes, memory's relation to the past changes. These changes extend over years; they are likely to span generations. The immediacy of violence yields to the ache of loss. The struggle to hold onto memory becomes a vivid moment of remembrance that captures something indelible. The lines are not always clear or separable; they may move simultaneously in several directions. Memory cannot be fixed in a single moment, but it is always nearby, ready to be called.

In the decades since the Holocaust, many artists have heard this call. Over this time, the works they have created trace the arc of memory, from capturing the shock of the awful moment of violence to finding, years later, solidarity in the remembrance of long-ago victims. Each of these phases of memory requires a different approach and different techniques.

The immediacy of violence, for example, tends to produce stark, brutal images that serve as a kind of documentation for events that must be remembered. These stark images have a two-fold purpose. Their most

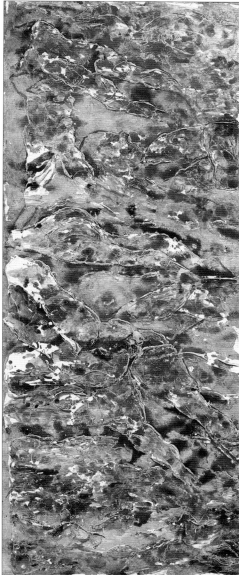

Kebedech Tekleab, The River in Rwanda; *1994.*

common use is as a form of testimony, demonstrating to viewers that the event in question actually happened. In their second purpose, however, these works reveal the challenge of confronting such painful realities. They also serve as a kind of reality check for the artist, offering a confirmation that the unbelievable did in fact occur, and can even be recreated. This proof is not just intended for viewers, but for the artists themselves. There is a deep need to state and to restate through the creation of such a work of art: This is what happened.

At the other end of the memory spectrum are works that acknowledge their distance from violent events.

Pelagie Gbaguidi, from the series The Shroud; *June 2007. Taken at the site of the Mauthausen concentration camp in Austria.*

The emptiness is a challenge to the imagination. It begs to be filled in because we know why and how it has been emptied.

These works try to gauge the weight of memory on the present. Brutality and violence are no longer the focus of works like these. Instead, they linger over the emptiness that began when the violence ended. Violence, they recognize, was the end point of countless lives, and the starting point of our collective memory.

The Legacy of Absence Collection follows the trail of memory across cultures and generations. Each of the works in this collection emerged from a specific creative inquiry, sometimes consciously linked to a historical trauma, sometimes only obliquely so. Each engages a moment of memory, sometimes in the immediate recoil of an assault, sometimes from an achingly long distance. All of them, though, stand on the far side of rupture, produced in a world that could not imagine the possibility of what they depict, up to the very moment that disaster occurred. Collectively, they are part of a global circle of reflection and witness. Made in the "afterward" of different cataclysmic events, these pictures illustrate the consequences, not the causes, of violence. They document a time of afterward, when the enduring effects of violence have taken hold of memory.

The collection is being presented in the Museum thematically, in order to highlight shared approaches to the varied problems of capturing memory over time.

Empty Places

At first glance, a series of empty landscapes appears far removed from the struggle of remembering. On closer inspection, these scattered places cohere around a single theme: In each of them, the emptiness is the result of a deliberate mass killing. Emptiness is all that the victims have left behind.

The artists drawn to these places came to confront a dilemma: How do you document what can no longer be seen? Naming the place, and thereby fitting it into a historic context, is a start. Once named, the empty landscape forces the realization that we are looking at something that needs to be seen. Yet we will never be able to see it, and the photograph has been made to remind us of this fact.

However, this reminder has another intent. We will never see what happened in these empty places, but these images will frame our imagining of what was once there. The emptiness is a challenge to the imagination. It begs to be filled in because we know why and how it has been emptied. With this knowledge, we cannot help but try to restore the victims to the landscape, though they are anonymous to us.

Many of these images were made in black and white, a medium that lends them a documentary quality and enhances their status as a kind of historical evidence. This quality makes them easier for us to approach, and gives us license to confront the difficult material that they portray. Thus, Drex Brooks's landscapes from the American West, or Simon Norfolk's images of Armenia and Rwanda, provide an opportunity to fill in the vast blank spaces that they have set in front of us. Because we understand instinctively how to react, black-and-white images seem appropriately historical, linking the emptiness to the moment of its creation. Yet their effect is distancing: We know that black and white is irrevocably linked to the past.

Perhaps inevitably, historical places are now being revisited in color as well, with an effect that is usefully unsettling: unsettling, because the conventions of historical documentation have been removed, replaced by the conventions of normality. These places are being revisited not only as historic sites, but as present-day places where mass violence occurred—only fitted into an everyday landscape. We are not accustomed to treating as normal those places that have been sanctified by their encounter with violence. And this shift is useful, however unsettling, because it brings the past more immediately into the present and asserts that this encounter has a continuing meaning in real time.

Also in the collection are color images made at the Mauthausen concentration camp site by Maria Theresia Litschauer and Pelagie Gbaguidi, artists from Austria and Benin, respectively. In each case, the documentary impulse is at the origin of the artist's project, but the emphasis on the sites as contemporary settings influences what each is trying to document. Litschauer made images of hundreds of places in Austria where Jews were forced into slave labor during the Holocaust; she captures these sites as part of the landscape of her native country today. Gbaguidi, on the other hand, was visiting Austria and began making photographs and short films of the landscapes around her. She wrote, "I tried to grasp what I could through the rustling of the leaves or the songs of the birds, everywhere that life underscored the presence of those who had disappeared there."

So Many Gone

Emptiness may be an entry into remembrance, but it is not enough. To return to the scene of the crime, to recreate the moment when mass murder was committed, is also a powerful impulse among artists. Victims are placed back into the frame of the work, but often they are so numerous, or so distorted by their ordeal, that the most we can see in them are human remains. Unfortunately, this does recapture the reality of mass murder. The individuality of the victims is irrelevant to the murderers. What remains after the killing is an indistinguishable mass of victims, stripped of identity and left to be absorbed by the landscape. One painting in Natan Nuchi's *Untitled* series portrays three concentration camp-like victims, their bodies in the process of disintegrating.

Zoran Music, in a print from his series *We Are Not the Last,* finds two sprawled victims staring off into the distance, their faces twisted beyond recognition. Kebedech Tekleab's *The River in Rwanda* captures a swirl of corpses in water, rather than on land. Josef Szajna likens his mass of victims to an ant colony, in a series that he began in 1978 and expanded over the next two decades. The theme recurs in all these works: always a landscape of people, never a glimpse of a person.

Who Were They?

The process of remembrance must go deeper, beyond mass victimization, into an exploration of who the victims were. Yet an inquiry into their individual lives is inevitably stymied by the fact that these lives were ended—or irredeemably altered—by what happened.

In some cases, artifacts left behind are all that remain. So, these are made to stand in for the missing. Naomi Tereza Salmon sorted through the personal effects of Jews murdered in Nazi extermination camps and made photographic portraits of their glasses, shaving mugs, and dentures. The poignancy of the glasses—some broken, some intact—contrasts with the rawness of the dentures. This juxtaposition, alert to the differing reactions it will stir, allows viewers a range of response that goes beyond any initial reaction. The complexity of our reactions to the different objects reminds us of the complexity of

Amer Baksic, Number 1, *from the series* Silhouette and Shadow (I); *1995–97.*

the lives that actually employed these seemingly mute artifacts.

For Eduardo Medici, the full individuality of the victims is irretrievable, yet must still be explored. He has made a collage of photographic negatives in various stages of disintegration, offering shadings of some, glimpses of others. The distress of the negative images evokes the fate of the unknown individuals captured within them.

Jung Won-chul sought out elderly Korean women who, when young, had been forced into prostitution by the Japanese army during World War II. Their portraits are proudly individual; they are focused on faces that look directly at the viewer. The expressions are mixed. Some are somber; others are welcoming. The lines in their faces are deepened by Jung's engraving technique. There is no attempt to avoid the shame or abuse these women suffered. Instead, they are given a chance to confront it directly. Through each gaze, the older woman reclaims the younger one.

Memory Fades, Memory Holds

We cannot remember clearly. We do not wish to forget. Memory moves between these poles, holding on where it can, slipping away when it can't. Creative works cannot resolve this dilemma, but they can capture it. In so doing, they

Ofra Zimbalista, a still from The Wedding; *2005.*

bring us closer to the subjects of our memory, since the struggle to remember is part of the human condition.

Ana Tiscornia worked with old picture frames in her installation *Portraits II.* Instead of using these frames to present portraits, however, she turns them to the wall. The back sides of the frames are used and tattered, like frames we all have at home. Instead of bringing us closer to our memories, the frames close the way to the past. Indeed, the work is based on photographs of the back sides of the old frames—the only element of the comfortable family portrait available to the artist.

Anna Bialobroda also juxtaposes an irretrievable image with a familiar setting. Working on boldly colored upholstery materials, Bialobroda paints figures in whites and grays, gesturing from inside of the fabric. In *Sport,* the background is vibrant and first catches the eye, while the figure itself is pale, if animated. This does not seem a portrait as much as an effort to catch any trace of whomever once sat on the upholstery.

A similar trace of a missing person appears in Samuel Bak's *Absence,* in which the outline of a young boy's arms raised to the sky is traced into the sky itself by the outline of the boy's figure cut into wooden boards. Evoking a famous photograph of a Jewish boy raising his hands in surrender to German soldiers during the Holocaust, Bak's painting searches out the memory of the boy, even while it acknowledges that he can no longer be found.

In a world where time is marked by a sense of afterward, memory is everywhere, covered in shadows. Amer Baksic traced these shadows lengthening along the streets of Sarajevo. Carrie Mae Weems found them in the swamps on the islands off the Georgia coast.

The Legacy of Absence Collection moves in and out of these shadows, following the artists as they pursue our shared memory.

Clifford Chanin, Curator
Legacy of Absence Gallery

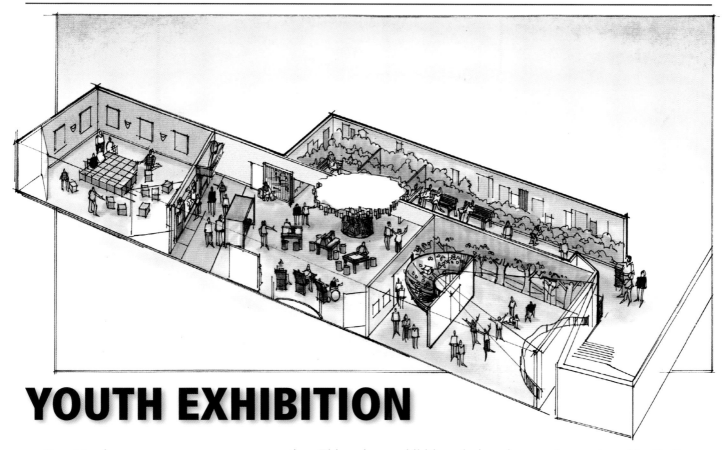

YOUTH EXHIBITION

An overview of the Youth Exhibition.

Dear Teacher,

I am a survivor of a concentration camp. My eyes saw what no man should witness: Gas chambers built by learned engineers. Children poisoned by educated physicians. Infants were killed by trained nurses. Women and babies shot and burned by high school and college graduates. So I am suspicious of education.

My request is: Help your students become human. Your efforts must never produce learned monsters, skilled psychopaths, educated Eichmanns.

Reading, writing, arithmetic are important only if they serve to make our children more human.

—Haim Ginott, educator, child psychologist, Holocaust survivor

The contents of this letter illuminate the Museum's goal for the Youth Exhibi-tion. This unique exhibition, designed for Museum visitors ages eight to 11, provides the opportunity to explore the lessons of the Holocaust and genocide in an age-appropriate, interactive manner. The Illinois Holocaust Museum and Education Center aims to encourage visitors of all ages to examine critical ethical questions derived from study of the Holocaust and genocide. Yet the Youth Exhibition seeks specifically to help younger visitors explore how to be responsible citizens and understand what it takes to care for themselves and others. It shows how to be an "upstander" and speak up for those being treated unfairly by bullies or bigots.

Visitors, whether they are younger children or teenagers, exit the experi-ence ready to act on the core values of respect, empathy, justice, civic virtue and citizenship, and responsibility for self and others. These core values allow individuals to form attitudes and actions that are the hallmarks of safe, healthy, and informed communities and serve as the foundation of our society. Young people want to know why the Holocaust happened and what they can do to make a difference. They also want to be able to explore these questions in a safe environment. The Youth Exhibition provides such a space.

The Museum believes that everyone should know about the Holocaust, but not everyone at every stage of their lives needs to know everything. The Holocaust must be introduced to young people in an age-appropriate manner. The history of the Holocaust is incredibly complex, and many—perhaps most—students are not ready developmentally to consider those ambiguities and gray areas before sixth grade. Younger students can't help but simplify, generalize, and stereotype when confronted with the behavior of individuals and groups in this history. And younger students are not ready to be introduced to the most gruesome aspects of this difficult story. Certain imagery and some vivid descriptions of what happened, which are essential to telling the truth about the Holocaust, can be frightening and alienating to younger visitors.

Holocaust education is not just about horror and atrocity, but rather examines a full array of human behavior. The Youth Exhibition, in particular, is designed to create critical thinking and employ multiple intelligences in order to prepare young people for a more detailed and complete study of the Holocaust at a later time. After visiting the Youth Exhibition, younger visitors will be more prepared intellectually and emotionally, beginning in late middle school, to interpret the history of the Holocaust, which is displayed in the Museum's Permanent Exhibition. The combination of character education, social-emotional learning, and an introduction to Holocaust studies enables students to identify and develop traits to help them become more responsible citizens.

Joseph Brodsky, a Nobel Prize winner from the former Soviet Union, states that "evil is not an aberration that stands apart from ourselves, but a mirror—a reflection of ourselves, of human negative potential." He maintains that we will never be able to combat evil unless we honestly examine the negative and positive aspects of our nature. It is

The Youth Exhibition's entry hallway.

important for young people to learn that the world did not just happen, but rather was the result of choices made by countless individuals and groups. Even the smallest of decisions can have enormous consequences for both good and evil.

The Youth Exhibition creates an immediate sense of community for the visitor. Youngsters experience a park-like setting filled with warmth, familiarity, and friendliness, yet they are challenged to investigate their assumptions and their choices as individuals within a community. This contextualizes the storyline that flows throughout the space. Park benches invite the young visitor to engage in discussion, to engage with the activities within the space, and to explore being an active participant in a positive way.

The Museum visitor interacts with several different "stations" within the Youth Exhibition, allowing for a truly engaging experience that will focus upon name-calling, bullying, being excluded from mainstream culture, standing up against prejudice directed at someone else, being a good friend, maintaining a strong cultural iden-

tity, and responding—in a variety of ways—to hate crimes. Through their involvement in these activities, visitors become involved in active listening and communication, building relationships, and employing social awareness, as well as practicing self-management, goal setting, problem solving, and decision-making skills.

The goal of the Youth Exhibition is for young visitors to leave having not only found their voices, but also wanting those voices to be heard. Having experienced the Youth Exhibition, these future generations of educators, doctors, politicians, artists, lawyers, and community leaders will have the tools to better reflect on their choices and be more prepared to interpret how they interact with others. They will have a better understanding of what they can do to make the world a better place for themselves and for those around them.

Noreen Brand,
Director of Education

Esther Netter and Vince Beggs,
Youth Exhibition Consultants

ABOUT THE BUILDING

In 2000 I was selected by the Board of Trustees of the Illinois Holocaust Memorial Foundation of Illinois to design their proposed Illinois Holocaust Museum and Education Center.

The Holocaust Memorial Foundation had come into existence as a manifestation of, and as a response to, the 1977 neo-Nazi marches that were planned for Skokie, Illinois, a community that was home to the largest concentration of Holocaust survivors with the sole exception of Jerusalem.

One significant result of these events was that the Holocaust Memorial Foundation of Illinois successfully lobbied the Illinois General Assembly to legislate Holocaust education in Illinois, making it the first state in the Union to put that educational imperative into place. As a result, large numbers of Illinois public school students came to visit the Foundation headquarters, which was located in a diminutive storefront on Main Street in Skokie. This created congestion in the residential neighborhood that abutted their modest headquarters; ergo, the need to design an expanded facility.

Architect Stanley Tigerman sketching at his desk; Chicago, 2008.

Even before my interview, I had first considered and then written about measurement and impermanence as constituent features of a "scaffold" in the context of buildings that I felt best represented the traditions implicit in Jewish prec-edent. A scaffold's ambiguity emanates from the uncertainty that its presence suggests. Given the often-transitory nature of buildings in the service of the Jewish project, the use of a scaffold as a device representing the temporal component in Judaism seemed appropriate. A scaffold either signifies that a building is in the process of demolition or the immanence of an impending structure. Arguably, a scaffold is either about absence or presence—or about both the transitory and the interpretive nature of Judaism. I am referring to the Ark of the Covenant described in detail in Exodus, in which measurement looms large in the design of the Sacred Tent, which in turn signifies a structure in-the-process-of-becoming and then continuously being relocated. On the other hand, the problems connected with permanence became a rationale for overturning the Solomonic Temple. That First Temple is significant because it was diametrically opposed to the fluidity implicit in the Ark of the Covenant as a repository for a language that was perpetually in a state of interpretation.

I also considered orientation important within the Jewish tradition of facing due east toward the rising sun, which for the Jews was further informed by the implications of immanence in anticipation of a Messianic Age. The subsequent orientation that succeeded the original eastern-facing ritual is a kind of post-structural deformed orientation in which the Jewish significant other was situated at the west wall of the Temple Mount. That suggested a deferential orientation toward the source of the flame; i.e., Jerusalem.

In the United States, the original eastern orientation signifying Messianic anticipation is sometimes refuted theologically as "a bankrupt concept." The eastern orientation is also sometimes refuted ecumenically as "negating the existential fact of Israel." After all, if messianic immanence is valid, then the existence of Jerusalem can be called into question.

* * *

Before explaining my approach to the Holocaust Museum project, I feel it is important to place my own formal and theoretical baggage on the table, since architects do not necessarily come to a project as innocently as a new, never-wetted sponge, as others might think. The reason that my preconceptions are germane to the project is because of my awareness of the Third Reich's determination to not only kill Jews but to eliminate the entirety of the culture—indeed, the whole history of the Jews as well. My response to such apocalyptic inhumanity is at the core of the architectural substance of my design.

Every architect wants, in some way, to communicate, which is to say that architects sometimes present more than one strategy in the design of a building so as to reach diverse viewers. In that spirit, there are several agendas at work in the Holocaust Museum project: 1) The representational model, wherein the "Holocaust Story" is framed by the architecture for the greatest possible effect; 2) The metaphoric model, wherein actual construction is utilized to convey the horrors to which architecture is sometimes employed at the service of the most reprehensible of clients; 3) the metonymic model, wherein the power of history is utilized for purposes of reiteration; and 4) the abstractionist model (e.g., measurement), wherein architecture-qua-architecture is exploited to reinforce the authority of a particular design. A fifth model, contradiction or slippage, comes into play between the biblical Temple era that is irrevocably absent and the current era that is inescapably present.

There is an unavoidable contradiction between the biblical secular cubit and the American standard construc-

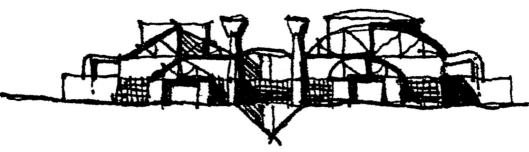

tion methods. That slippage suggests an ambiguity consonant with the concept of employing a scaffold in the service of a building that would have never come about in the first place—that is, if certain circumstances had not occurred at that infamous January 1942 conference that Reinhard Heydrich convened at the sumptuous villa at Wannsee just outside Berlin. It was there that German officials discussed the Final Solution.

* * *

There was nothing ambiguous about the slippage that occurred between the tribal protocol defining the era of the Ark of the Covenant and the city-state that King David envisioned when he dreamed of the temple that his son Solomon would later build in deference to one singular divine being. The gravitas of a city-state enforcing a census (cults believe that counting is the work of the devil) is embellished by measurement. Both of these are expressions of the magnitude of change between tribal and polis policies; i.e., that which is fluid versus that which is fixed.

Did God thwart King David's initial plan to build a fixed monument to Him, where the word would be interpreted within an unchanging structure when its movable predecessor was intrinsically fluid as it moved from place to place? Where the father, David, could not bring his notion of the Temple to fruition, the son Solomon's Temple was presaged by the repeated use of measurement in Exodus so as to describe the Ark of the Covenant.

* * *

Designing a building like the Holocaust Museum understandably

A sketch by Stanley Tigerman of the Illinois Holocaust Museum and Education Center.

Stanley Tigerman observes construction of the Illinois Holocaust Museum and Education Center; July 2008.

engenders thoughts about building at all in a world that tolerated activities brought about by city-state administrators who carried out the will of the Third Reich's leadership—those who systematically brought their inhumane devastation into being. I always thought that architecture was intrinsically optimistic, yet Holocaust museums are built by architects, some of whose predecessors designed death camps. Where is the logic connected with that slippage?

Then there is the slippage between tribal conceits and their nomadically considered temporary structures and the protocols required to administer a fixed establishment as monumental as a city—or by extension, even a single pukka building constructed out of materials that suggest longevity, if not indeed permanence.

All of these conflicts suggest an overarching conflict that hovers over the design of all buildings dedicated to the Jewish project, one of which is the Illinois Holocaust Museum and Education Center.

* * *

The representational model that discloses the one and only story of the Holocaust represents by definition a client consensus that was destined for fulfillment. In any case, the Skokie site resonated with the controversial past of 1970s neo-Nazi demonstrations that flew in the face of a democratic society. An unusual pattern of movement throughout the building brings forward a theory that one can never return: Thus, one enters the structure one way and exits another way.

Then there was the metaphoric model. In the case of the Holocaust, industrially informed modern architecture was utilized by the architects of the Third Reich to intimidate—indeed, to terrorize—a population predestined, in the Nazis' collective hatred of Jews, for extermination. That the field of architecture, arguably the most optimistic of artistic disciplines, could even be envisioned for such contravening usage boggles the mind. In any case, it is a stunning perversion of the optimism intrinsic to architecture, to say nothing of an overriding of modern architecture's well-documented agenda that, at least in part, came about to address issues connected with social cause.

Under normal circumstances, morality and ethics are the wellsprings that inform architecture. To build is to overcome a level of inertia always exerted against those who would challenge the status quo. To confront such inertia, an architect must have a provable ethical quotient so as to overcome such inertia. Mies van der Rohe was just such an architect. He was once introduced at a formal event as someone "who had to will his buildings into existence." Mies's architectural philosophy was sufficiently avant-garde; he needed an ethical core that he could draw upon to overcome those who would otherwise stymie imagination. Architects who lacked such an ethical will and who could allow themselves to be used to design death camps is for me incomprehensible.

The metonymic model, where the power that history holds over us is too often utilized for the expressed purpose of establishing authority, is a model that we architects often exploit so as to attain continuity with a distant past, thus validating our architectural production. In the case of the Holocaust Museum, I too exploited the metonymic model by referring to classical antecedents that had informed the architecture of the Third Reich.

The Holocaust Museum program called for a tripartite solution: museum, memorial, and education center. The solution juxtaposes a dark rectangular building orientated toward Jerusalem—which is approximately 6.5 degrees southeast of the Skokie site—that represents the descent into darkness; a light building orientated due east in anticipation of a Messianic Age; and a book of remembrance that is situated at the intersection of the two rectangular parallelepipeds. The overall structure establishes a single directional progression through it, beginning with a descent into darkness and ending in an ascent into the light. The book of remembrance memorial is on a level above the main one centered between the two structures, which in turn is devoted to a German box car that symbolizes the transportation utilized to send Jews to their apocalyptic end at one of the six death camps in German-occupied Poland.

While the cleaved space between the two main bodies of the building is literalized, it is uninhabitable. The resulting virtual space cannot be understood through the use of the two Jewish histories with their disparate orientations, but is instead the space of a significant other—a kind of dybbuk—which is in fact a disembodied cleave where each side has the potential of embodying its significant other. The book of remembrance is portrayed as a hinge between the two significant Jewish traditions, both of which were vulnerable to the Nazis' determined attempt to eradicate each in their entirety.

Both dark and light rectangular buildings, together with the hinge, are in aggregate—as buildings tend to be—literal. That literal quality refers back to the first literal structure erected in the service of Judaism—the one that David envisioned but Solomon built: the first Temple (c. 950 BCE). Before that time, tribal configuration precluded a political solution that might embrace the several ambitions that many tribes aspired to individually. Bringing the tribes of the Jews together was David's dream, but one that would only be realized by his son Solomon. The nomadic quality representing tribalism is best understood architecturally by the mobile design of the Ark of the Covenant.

Looking back on my design for the Holocaust Museum and having some distance from it, the results might have come about in a way other than one that I used to engender a literal building. For one, that the dark side focusing on its significant other at the West Wall of the Temple Mount in Jerusalem is actualized when its post-structural other is in another location, suggests the possibility that "otherness" might be posited in a way other than one that became literal: What that might have been remains mute. For another, that the light side suggests an anticipation of a Messianic Age, infers something other than a conventional building—perhaps a more distinct scaffold in anticipation of becoming rather than the presence of measurement as a signification of a scaffold.

I'm not sure that building-qua-building is an appropriate response to something of the horrific magnitude that the Holocaust deserves. No building in and of itself can ever adequately portray the devastation that such an event engendered. Monuments and memorials abound, but each in its own way somehow falls short of representing the agony that was visited upon so many lives. Perhaps an oral tradition does have a place in the Holocaust; I'm not really sure that something as literal as a building can ever invoke something that perhaps only the *unheimlich* can deal with.

Stanley Tigerman
Architect for the Illinois Holocaust
*   Museum and Education Center*
Chicago, 2008

The overall structure establishes a single directional progression through it, beginning with a descent into darkness and ending in an ascent into the light.

AFTERWORD

Each of us goes about our daily routine—home, work, school. We interact with family, coworkers, strangers, and colleagues. We cook, order, and eat meals; we prepare for and attend meetings. We read, we write, we play and watch sports. All of us acknowledge the passage of time, but most of us pay scant attention to our role in the larger scheme of things. Only a few of us are cognizant of our impact on the world and are aware of our place in its history.

We who survived the Holocaust have come to recognize that the era during which our families, our homes, and the world we knew were destroyed is a very important chapter in the history of mankind. Our being there did not create this importance. Our presence was accidental. Our survival was miraculous. But what has followed, the journey each of us has taken, has resulted in a collective statement that testifies to the resilience of the human spirit. We emerged from a nightmare and began a return to life. We made new homes, started new families, and found ways to contribute to our communities.

In the wake of the attempted Nazi march in Skokie in the late 1970s, a number of survivors recognized that the time had come to become proactive in educating the community about the Holocaust. An organization, the Holocaust Memorial Foundation of Illinois, was created under the leadership of Erna Gans, and was further expanded under the leadership of Lisa Derman. While each served as organizational president, from 1981 to 2002, we grew from meeting in members' homes to having a post office box to renting a storefront to owning a 6,000-square-foot facility. We have spent many years talking about our experiences, using education to share the lessons of the Holocaust. We who were victims of prejudice and intolerance taught the next generation to guard against hatred. We taught them to speak out against injustice. In fact, every time we have spoken, we have been carrying out the motto of the new Museum: Remember the past. Transform the future.

In 1999 our organization began to consider whether we should attempt to build a new center. I volunteered to oversee this process. Immediately, a rush of adrenaline went through me with the knowledge that a significant museum would be built. It was clear that this was a project whose time had come. Survivors believed in it. Members of our Board of Directors jumped in with an enthusiastic unanimous vote. We attracted the attention of some of this region's most generous individuals. And, as in our organization's past, we had the help and support of the community of Skokie. The mayor and village leadership became our proud partners, bringing our message to the broader community and helping ensure our ultimate success.

We have watched this new Museum grow from an idea, a nearly impossible dream, into bricks and mortar, exhibits and resources. From the day of our ground-breaking to the beam signing to such landmarks as the placement of the railway car, survivors have been present. Nothing could be more fitting, because this Museum is much more than a building composed of concrete and steel and glass. It contains the whispers and faded images of our families, and preserves them for coming generations. Those of us survivors who have been involved in the creation of the Illinois Holocaust Museum and Education Center have been part of a wonderful process that nourishes the human spirit. We have shared in a journey we could not have taken alone, and arrived at a destination few of us dreamt we would witness.

Remember the past. Transform the future.

We, the survivors, the eyewitnesses, are examples of living history. Through us you can glimpse the dirt road of the *shtetl,* the vibrant pace of the big city, the bustling commerce of the marketplace, and the Torah discussions of the *yeshiva.* Listen and we can bring you closer to the sound of a Yiddish lullaby and the smell of *cholent,* the Sabbath stew. Through us you can also approach the sights and sounds of the Six Million, one and a half million of whom were children, whose memory we have tried to honor with all that we have done. But when the time comes when we are no longer here, we will continue to speak through this Museum. Our voices will continue to be heard and our stories will continue to be shared. Through the Illinois Holocaust Museum and Education Center, the history we lived will teach generations we will not have the opportunity to meet in person that one person has the opportunity to make a difference in this world. All who pass through the doors of the new Museum will become part of the history we lived, as they accept the responsibility to improve history through their own lives and actions. This, I believe, was *bashert.* It was meant to be.

Samuel R. Harris, President
Illinois Holocaust Museum and Education Center

Picture Credits

The **Illinois Holocaust Museum and Education Center** wishes to thank all those who provided images for the Museum and this book. The photos, documents, and artifacts used in this book appear courtesy of: the Abramovitz family; Rose Abrams and Edith Adlam; Victor Aitay; Livia Ayal; the Bernard H. Baum family; the J. W. Beer collection and the Zindell family; Michael and Melissa Berenbaum; Sonia and Ted Bloch; Carole Boron; Yoram Braginsky; Felicia and Gershon Brenner; the Charak family; Stanley Chencinski; Gordon Derman; the Derman family collection; Max Epstein; Alfonse Farruggia; the John Fink family; Cantor Leopold Fleischer and his family, in memory; Helga Franks; Fritzie Weiss Fritzshall; Bridget Gallagher; Vern Gideon; Jerome J. and Ruth B. Glass; Bernard Goldberg Archival Collection; Bertha Green; Leah Grotchowsky Gutman; the Har-El family; Sam Harris; the Jack Heiman family; the Janger family; Boris Kacel; Melissa J. Kahn; the Koster (Krotoschinski) family, in memory; the Kredow family; the family of Renny Greenblatt Kurshenbaum; the Poeller Teschner Mandel Landes family; Dan and Regina Lipman; Kate Lipner; Yitzchak Mais; Hannah Messinger; the Ner Tamid Ezra Habonim Congregation; Irene and Albert Poll; Dr. Gertrude Pollitt; Ralph Ponfill; the Helen Rappaport family; Walter W. Reed; the Rehbock family; Zev Rogalin; Lynn Romanek-Holstein; Ruth Rontal; Samuel Rosen; Abe Rosenblum; Sylvia, Linda, Mimi, and Stuart Rosenbush; Meyer and Esther Rubinstein; the Schaap family, in memory of Klaus Schaap; Hedy Sered; Adam and Pela Starkopf; the Stearns family; Barbara Steiner; Hilda Stern; the Stiefel family; Matus Stolov; Mr. and Mrs. Michael G. Strauss; the Suppo family; Tom and Steve Ungar collection; Ruth and Sigi Veit; the Waldman family; Mark Weinberg; the Weinblum family, in memory; Aline Wintergreen; Rabbi Albert Wolf and Meyer-Wollman-Wolf families; Ilse, Liesel, and Susan Wollman; Deborah Lust Zaluda.

The **Illinois Holocaust Museum and Education Center** wishes to acknowledge those who provided fine art for the Legacy of Absence Collection appearing in this book: *Final Movement,* 1998, by Samuel Bak, gift in honor of Danna Nolan Fewell and Gary Phillips, courtesy of Sue and Bernie Pucker; *The River in Rwanda,* 1994, by Kebedech Takleab, photo from the series *The Shroud* by Palagie Gbaguidi, taken at Mauthausen concentration camp, June 2007, and Number 1 from the series *Silhouette and Shadow (1)* by Amer Baksic, 1995-97, on loan courtesy of the Pritzker Family; still from *The Wedding,* 2005, by Ofra Zimbalista, from the Illinois Holocaust Museum and Education Center collection.

Images from the **U.S. Holocaust Memorial Museum** appear courtesy of: Myriam Abramowicz; Archiwum Panstwowego Muzeum na Majdanku; Beate Klarsfeld Foundation; Belarussian State Archive of Documentay Film and Photography; Belgium Radio and TV; Bibliotheque Historique de la Ville de Paris; Central Zionist Archives; Lydia Chagoll; the Deutsches Historisches Museum GmbH; Aaron Elster; Federation of the Romanian Jewish Communities; Harry Fiedler; Paul Flacks; The Forward Association; Franklin D. Roosevelt Library; Frihedsmuseet; Sylvia Laufer Goldberg; Abraham & Ruth Goldfarb Family Acquisition Fund; Beit Lohamei Haghetaot; Harry S. Truman Library; Imperial War Museum; Instytut Pamieci Narodowej, Warsaw, Poland; Israel Government Press Office; Leon Jacobson; Robert Kempner; KZ-Gedenkstætte Dachau, Fritz Melbach; Misha Lev; Library of Congress; Linda Mittel; Marcello Morpurgo; John W. Mosenthal; Al Moss; Muzej Revolucije Narodnosti Jugoslavije; Muzeum Okregowe Konin; Muzeum Regionalne w Tomaszow Lubelski; Muzeum Sztuki w Lodzi; Muzeum Wojska Polskiego; National Archives, Washington, D.C.; National Archives and Records Administration, College Park; Nederlands Instituut voor Oorlogsdocumentatie; the New York Times; Shulamith Posner-Manbach; Rafael Scharf; Samuel Schryver; Jizchak Schwersenz; Leah Hammerstein Silverstein; Hiroki Sugihara; United Nations Archives; Thomas Veres; Tibor Vince; Jehuda Widawski; Yad Vashem Photo Archives; YIVO Institute, photographer Mendel Grosman; Eliezer Ziber.

Cover photo courtesy of the **U.S. Holocaust Memorial Museum,** courtesy of Yad Vashem Photo Archives, Bernhardt Walter/Ernst Hofmann, photographers. Cover artifacts from the **Illinois Holocaust Museum and Education Center;** Scroll of Esther courtesy of the Janger family.

Additional photos provided by: **AP Images,** 198; **Bayerische Staatsbibliothek Munchen,** Fotoarchiv Hoffmann, 25 bottom; **Beit Lohamei Haghetaot,** 104; **Beth Hatefutsoth,** Photo Archive, Tel Aviv, 175 top; **Bibliotheque Historique de la Ville de Paris,** 43 bottom; On loan courtesy of **Marlene Brandis,** 16 top; **Bundesarchiv,** Bild, Fotograf: Koch, 212, Fotograf: Cusian, 214; **Corbis,** 39 top left, 46, 131, Olivier Fitoussi, 200, Ira Nowinski, 199, Sygma, 201; **Dioezesanarchiv Limburg DAL,** Nachla Pfarrer Becker: Germany c.1941, 49 bottom; On loan from the **Graundenz** family, 151 top right; **Hamburger Institut fur Sozialforschung Fotosammlung Jaohannes Hehle,** 71; On loan from the **Walter and Gisela Hesse** family, 9; On loan from **Dovie Horvitz,** in memory of the Vivette Ravel family, 15 bottom; **House of the Wannsee Conference,** Berlin, 75, 76; **Jacob Rader Marcus Center of the American Jewish Archives,** 124 top and center; **Jewish Historical Institute of Warsaw,** 60 top; **Landesarchiv,** Berlin, Germany, 37 left and right, 78; **Leopold Page Photographic Collection,** 152 top and center; On loan courtesy of **Esther Levin,** 151 inset; **Moreshet—The Mordechai Anielevich Memorial Holocaust Study and Research Center,** 107; Courtesy of the **New York Library,** 218; On loan courtesy of **Margot Schlesinger,** 193; Courtesy of **Stadtarchiv Muenchen,** Fotograf: Weiler, 205; Courtesy of **Stadtarchiv Nuernberg,** 85; **SuperStock, Inc.,** 53 top; **Swiss Federal Archives,** 73; **Ullstein Bild/The Granger Collection,** New York, 45, 47, 76, 126; **Yad Vashem Photo Archives,** 62 top and bottom; **YIVO Institute,** 137.

Black & white survivor portrait photography by **John Reilly Photography.**

Artifact and document photography by **Deborah Van Kirk.**

Additional photography provided by **Rebecca Gizicki** and **Ron Gould Studios.**

Youth Exhibition illustrations provided by **Kraemer Design and Production, Inc.**

Maps illustrated by **Susan and Mark Carlson.**